Caitlin Davies is a freelance journalist, regularly writing education features for the *Independent*. She lives in London with her daughter Ruby.

# PLACE OF REEDS

Caitlin Davies was in her twenties when she met and fell in love with Ron. When he returned to his home in Botswana, Caitlin joined him in Maun, the 'Place of Reeds'. Eager to absorb the culture of the Setswana, the headstrong Londoner became part of Ron's large extended family, and fell in love with both the country and its people. Eventually, with the birth of their daughter Ruby, Caitlin's happiness seemed complete . . . But the Botswana of the 1990s was changing. AIDS had taken its toll; violence was on the increase. When, with her child in her arms, Caitlin was brutally attacked, Ron's family closed ranks and Caitlin found herself ostracized by the people she had grown to love . . .

CAITLIN DAVIES

# PLACE OF REEDS

*Complete and Unabridged*

# CHARNWOOD
*Leicester*

First published in Great Britain in 2005 by
Simon & Schuster UK Limited
London

First Charnwood Edition
published 2006
by arrangement with
Simon & Schuster UK Limited
London

Landscape photographs taken by
Hassan Sanusi Kadir
Maps by Martin Collins

British Library CIP Data

Davies, Caitlin, *1964 –*
Place of reeds.—Large print ed.—
Charnwood library series
1. Davies, Caitlin, *1964 –*   2. English—Botswana
—Biography 3. Large type books 4. Botswana—
Social life and customs
I. Title
968.8′3032′092

ISBN 1–84617–271–3

Published by
F. A. Thorpe (Publishing)
Anstey, Leicestershire

Set by Words & Graphics Ltd.
Anstey, Leicestershire
Printed and bound in Great Britain by
T. J. International Ltd., Padstow, Cornwall

This book is printed on acid-free paper

*To my sister and to my brother*

I'd like to thank the Society of Authors
for a grant from the K. Blundell Trust.
It gave me the time and confidence
to start writing this book.

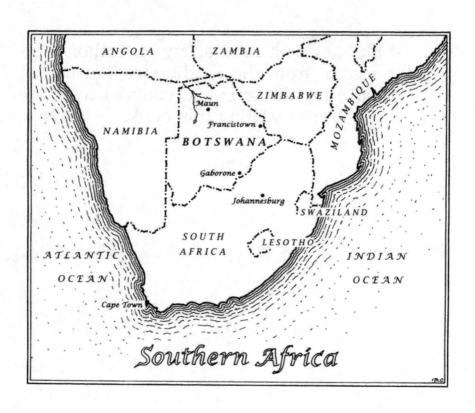

Southern Africa

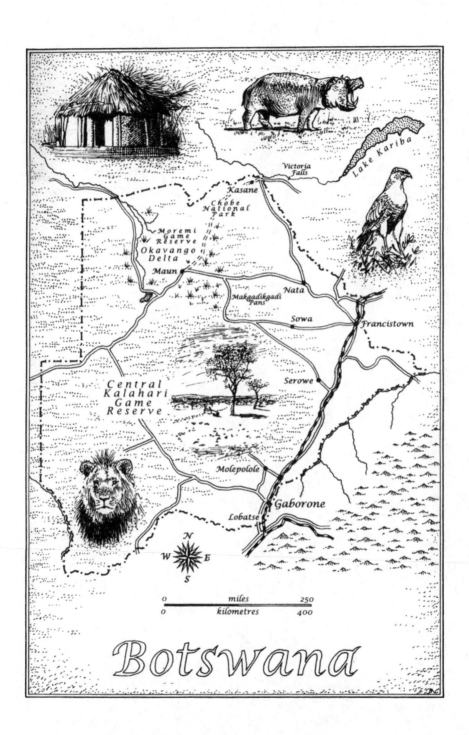

Lake Kariba

Victoria
Falls

Kasane

Chobe
National
Park

Moremi
Game
Reserve

Okavango
Delta

Maun

Nata

Makgadikgadi
Pans

Sowa

Francistown

Central
Kalahari
Game
Reserve

Serowe

Molepolole

Gaborone

Lobatse

N
W        E
S

| 0 | miles | 250 |
|---|-------|-----|
| 0 | kilometres | 400 |

Botswana

# PROLOGUE

I'm not quite sure how I got here. Until a few months ago I was living in Maun, a southern African village on the edge of the Okavango Delta, a miraculous inland swamp in a land of desert. Maun was my home and I never thought I'd leave. When I sat at a computer screen then, it was in my small thatched office in the western corner of our plot. It was a round building with a conical roof that fitted like a hat, its white walls bumpy to the touch and dappled with shadows from the purple flowering bougainvillea trees. Normally the office door was open, to let in a breeze, and just by the step grew two giant pawpaw trees whose fruit clung to the branches like orange haemorrhoids. Beyond the trees and the flimsy metal fence of the plot I could see children playing on the banks of the Thamalakane River. I would watch the river glittering, its surface covered with water lilies, the undersides brown like wet liver.

At night I worked with a mosquito coil burning away on the desk and next to that an industrial-sized torch to light my way back to the house. If I worked late then I had to worry about walking past the hippopotamus which, depending on the season, appeared at around nine and began foraging next to the fence. Afraid that the hippo would trample down the fence and enter our plot, I would walk quickly back to the house, its dark-green walls camouflaged even in daylight against the leadwood trees. The hippo appeared during the day as well, its grey hulk half-submerged in the river, sunlight outlining the thick muscles of its enormous nose.

Now I'm in London. It's summer and in my street all the windows are open. It doesn't seem right that today the forecast is 100 degrees. London, in my memory, is a dark and rainy place. It's a place of steamed-up windows on the top of a double-decker bus, of wet pavements and black umbrellas, of Christmas trees in shop windows. But then it's been twelve years since I saw the city in summer.

I look out of the window. It's only on the second floor but it seems very high up to me because in Maun nearly everything is on ground level. Above the slate roofs, chimney pots and satellite dishes, the sky is a hazy blue. Down below, on the street, I see a familiar figure walking slowly along the pavement. It's the owner of a Maun safari company and I wonder why he's not wearing khaki and doesn't have a walkie-talkie in his hands. He looks thin, I think, and I find myself assuming that he has HIV. Then the figure looks up and I almost wave until I realize it's not the person I'm thinking of at all, because I'm in England now. Further down the street I can hear a woman screaming at her children. She's telling them to get a fucking move on. In Maun someone would report her to the chief for using abusive language. In a house opposite a man is in the bathroom. I can't believe he doesn't realize he is

2

on full view. I see the man sniff delicately at some underwear he has just removed. I turn away, unused to having neighbours whose houses I can look straight into, even if most of them have net curtains. Then I think I can hear Ruby waking up. I must wash the syringe so her medication is ready. She's not supposed to go more than twelve hours without it. Then she cries out. From habit I rush to her, propelled by visions of puff adders sinking their fangs into her legs.

'Mama!' she says, smiling. She's standing at the doorway to the bedroom, her plump legs planted solidly on the floor but the rest of her body a little wobbly with early morning uncertainty. She looks sticky and baffled.

'I had a dream,' she says, holding out her arms so I will pick her up.

'Yes?' I ask, trying to sound unconcerned. I feel the unfamiliar softness of a carpet under my bare feet.

'I was in Africa at the farm. With my dada. And small grandma. And big mama. And Alice and Ene and Gabs and Gogo.'

'That's a nice dream,' I say, though it sounds more like a nightmare to me.

'You're wearing shorts,' Ruby says, looking down at my legs.

I look down as well. My legs are sun-tanned brown, and the scars on my thighs have shrunk to silvery streaks as if a worm has burnt its way across my skin. No one else notices these scars, they are far too small.

'I miss Africa,' Ruby says plaintively.

I smooth down her thick curly hair but say nothing.

This isn't good enough for her. She's three and a half years old and very determined. 'When are we going back to Africa?' she demands, fussing in my arms until I put her down.

I'm not sure how to answer her. I want her to be proud of being an African, to love Botswana with the intensity that I once did. And I want her memories to be uncoloured by what happened to me.

'Look! A fly!' she says and we stop on the stairs so we can both stare at the motionless black fly. I can't work out why it's so fascinating until I realize it's been months since I saw a fly, or a spider, or a beetle, or any sort of insect inside a house at all.

The phone rings and Ruby rushes down the stairs to answer it. It's an old-fashioned phone and not a touch-tone phone that everyone else seems to have. When I made phone calls last week to set up gas and electricity accounts a recorded voice told me to press a number according to what type of help I wanted. I dialled a number, and kept on dialling a number, but nothing happened. I must get a new phone. Everything seems odd and out of place, especially me.

'Hello?' Ruby says confidently into the receiver. 'There's no one there,' she says, handing it to me.

I take the phone and know immediately from the static on the line that it's a long-distance call. I prepare myself for bad news.

Someone must have died.

'Cait, o are eng?' It's Ron's voice, deep and familiar yet very far away. He sounds relaxed.

'Fine,' I say in English. I realize, shocked, that I have nearly forgotten how to speak Setswana.

'Dada!' Ruby lunges for the phone and rips it away from me. 'Where are you?'

I hear him answer that he's at the farm. My heart sinks. I hate the farm.

'Where's big mama?' Ruby asks.

My heart sinks further. I assume the old woman won't want to talk with me.

'It's Gabs!' Ruby tells me now, still talking on the phone.

The old prickles of resentment begin to run up and down my spine.

'Bye bye, Dada!' Ruby says brightly and she hands over the phone. She sits down on the floor by a pad of paper she was drawing on last night. These days everything she draws contains a mother, a father and a baby. Even in the toilet she points down the white porcelain bowl and says, 'There's a daddy poo, there's a mummy poo, and there's a baby one.'

Although Ron is talking to me on the phone, I'm watching Ruby closely, scanning her face. 'Watch I can do,' she says, standing up again, hoisting up the phone book and trying to balance it on her head. It's only the north London residential phone book but it's far fatter than the phone book for the whole of Botswana.

'Is everything okay?' I ask Ron.

'Ee,' he says. He pauses. He will not say what he really thinks because he never does. Perhaps

5

his mother is with him. Perhaps he's standing alone in the bush, sweat on his face from hacking down trees under the searing African sun.

Outside I hear the milk van trundling along the road. Someone rings my doorbell and I feel uneasy. A police van has just turned into my street and I crane my neck, convinced it will stop outside my house.

I put the phone down and leave Ron to return to his morning job of tracking down missing goats on the farm. I wonder, briefly, if the lions have been there again.

'Don't do that,' I tell Ruby who has started scratching on the windowpane with a pen.

She ignores me and scratches harder.

'Ruby . . . ' I warn.

'I WANT TO GO BACK TO AFRICA!' she suddenly explodes, throwing herself face down on the floor so her drawings scatter.

# PART ONE

PART ONE

# 1

I first met Ron at a fancy dress Hallowe'en party in America. It was 1988 and I was studying at Clark University in Worcester, Massachusetts, home of the first space rocket and the birth control pill. The party was on the ground floor of a white clapboard house and I drove there in my battered Dodge Aspen, a vast boat of a car with a front seat that could fit three. On the bonnet I'd glued a plastic figurine of Margaret Thatcher. It was the only car in our street that had never been broken into. On the way to the party I stopped twice when the Dodge stalled, running out in the freezing cold to the front, opening the bonnet and ramming a toothbrush in the carburettor to get it going again. I'd just finished a car mechanics course and this was the only thing I'd learnt.

I was dressed half-heartedly as Little Red Riding Hood, having found a red cape and a wicker basket at a thrift store on Main Street. I walked up the wooden steps to the party, passing under the red foliage of trees lit up by the streetlights. It was autumn and outside the city the trees were aflame. On the porch of the house were two pumpkins; giant-sized the way most things in the United States still appeared to me although I'd been in Massachusetts for a year. I was twenty-four years old and halfway through my Masters degree.

The door was open and I hurried in, looking for Debbie whose house it was. It was crowded inside and I grabbed an empty spot on a sofa next to a tall man with baggy white trousers and overgrown hair. He was sitting very still, surveying the room while his finger gently traced tiny circles on the tip of his chin. He glanced at me as I sat down, fiddling with my red cape. All around us hung orange and black Hallowe'en decorations, cut-out paper masks, grinning pumpkin faces, witches riding black cats.

'Looks nice in here,' I mumbled.

'It's a strange celebration,' said the man next to me and I wasn't sure if he were talking to me or to himself.

'Yes,' I agreed. 'Witches and ghosts, the living dead and scary things.'

'But not as scary as *Friday the 13th*,' said the man. 'People here, I find it strange. They like to show very violent horror movies and then they are shocked when in real life some nut goes out and shoots people with a military weapon.'

'Where are you from?' I asked, unable to place his accent. His English had a slightly stilted quality about it. He was definitely not an American.

'Botswana.'

I nodded.

'Do you know where that is?' he asked with a slight challenge in his voice.

'Africa,' I said, although I knew virtually nothing about Africa and had no intention of ever going there. I hoped he wouldn't ask me where exactly in Africa Botswana was. 'Your

English is very good, very . . . ' I wanted to say that apart from the Americanisms he used it was very exact, almost formal, but he had already taken offence.

'That's because you people colonized us.'

The man lit a cigarette and held it delicately between his fingers. He turned to look at me directly now. His face was long with a straight nose; his chin framed with the beginnings of a beard and below his bottom lip sat a little tuft of hair.

'What's your name?' he asked.

'Caitlin.'

I smiled because he repeated it back to me and it sounded odd the way he drew it out into three syllables, as if my name were the beginning of a song.

'And yours?'

'Ronald,' he said.

'Oh,' I said, 'that's not . . . '

'Not very African?' he asked and I had a feeling that we were alike, both the sort of people who were quick to find fault.

'What are you studying here?' I asked.

'Computers.'

'Oh.' I shifted on the sofa; I had never used a computer.

Then Debbie appeared and I went to chat with her. When I later returned to the sofa, Ron had gone.

The second time we met it was again at a party. It was early spring and I was standing in a kitchen full of fraternity types helping themselves to beer from a huge keg in the corner. I was arguing with one of the men who was telling me what a good job Reagan had done and how in comparison George Bush was a wimp.

'You're not listening to her,' said Ron, coming up behind the man who, to drive his point home, had cornered me next to a window.

The man turned, confused. 'Yeah, buddy,' he said to Ron, and attempted the sort of complicated handshake white American students often tried on black men.

I smiled as Ron gave the man the cold shoulder.

'So, how are your courses going?' I asked, relieved to see the fraternity brother head off to the other side of the kitchen. Men in general annoyed me; I had just broken up with someone who had turned out to be everything I had thought he was not.

Ron shrugged. He wore beige trousers and a striped rugby shirt. His hair seemed longer, his beard more pronounced. As he stood next to me I saw we were exactly the same height. 'My computer courses are pretty boring. What are you studying at Clark?'

'Electrical engineering,' I said quickly.

He looked caught off-balance. 'That's an interesting course for . . . '

'For a woman?' I laughed, spilling my drink. 'Yes, our breasts do tend to get in the way.'

Ron looked slightly shocked.

'No,' I said, 'English. I'm doing an MA in English. My mission is to further the aims of British colonialization.'

Ron giggled and sipped from his cup of beer.

'Dude!' said a man coming up next to Ron and clapping him on the shoulder. He was dressed in a multicoloured shirt, with bracelets on his wrist and straggly blond hair.

'Thomas,' Ron said and nodded politely in acknowledgement.

The man bounced up and down on the spot. 'Are we going this weekend?' he asked. 'The Dead are playing. I can get tickets, dude!'

'You don't like the Grateful Dead?' Ron asked, seeing the look on my face.

I grimaced.

'I've only been to one show myself,' Ron continued. 'I didn't have a ticket so I put a sign around my neck: Dumb African Never Seen The Dead. I got two tickets, three tabs of acid and a bean burrito.'

We both laughed and then Ron began stroking circles thoughtfully on his chin.

'Do you miss home?' I asked.

'Dreadfully,' he said and his whole body appeared, for a second, to flag.

'Where are you from? A city?'

'I am from Maun. It's a village in northern Botswana, near the Okavango Delta.' As he spoke he savoured the place names as if they were sweets. 'Do you know of the Okavango?'

'Not really, is it nice?'

'It is beautiful beyond any singing of it,' he said and smiled. His face grew soft and he became animated, the words tumbling out as if he hadn't spoken of home for a very long time. 'When I was a child, there was water as far as you could see, and there were animals

13

everywhere. In those days, even Maun was a swamp. I walked out of my house in the morning and I was in the water. As a child I used to go out on the *mokoro*, the canoe, and fish with my uncle. This one time he was going after a huge barbel and when he threw in the line it got caught on his ear and the hook, it ripped off his, what do you call? . . . his ear lobe . . . ' Ron smiled at the memory. 'I'm sorry, I usually don't talk this much.'

'You don't?'

'No, normally I don't talk at all.' Ron's whole face tightened. His eyes went blank and he seemed to shrink into himself. A woman passed behind him and patted his head.

'Your hair's so cool,' she beamed.

Ron scowled.

'So there are lots of wild animals in the Okavango Delta?' I asked politely.

'Oh, there are incredible wildlife populations in the swamps,' Ron said, looking round the room for a moment. 'In fact Americans very much enjoy coming over and shooting them. They call it sport hunting.'

'And what do you miss most about Botswana?' I asked, moving nearer, pulled by the sound of longing I had heard earlier in Ron's voice.

'My grandmother Madintwa,' Ron sighed and smiled at the same time. 'She brought me up. She is a very kind somebody, although her name might suggest otherwise.'

'Why, what does her name mean?'

'Well . . . ' Ron drew a deep breath. He had a leisurely way of speaking, as if he had all the time

14

in the world. 'She was given her name because of what happened shortly before she was born. What happened was this. One day my grandmother's mother was digging for water-lily roots in the Thamalakane River when a crocodile grabbed her on the shoulder — '

'A *crocodile?*'

'Yes. It grabbed her and its teeth came right through the bone. But she was a very strong woman and she fought the crocodile off with her knife, managing to drag herself to the riverbank where she collapsed.'

'So she was okay?'

'Yes. She stayed there on the riverbank for quite some time until some passers-by found her and put her on a sledge. Now, her husband heard about what had happened but he wasn't much help, so my great-grandmother went and stayed with a sister. And this was where she met another man, I believe he was a foreigner from Angola. Well, when she got hitched up with him there was a tremendous fight and everyone was called to a meeting. In the end it was agreed that the man pay the husband some cattle and then he was allowed to stay with my great-grandmother. And it was around that time that my grandmother, Madintwa, was born. Madintwa means the mother or owner of fights, because she was born at a time of family fighting.'

I shifted on my legs. I had been standing listening, engrossed in the story, for so long that now I felt cramp in my calf. And while I had been listening I had been there in the Okavango

Delta, in a place where women gathered water-lily roots and fought off crocodiles with knives. I took in my surroundings again, the fraternity men chugging weak American beer from paper cups emblazoned with the Stars and Stripes, the peanuts spilt on the floor, the waft of marijuana coming from the porch. 'And what does your grandmother think of you being here, in America?'

'I think it's breaking her heart,' Ron said, his voice low. 'I don't think she really even understands where I am, or whether I'm coming back. And, you see, I'm my mother's only child.'

'Is that unusual?'

'It is in Botswana,' Ron laughed.

'Do you often speak to your mum?'

'I can't.'

'Why not?'

'Because there are no phones in Maun.'

'Oh.' I felt foolish. I didn't know what it was like to live in a place without phones. 'So, you write to her?'

'No. She can't read.'

We talked on until two in the morning, until most of the people had left the party and I'd had too much to drink to drive my Dodge Aspen home. Ron lived nearby on Oberlin Street in a two-storey house made from horizontal white wooden slats. Four crooked steps led up to a little porch area with thin white pillars like a poor version of a southern antebellum mansion. Walking up the dim stairway we could hear someone coughing their lungs out. Inside the flat it smelled of stale beer and the windows were wet with condensation.

'Is this your room?' I asked, peering through an open doorway. Inside, the room was empty but for a large mattress on a wooden floor, a guitar, a pair of trainers and a sports bag. But on the bed was a massive blanket, a bright cobalt blue the colour of a swimming pool, with intricate black flower designs.

'That's an amazing blanket,' I said, attracted by the brightness, bending down to feel it was thick and soft.

'I brought it with me,' Ron said, putting on a bedside lamp.

'You brought this massive blanket with you, from *Africa*?' I asked, incredulous.

Ron nodded seriously. 'I had been told it was very, very cold in America.'

★  ★  ★

Later in the morning I woke to hear swearing in the kitchen.

'Dude!' a man yelled, putting his head round the bedroom door.

I covered myself, alarmed. It was Thomas the bad-tempered hippy from the party.

'Oh,' he said, seeing me in the bed. He beamed conspiratorially at Ron. 'Good party, hey?' He winked.

'Do you mind?' said Ron raising one eyebrow. 'Do you people not knock before you enter someone's room?'

Thomas ignored him. 'Look, asshole, it's freezing in here.'

17

I watched while Ron leapt up and put a dressing-gown on.

'The boiler has broken again. For some reason our American friend is incapable of fixing it. I'm just going downstairs.'

I watched while he left the room, relieved to find that the man I had spent the night with was just as beautiful-looking in daylight as he had been the evening before. There was something very calm about him, his movements were measured, he thought carefully before he spoke, both his language and his stance were graceful. I lay there feeling, for once, that everything was possible.

Ron made tuna melt for breakfast, producing a huge pile of slightly burnt toast with tuna and melted cheese on top. He did it smoothly and without fuss. Then he piled it all on one plate.

'In Botswana,' he said, 'when you are very close to someone, you share from the same plate. Or do you want a separate plate?'

'No,' I smiled, 'this is fine. Do men cook in Botswana?'

'As boys, yes. We are all taught, of course, how to make a fire and to prepare fish, and porridge and so on.'

'That's a healthy upbringing.'

'Well, our society is more equal than yours.'

'And how exactly is that?' I asked, a touch of sarcasm in my voice.

'Well, firstly, we are a peaceful country. We have never been to war and we have never been invaded. Secondly, we believe in equality between men and women.'

'Oh yeah.'

'Yes. We do not have pornography, for example. Furthermore, in Botswana everyone is free to speak their mind and is listened to respectfully. When decisions are made then people are called to the Kgotla, likewise when criminals are tried.'

'And what is the Kgotla?'

'A public meeting place, the place where the chief resides.'

'What, and anyone can talk, whoever they are? They don't have to be politicians or something?'

'No. They can say what they like for as long as they like.'

★  ★  ★

As summer arrived in Worcester the days got humid and sticky. One after another the universities I had applied to, to do a PhD, rejected me.

'I don't know what I'm going to do,' I moaned to Ron. We were sitting on his apartment's small second-floor balcony. It was so hot I was eating ice.

'You should come to Botswana,' said Ron. He was crouched on the floor of the balcony, sewing up a skirt of mine. I had bought it at a thrift store as a dress and then cut it up to make a skirt, but I hadn't done a very good job. As usual I had done it on impulse, without thinking it through, and had made a total mess. Ron was repairing the skirt with such delicate stitches that it looked like a Beatrix Potter

19

mouse was at work.

'But why, why should I come to Botswana? I mean, I know you've told me what a wonderful country it is, but what would I do there?'

'You'll get a job easily.' Ron bit some thread between his teeth.

'But as what? I don't want to go to a country I've never been to before and just be someone's girlfriend.'

Ron looked offended and he held his needle up in mid-air.

'Look,' I said, 'it would make me so dependent to go there like that. Anyway,' I relented, 'I was thinking of doing a teaching course, it would take a year . . . '

'In England, do you mean?'

'Yes.' I nodded as if I had it all planned out, although I had just that second decided this was something I was going to do. I had never wanted to be a teacher, now suddenly it seemed like such a good idea that I wanted to do it immediately.

'Ah,' Ron sighed. 'My love, I will miss you.'

I smiled. 'Don't be so soppy.'

'When I say 'my love',' Ron said looking worried now, 'I'm just being protective, not possessive, okay?'

'Okay.'

'I had this very strange dream last night,' Ron began, laying the finished skirt on a chair.

I settled down. I loved it when he began a story, even if it were just a dream, for his voice was calming to listen to and lulled me into a different place and a different time.

'The dream was about Maun and my family. Now, there is a main road in Maun, well, actually, there is just one road in Maun, and just off this road is a fresh produce shop. My father was the one who built this shop and there is very little on sale because the trucks with the food have to drive three days up from South Africa. In my dream, I was sitting on a bench at the back of this shop with my grandmother Madintwa. She was looking very well, very fat and happy, and she was wearing her best shawl. My grandmother turned to me and said, 'So, Ronald, tell me when you want to get married and I'll find you a good woman who wants to marry you.' To which I replied, '*Mme*, or mother, if I do get married, the woman I'm going to marry is right here' and then I turned to my left and pointed at you. You were sitting on another bench talking with Kgomotso . . . '

'Who?'

'Kgomotso, my grandmother's sister's grand-child. And my grandmother looked at me, after I had said this thing about marriage, and gave a rather shy smile. Isn't that a funny dream? Besides, my grandmother would never really say that.'

'And I would never want to get married,' I said.

'Nor would I,' agreed Ron.

# 2

It was pissing down. A gale was sweeping up from the Sussex coast and the glass walls of the Stanley Deason staff room were taking a battering. Outside, on the school playing fields, the air was misty with salt-water spray. Lunchtime was almost over and I sat near the head of the English department, a soft, gentle woman who was trying to teach me how to raise my voice without shouting. Opposite sat another member of the English department, staring blankly at her lunch. She was on a diet, as she always was, and today it was a sticky lump of cottage cheese with two carrots, which had turned brown in the Tupperware box. The room was large but I felt claustrophobic and moved to the window where outside I could see a boy huddled up against the wall crying convulsively.

'That boy is really crying, I think he's been beaten up,' I said to a male teacher from the maths department who was washing his teacup at the sink.

The teacher turned and looked through the window. He was an aggressive, bullet-shaped man whose face was always flushed. He was a year head and an old-timer at the school and he had little time for trainee teachers like me.

'Him?' he asked, looking out into the rain at the boy still huddled by the wall.

'Yes.'

'Well, he's a little dickhead anyway, isn't he? I suggest if you have any dealings with him you come down on him so hard his teeth rattle. The fucking little poof.'

I stood at the sink, my back rigid. A month ago the year head had accused me of being a bleeding-heart liberal fresh from university with no idea of the real world.

By the time I had made my tea the boy outside had gone. I felt useless, as I often did at Stanley Deason. I had been on my teacher training course for several months, each week spending two days at Sussex University and three days at my placement school. At university we were taught ways of making English classes interesting, thirty-one ways to teach a book, twenty ways to teach a poem, the importance of colourful wall displays. And then we came into our schools and found that our job was to control rooms full of children who didn't want to be there and who were taught by adults who didn't want to be there either.

A few weeks before the end of my course I saw a British Council advert recruiting teachers for Botswana. It was a glorious March day, the sea was calm and almost inviting-looking, the air was full of seagulls. I walked on to the West Pier, or what was left of it, near the square where I lived. Ron had told me that almost a hundred years ago three chiefs from Botswana had walked down this very same pier in their top hats and overcoats waiting for a meeting with Queen Victoria. Their plan was to appeal to the queen to continue to 'protect' Bechuanaland rather than handing it over to Cecil Rhodes and the Boers.

I replied to the advert and was called to London to attend a selection board. At the British Council offices I was left to wait in a small, warm room, its shelves lined with books, folders and magazines. I tried to read the information pamphlets laid out on a large glass table, but the impending interview made me nervous. Finally I was called next door and told to sit at a table opposite three suited men. The man in the middle was the representative of the Botswana Ministry of Education.

'So my dear,' he said kindly after I had answered some questions about my teaching experience. 'What do you know about my country?'

'Not much,' I admitted. 'It's in southern Africa, just north of South Africa . . . '

The man nodded.

'It's a land-locked country, with a lot of desert. It gained independence from Britain in 1966.'

The man nodded again. He must have heard all of this a million times. It was the information contained in the pamphlets in the room where I been left to wait.

'And where would you want to be posted, should you be appointed a teacher in Botswana?' the man asked.

'Maun,' I said immediately. It was Ron's home village. It was the place I had heard about endlessly. It was where Ron was heading when he finished his studies in the States and it was where I wanted to go as well.

The man started laughing, at one point banging his hand on the Formica table he was laughing so much.

I laughed too, although I wasn't sure why.

'How on earth do you know of Maun?' the man asked, wiping tears from the corner of his eyes.

'Oh . . . ' I said vaguely. I was a bit alarmed at the man's reaction after the lyrical way Ron always spoke about his home village. 'I know someone from there.'

'Do you?' The man raised his eyebrows. 'Maun!' he said, turning to the two men from the British Council who flanked him at the table. They smiled politely but they didn't get the joke the way the Botswana man did.

★　★　★

'Need a cab?' asked the taxi driver as I stood a little uncertainly in the car park at Farnham station in Surrey. I had passed the interview and now I was about to attend a two-day pre-departure briefing before setting off for my new life in Botswana. The idea of a briefing session sounded secretive and a little exciting as if the newly recruited teachers were espionage agents preparing for a tough overseas assignment. We had been kindly requested in advance to wear our name badges at all times and as I got into the cab I began to I fiddle with mine, not sure whether I really had to put it on.

'Going abroad?' the driver asked.

'Yes, I'm going to Botswana,' I said happily, glad to be on the move after a long train ride from Brighton.

'I wouldn't want to go there,' said the driver ominously, swerving left and looking at me over his shoulder.

'Why?' I was surprised he'd even heard of Botswana. Most people hadn't when I said I was going there.

'I was in Nigeria,' he said as if that should explain things. 'Where is it, then? In the west?'

'No, southern Africa.'

'South Africa?' The taxi driver eyed me in the rear-view mirror.

'No, it's a separate country, it's just above South Africa.'

'Do you think Nelson Mandela will become president?' asked the driver. 'Did you watch him being released from jail?'

I nodded; I had been glued to the TV screen on the day he was let out four months ago.

'Twenty-seven years, imagine,' said the driver. 'History in the making, isn't it? Say hello to him from me!'

I wanted to say again that I was going to Botswana, not South Africa.

The driver fell silent then and a couple of minutes later we arrived at the castle, instantly recognizable from the glossy aerial-view photograph I had been sent. I got out of the cab and there were the little medieval turrets, the flagpole, the huge lawns and dainty flowerbeds. Originally founded in 1138AD by a grandson of William the Conqueror, the castle was now

26

home to an international briefing and conference centre. It looked like a stately home, old and grand but a little bedraggled, the beige stone walls with patches of red like a skin disease.

I paid the taxi driver and walked through the entrance of the castle, following the signs to the Great Hall. There were already twenty other teachers gathered in the echoing stone room and we smiled anxiously at each other, knowing we'd be sharing rooms for the next two nights. Ancient leather chairs were dotted around the hall and a group of five teachers stood by the wide fireplace as if posing for a magazine spread on the state of the nation's aristocracy.

From the Great Hall, we were instructed to go to a conference room upstairs, where we took our seats and waited for the briefing to start.

'Good afternoon, ladies,' said a woman in a pale-pink chiffon shirt, her blonde hair arranged stiffly around her head, 'gentlemen. I hope you've had a chance to relax and get to know each other.'

A handful of people sitting at the front on black plastic chairs nodded and two got out notebooks and pens.

'The programme for this afternoon begins with a short slideshow to give you a general feel for Botswana.' The woman hesitated for a second as if expecting applause and then took her seat on a small stage at the front of the room. I watched as a man in a bright-blue suit rolled down a large white screen and asked that the lights be dimmed. Two young women hurried round the hall handing out wads of photocopied sheets and then the first slide clicked on to the screen.

'Botswana is a land-locked country bordered by South Africa, Namibia, Zimbabwe and Zambia,' intoned the man. 'It is a largely arid country, approximately the size of France. The Kalahari Desert covers over eighty per cent of the total land mass.'

On the screen came a map of Botswana which had very little marked on it but for a railway line, some roads and two small areas of blue, one to the east and one to the north. The next slide showed a flat brown landscape dotted with spiky-looking trees into which a small boy was leading a herd of fat white cattle.

'The population of Botswana is small,' continued the man, 'currently standing at one point two million people. There are three times as many cattle as people. The heaviest population density is here, on the eastern corridor to Zimbabwe and South Africa.' He pointed to the railway line that cut across the right of the map.

'Botswana gained independence in 1966, led by the visionary Oxford-educated first president Sir Seretse Khama, and it remains one of Africa's shining success stories. Some would say an African miracle,' he said with a smile. 'The national language is Setswana and the official language is English, so you won't have any problems there. And because Botswana had very few colonials before independence, there is little post-colonial resentment. Rather, expatriate

28

expertise and technical know-how is welcomed with open arms.'

The man clicked another slide into place and on the screen came a photograph of people at an outdoor meeting. A row of elderly men in suits sat on small wooden chairs, clutching walking sticks, trilby hats on their heads. To their right, and in the background, women sat on the sand, bright scarves around their heads.

'The Botswana are a very garrulous people. They are known to hold long informal conversations on every topic under the sun. In general it is a place where constructive criticism and opposition are actively encouraged.'

The image faded and was replaced by a beaming schoolgirl. She sat at a wooden desk, dressed in a starched red and white uniform, a pen in her hand.

'Botswana's citizens have access to both free health care and free education,' explained the man. 'This is thanks to rich diamond deposits, first discovered in 1967, which the government controls in partnership with the multinational conglomerate De Beers. And there are other natural resources as well, namely wildlife. Botswana is today regarded as one of the world's last remaining Edens and the government is firmly committed to conservation. The country is divided into several regions, the most famous being perhaps the Okavango Delta.'

I sat up a little straighter. Now we were getting to the bit I had heard about, the part of the country where I would be going.

'The world's largest inland delta, the Delta is

home to some of Africa's biggest free-roaming wildlife populations, including herds of buffalo, zebra and elephant. Botswana, as I'm sure you will know, is home to the Big Five and the country is famous among both trophy hunters and photographic tourists.'

On the screen came a landscape scene, an almost surreal image of a blue snake of a river sliding its way across a flat green landscape. The next photograph showed a single bull elephant standing majestically at the water's edge as a sinking sun bathed clumps of papyrus in gold.

'The watery jewel at the edge of the Kalahari,' said the man reverently. 'The local people still live off the river, here we see some of the Delta's Bayei tribe using the dug-out canoe called a *mokoro.*'

I leant forward, feeling a little shiver. Ron's family on his mother's side were Bayei and I had begun to feel I knew them after all the stories Ron had told. But now here in the conference room I was looking at anonymous people sitting half naked in wooden canoes and I felt uncomfortable.

'This is Maun,' said the man in blue, his voice adopting a lighter tone. He pronounced it differently from Ron, making the sound short and round. 'A village on the edge of the Delta, traditionally somewhat of a frontier town with a rough and ready image.'

I felt a little shiver again at the sound of the word Maun and I fiddled with my name badge, staring hopefully at the white screen. The slide showed an aerial view of a flat brown land, a hotchpotch of round houses interspersed with shiny rectangles of tin roofs. After the scenes we had been shown of the Delta, the village looked dry and rather bleak.

'Ladies! Gentlemen!' called out the chiffon woman, getting back on the stage. 'We are now having our talk on health.'

I looked around for paper to write on. While I wasn't much interested in wildlife, I did want to know about health. But as I listened I began to think I was entering a danger zone. AIDS was rampant in the region. I was to be on the lookout for a certain type of fly that burrows its way into your skin and erupts in maggots. I should only tourniquet a snakebite if I was sure the snake was a mamba. I was to have several vaccinations before leaving: tetanus, polio, TB, yellow fever, cholera, and an injection of the sci-fi-sounding gamma globulin. A paragraph at the end of the health notes advised me to make a will before my departure.

The following afternoon I took a train back to Brighton, absconding from the orientation a day early, and I spent the journey reading a British Council handout on living conditions. I flipped through a list of what I should know about life in Botswana until I came to 'what to bring with you'. This began with: linen, china, glass, cutlery . . . none of which I owned so I turned the page to a section on domestic help. The general standard of honesty is good, I read, but the maids can't shop or cook without guidance. Safari suits are recommended for men, cotton dresses for women with a warm wrap for evening

31

parties. What on earth was a safari suit? Where would I get a warm wrap?

Still the train hadn't arrived at Brighton so I examined another handout which informed me that I would find the Batswana people very courteous and polite. When giving or receiving a gift the 'following procedure is observed: one hand is extended, the other is placed over the outstretched arms and a slight curtsy is performed'. I read this very carefully several times, unsure which arm to put where and glad there was no one sitting near me on the train to watch. Finally I was advised against swearing with the saying: *'Tshwene e bonye mapalamo mafologo ga e bona'* — the baboon found the way up, but he could not get down. In other words, weigh up the consequences before you do anything.

★ ★ ★

A few weeks before I left the UK Ron arrived, en route from the States to Botswana. There had been a mix-up over the flights and he was given a free night at a hotel near the airport before continuing his journey. My first surprise when I met him at Heathrow was his hair. The long curly locks had gone and his hair was short, giving him a slightly military look.

'Oh, my God!' I said as we got on the bus to the hotel.

'You don't like it?'

'Well, it will just need some getting used to. I guess it will be better, in the heat and everything.'

'No, I had to cut it off because of what people will say.'

'How do you mean?'

'People in Botswana, they don't like long hair.'

'Well, you're allowed dreadlocks aren't you?'

'No way!'

'What, you mean there are no Rastas in Botswana?'

'Not that I'm aware of.'

'So your family wouldn't like you with long hair, then?'

Ron smiled and we held hands on the bus. 'My mother would go ape shit.'

I sat back, surprised that hair should be such an issue, and that Ron would cut his off because of what people, especially his mother, would think. In America Ron had never been bothered about what other people thought.

That night in Ron's hotel room he had a second surprise.

'I'm going up to the Lakes next week,' I said, 'to say goodbye to mum and dad. They're up in the Lake District for the summer.'

'And when do you arrive in Botswana?'

'August,' I said. 'I can't wait.'

'I have to tell you something,' Ron said, his voice low, a little shaky in the semi-dark.

'What?' I sat up in bed, fearful.

Ron hesitated.

'What?' I said again.

'I have a child.'

'You have a child?' I repeated. 'What do you mean you have a child? Where? With who?'

'I didn't know,' Ron said softly, watching my

face. 'Rita, my sister just told me. She's called Alice. She was born just before I went to the States. But no one told me. Her mother never told me she was pregnant. I had no idea. I've been meaning to tell you. I thought you'd hate me for it.'

'Why would I hate you for having a child?'

'Because you're always saying how men don't take being a father seriously.'

'I am?'

'Yeah. How they get women pregnant and then dump them and walk out.'

'But you're saying you didn't *know* you had a child.'

'Yes, I had no idea. Really, I had no idea.'

'So how old is she, Alice?'

'I guess about three.'

'Wow.' I thought about this. If Ron had a child then he had a child, it was something that had happened before I had even met him. And it was not like I wanted children myself, both Ron and I were certain about this. I liked children, as long as they weren't mine. 'And you've never met her?'

'Of course not,' said Ron miserably.

We lay in the bed quietly for a while.

'So this is going to be some homecoming?' I smiled and snuggled closer.

# PART TWO

# 3

My first glimpse of Africa was a red hill in Angola. It was August 1990 and I was on a cramped British Airways flight to Gaborone. As the plane stopped to refuel, I peered out of the window at dawn breaking over the red Angolan earth. It looked hot and silent, the hazy landscape empty but for the silhouettes of two soldiers just visible at the summit of a small hill. And then we were in the air again and on our way.

I walked across the tarmac at Sir Seretse Khama airport feeling jet lagged but excited. The worst bit was over, for I hated flying, and at last I had arrived. A heat haze shimmered on the horizon and in the distance I could see the harsh outline of a rocky hill. To my left a group of soldiers were standing guard next to a military-looking plane, while beyond that I could see three small planes, so small I couldn't believe they could really fly.

The arrivals hall was a modest glass building and I was quickly ushered through immigration to wait for my luggage. Considering I had travelled halfway across the world my bags were light. I had had no idea of what to pack for a two-year trip and so I had thrown in some teaching materials, a few clothes, some favourite books.

I walked through customs and out into the

airport terminal, so busy looking for Ron that I walked straight into two British Council women. The women were blonde and pale, they held clipboards in their hands and they had already worked themselves into a flutter of preparation.

'Are you one of the teachers? Unified Teaching Service?' asked one.

'Yes.'

'And your name is . . . ?' The woman ran a red fingernail down her sheet of names. 'Right, here you are. If you could just wait over there . . . '

But now I had seen Ron standing a little back from the barrier on the shiny airport floor. He was standing with another man who I assumed was Duncan, a relative I knew Ron was staying with in Gaborone.

Ron saw me and, beaming, he rushed over. We stood there awkwardly for a moment, perhaps stunned by the fact we were now both in Botswana, and then we hugged. Although I had seen him just a couple of months ago he already looked different; his complexion was darker and his hair was now even shorter. He looked smarter somehow, his clothes clean and ironed. He had put on a little weight and I could sense, just by the way he stood and the expression on his face, that he had about him an air of confidence as if he were finally at ease.

'Where do you think you're going?' exclaimed one of the British Council women, rushing after me.

'Oh,' I said, disengaging myself from Ron. 'Sorry.'

The woman looked suspiciously at the two men.

'*Dumela Mma*,' said Duncan, holding out his hand.

The British Council woman smiled frostily.

'And you must be Caitlin,' Duncan said to me. 'Welcome to Botswana. You are very very welcome.'

'I'm sorry, but you must remain with the other teachers,' said the British Council woman.

'Where are you staying?' shouted Ron as I was steered away.

'Gaborone Sun.'

'I'll call you later,' he promised.

'This way please,' said the woman. 'How do you know him?' she asked suspiciously, glancing back to where Ron stood.

'He's my . . . boyfriend,' I said weakly.

She raised her perfectly plucked eyebrows. 'Well, I'm sorry but we do need all the teachers to stick together. We have an awful lot to get through this morning.'

The British teachers were herded out of the airport and we stood on the pavement facing a row of huge cactuses planted amid large brown stones. It was eleven in the morning and the sky was a cloudless blue. The air was hot but light, without the oppressive sense of humidity I'd experienced in the UK or on the east coast of the States. There was also a certain sort of light I had never seen before, very clear, very bright, so that I wanted to squint even while standing in the shade. I had been told that this was winter, but it was far hotter than I had imagined. I watched as

39

hotel buses pulled up at the terminal and tourists dressed in khaki got on board. Then the teachers were ushered on to a small white minibus known as a combi and driven to where we would be staying: the Gaborone Sun Hotel.

I sat by the window near the front of the combi, trying to take in everything around me. I had experienced the Farnham Castle briefing with its slide-show and handouts, and I had asked Ron numerous questions, but I still didn't really know what to expect. There was a part of me that still thought of Africa in terms of the Saturday morning *Tarzan* films I used to watch with my brother when we were kids. That Africa was jungle-like, full of wild animals and occasional natives, a place of adventure and danger. As an adult, the rare times I had seen images of Africa on TV they were of protests in Soweto with children beaten, police with riot shields and burning cars, or more recently horrific reports of people dying from famine in Ethiopia.

As I sat in the combi I couldn't help but press my face against the window. We were being driven incredibly fast along a dual carriageway which was bordered on each side by sand. For a mile or more we passed small bushes and thorny trees and little else. Then the buildings began; everywhere there seemed to be houses or offices going up. We passed one construction site after another until we appeared to enter the city itself. Chosen as Botswana's capital in 1966, I knew that Gaborone was one of the fastest growing cities in the world, yet it still had only 130,000 people. The houses now were large and low with sturdy white walls and ornate gates. The roads became busier and many of the vehicles were huge four-wheel drives empty but for the driver. On the pavements women walked with bags balanced on their heads. There didn't appear to be many traffic lights or street signs.

At last we approached the centre of the city, passing a tall glass-fronted building which we were told housed the offices of the Unified Teaching Services. Far off in the distance our attention was drawn to the grand Orapa House building where Botswana's diamond wealth was sorted and sent off across the world. Yet next to the immaculate tarred roads I could see that the land was still sand as if the city had just been built, carved and tarmacked out of the semi-desert.

We pulled up at the hotel, a grand building with doormen in full uniform as if guarding the Queen at Buckingham Palace. Inside the plush air-conditioned reception area there was a tinkle of glass chandeliers and in the corner a man playing 'As Time Goes By' on the piano.

We waited until we were checked in and then set off wearily along the silent, carpeted corridors to our rooms, passing uniformed women pushing trolleys piled high with toilet paper and complimentary soaps.

Once inside my room I sat on the bed for a moment and went into shock. Where was I? I mentally pictured a map of the world, marking with a cross a city near the southern tip of Africa. Then I worked my way aimlessly round

41

the room, picking up a 'Gaborone Sun Super Fun Book' from the bedside table which offered me a 10 per cent discount from the Bushman Gift Shop and eighteen free holes of golf. We had been told that accommodation in Gaborone was hard to find and that teachers posted in the capital could expect to spend months in a hotel. Although I had asked to be posted to Maun, I'd been told this was unlikely as teachers were needed in the south and the Gaborone area. I dreaded the idea of staying at the Gaborone Sun for weeks on end, sneaking out to meet Ron or perhaps sneaking him in. I opened the white curtains and stared out at the green lawn and the swimming pool, its water an almost impossible turquoise blue. The phone rang and I rushed to answer it.

'Hi, my love,' said Ron and I could tell from his voice he was smiling.

'Where are you?'

'At the end of the road.'

'Which way do I go?' I asked, feeling disorientated.

'Just come out of the hotel and turn left. I'll be at the corner of the third road on the right.'

Since Ron had returned to Botswana he had quickly got a job at a computer company in the African Mall. As we assumed I would be posted to a school in Gaborone, Ron had been home to Maun but was now settling down in the capital. He was staying with Duncan, a senior banking man, and his wife, Cecilia. I set off out of the hotel, following Ron's directions. The roads were busier now, and the pavements fuller with pedestrians. I felt light-headed as I walked, eager to take in everything new. As I passed a sports stadium on my left I saw a group of young men by the road, building what appeared to be a lookout post. As I passed them I realized I had, for a second, held my breath, bracing myself for them to call out the way builders in England or America would. But they had taken no notice of me, and I remembered reading that Botswana was one of the safest countries for a woman alone to travel through.

I caught sight of Ron standing on the corner and I tore across the road, dodging two combis which beeped at me as I ran.

'Oh, my God,' I said in a rush, 'I can't believe I'm here!'

'Nor can I.'

'Quick, let's go before the British Council women track me down.'

We set off along the road to Duncan's home, passing large white houses with front lawns and guard dogs. There seemed to be plenty of space here, the houses were not built on top of each other the way they were in England, rather they were situated on their own plot of land, part sand and part grass. Next to each large house was a little white building.

'Are those garages?' I asked.

Ron laughed. 'They are servants' quarters.'

'Wow,' I said. 'So everyone has a servant around here?'

'Pretty much.'

'What, like butlers or something?'

'Oh, maids, gardeners, nannies, you know.'

43

'No,' I laughed, 'I don't know. Is it normal then, to have a servant?'

'Not where I come from,' Ron said.

We stopped outside Duncan's house and I hesitated at the gate, feeling tired and scruffy all of a sudden. Ron led the way up a stone path and I hung back at the sound of dogs barking frantically.

'It's okay, they're chained up,' Ron said, opening the front door.

We walked straight into a large living-room, spacious yet full of colour and objects and furniture. The television was on and a South African gameshow was blaring out. There was no one in the room, and yet I felt somehow that I was being watched. I followed Ron under a small archway that led to another room, a dining area with a large oval wooden table. In the corner was a huge fridge-freezer, bigger even than anything I had seen in America. And then I saw it, the object that was making me feel watched, a stuffed buffalo head mounted halfway up the wall. I stopped nervously in front of it, the huge hairy face level with mine, its nose as wet as if it were alive. For a second I imagined that the rest of the buffalo's body were on the other side of the wall. As Ron walked across the room and through an open doorway, I hurried after him, trying to avoid the animal's yellow glass eyes. I knew Botswana was a hunter's paradise, but I hadn't expected dead buffaloes in the midst of what felt like suburbia.

Ron led the way through the kitchen and out into the sand yard at the back. In the corner two

Dobermans were chained up against the fence. Near the dogs, and apparently oblivious to their mad lunges at the chains, a woman sat on the sand, pounding clothes in a metal bath full of water and suds.

Ron spoke to her and she replied, laughing.

'Hi,' I said, embarrassed. I had asked Ron repeatedly about how to say 'hello' but although I knew the words I just couldn't bring them out of my mouth.

The woman looked at me, her arms resting on the side of the tin bath. '*Ee*,' she said, the 'ay' sound drawn out like someone agreeing mightily with someone else. Then she returned to her washing.

'Who was that?' I whispered as we entered the servant's quarters.

'She does the washing,' said Ron.

'I can see that. So she's a maid?'

'No, not really, she's Cecilia's sister's child.'

'Oh.'

Then we closed the door. The room was simple, empty but for a mattress on the floor and a small wooden chair. On the chair Ron had placed a card he had made at work, a card to welcome me to Botswana.

★   ★   ★

By the time we came out of the servant's quarters it was dark outside. Walking across the sandy yard, I looked up to see the biggest night sky I had ever seen. I felt dizzy and exhilarated as I stared up at the vast blackness imbedded with

45

the sharp glow of hundreds of stars. I had a feeling of weightlessness, as if for a moment I had lost all sense of gravity.

Inside the kitchen a woman was at the gas cooker stirring what looked like porridge in a huge pot.

'Hi!' I said to the woman, thinking wrongly that she was Cecilia. She was busy stirring, pounding a stick in and out of the pot. As the stick came out of the pot I could see it had hoops of metal at the end, like an egg whisk.

In the dining-room Duncan was sitting at the table working through the contents of a briefcase, a glass of beer by his side. I accepted a beer from Ron, wondering if women in Botswana drank beer, feeling self-conscious as I sat down to drink it. In the living-room a girl and two boys were sitting on the carpet watching TV.

'There is the food,' said the woman from the kitchen, coming in and placing several plates on the table. I took one of the plates and looked at it worriedly. There was a large piece of gristly brown meat on the bone and then a mound of something sticky and white. My stomach lurched; I was a vegetarian and meat made me nauseous.

'She doesn't eat meat,' Ron told the woman.

The woman stopped in her tracks on the way back to the kitchen. Ron said something in Setswana and the woman stared at me, as if not understanding.

'But this looks nice,' I said, pointing at the white mound.

'This is *bogobe*,' said Ron. 'It is made from sorghum, people call it *phaletshe*.'

'Oh.' I looked around for a fork.

'For your hands,' said Ron as the woman came back from the kitchen carrying a bowl of warm water. The woman offered first Duncan, then Ron, and then me, the water. Then she offered each of us a cloth to dry our hands on. Not a word was spoken during this procedure and I felt increasingly uncomfortable at being waited on. There was a clear hierarchy in the household. The men came first, then me — either because I was the guest or because I was white — and then the women. But just as I was thinking this there was a commotion in the other room, outside the dogs began barking and the children rushed to the front door.

'*Ko ko! Dumela!*' I heard a woman call out in a quivery voice.

Immediately Duncan rose and went into the living-room. An elderly woman was standing in the centre of the room, having some difficulty negotiating her way around the furniture with her walking stick. Duncan went to help her, easing her into a chair, calling at the boy to move a table and the girl to fetch water.

'Who's that?' I asked Ron.

'I think it's his aunt.'

I waited while the entire household rushed around the elderly woman who now sat on a soft wide chair. One by one the children and then the woman from the kitchen bowed before their elder, replying to her greetings and her handshake. I was amazed that the woman

47

commanded such respect purely because of her age.

When we had finished eating Ron gathered up the plates and took them into the kitchen. But the moment he started washing them in the sink the kitchen woman hurried over, alarmed.

'*Ao!*' she said and then spoke animatedly in Setswana.

Ron said something in reply and the woman howled with laughter. I had never seen Ron make people laugh in America. But I could tell that he wasn't yet comfortable with Setswana, that he was having to try quite hard to speak fluently. It had been years since he'd spoken his own language.

With the woman still laughing, Ron returned to washing the dishes.

'People will think you've bewitched him,' said Duncan, coming into the kitchen behind me. 'Next he will be carrying a baby on his back!'

'She has bewitched me,' said Ron with a smile.

I found the many visitors to the house that evening polite but not interested in the presence of a stranger from England, or at least I was not asked any questions about who I was or what I was doing in Botswana. I couldn't tell if people were not curious about my presence or if it were somehow rude to bring attention to it. One of the few times there was a comment was around midnight when I overheard a man saying to Ron in the kitchen, 'Well at least she's not *that* white.'

★　★　★

The next morning I woke early, worried about getting back to the hotel before our orientation began. And I hadn't been able to sleep well because of the unfamiliar sounds outside. A cock began crowing while it was still dark outside and it didn't stop until the whole room was bathed in light. I could smell smoke. I could hear people talking in the lane that ran behind the servant's quarters and a rhythmic, sweeping sound.

'What time is it?' I asked Ron.

'Half five.'

'You have to be kidding? Half *five*? It's the middle of the night. What time do you have to be at work?'

'Seven thirty.'

'How the hell do you manage that?'

Ron shrugged. He had already washed, shaved and dressed. I couldn't believe this was the same man who routinely slept through his midday classes at Clark University.

'Oh, my God,' I said, covering myself with the sheet, longing for more sleep.

In the yard I found a woman sweeping the sand. She was bent forward from the waist, with one hand resting horizontally across the pit of her back. The broom she used was flat and broad at the end and she was raking at the sand, making neat little lines across the yard. I wondered if she did this every morning, for surely the wind would soon blow the sand all over the place again.

Inside the main house two girls were at work. One was frying eggs, another was washing dishes.

'Where's Cecilia?' I asked Ron, for I had still not met her.

'She's gone to Kasane. This is Duncan's sister's child,' he said, gesturing to the girl at the sink. She turned and smiled shyly at me, doing a little curtsy before returning to the washing-up. The house seemed very busy. Everyone had their tasks and I wasn't sure what to do with myself.

'I've got to get back to the hotel,' I said.

'Take it easy, Cait,' said Ron accepting a cup of coffee from the girl who had now finished frying the eggs.

'But don't you have to be at work?'

'Yes.'

I sat down at the table and tried to relax. But I wasn't good at staying at other people's houses; I wanted my new life to start at once.

'I don't like being waited on,' I whispered to Ron when the girls left the room.

'Nor me,' he said. 'But they are just being respectful.'

*   *   *

I returned to the hotel where the other teachers were recovering from a five-course breakfast. We spent the rest of the day getting work permits and then in the afternoon I went to meet Ron again. We strolled around the main Gaborone mall, a long concrete axis paved with stones. On either side were low buildings, banks, a post office, a cinema, clothing and furniture shops with large window displays offering customers

50

the chance to buy on hire purchase, urging them to Lay Bye Now!

The atmosphere in the mall was relaxed and people seemed to be returning from a day's work. Men in suits strolled by, one or two holding hands. On either side of the long central pathway stalls were set up on the paving stones, selling leather bags, wooden ornaments and a few clothes. The women selling the goods sat well back from their stalls, chatting with each other in the shade of acacia trees. There was no sense of harassment or bargaining, no enticement of buyers at all, even when a white couple suddenly appeared, the man fingering his way through a wallet stuffed with paper money.

We walked from the main mall, across a main road, and along a sandy path to the African Mall where Ron worked. Here the low concrete buildings looked far older than in the main mall and the types of shop more modest. Dusty-looking pick-up trucks were parked in rows outside a fast-food restaurant. At the corner of the parking area two women were selling fruit and veg. They wore thick padded jackets which reminded me that this was supposed to be winter and not the summer it felt like to me. I glanced at the produce, expecting mangoes and pine-apples and hot-country fruit but there was just a pyramid of withered oranges next to a big pile of onions.

★ ★ ★

After three days spent idling away our time at the Gaborone Sun, the British teachers were finally moved en masse to Molepolole, a village some 50 kilometres north-west of Gaborone. We were driven there in two combis and we chatted about where we wanted to be posted and swapped what we had heard about Iraq's sudden invasion of Kuwait.

Most of us were growing restless, our paperwork was in order and while we were keen to begin a short course of language lessons, the orientation was proving haphazard. We were assigned dorms at the local college of education, and we ate in the student dining-room, which smelt at all times of instant coffee, boiled milk and fried eggs.

Each day we waited hours for our orientators to arrive from where they stayed in comfort in Gaborone. On the second day we were told we were to be addressed by a senior representative of the Ministry of Education at 9 a.m. So well before 9 a.m. all the British stood in a line outside the lecture hall. We were still waiting there at 11 a.m. when the speaker finally arrived.

'What are you waiting for?' a woman yelled, having arrived with the ministry representative several hours late. 'Get into the hall!'

The notion of time, we soon realized, was not what we were used to. It was referred to as 'African time'. African time meant things happened when they happened, not when your timetable said they would and the British were getting increasingly desperate.

On the third day an elderly white man from

52

the Unified Teaching Service came to talk to us. He told us with pride that he had been in Botswana for twenty years and still didn't know any Setswana. Then he warned us that the African names of our students might be a bit of a problem to pronounce and that it was much easier to assign them numbers and use those instead.

★ ★ ★

As the week wore on still none of us had been told where we would be posted and everyone was feeling aimless and a little depressed. I still hadn't got a good impression of Botswana, having just seen the inside of a posh hotel, Duncan's house and a drab teaching college. So one morning I walked into Molepolole, the village in which the education college was located. It was my first experience of village life and I decided to practise the little Setswana I had been taught.

'*Dumela*,' I said to a woman on a sand pathway, stressing the second syllable the way our language teacher had taught us. The woman had a scarf around her head, like all the women I had seen, and a baby was on her back, wrapped tightly against its mother with a large white shawl.

'*Dumela mma! Le tsogile jang?*' said the woman, responding to my greeting and asking me how I was.

By the time I had got the reply out of my mouth the woman was half a mile down the path. I couldn't imagine how I would ever be able to speak the language when I couldn't remember a new word from one day to the next. We had spent our first two language lessons just on greetings, which had so many variations I was beginning to panic. There was a way to address men and a way to address women, and the problem with addressing men was that I just couldn't roll the 'r' in 'Rra'. There were ways to address an age mate or peer, and ways to address a child. There were formal and informal ways of greeting. Polite procedure meant the person approaching began the greeting, however you did not ask an elder how they were, but rather waited until they asked how you were. When the words I wanted flew out of my head during our language class I resorted to a loud 'Ee.'

Everywhere I went I could hear people saying Ee! It was in every sentence, punctuated every comment, answered every question. Ee meant yes, but it also meant: yes, I see what you're saying, yes, now you understand, yes, that's exactly right, yes, I couldn't agree with you more. Setswana seemed to be a language of agreement.

I walked on, passing hundreds upon hundreds of round houses. The walls were made from mud and the conical roofs of thatching grass. It was the most beautiful architecture I had ever seen, so compact, so well blended with the land. Some of the houses were left the colour of the mud they were made with, while others were painted a white so bright I wanted to shield my eyes as the sun bounced off the walls.

Walking through Molepolole it became clear that village life in Botswana was lived outside. I felt like a voyeur as I passed compound upon compound whose inhabitants were building fires, cooking, preparing vegetables, listening to the radio, washing, chatting, cleaning. Everyone seemed busy and yet everything seemed to be being done at such a leisurely pace. The atmosphere within the shops and the bank I entered was incredibly laid back: no queues, no sense of urgency. I began to wonder if the way people related to each other, the amount of time they spent greeting each other and agreeing with each other, the ingrained respect for elders, the sense of hard work but without any accompanying urgency, had made Botswana what it was: a haven of peace in a troubled region.

I took the main sand pathway back to the college and as I passed one homestead a group of young boys called out from behind a mud wall. '*Lekgoa!*' they shouted and the word was quickly picked up. '*Lekgoa! Lekgoa!*'

I knew this was the word for 'white person' but when I asked what it meant explanations varied. Some said it came from the verb *go kgwa* meaning to vomit, referring to those spewed up by the ocean. I was told the term wasn't very nice but the way it was sung out didn't appear insulting. Perhaps it was true, as we had been told on our orientation at Farnham Castle, that white expatriates were welcome here.

# 4

Bernie and I stood outside the Peace Corps building in central Gaborone, dying for a pee. The day before we had finally been given our teaching posts and Bernie and I were the only British teachers to be posted to Maun. An English teacher from London, Bernie had just spent several years teaching in Malaysia, where she had met and married her husband, Hassan. Now we stood sweating and moaning outside Peace Corps headquarters. We had arrived two hours ago from Molepolole, but before we set off on our trek to Maun we first had to pick up some Americans. I would have to travel the long journey north without Ron, because he still had to pluck up the courage to resign from the computer company he had just joined in the African Mall. Delivering bad news wasn't something Ron was good at, and he felt embarrassed that he had to tell his boss he was leaving.

'I *really* need a pee,' I said, dancing on the spot.

'Me too,' agreed Bernie.

'Excuse me,' I said to a man at the fence which marked off the Peace Corps headquarters. 'Can we just use the toilet?'

The man frowned. 'American?' he asked.

'No. British. We just want to use the loo.'

The man went off to consult with a superior

and then came back. 'They say you need an American passport.'

'What? To get to the toilet?'

Eventually we were allowed into the Peace Corps director's residential house next door. Then we were ordered into the combi where we sat and sweated for a further hour. Finally we set off, Bernie, Hassan and I, three Peace Corps volunteers, and four British teachers who would be dropped off in Francistown. We drove the whole day through endless unchanging land-scape of brown bush and small trees. Sometimes we were on the tar, sometimes on the sand and we bumped up and down in the little metal combi and complained. Often we couldn't see anything at all out of the windows because the truck in front of us which carried our luggage threw up such a storm of white dust that we coughed, even inside the combi. And the journey was made all the worse by a Peace Corps man who spoke into a little tape recorder the whole way.

'Now we're leaving Gaborone,' he began. '*Man*, is it hot!'

The British gave each other looks but the man didn't notice.

'Now we've been on the road for six hours and I've eaten all my candy. Now we're arriving in a small settlement, what's the name of this place guys? and we're stopping so Debbie can barf.'

I wondered who he was sending this tape to, or whether he was keeping it for himself. The last straw was when the Americans began singing 'Kum Ba Yah, My Lord, Kum Ba Yah.'

Finally, in the dark, we arrived at Francistown, Botswana's second largest urban centre and home to around 60,000 people. The town was several hundred kilometres north-east from Gaborone, situated on the railway line I had seen on the map. Francistown was the last train stop in Botswana. It was far older than Gaborone and its name came from an English gold prospector back in the 1860s when gold had been found along the Tati River, sparking off southern Africa's first gold rush. There were few streetlights, but I could see that we were travelling along a wide tarred road lined on either side with trees and short, squat office-looking buildings. I thought I saw a sign for Woolworth's. I wondered if there were still gold mines in the area and if so where exactly they were.

The next morning, Bernie, Hassan and I asked the truck driver if we could sit in his vehicle and a German man, Thomas, joined us. He had been in Botswana before and loved the place so much that he had returned for another contract. He knew the area a little and he spoke some Setswana too. We quickly moved the suitcases around and made ourselves comfortable, sitting up high with clothing wrapped around our heads and faces to keep all the sand and dust away. It was the way to travel, up high and in the open air. Now the tar road had ended and urban life disappeared behind us. It felt like we were embarking on a great adventure in a huge country where it was possible to drive for hours without seeing a living soul. The air smelt of wild sage. There were no shops, no houses, no motorways, just four ostriches hurrying in a loopy-legged fashion along the road.

A few hundred kilometres later, the landscape changed and there were palm trees and houses. We crossed a small bridge over a dry riverbed and entered the village of Nata where we were to stop for lunch. A German woman who was acting as our chaperone told us a booking had been made to feed ten people, but I couldn't see how as there were no phones anywhere and I hadn't seen a post office either. All I saw were the by-now familiar round houses, women walking with buckets of water on their heads, men sitting in their yards, goats and donkeys everywhere.

After lunch at Sua Pan Lodge we got back on the truck, retied the clothing on our heads and settled down. But now the ride was really bumpy and we were thrown around, moving grindingly slowly in thick sand and then suddenly spurting forward, then coming to a stop and then starting again. The land around us was flat with sandy dips that looked as if they had once held water. On our left we passed an enormous baobab tree, its trunk wider than our truck, its thick branches twisted up towards the sky.

Thomas, the German man, sat up high on a tyre and looked around.

'There is a leopard,' he said just as the sun was fading.

I laughed.

'No, look, there, it is a leopard. I can tell by the way it's sitting.'

59

We peered across the flattish scrubland, the grass brown in the dying light and the tips of the trees golden and glowing, to a stone with a shadow on top. It seemed completely bizarre, a lone leopard in this desolate bush. What did it eat, where did it sleep? I had only ever seen a leopard before pacing up and down in a cage at London Zoo.

We arrived in Maun just as night was falling. One minute we were in the bush, bumping up and down, and the next we slid on to a tarred road and there were lights all around us. Not electric lights but lights from hundreds of compound fires. After six hours of bush we had arrived at civilization and we all hung over the side of the truck as we crossed a river containing the first sign of water we had seen for two days. Again I wanted to place myself on a map, to pinpoint this sudden explosion of life in a place that could only be reached by a torturous sand path from Francistown, 500 kilometres away.

Maun was extremely flat. I couldn't work out where it began and where it ended. We were obviously travelling along a main road but on both sides houses disappeared far into the bush and the night. Nothing was higher than the dense acacia trees and the sky hung over the village like a massive black umbrella. I felt as if I had arrived somewhere totally self-contained, inaccessible and removed from the rest of the world. This was the Wild West's frontier town I had heard and read so much about. Established in 1915 as the capital of a group of people called the Batawana, the name Maun meant 'the place of reeds'. I had read that this was derived from the San word 'maung'. But Ron had told me it came from a word in Seyei, the language of his mother's people, one of the dozens of languages spoken in Botswana. The Seyei word described a part of the Thamalakane River where the banks were elevated and covered with reeds. The truck came to a stop and so did the combi. It was dark so it was hard to see why we had stopped or where. Thomas told us it was Riley's Hotel, and that we would stay here before being placed in our schools. A pick-up truck went past us and the men in the back shouted and waved and laughed.

'What are they saying?' I asked Thomas. It was beginning to drive me crazy that I couldn't understand what was being said around me. I didn't know what people on the streets were saying, what people in shops were saying, or what announcers on the radio were saying.

'Um,' said Thomas and he shrugged.

'Go on, what are they saying?'

'They are saying something like . . . ' He coughed. 'Fuck off back to your own country.'

Bernie and I laughed. 'I thought we Brits were going to be welcomed with open arms?' I said. 'That's what they said at Farnham Castle.'

The German woman came out of Riley's Hotel, of which all we could see were some electric lights in the trees. 'I'm sorry, they say we can't stay here. We'll try Island Safari Lodge.'

So we bumped our way through Maun, the tar road having ended as suddenly as it began, carrying on through deep dark bush for another

10 kilometres until we arrived at Island Safari. Getting out of the truck I could smell we were near water. We made our way along a narrow pathway bordered by huge trees covered in creepers. A sign on a fence lit up by the orange glow of a light read: Island Safaris. Photographic Safaris, Expeditions and Outfitting.

Thomas led the way to a thatched brick building. Instead of glass, the windows were open to the night sky and I could hear a buzzing sound that I thought might be cicadas. Inside the room people were drinking beer and playing darts. It was hot, noisy and cheerful. Some of the darts players turned to glance at us as we walked in and then returned, uninterested, to their game.

An hour later we sat at a table eating pizza, our energy restored, our legs stretched out on the cement floor. Then suddenly we stopped with the slices halfway to our mouths as a deep, explosive sound came from somewhere in the dark outside. The sound came three times, an echoing, bouncing, deep-throated chuckle that gave me goosebumps along both arms. Then it was silent again.

'Hippo,' Thomas said. 'That's a hippo.'

'Where is it?' I whispered.

'In the river outside.'

'Oh.' I remembered reading about hippos in a guidebook. I had read that you should never get in between a hippo and water. And if you were on a boat and saw a hippo, then you were to warn it of your presence by tapping on the side of the boat or talking loudly.

* * *

I woke up on that first morning in Maun to the warmth of the sun coming in through the zebra-patterned curtains and the sound of doves and a bird singing 'go awaaa, go awaaa'. I knew what this was; it was the Go Away bird. Moving around quietly, as Bernie and Hassan were still asleep on the other bed, I looked outside the window and watched two dogs barking at the foot of a huge gnarled tree. I craned my neck upwards and finally realized I was looking at some monkeys. They were running along the branches, stopping to bounce up and down, scratch their armpits and make faces, deliberately driving the dogs wild. 'Bernie,' I hissed, unable to appreciate this alone. 'There are bloody *monkeys* outside.'

I went out and walked towards the Thamalakane River which was right in front of the room. The scenery was stunning. The river was wide and sparkling, its surface crystal clear. This, I had been told, was the month when the Thamalakane was highest. It was the time of year when the floods which originated in Angola had made their way through the channels of the Okavango Delta and into Maun. I walked back to the bar area and saw the windows and doorway were now boarded with matted screens. So I sat on a brightly coloured bench overlooking the river. It looked inviting even though the German woman had warned us the night before never to trail a hand in the water when on a boat because a crocodile would bite it off. I scanned the surface of the river, not seeing any crocodiles, not really believing there really were any crocodiles. And, if they hibernated in winter as I had been told, where were they now?

Before me the white walls of the lodge led down to the water and at the end of a little jetty a large wide boat and several small speedboats were tied up. I watched while a man came out from a building behind the bar and set off down the steps to the pier. He pushed out a canoe, took a long pole, and climbed in. On the other side of the river three women in green and white uniforms were standing, waiting for the man to reach them. It seemed an amazing way to go to work, to be poled across a river. But as the man reached halfway across the river the women began to shout and wave their arms. The man appeared to stop for a second, he shouted something back and the women began waving again, indicating that he should steer to his left. I peered at the water, not seeing what the drama was about.

The man reached the other side and the women waiting on the riverbank clambered into the canoe. I thought they looked nervous and the man was now poling quickly. As they reached the jetty they all leapt up on to the steps while the man tied up the canoe. Suddenly there was a terrific splash and burst of spray, and a hippopotamus shot out of the water, its massive mouth opening to display teeth so large they looked like tusks. The women stood on the jetty, rearranging their clothes and laughing. Then the hippo sank back into the river and the surface was clear and smooth again, as if nothing had happened at all.

★　★　★

After the usual breakfast of instant coffee and fried eggs, we got back on our truck ready to set off back to Maun. That's right, I reminded myself, we weren't here on holiday but to start a new job. Just as we left Island Safari Lodge an American woman joined us. We were told that she knew Maun well and would be able to get us all to our different schools in the village.

'How you guys doing?' she called as she swung herself into the front of the truck.

Bernie replied politely. Hassan lit a cigarette.

'*Go siame!*' the woman yelled to one of the lodge employees who stood and stared impassively as we drove off. Then the woman opened the window connecting the cabin of the truck with the back, so she could talk to us as we travelled.

We drove back through the bush, bumping up and down as we left Island Safari behind us. In daylight the bush was less mysterious than it had been the night before. Now we could see the wide sand path before us, winding its way through a forest of acacia trees whose branches tore, screaming, along the metal sides of the truck. There were no houses and no people, just sand and thorns and the blue sky.

After half an hour we came to a crossroads in the sand and, turning right, we travelled back in the direction of Maun. The path was smoother now; the sand less deep, but still the going was slow. We passed termite mounds which looked like sand sculptures, a couple of rectangular mud houses, their iron roofs held on with stones, and large thorn trees like spiky mushrooms.

'That's the new hotel!' called the American woman, waving her arm to the left. We looked to where she pointed and saw a clearing had been made in the bush half a kilometre from the road. There stood a large, glaringly white building with pillars in front and steep wide stone steps leading down to a sand courtyard. The size, and the colour, seemed shocking somehow after all the muted shades of brown and green in the bush. The hotel looked so out of place, so new and concrete, that it could have just been dropped there, ready made.

Ten minutes later we reached Maun's one strip of tar road and suddenly we sat comfortably, moving quickly, our eyes free from the sand and dust.

'Safari South!' yelled the American woman as we passed a low building on the left, set away from the road, its corrugated-iron roof glinting amid a clump of tall dark-green trees. 'Oldest safari company in Maun!'

As we passed, I glanced to my right and saw a turn-off for the airport. A collection of hand-painted signs on wooden sticks that had been sunk into the sand advertised a Bushman Curio Shop and the Duck Inn. We continued along the road, looking this way and that as things became more crowded with people and buildings. The road was bordered now with low white buildings, the doors and windowsills painted a pale blue. Each house sat squarely in its own plot, identical in size and appearance to its neighbours. The yards had freshly raked sand and little else.

'Cop shop!' yelled the American woman. 'Magistrates' court!' I turned to my left to see low dark-red painted buildings that were connected to each other, forming three sides of a square.

'Oldest building in Maun!'

As we sped past I craned my neck trying to see which building the American woman was referring to. For a second I expected to see the sort of old building I would see in north London, several storeys high, Edwardian and in need of repair. But all I could see was a very small whitewashed round house, its walls slightly crooked, its thatched roof a burnt brown.

As we continued on our way to our schools we passed a sign for a prison and then came to what appeared to be the most commercial part of village.

'Downtown Maun!' laughed the American woman as we passed a sign to Riley's Hotel, a pale-yellow stone building that belonged to a safari company, a clothing and gift shop, a garage and a small food shop. Yet opposite this array of shops and offices, on the other side of the tar road, the land was total bush, brown and overgrown except for a barren cleared area where a football match was in progress.

Then we turned off the tar road and into the residential part of the village. Now all the land was sand and everything seemed to be different shades of brown — the trees, the houses, the thatching of the roofs, the low mud or high reed walls that appeared to mark off different compounds. Everything looked the same; how would I ever find my way around? We passed one signpost with a handdrawn picture of a phone but never came across a phone.

Then the truck came to a stop and we lurched forward. Two donkeys, their flanks the colour of chocolate and dust, had run into the road, braying manically. In the middle of the pathway they suddenly stopped and stood there silently, motionless but for their tails that switched away the flies. The truck driver put his arm out of the window and gave one of the donkeys a resounding slap across its back. The donkeys ran off and we drove on, passing a butcher's shop with wooden posts outside that looked as if they might be used for tethering horses. On our left was a sign for the Kgotla, the traditional court and meeting place, while on our right several buildings were in the process of either going up or crashing down. In one yard was a new, concrete house with no window-panes. Next to it was the skeleton of a round house, the stripped lengths of wood forming a perfect circle on the sand.

Finally we swung through the metal gates of Tshwaragano Community Junior Secondary School and into a sand courtyard. Things seemed very peaceful and quiet, though we were in fact arriving late and school would start tomorrow.

I took my bags down off the truck and waved goodbye to Bernie and Hassan. As the truck drove out of sight I realized I didn't have Bernie's phone number at her new school, but then I thought perhaps the school didn't have a phone anyway. I stood with my bags on the empty courtyard, wondering what to do and which way to go. Then the headmaster appeared, a short plump man in his forties wearing shorts and a torn T-shirt. He took me to my new house, a perfect concrete square with one window at the front and one on the side. Around the house was dry grass but it looked as if someone had tried to grow vegetables not too long ago for I could see the withered remains of two tomato plants.

'This is your home,' said the headmaster. 'You must feel comfortable here. You are welcome.'

'Thanks, thanks a lot.' I kept on grinning stupidly. I was so happy to have arrived, to have finally made it to Maun. 'I'm sorry we got here so late, we had to . . . ' I began, but the headmaster just waved my apology away.

Amazingly some clouds had gathered in the sky and I looked up and asked, 'Do you think it's going to rain?'

The headmaster thought for a while. 'In Africa,' he said, 'we do not ask, 'Will it rain?' When it is raining, then we say, 'Now it is raining.' '

'Oh, right.'

My new home smelt of flaky cement and mosquito spray. The front door led straight into a small living-room, its walls painted a faded peppermint green except for half a metre all along the bottom which was painted a shiny gloss blue. Before me a crooked archway led into a tiny kitchen where there was a sink and a stove, and a window with a view over the pathway that ran behind the back of the school. To the right of the kitchen was a small shower room and toilet. The walls were again peppermint green and there were brown stains around the showerhead. The tiny bedroom held just a bed frame and bare mattress.

I went back into the living-room with a satisfied feeling. I had arrived. I opened my suitcase and took out my wrinkled clothes and books. Damn, forgot to bring the linen, the glass and the cutlery, I laughed to myself. Then I wondered what exactly I was going to sleep on. I didn't have a bowl or a spoon to eat with, a pot to cook in, any gas for the cooker to cook with. I didn't even have a tea bag. That night I slept badly on the bare mattress. It was too hot, much hotter than it had been in Gaborone or Molepolole, though officially it was still winter. The mosquitoes drove me crazy and I had nothing to fight them off with. At least, I told myself, this wasn't the malaria season. I hallucinated about flying insects in the air, heard strange singing voices and woke sitting upright on the hard bed. Later the students told me the school was built near a graveyard and people had seen spirits here.

In the morning I washed with cold water and headed to the school building. But when I got to the staff room I nearly ran back home. For the relaxed headmaster from the day before was now wearing a crisply ironed black suit with a sparkling white shirt and gold cuff links, all the men wore ties and all the women were decked out in their teaching finery. Batswana, I realized, were a very smart group of people and no one would dream of going to work without being thoroughly overdressed.

The bell went for morning assembly and I followed the other teachers outside to where all the children were lined up in the back courtyard. The teachers stood in a row in the shade of the staffroom roof, the children stood stiffly in the glaring sun. The girls wore deep-red tunic dresses with white shirts, white socks and black shoes, the boys red trousers and white shirts. Suddenly, although they must have been told to do this, they began to sing the national anthem.

'*Fatshe leno la rona, Ke mpho ya Modimo* . . . ' they began slowly, their voices low. *This land of ours, is a gift from God*. And then the anthem progressed and the voices grew strong and loud and the sound was so beautiful, the children's faces so serious and so proud, that I felt an awkward lump in my throat.

'*Tshogang, tsogang! Banna, tsogang!*' they sang, their voices rousing, filling the courtyard as they called on first men and then women to rise and stand. I looked along the row of teachers and all of them were singing as well, the eight black Batswana teachers, a young white American man, and a middle-aged Indian woman. '*Ka kutlwano le kagisano, E bopagantswe mmogo,*'

71

they sang, *Through our unity and harmony, We'll remain at peace as one.*

As the anthem finished, I began to shift worriedly. I assumed the headmaster would introduce the school's new teacher and I didn't look forward to having all the children turning to stare in my direction.

'*Bomma le Borra*,' intoned the headmaster, nodding to the teachers, 'Girls and boys, you are welcome to a new term at Tshwaragano CJSS. Now, before we begin I would like to talk to you, to *advise* you, on certain modes, or one could say *methods*, of behaviour expected from you this term . . . '

I tuned out as the headmaster spoke and began thinking about how to get a gas bottle so I could cook that evening.

'Remember, we are your parents,' continued the headmaster. 'Respect us as you would your parents. And we will discipline you as needs be, as your parents themselves would do. There will be *no* fighting at breaktime over food . . . '

Two of the teachers standing near me chuckled and one began rubbing his fingers up and down the stick he held in his hand.

'And today we welcome a new teacher to our school. She is from *England*. Mrs Davies . . . ?'

I smiled as the children looked my way. Their faces were turned toward me, but their eyes were averted to the ground. One or two took quick glances at my clothes, my face, and then returned their eyes to the sand. I felt as if a spotlight were on me. I smiled again, despite myself. I didn't want to smile; I knew from my

72

experience at Stanley Deason that a new teacher must come in hard. She must appear to be firm, in control and preferably a little scary. But still I smiled.

# 5

I was sitting on the stone step outside my new home at peace with the world. School was over for the day and Ron, who had just arrived from Gaborone, was in the kitchen cleaning fish. I had had a strange morning. One of the students had asked me about AIDS and the others had laughed at her, saying as long as you didn't share a blanket with a white person then it was impossible to become infected. A senior teacher had then taken me to one side and said such things should not be talked about with children.

I was enjoying teaching at Tshwaragano, yet I felt I had to tread carefully for the school was nothing like what I was used to. When I entered my classroom each morning the students were ready and waiting, sitting to attention at their wooden desks. None spoke until I did, and every response, every enquiry, was prefaced by the word 'Madam'. The students were to do as they were told, and if they didn't then they were beaten. While the undercurrent of physical violence unnerved me, the existing sense of discipline meant that I was free to teach. I didn't have to send students out, I didn't have to quieten them down, instead, I longed to get them to speak, to lose their fear of asking questions.

From where I sat outside my house I could see a clump of mophane trees and, perched on the highest, was a paradise flycatcher shaking out its multicoloured tail like a peacock. Although the winter landscape of Maun was so dry, the trees bare, the grass brown, there were moments of brilliance like this, the plume of a delta bird or the sudden sinking of the sun. It was September and now, a few hours from dusk, the heat of the day was beginning to lift and the air was growing cool. This evening I was going to meet Ron's family for the first time.

On the pathway to the left of our house I could see Rra Pitso, the school's watchman. In a few hours he would begin his nightly rounds. He was in his seventies, and I couldn't work out why the school had hired someone so elderly as a watchman unless it was because they had no fear of crime. Each night Rra Pitso made his way tortuously slowly around the school property, the beam from his torch shining in a wobbly fashion on the sand, as he talked and muttered and laughed to himself.

Sitting on the step, looking out across the land, I could hear the playful shouts of children on their way home from school, calls of 'Oa yaka!' — You are lying! — coming high and clear across the earth. There was something about the flatness of Maun that made it possible to hear conversations even in the yards outside the school grounds. In the mornings I lay in bed and listened to people in nearby reed houses exchanging greetings.

*Dumela Mma.*

*Dumela! How have you risen?*

*I have risen well. And you, have you risen?*

*I have risen well.*

And as the sun rose each day particles of sand and dust hovered in the air and the tips of the reeds looked as if they were on fire.

'Shall we go?' Ron asked. 'It's getting late. People around here, we don't really visit at night, and my grandmother is waiting for us. She'll think something terrible has happened to me.' It had taken several weeks before Ron had felt able to resign from his job in Gaborone, and then several days for him to travel up to Maun. Now that he was here life was becoming easier. I had a friend and a guide, and now at last I would meet his family.

We set off through the school grounds and out along the sand path. Walking on an evening such as this was almost like swimming, for it meant walking through patches of hot air and then patches of cool air, like suddenly coming across a warm spot in the sea. I assumed it was something to do with the seasons, with the fact that winter was coming to an end and now summer would begin.

By now I was familiar with the main sand path from the school to the Maun shops, the nearest of which was P.A.W Supermarket, a tiny stone building with tinned goods and an off-licence next door called a bottle store. A few days earlier I had passed a young man, sitting drunk outside the bottle store. His head had been held up so he faced the sun and he was saying one word over and over again: 'Saddam, Saddam, Saddam.' He said it with reverence, as if Saddam Hussein were a hero of his.

But although I had walked many times down this path, I had not ventured into the village itself and I had no idea where Ron's family lived. I found it exhausting walking on sand. I was used to being a fast walker and I was used to tar roads and pavements and now suddenly I couldn't get up any speed. And in Maun the whole land was sand, white like a vast beach but without any sea in sight. Sometimes, walking on the sand at dusk like this, I could almost believe I was on a beach, that if I just walked a few more kilometres I would suddenly come to the sea. In the very early morning, and again just before the sun set, the sand appeared almost purple, dark and bruised where trees cast shadows or where footprints dug deep.

As we walked I could hear the jangle of cows' bells in the distance. Goats were everywhere, standing on their hind legs, tearing determinedly at the spiky branches of small thorn trees. Outside compounds people leant on gateposts chatting. We passed a small boy in shorts pushing a wire car with a long metal handle and he paused to let us pass as if he really were driving a car and we had right of way.

I looked down at my legs, worrying that my skirt might be too short.

'Are you sure this is okay?' I asked Ron.

'Of course it is,' he said, easily.

'I mean, do you think I should have worn a dress?'

'My grandmother won't care what you are wearing.'

'And your mother?'

Ron just laughed. He stopped as a dusty yellow pick-up veered off the road and came to a halt beside us. 'Hey, Mozambia.' The driver laughed and waved, hanging his hand out of the window and catching Ron's fingers. Ron's nickname was Mozambia because, growing up in Boyei ward, he had looked out of place with the light complexion he had inherited from his white South African father and his long, straight nose. Mozambia meant, literally, person from Zambia.

Ron and the man stood there holding hands and joking. In the back of the vehicle was a huge mound of rotting vegetables and, on the back of the spare wheel, two women sat perched like chickens.

'This is my friend Caitlin,' Ron said.

The man looked serious now. He turned off the engine and got out. He was tall, far taller than Ron or I, and he had to turn sideways to get his large body out of the car. As he straightened up I saw how smartly he was dressed in a black collarless shirt made from a silky material. Around his neck he wore a gold chain with a silver Africa that glinted in the sun.

'*Dumela Mma*,' the man said to me, taking my hand. '*O tsogile jang*? I am Bashi. I am Mozambia's very old friend. Isn't that so?' He turned to Ron. 'I knew your husband here when he was still wearing little shorts! Welcome,' Bashi said, letting go of my hand and opening out his arms, spreading them out as far as they would go. 'Welcome to our beautiful Botswana! Is Mozambia teaching you Setswana? I will be your teacher; I will make an African of you! And where are you two going? Can I give you a lift?'

'We're going to Ron's mum's,' I said.

'That is good, yes. That is the African way. You must visit your in-laws, for you are our daughter now, isn't it?' and he laughed uproariously and slapped Ron on the back. 'Tsamaya sentle,' he called, getting back in the car.

'He seemed nice,' I offered as Bashi drove off in a cloud of dust.

Ron smiled. 'He was pretty much the only one who wrote to me while I was in America.'

'What does he do?'

'This and that,' he said, not sounding sure. 'He used to be a farmer, now he's trying to buy up land. He says he wants to build houses and rent them to white people!' and Ron laughed as if this were a reckless idea.

We walked a further couple of kilometres and then turned left into Boyei ward. In Maun each population group had their own traditional area and this is where the Bayei lived. Setswana was a language of prefixes — so the country was Botswana, people were Batswana, a person was a Motswana and the language was Setswana. Ron's mother and grandmother also belonged to the Bayei people, each was a Moyei, they spoke Seyei and lived in Boyei ward. All around the land was dotted with round mud houses with thatched roofs in sandy yards. Nothing seemed to be growing in any of the yards, and on the bushes on the side of the path plastic bags hung like weird white fruits caught on the thorns.

'So this is where the Bayei live? All this, this is their ward?'

'This is where we were told to stay, yes,' said Ron. 'When we were still slaves.'

'Which was when?' I asked. The word slave was shocking; I could not imagine that Ron's grandmother had ever been a slave.

'Oh, a while ago,' said Ron.

'And by who? Who made the Bayei live here?'

'By whom,' corrected Ron.

I laughed, exasperated. Ron was always correcting my English.

'So who told you you had to move here, the Ba . . . the Ba . . . the Ba who?'

'The Batawana,' said Ron. I knew the Batawana were one of eight population groups to be officially named as 'tribes' under British rule, and they remained the only eight tribes recognized in Botswana's modern constitution. But I was still unsure how the Batawana had come to rule over the Bayei. I wanted to ask Ron more, but now that we had entered Bayei territory he was distracted by having to stop every few yards as people called out to him.

'Mozambia!' an elderly woman cried.

Ron introduced me to the woman, his grandmother's elder sister, and I smiled obligingly. She was a tiny woman, with a deeply lined face and a bent back. In her arms she held bunches of white and blue plastic bags. It looked as if she had been collecting them. As I looked closer I saw pieces of plastic peeping out from where she had stuffed them down the front of her dress.

'*A ka ka ka!*' the woman laughed. She took my hand and turned it so the palm was facing up.

Then she sprinkled it with little dry kisses. I smiled, embarrassed.

'*Dumela Mma,*' I said.

The woman laughed so hard she had a coughing fit, and then she began talking quickly, and as she did so she poked protectively at the plastic bags down her dress.

'What's she saying?' I whispered to Ron.

'She says that you are her daughter and that you can already speak Setswana.'

'Oh, I can't,' I protested. 'Tell her I can't.'

Ron shook his head. 'I can't contradict an elder.'

I looked at him as if he were mad.

The woman finally let go of my hand and we beamed at each other. Then she hurried away.

'Is she collecting those bags?' I asked.

'It looks that way.'

'But why?'

Ron looked sad. 'She's a little unbalanced. She didn't used to be that way. I don't know what happened.'

'Can we help?' I asked. 'She looks emaciated.'

'She has children,' said Ron. 'They are the ones who should be helping her.'

We stopped several more times before we reached Ron's family's compound. By now I was getting confused. 'Who was that?' I asked as we moved from one well-wisher to another.

'My aunt.'

'Your mum's sister?'

'Yes.'

'But I thought your mum doesn't have any sisters?'

'Well,' Ron paused in order to think about it. 'It's my grandmother's sister's child. You know my grandmother was married, then she left her husband and he married again. He had several daughters from the second woman and one of those . . . '

But he had lost me already.

'Are we here?' I asked, as Ron slowed down.

He nodded.

'Are you nervous?' I asked for Ron was stroking his chin in the thoughtful way he did when he had something on his mind.

'Of course not,' he said.

I looked around, not sure if I would be able to find my way here on my own. I thought that without Ron I would be totally lost. One sand pathway gave way to another with no landmarks that would ever stick in my mind. There were no streets, no street names, no billboards, no big buildings. On my left was a fence made from wire mesh, tied to tree branches sunk into the sand. The fence had sagged and was so low in parts it would have been easy for me to simply step over it. But it seemed to mark a pathway that ran between the mass of compounds and it served as a washing-line for I could see a row of white T-shirts hanging out to dry. On our side of the fence were three palm trees, the lower branches brown and shaggy, and a giant root of a tree that looked as if it had been felled by something violent, perhaps lightning.

Ron had stopped in front of a tall reed wall. The dark-brown reeds stood vertically in the sand and were tied tightly together, although they were fraying a little at the top. Four strands of reeds ran horizontally along the wall, keeping the structure in place. I could see why Maun was the place of reeds: they were the basic building materials that nearly everyone used to construct their homes.

There was a gap in the middle of the reed wall, which served as a doorway. Over the top of the wall I could see wisps of fire smoke and the tip of a thatched roof.

'*Ko ko!*' Ron called as we approached the gap in the reed wall. *Ko ko!* was the easiest Setswana expression I had learned. It was the equivalent of saying 'knock knock' and it was said when arriving at anyone's yard because, of course, there was no door to actually knock on.

'*Ee,*' a woman's voice called out from within.

As we walked forward I remembered how Ron had described his one ambition as a child. He had a dream of entering his mother's compound with money in his pockets, with the ability to finally look after the women in his life the way they had for so long looked after him. I thought it was touching, the way he had never turned his back on his roots.

We walked through the gap and into the yard itself. The white sand was freshly raked and there wasn't so much as a stray leaf on the ground. The way the reed wall surrounded the entire yard made it feel like I was entering a private sanctuary cut off from the village around it. No one passing on the pathways outside could see what anyone was doing in here, and although I could hear voices, the wall was high enough that I couldn't see out.

The yard was bare but for a roll of wire mesh, a tin bath, a white plastic container and a thick log of wood. But I had the impression that the yard had just been cleaned, that things had been cleared away and that normally it was a busier, more crowded place. And it was clear that the people sitting in the compound were all waiting for me. As I counted first two, then three, then six people, I felt a sense of panic. Which one should I address first? How should I behave?

In front of me two elderly women sat on a piece of green tarpaulin, their legs stretched out before them, scarves on their head. Their faces were serious; they looked as if they were wearing their best clothes. To their left, a small girl in a pink dress was building a fire, arranging a pyramid of sticks, and then placing a black, three-legged pot on top.

'*Mozambia we!*' one of the women sitting on the sand sang out, clapping her hands. This had to be Ron's grandmother, Madintwa. I had heard all about her, from how she had got her name, to the fact that she was the only elder not to have beaten Ron as a child. At night they used to sleep together, Madintwa giving Ron's little toddler legs a pinch when he strayed on to her side of the mattress.

Ron went up to his grandmother and shook her hand, speaking softly and making her laugh. She looked up at him, drinking in his face, his presence, appearing to forget entirely about me.

Next to Madintwa sat another elderly woman, frowning in concentration. Behind the women an

84

elderly man sat on a wooden slatted chair. He wore a three-piece grey suit and had a white handkerchief tied round his head, knotted in the corners like an old man sitting in a deckchair on Brighton beach. Behind him a younger man stood, his head was shaved and he had a very dark complexion with sharp cheekbones. He half nodded at me and then looked away.

'*Dumelang Borra le Bomma*,' Ron said to the people in the compound, releasing his grandmother's hand. The people responded and Ron went round each one, even the little girl, shaking their hands. He had seen his grandmother the day before, and yet here they were greeting each other so formally. And it was the formalities, I thought, that set the pace of life in Botswana, slowing it down. It was hard to be in a rush if you had to greet each and every person, ask how they were, say how you were, before even getting to the purpose of any visit.

I was about to do the same, to tour the compound shaking hands, when a boy rushed into the yard dragging a white plastic chair. He set the chair very purposefully next to my legs.

'No, it's fine, really,' I said, wanting to sit on the same level as the women. I suddenly realized that I was yet to see a woman in Maun actually sitting on a chair, unless she was a teacher in the staff room. As the boy stood there determinedly with the chair, I thought perhaps it would be rude not to take the seat I was being offered. I sat down a little stiffly and looked around. There were two houses in the compound. The one on the right looked weather-beaten, there was a

85

doorway but no door and stakes of wood held up a sagging roof. In front of the house a woman sat slumped against the step. She had her head down and she wasn't moving.

But it was the house in front of us that drew my real attention. Like its neighbour, it was a round house, but its coffee-coloured walls were entirely smooth, and it had a wooden door as high as the roof. The roof itself was a burnt brown and the rim rippled unevenly around the top of the walls. At the bottom of the walls, running all the way round the house, was a little step. This, I told myself, was the house in which Ron had grown up, the place where he had spent his childhood. I could not, for a second, imagine how he had moved from this to the skyscrapers of Massachusetts.

Everyone in the compound was talking now and it sounded, for a second, as if they were arguing. I could not understand a word, except for the frequent use of '*Ee!*' and I wondered if they were discussing me.

Madintwa gave a sudden exclamation and held out her hand. She had to be talking to me. I leant out of the chair, almost falling over, and then got down and squatted on the sand. She took my hand with a warm, hard grasp and pulled me nearer. Her hands were large and strong, with marked veins along her forearms. She pulled me towards her until I was kneeling in front of her, just inches away from her face. She smelt of fire smoke and baby oil.

Madintwa was not as old as I had imagined, certainly not as old as my much-loved grandmothers, both of whom had recently died. She had a round, unlined face and her eyes were a little slanted, giving them a beseeching look. She wore a two-piece shirt and skirt, the top a riot of yellow and purple and blue. Her scarf was also yellow, but with a pattern of deep-blue flowers. She wore it tight across her forehead, a little like a pirate, and above each ear peeped black hair tinged with grey. I could see that her eyes were a little blurred with the beginning of milky-white cataracts in the corners. To the left of her wide broad nose was a little bobble of skin. Her ears ran straight down to her jawline, with no ear lobes at all. When she smiled, as she did now, her cheeks filled out and to my relief she no longer looked serious but mischievous and playful.

Madintwa began to speak in a deep, melodious voice. For a moment I felt as if I were in church and she were the preacher. She talked on and on, grasping my hand, looking me directly in the eyes as if believing that the more she talked the more likely I would be to understand.

'She's welcoming you to Botswana,' Ron explained, as at last his grandmother paused for breath.

Madintwa said something to Ron, and then waited for him to translate.

'She's says you're very welcome here.'

I smiled and was about to stand up when I realized Madintwa was still holding on to my hand.

'Thank you,' I said.

'*Ee!*' Madintwa laughed and slapped one of her legs joyfully. She let go of my hand and sat back. A Peter Tosh song suddenly blared out from a compound somewhere on the other side of the reed wall. Madintwa beamed and shook her shoulders, doing a little dance. Then the woman next to her began to talk. The two women looked at me, looked at each other, and began to laugh.

'What?' I implored Ron, as I got back on to the white plastic chair.

He smiled. 'My grandmother says, 'Here is the woman whose hair falls over backward'.'

I touched my hair self-consciously.

'And she says we look the same, you and I.'

'We do?' I frowned, puzzled. This was the third time I had been told Ron and I looked alike but I couldn't see the similarity myself. 'Who are the other women?' I asked.

'The one next to my grandmother is her neighbour. That is MaBoipelo, my grandmother's sister, there . . . ' He nodded to the woman sitting outside the broken-down house who still hadn't moved.

'Is she okay?' I whispered.

'No, she is sick.'

'With what?' I looked over at the woman. I wondered why she didn't lie down if she were so sick, and why no one seemed to be looking after her.

Ron shrugged. 'They are taking her to the traditional doctor to find out. The suspicion is that she's been bewitched.'

'By who?'

'Now is not the time,' said Ron irritatingly.

'And the men?'

'This is my grandfather,' he said indicating the elderly man on the chair who was busy picking something out of his hair, the white handkerchief off now and lying limp in his lap.

'Good evening and how are you?' said the man in sudden, faultless English. He held out his hand and I got off the chair again to take it. All around me everyone was laughing, including Ron. 'I've never heard him speaking English before,' he said. 'My grandmother says he is showing off.'

I shook the old man's hand and stood there as he continued to hold it. Batswana liked touching hands, but I felt awkward, not sure when it was appropriate to take mine away.

'And how are you?' he asked.

'Fine,' I smiled. 'And you?'

But his reply was drowned by Madintwa's laughter, she was shaking her finger at him and the old man looked disgruntled.

'I fought your war,' said the old man to me. 'That was World War Two.'

I nodded until at last the old man dropped my hand and went back to picking at his hair.

'And this is my uncle, OT,' said Ron, leading me to the man standing by the house. I had heard quite a lot about OT, for Ron admired his uncle and he had fond memories of how they used to hunt together when Ron was a child. He also felt sympathy for OT, who many years ago had been recruited to work in the gold mines in South Africa. Mining agents used to fly into

Maun and elsewhere in the Okavango Delta and entice men to the mines with a free flight in an aeroplane and the promise of good pay and good leave. But the mines were terrible places, especially perhaps for a young village man like OT, who had grown up in a peaceful, non-racist country and then found himself underground and abused in Johannesburg.

'Ee,' said OT and he shook my hand briefly. He seemed a little abashed and when he smiled I could see his three top teeth were missing. I thought that was why he had kept his mouth closed until now, and with it closed he had looked stern and a little threatening.

'So, where's your mum?' I asked, returning to my seat. It was getting cold now and a sudden wind whipped up a mini tornado of sand, whirling in the air and then flying furiously over the reed wall. The young girl in the pink dress took the pot of boiling water off the fire with her bare hands. I watched, astounded that she hadn't burnt herself. Then she poured the water into a brown metal teapot, added several large spoonfuls of tea leaves, and gave it a thorough stir. Next she struggled to unfold the legs of a stand-up metal tray. It was exactly the sort of tray one of my grandmothers had used when she gave me tea in her bungalow in Carlisle. With the tray finally up the girl set it before the elderly man, and then began unfolding another one on which she placed three cups. She handed one to me and then took a large metal one, and bent down facing Madintwa, doing a curtsy with one hand on her knee. She stayed in that awkward position while Madintwa slowly, still talking, took the cup, poured the tea on to the saucer, and then slurped away.

I picked up my tea and found it scalding; full of boiled milk, and with so much sugar it burnt my teeth.

'*Monna we*,' instructed Madintwa, gesturing that Ron should move nearer to her. She had finished her tea and was now ready to talk again.

'What's she saying?' I asked.

'She says she can die happily now that her husband has returned.'

'Her husband?' I asked, confused.

'She means me. She says she's going on transfer soon,' Ron continued.

I frowned, thinking she had an employer who was going to transfer her somewhere.

Madintwa laughed again and threw a long strong arm into the air, pointing at the sky and shouted something out. I realized she was being transferred to heaven and I laughed obligingly. In response Madintwa leaned over and patted me on the knee. I had thought people would be less welcoming than they were, suspicious that their son had returned from America with a white woman. But the people in this compound seemed accepting in a calm, inclusive sort of way. I felt like a special visitor who had been away and was now being welcomed home. Suddenly Madintwa got excited. She hauled herself up from the tarpaulin, pushing her bottom up with the palms of both hands on the sand, bending her legs until she was upright. Then she adjusted her headscarf and smoothed down her skirt before walking up to my chair and peering at my face for a second. Then she yelled an order at the girl. 'What's happening now?' I asked.

Ron smiled, pleased. 'My grandmother wants to welcome you in the traditional manner.'

'What should I do?' I asked, as the girl came with a large metal bowl of water and placed it before Madintwa.

'Nothing.'

Madintwa sat back down on the tarpaulin and took the bowl in both hands. She lifted her eyes to the sky and spoke earnestly for a few minutes, appearing to be listing something, perhaps people's names. Then she took a large mouthful of water, so large that her cheeks bulged, and beckoned me towards her again.

I got off my chair and knelt down on the sand. Madintwa tipped her head back slightly and then, catching me completely off guard, spat a spray of tepid water all over my face.

'*A ka ka ka!*' she laughed.

I sat resting on my knees, a little shocked, the water running down my forehead, over my eyes and into the corners of my mouth. I wondered whether I was supposed to leave it there or whether I could wipe it away.

'MaMozambia!' yelled the girl who had served us tea.

'Is it your mum?' I whispered to Ron.

He nodded. Madintwa straightened up, rearranging her hands on her lap, her face becoming serious again. I wiped the water away and got back on my chair.

'*Ko ko!*' came a soft, flat voice from behind us and I turned to see a tall, thin woman entering the compound. She was walking slowly and purposefully, bearing a large blue and white bag on her head.

'*Ee!*' said Madintwa with gusto and began talking ten to the dozen as her daughter came further into the yard.

I got up, expecting to shake Ron's mother's hand. '*Dumela mma*,' I said self-consciously, although she hadn't greeted me yet.

'*Ee*,' said Eliah quietly. She touched my hand with hers, which was hot and rough. Then she removed the bag from her head. Her bearing, while she did this, was utterly regal. She could have been a queen acknowledging the presence of her subjects. She moved in a measured way, much like Ron, and every gesture looked as if it had been thought out beforehand. Her face was serious with not even the glimmer of a smile. Then she put the bag on the ground and sat down on the log. She tilted her face up slightly, so that she was almost looking down on me. There was very little physical resemblance between Ron and his mother, except perhaps an air of confidence. She was dark-skinned, with a strong jaw and a beautiful mouth that had a little dip in the middle and made it look, momentarily, as if she were smirking. I had a very strong urge that I wanted her to like and approve of me. I wanted to be liked anyway, to fit into this new country, but especially I wanted to be liked by Ron's family. And yet it wasn't quite that I wanted to fit in, but that I wanted to understand.

I wanted to know how people did things and why. I was a visitor and I wanted to be polite.

Eliah leant forward and without speaking opened the bag she had taken off her head. Inside was a pile of shiny new aluminum pans, one inside the other. She pushed the bag towards me.

'They're for us,' Ron said.

'Oh, thank you,' I said to Eliah.

'*Ee*,' she said and smiled slightly.

'That's really kind of you,' I continued.

'She thought we would be staying with her,' Ron said quietly as his mother and the other women began to talk.

'Really?' I looked around. I couldn't see how we would all fit in the round house in front of us.

'That's nice of her. Did you tell her I've got a house at the school?'

'Yes.'

'You wouldn't have *wanted* to stay here, would you?' I asked.

'God no,' said Ron and while the women weren't looking we squeezed each other's hands.

Eliah spoke briefly out of the corner of her mouth and the girl in pink rushed off. She came back with a tin cup of water, and Ron's mother lifted the cup and drank until the water was gone. Then she put her hands on her knees and began to speak.

'She says she had a dream, last night,' Ron explained.

'Oh?' I brightened up. I was always having dreams, portents of both good and bad, and I was a great believer in dreams that came true.

'She says we should stay away from tall buildings.'

I stifled a laugh. Maun didn't have any tall buildings.

'And she wants to know if we've been to see my father. I told her we haven't.'

'Oh,' I said, thinking Eliah looked a little displeased. 'When will we go and see him, and your stepmum, Selina?'

The word 'Selina' had an electrifying effect on Eliah. She spat to one side on the sand and then she and Madintwa had a heated exchange. Then Eliah turned back to Ron and the two of them began to chat.

'My mother is going to Morutsa tomorrow,' Ron explained as I sat listening, desperate to understand. 'It's in the bush about twenty kilometres from here, where they get reeds and thatching grass. I haven't been there for years. My mother wants me to go with her but I'm trying to explain that I have to go to work.'

Ron had got a job the moment he'd arrived back in Maun at a newly formed computer company, the first computer company in the district, run by an American man with a passion for wildlife conservation.

I sat and watched Eliah who was now bringing things out of the house and piling them on the sand. She put down a huge thick blanket, two jerry cans, a large white container, and three boxes. On the side of the boxes I could see the word *Power*.

'What's that?' I asked.

'Power,' said Ron. 'It's a home brew. They take

it to Morutsa and cook it up and sell it to the men there. Sometimes they exchange it for reeds.'

'It's alcohol?'

'*Ee.* It's against my mother's church to use or sell alcohol, but my grandmother says it's a good way to make money.'

We sat there while Eliah continued to pile her possessions on the sand. Now that she was in the compound the other people seemed more subdued, as if she were the head of the household and they had to have her permission before talking. I felt a little nervous in her presence. I told myself it was kind of her to give us the pans, but I wondered at her expectation that we would live with her.

'Shall we go?' Ron asked and we both stood up. Then he went around the yard shaking each person's hand and saying, '*Go siame*' — Go well — to each in turn. Madintwa grasped my hand as I said good-bye and, like her elder sister whom we had met on the pathway earlier, she turned my palm upside-down and sprinkled it with kisses.

★　★　★

Two weeks later I was walking to the Maun mall on my way to Ron's office. I came here most days for it was here that most of the shops were. As I entered the mall from the direction of the school, I passed the Maun co-op on my left and then a butcher's shop owned by a German man. I could smell, through the open screen door, blood and wet meat. At a right-angle to the butcher's was a chemist run by a thin white Englishwoman who had been midwife to hundreds of women in the area. It was here I bought my mosquito spray and other supplies. Across the sand was a clothing shop, Cash Bazaar, a South African chain store which sold cheap school uniforms, blankets, pots and pans, and stiff green and blue maid's dresses. It seemed to be the only shop in Maun run by Batswana, for while there weren't many non-Africans in the village, it was the white people and the Indians who appeared to own all the businesses. I walked diagonally across the mall, heading for Baagi House, a two-storey concrete building with round walls and a small porch. The computer company Ron worked for was on the second floor. It was a Friday afternoon and I was sweating, dying for some water to drink after my trudge through the sand from school. Under my arm I held a newspaper, *Mmegi*, that I had just bought in Maun's one newsagent's. It was delivered by bus every Friday and from midday people stood around the newsagent's waiting for it to arrive. Sometimes the bus from Gaborone broke down and no newspaper reached Maun at all until the Monday.

All across the mall people were strolling, greeting each other, wandering in and out of the shops. Twice people called out, 'MaMozambia!' and I stopped to answer, having no idea who they were or how they knew me. But Maun was small and there weren't many white people so those who did live here were easily recognizable.

'Hey, MaMozambia!' I turned at the sound of a man's voice close by and saw Bashi striding across the mall, hand in hand with another man. In his free hand he held a bunch of green sticks.

'*Dumela Mma,*' Bashi said. '*O tsogile jang?*'

Bashi was the only person who spoke in the formal way our Setswana instructors had taught us in Molepolole.

'*Ke tsogile sentle,*' I replied, enjoying the chance to practise what I had learnt. '*Wena o tsogile jang?*'

'Excellent,' said Bashi. 'Your pronunciation is very good.'

I smiled; I knew it wasn't.

Bashi took one of the sticks from his hand and held it out. 'Sweet reed,' he said, lifting it to his mouth and tearing off a strip of green bark.

I followed suit, stripping off the bark and then taking a bite at the white stringy flesh. My mouth almost collapsed at the sweetness.

Bashi laughed. 'This is one of our local foods. And another one is *tswii.*'

'What's that?'

'It is water-lily root and it is a delicacy round here. People in the south, they laugh at we Batawana eating tswii, but then what do these urban people know? They are so busy eating *hamburgers* and talking like Americans that they don't even know who they are any more! You know the best *tswii*-maker in Maun?'

I shook my head.

'*Ee.* It is Ronnie's mother. She is the best *tswii*-maker in Maun. Where is Mozambia?'

'At work, I'm just going to see him.'

'Good, good.' Bashi shook my hand again. '*Tsamaya sentle*, my sister.'

I reached the steps to Baagi House and climbed up to the porch, and then I suddenly caught sight of Ron's mother walking across the mall from the direction of Cash Bazaar. She was walking slowly, her head held high, with a huge stiff bag balanced on top. I waved but perhaps she was too far away to see me. So I waited on the porch until she came closer. Surely she could see me now, I thought, as she stopped at the bottom of the steps and I went down.

'*Dumela Mma*,' I said. It had been two weeks since I had met her and after that visit I had asked Ron what his mother thought of me. 'She likes you,' he said. 'But she told me that people can change.' 'Oh,' I'd said, annoyed by such a cryptic comment.

As we stood facing each other outside Ron's office I held out my hand, but when Eliah didn't move to take it I took it back.

'*Ee*,' she said, looking at me and then looking away.

For a dreadful second I thought it wasn't her, that I had lost my mind and just greeted someone else, not Ron's mother at all.

'Are you looking for Ron?' I asked. '*O batla Mozambia?*' I struggled in Setswana.

'*Ee*,' Eliah said, looking at me at last.

I smiled brightly and hurried back up the steps and up the precarious twisted stairway inside Baagi House. Ron was sitting at a table in front of a computer. The screen was blank.

'Hiya,' I said and he turned. 'Power cut?'

He nodded. 'I am going mad! It's been down for hours.'

'Your mum's outside.'

'Okay.' Ron didn't move.

'But,' I looked around, seeing there was no one else in the office, 'she sort of blanked me. I mean, I said hello and everything and she just sort of, well, blanked me.'

I waited for Ron to reassure me. He got up and stretched his arms, flexing them over his head. 'She probably thinks you don't want to know her.'

'But I greeted her!' I objected. 'Why would she think I don't want to know her?'

'Because,' said Ron, 'she's poor and you're white.'

# 6

It was a sweltering hot day in December and Ron and I were waiting inside the house for Roy, his brother. It was so hot that the evening before I had opened a can of tomatoes and the lid had popped, spraying hot red juice all over the walls. For the past week it had been over 100 degrees every day and by seven in the morning a haze of hotness lay shimmering, suspended over the school grounds. This was supposed to be the rainy season, but as usual there was not even a cloud in the sky.

'I thought he was coming first thing in the morning?' I complained, impatient to set off. Roy was taking us to Last Chance, the bar Ron's stepmother, Selina, owned.

'You know Roy,' Ron answered.

I had met Roy a few times and he never, ever did what he said he was going to do. He was a few years younger than Ron and physically they looked quite alike. But unlike Ron, who had a measured and moralistic approach to life, Roy was altogether a looser individual. He was impulsive, talkative, and he could never sit still.

'What the hell is that?' I got up and went to the open door as a monstrous green truck came hurtling down the path towards our house, sand flying.

We climbed on board and, as we drove back to the school gates, people came out of their houses to see what the noise was about. They waved at Roy, for he was a familiar figure in Maun. He was a renowned mechanic and had worked for village garages, for car-hire companies, for construction sites and road builders. And at each place he had left a trail of disorder, of missing vehicle parts and unpaid debts.

Eventually Roy brought the truck to a stop some ten kilometres outside Maun. I saw we had stopped a little way from the main sand road, in front of a two-room concrete building painted a bright orange. There was a hand-painted sign on the porch which read *Last Chance Bar and Bottle Store*. I couldn't tell if the sign was about to go up or whether it had been up and had fallen down. But it was clear why it was called Last Chance, for there wouldn't be another bar or bottle store until Francistown 500 kilometres away.

'Daddy's here,' Roy said, passing behind a blue Land Rover. Ron nodded.

I smiled; I found it odd how the men called their father Daddy, but I didn't seem able to explain how archaic this sounded to me.

'And Mummy,' said Roy, stopping to light a cigarette next to a battered white pick up.

Ron shrugged. Selina was Roy's mother, not his, and they had a somewhat volatile relationship. Selina and Ron's father had brought up six children together but now they appeared to be separated. Selina ran the Last Chance bar and Ronald senior lived in Maun where he was deputy sheriff. I had thought this sounded an exciting, Wild West sort of job, until I realized it meant repossessing people's goods when they failed to pay debts.

We walked along the porch of the bar and round the back of the building into a courtyard. The place was swarming with people. Children ran around in party dresses, two men were slapping huge slabs of beef on to the *braai*, an oil drum cut in half with a tray on top. Stephen, Ron's youngest brother, was standing watching the men, every now and again poking at the meat with his fingers. I hung back for a second by the back door to the bar. This side of Ron's family was so different from that of his mother and grandmother. At the compound in Boyei ward the family always appeared as a unit, sitting close together on the sand encircled by the reed wall. But here the family seemed scattered, spread out in the courtyard, each in their own individual area.

As I stood there I had a strange feeling that the different members of the family had noted my presence as if they had somehow been waiting for me, and yet not one of them looked my way. Then Rita, one of Ron's three sisters, called me over.

'Caitlin!' she said and waved. She looked as if she had just walked out of a hair salon, for her hair was woven in an intricate design that must have taken hours. She wore, as she usually did, a miniskirt and high heels and I thought it must take a lot of practice to walk in the sand in heels. 'Where have you been?' Rita asked, waving a can of Hunter's Gold.

'What do you mean?' I asked. Rita was always

very welcoming when I saw her, but she always put me immediately on the defensive.

'You haven't visited us,' she said.

Well, I thought, you haven't visited me either. I decided it was just her way of being friendly so I tried to lighten up. Sometimes I took things too literally. People often asked, *Ntse o teng?* — Are you still around? — and I took this to mean they were surprised I had not returned to England.

'Look at Mozambia, he's so *thin*,' said Rita.

'Not really,' I muttered, taking the comment to imply that somehow he wasn't happy in life.

'And just look at all these children . . . ' said Rita.

'Yes.' I turned, watching them rushing around the courtyard, eating crisps and drinking Coke, having fun and shouting.

'Have you met all of them, the children?' Rita asked.

'Yes,' I said, sensing Rita was trying to draw my attention to something.

'Caitlin,' said Patricia, Ron's eldest sister, appearing from round the corner of the building. Unlike Rita, Patricia looked very formal in a purple and white flowing African print dress with matching turban. She had an older, more settled face, but like Rita she was immaculately made up, her eyebrows plucked into tiny black lines.

'You look amazing, your dress is stunning,' I said.

'Ooh, Caitlin,' Patricia laughed, taking my hand.

'I'd better go and say hi to your mum and dad,' I said, thinking it odd that neither Ron's father nor his stepmother had made any move to greet me. I told myself that I was still thinking in an English fashion, that as I was the guest I had to be the one to initiate the greetings.

I could see Ronald senior sitting on a chair far apart from the others, sipping from a small glass of whisky. I had seen him twice before and he was the quietest, stillest man I had ever met in my life. He could sit, in silence, for an hour or more. And his silence made me nervous; so that I talked far more than was necessary and ended up feeling a fool.

'Hi,' I said.

'Afternoon,' Ronald senior nodded. His pale skin was reddish from the sun and his lips looked a little sunburnt. His hair was white, growing in waves back from his forehead, and he wore small rectangular glasses which rested halfway down his nose and made me think of Doctor Doolittle. I knew Ron's father had moved to Botswana in the 1960s from South Africa, but Ron didn't seem interested in telling me much more than that.

'Hot isn't it?' I said.

Ronald senior nodded.

'Boiling,' I added. I sat down next to him and we remained in silence for a full five minutes.

'Mmm,' said Ronald senior at last. 'Is Ronnie here?'

'Yes,' I said, but looking around I couldn't see him. I wondered why he hadn't come over to greet his dad. But then Ron and his father appeared to have a rather strained relationship. As a young child Ron had been taken from Boyei

105

ward and sent to stay with his father and Selina. And instead of being grateful to his dad for bringing him up, Ron seemed to resent him for doing so. Because by bringing him up, Ron had been taken from his mother and, more importantly, his grandmother.

'When do you think it will rain?' I asked hopefully.

'Hmmm,' Ronald senior said, and he tilted his head up and surveyed the blue sky. 'I think Selina is trying to get your attention.'

'Oh.' I looked across the courtyard to where Selina sat with two friends. She was waving, so I got up and made my way over. Like Rita, Selina wore a short skirt, her hair was freshly done, and gold jewellery jangled around her wrists.

'I love your skirt,' said Selina as I came up and shook her hand.

'Thank you,' I said, surprised.

'Yes, it's almost a miniskirt. You should wear a miniskirt. You have nice legs,' and she clapped one of her friends on the shoulder and howled with laughter. Selina had a very liquid face, the features moving and rearranging as she looked me up and down. I was affronted by the way she examined me, but I was learning that Batswana felt it was perfectly acceptable to comment on and assess people's bodies. The headmaster's wife at the school had taken to sitting outside her house and calling to me as I walked home. 'Hey, MaMozambia,' she would yell, 'you have really put on weight. Yes, now you are *fat!*' I bristled every time she did this, torn between wanting to explain that in England this would be an insulting way to talk to someone, while appreciating that being fat in Botswana was still a compliment. Fat meant healthy, it meant you weren't poor, you had plenty of food, you were in general being looked after.

'Where are your children?' asked the woman sitting next to Selina.

'I don't have any,' I replied.

'What? You don't have *any* children?' The woman sounded appalled. 'Not even *one*?'

'Not even one,' I echoed, trying to smile. I was repeatedly being asked where my children were; it was the first question a Motswana woman ever asked me. I was already beginning to give up trying to explain that I didn't want anyway, for this was like saying I was a vegetarian and didn't eat meat. However much I explained I just didn't seem to be able to make sense to my listener.

'Where is Mozambia?' Selina asked.

'There.' I pointed.

'Ronnie!' Selina shouted.

'*Mma*?' Ron came over a little reluctantly.

'Ah, Ronnie,' Selina cajoled. 'We haven't eaten meat for so long . . .'

I frowned, there was an awful lot of meat-eating going on, what did she mean?

Selina seemed to be waiting for something. 'I am his mother, you know,' she said to me suddenly. 'I brought him up. So I am his mother.'

I nodded. Her voice was rising and I thought there might be a scene. 'We need meat, we need bar stock, the car needs repairing.'

Ron stood and nodded politely. Then suddenly

he stiffened. I followed his gaze, looking out across the bush land behind the bar where the children were playing.

'What is it?' I asked.

'Over there,' said Ron. 'You see that girl? That's my child. That one, that girl there.'

'Yours?' My heart fluttered. 'You mean that's *Alice*, over there?' In the five months since I'd been in Botswana I had not met Ron's child. Each time I asked about her I was told that Alice was with her mother, that she was in the bush, that she was with a relative in the Delta. Somehow she was just never around and there didn't seem to be any expectation that she would — or even needed to — be around or be with her father. Ron worried about this, about what his role in relation to Alice should be, and it was something that hung over him. But he worried in his own way, holding it close to him, chewing it over.

'What should I do?' Ron turned to me, his face unsure, a slight tremor on his lips.

I was about to ask if he were sure that the girl was Alice when the children ran nearer and I saw she had to be. She looked about four or five years old, tall and thin with knobbly knees under a worn yellow dress that was far too small for her. Her face was long and dark-skinned, her hair cropped but in need of a comb. She was running with the other children but the way she moved was awkward, her chest thrust forward, her legs trying to catch up with the front half of her body. She stopped then and stood slouching on one leg. It was exactly a position Ron sometimes adopted. And her sharp, defined collarbones, I saw now, were the spitting image of his. There was something so bony, so vulnerable, about her that I felt immediately protective. She wasn't laughing or shouting like the other children, she wasn't saying a word. And as I continued to watch it was as if she were only on the periphery of their game.

'Have you met Ron's daughter?' Rita asked brightly, coming up next to me. 'Mummy thought she should come and live with us.'

Ron scowled.

'I named her, you know,' Rita said to me.

'Did you?' I asked, but I wasn't really listening, I was wondering how Ron's daughter could be living with Rita and Selina, why no one had told us this. And instead of being told this, we had been brought to Last Chance and presented with what had already been done.

Ron still hadn't moved. He looked rooted to the spot, stroking his chin and gazing far off into the bush. Then, eventually, he shifted from one leg to another, and walked slowly off towards the children.

'Ah, Caitlin,' said Patricia coming up to stand with Rita and I, 'Ronnie has a child, a daughter . . . '

'Yes,' I said angrily, 'I know that.'

'You knew that already?' Patricia looked surprised.

'Of course I knew that already,' I said a little too loudly, astounded that Patricia thought her brother, or anyone else, would keep something like this a secret. 'He told me. In England.

Before we came here.'

'Oh. Well, I didn't think he'd told you.'

'Well, he had,' I said. This, I felt, was what everyone had been waiting for, why they had been watching me closely, ready to reveal that my boyfriend had a child with another woman. 'I'm going to the loo.'

When I came out of the toilet it had grown suddenly dark but for a string of coloured lights lit up along the front porch of the bar. Inside the bar there were twenty or so people drinking and playing darts. The place was getting raucous. I looked up, expecting to see the usual array of stars but instead I found thick grey clouds chasing each other across the sky. A sudden wind came up, cool and wet-smelling, and I wondered if at last it would rain.

I couldn't see Ron and I couldn't see the kids. I went and looked around the front courtyard, peering into the green truck but finding it empty. The trees near the concrete toilets began to sway violently and I heard a crash from somewhere in the bush as if a branch had been felled. Then a flash of lightning cracked horizontally across the sky like a jagged silver rip along a piece of blackened paper.

Storms in Botswana were not like storms in England, here they took a long time coming and were dramatic and intense and even a little frightening. Twice in the past month I had witnessed displays like this, but they had disappeared as quickly as they had come, delivering no rain, leaving the land still dry and brown and parched. I couldn't wait for rain, and in a drought-stricken country like Botswana rain was always good news, a sign of fortune and the ancestors' pleasure. *Pula* — rain — was even the name of the country's currency. But still the power of a Botswana storm could be scary.

A rumble of thunder rolled across the night and then a sudden explosion bounced and echoed off the walls of the bar. Instinctively I ducked, as if the thunder were coming down on me. I glanced quickly into the pick-up truck, still looking for the kids, and then passed slowly by the back windows of the Land Rover. At last I saw signs of life. Inside a group of children were lying on their tummies, on the seats and on the floor, apparently asleep. I gently opened the door to the driver's seat and got in. I turned round so I was kneeling on the seat and waited until my eyes adjusted to the lack of light. I could see Rita's daughter Kookaburra, she was sitting upright now smiling at me, her arm dangled affectionately around her cousin Chili.

'Aunty Caitlin,' said Kookaburra, 'do you know how many stars there are?'

'No, Kuka,' I said, 'I don't.'

'Aunty Caitlin, will you sit back here so I can stroke your hair?'

'Okay.' I clambered over the seat and pushed the children over until I sat in the middle. Kuka began to plait my hair, Chili went back to sleep. As I sat there, feeling quite dreamy myself, I sensed Alice moving towards me. She didn't come too near, but I felt a hand come out in the semi-dark and pat my hair. The hand came away quickly, as if she hadn't liked what she found.

Then she patted me again.

We sat that way for some time. Outside I could hear the rain pelting down, as if making up for all the dry months when barely a drop had fallen. Two men came out of the bar and stood on the porch, arms up, welcoming the storm. More cars began to arrive, led by a Land Rover full of Korean road builders clutching beers. Then Ron's face appeared at the window.

'Are we going?' I asked, winding down the window, feeling the spray of rain in my face.

'Ee.'

'You okay?'

'Ee.'

I disentangled myself from Kookaburra and got out of the car. Lightning lit up the courtyard and I ran to the green truck, drenched. We climbed on board, drawing a piece of black sheeting around us. Roy handed us plastic bags and we tore them open and put them on our heads. I looked at Ron, a bag round his hair like an old woman's shower cap, water dripping down his face.

'Did you talk to Alice?' I asked, huddling nearer.

'Ee.'

'She was in the car just now. She's sweet, isn't she? But God, she's shy. She does look like you, she really does.'

'Do you think so?' Ron asked and I was surprised at how proud he appeared by this comment.

'Has Selina *really* adopted her then? I mean, does she want to live at Last Chance? What about her mum, what does she think?'

'I've no idea,' Ron said, moving the sheeting a little. 'They're meddling, Rita and Selina, they always do this.'

'But where is she going to live then?'

'Wherever is best for her.'

'I'm sorry,' I said, feeling annoyed rather than apologetic, 'but to me it's really odd. I mean, this isn't pass the parcel is it? First she's with her mum, then she's at the bush or somewhere. Now she's with Selina and them. Has anyone asked her where *she* wants to live?'

'As I said, she will live where it is best for her.'

We didn't usually argue, Ron and I. We had heated discussions about things we had seen, or heard, or read about. But on everything else we agreed. And we never argued about anything personal. I knew Alice was not my child, that there was no real reason for me to get so heated about her welfare, but the way children were moved around was an aspect of Setswana culture that I found hard to understand.

'You mean just like you were moved to your dad's? Because that was 'best for you'?'

Ron stared at me. I thought I had made him angry now.

'And now look how you are. You're furious with your dad for taking you from your mum and grandma and you have this dreadful responsibility to them, that you have to look after them because for a long time you weren't there.'

'It is not dreadful.'

'Okay, fine, it's not dreadful. But did anyone ask you where you wanted to live?'

113

'Cait, what's the problem?' Ron frowned and took his arm away. 'Alice will live where it's best for her. Just because the way we do things here is a way you're not used to, it doesn't mean the way you people do things is any better.'

'You didn't answer me, did anyone ask you what you wanted before you were removed from your mum and grandma?'

'No, they did not. But that's different, he was my dad. Selina and Rita are meddling here, no one asked them to take Alice. Selina knows my mother wants Alice to live with her.'

'What?' I took the plastic bag off my head and ran my hands through my wet hair. '*Your* mum wants Alice to live with her?'

'Well, Alice is her grandchild,' said Ron, folding up the plastic sheet. 'Are you saying my mother would not be capable of looking after Alice well?'

'No,' I said carefully.

'So what is it that bothers you so much? You want Alice to come and live with us?'

'Yeah, as if,' I laughed and Roy put the truck in gear and we roared off into the night.

# 7

Christmas just wasn't Christmas the way I was used to it. There were no Christmas trees or twinkly lights or plastic snowmen in the Maun shops, no tinsel or baubles for sale, no billboards or television advertising mince-pies or dolls, and most of all there were no cold dark afternoons with the promise of snow. There was never even any possibility of snow in Maun, because such a weather condition only existed in the far south in South Africa.

For once I would forget about Christmas altogether. Instead, we were going on a road trip. Ron had bought a Land Rover, a sky-blue vehicle with a white roof and an open back. It was so high off the ground that it felt like boarding a bus and it moved like a tank. Now, said Ron, we would be able to go anywhere, even into the bush. School had closed for the long summer holidays and we were to visit relatives in a village in the far north called Satau. I wasn't quite sure who we were visiting or why but I was coming to terms with the fact that asking questions sometimes didn't get you very far. And I was realizing that what I thought were Ron's characteristics were in fact national characteristics — in that plans that had been made and discussed could suddenly change, and in that people did not ferret out information, they waited to be told. We left the school grounds half

115

an hour after the sun had come up. Roy was coming with us and we were heading for the place where Veronica, his girlfriend, stayed.

It had rained the day before and my neighbour at the school had spent the entire evening standing at the door to his house catching flying termites and popping them into his mouth. The rains had released a whole world of insects I had never seen before, and the termites had came flooding out of holes in the ground, whirling upwards like fluttery tornadoes. It was impossible to stop the termites coming into the house, and even with the door and all the windows shut I still woke to find a crunchy carpet of insect wings on the floor. In the morning, outside on the sand, I found another variety of insect, red creatures as small as pins which seemed to be made from crimson velvet. At first I thought they were tiny drops of blood, then I bent down and touched one. Now I had noticed one I began to notice they were all over the yard, like flowers that had burst into bloom all at the same time.

'Have you known Veronica for long?' I asked as Ron drove. I was staring out the window, impressed at how, after just a few hours of rain, Maun had been transformed. Now the sand was a field of green, except for areas of white sand around people's houses like bare patches on a carpet.

'Roy and she have been going out since they were teenagers.'

'So why isn't she coming to Satau too?'

'She can't, with the baby.'

'Baby? What baby? Roy's never mentioned a

baby. Jesus, you people keep things to your-selves.'

'No one is keeping anything from you, Cait,' Ron chuckled. 'She's just come out of hospital. This baby is brand spanking new.'

I shuddered a little. I wasn't that fond of little babies, they all looked ugly, and if someone put one in my arms I thought I would drop it.

Ron stopped the Land Rover outside a large metal gate and then we drove into the Ramsdens' yard, where Veronica stayed. At the doorway to the house stood a short woman with loose curly hair, a flowered pinafore wrapped around her generous waist.

'*Dumela Mma*,' she said as I approached. 'You must be Caitlin. I'm Penny, Veronica's aunty.'

I shook her hand and waited while she led the way into the house. When she turned and smiled at me her eyes almost disappeared into her face. I followed Penny into a dark, square room. For a moment I was surprised to be going inside at all, for I was growing used to the way life in Botswana was lived outdoors and rarely, if ever, did you go into someone's house. It was quiet and cool inside and it took me a moment to get my bearings. Then, on the sofa before me, I saw a woman with a baby at her breast.

'Yeah, *mosadi*!' Roy shouted cheerily, coming into the room behind me, bounding on to the sofa and ruffling Veronica's hair. Then he bent and popped Veronica's nipple out of the baby's mouth. The baby screwed up its eyes and began to cry. Veronica slapped Roy on the arm, readjusted herself and the baby continued to

117

feed. I watched Veronica while she did this; she looked older than Roy, perhaps my age, with cropped hair and pearl-drop earrings. Her face was round with a strong wide nose and the way her top lip jutted out a little made her look amused.

'So you're going to Satau?' Veronica asked, swinging a breast to one side and holding the baby up against her shoulder. I was used by now to seeing breasts, the girls at school frequently undid their shirts during the hottest days, and they were always naked from the waist up when they performed traditional dance. On the streets and in shops women often walked around breastfeeding a child; there was nothing sexualized about breasts in Botswana.

I watched Veronica burp her baby. She looked tough somehow, the way she sat, the firm way she did things.

'Come and sit here,' she said kindly. 'After all, we are sisters-in-law, isn't it?'

'I'm not married to Ron . . . ' I began.

Veronica laughed. 'And I'm not married to Roy.'

I moved next to her, thinking I should at least ask about her baby. 'It's a boy . . . ?' I hazarded a guess.

'Yes. And he was very very late. I tried by all means to get this baby out for four days. Hey, the pain, you can imagine. Late, a very late baby, just like his father.'

Roy laughed.

'Here,' said Veronica, 'you can hold him. Lloyd, this is your Aunty Caitlin.'

118

I drew back but Veronica had already put him in my arms. Despite the heat he was swaddled in a thick white blanket with a blue woollen hat on his head. He struggled a little and I lifted him upright. 'Oh,' I said, feeling something wet seeping on my lap. Veronica laughed, tipping her head back against the sofa as if she hadn't heard a good joke for a very long time.

Back in the sand courtyard Roy stacked his belongings in the back of the Land Rover, piling in a suitcase and a blanket and a tool-kit, shoving to one side the cooler I had so carefully stocked with ice blocks, Castle beer, hard-boiled eggs and chocolate. I had looked on a tourist map and knew we would be heading north-east from Maun on the sand road that led to Shorobe. From there we would skirt the eastern tip of Moremi Game Reserve and then drive north through Chobe National Park. The village of Satau wasn't on the map, but I knew it was somewhere up there towards Kasane where four countries locked — Botswana, Zambia, Zimbabwe and the tongue of land called the Caprivi Strip which some said belonged to Namibia and some said not.

We drove out of Maun and on the either side of the road the bush was green and dense. I could recognize different species of trees now, like the mophane trees which dominated the landscape and were no longer dry and bare but full of lime-green butterfly-shaped leaves and tiny little yellow flowers. I could recognize the majestic morula trees with their wide-spreading crowns and their grey, mottled bark which peeled off in flaky discs. Hidden in the depth of the trees were young, round green fruits. The camelthorn acacias with their furry grey pods shaped like ears were so familiar now that I barely noticed them. But each time I saw a sausage tree, with the fruit that hung down like baseball bats, I stopped in amazement to stare.

'Morutsa is that way,' Ron said after a while. I looked left out of the window, seeing no road, no sign, nothing to indicate that a settlement lay in that direction.

'Where your mum goes, to get reeds?'

Ron nodded and, as we sped by, I saw that in fact there were signs. On one tree was nailed an old car number-plate, on another a metal plate, on a third two old flip-flops which Batswana called patter patters.

We passed the turn-off to Morutsa, and then drove through the village of Shorobe, until we were travelling on a thick, wide road of soft churning sand. I judged that we were not far from Moremi and I expected to see a fence demarcating the boundary of the game reserve. I had read that the idea of a game reserve at Moremi harked back to the 1960s prior to independence and its borders had been expanded several times over the years until now it contained almost 20 per cent of the entire Okavango Delta.

'Elephants,' Ron said after a while.

I looked out of the window at an enormous dome of beige shit on the path below.

'Oh, come on,' I said.

Ron shrugged as if he couldn't care less that

I didn't believe him.

'Really? Is that really elephant shit?'

'*Ee.*'

'But are we *in* the game reserve?' The landscape seemed too normal, somehow, for elephants. I had imagined the game reserve would be like a wild-animal park in England, Whipsnade perhaps, where you drove in, closed your car windows, and then filed past various wild animals. And elephants, to my mind, belonged in a Tarzan sort of landscape with jungle trees and monkeys, not this gentle bush.

'What's elephant in Setswana?'

'*Tlou,*' said Ron, and the word had a deep finality to it, as if it were the end of a discussion that couldn't be argued with.

Roy and I took turns sitting in the passenger seat and Roy was in the open back when we came across our first elephant. It was just there, this massive bulk in front of us blocking the entire sand pathway. It had appeared from nowhere, made no noise to announce its arrival, it was just there on the path. For a second it looked familiar. I had seen photos of elephants, I had seen children's books and cartoons with elephants in them, and the creatures were big and sweet but a little stupid. I had even seen them in zoos. But this was a real one, standing in the place where it belonged. As we drove a little closer I couldn't get over the animal's size. If I got out of the car now I would probably be as tall as its knees. I began to take in details, the way its body sloped down to its tiny muscle of a tail, the way its skin sagged down around its legs in giant dark creases as if it were wearing clothes too big for it.

I put my hand to my mouth. 'Jesus Christ.' I couldn't see what we were going to do. We couldn't continue driving, for we would smash right into the elephant. I wondered for a crazy second if we could just drive in-between its legs, passing the Land Rover under its tummy and out the other side.

I could hear Roy laughing from the back. 'Give me the camera!' he yelled.

I turned to hand it to him and when I turned back again, miraculously the elephant had begun to move off, walking absolutely silently across the path until it disappeared into the bush.

We drove on, the going getting tougher in the sand. We were hardly moving at all, I could feel the strength needed to keep the wheels of the Land Rover in the grooves other drivers had made. Then Roy yelled from the back again. 'It's charging!'

I looked behind and saw an elephant, the same one, another one?, running after us. Its trunk was up and its ears were flapping and it was making a terrible, deep, agonizing cry, sand flying as its enormous feet thundered along the path.

'I'm scared,' I said, my voice trembling.

'So am I,' muttered Ron.

But you're not allowed to be scared, I thought, mentally urging the Land Rover on. Don't get stuck, I prayed, don't get stuck.

'How fast can an elephant run?' I asked.

But Ron was busy sliding around on the sand trying to keep the vehicle going.

Finally I turned round again to see the elephant had stopped.

'Only a mock charge,' laughed Roy from the back.

The elephant was disappearing behind us, its body getting smaller and smaller in the distance. But my body was tingling with fear and my hands, as I stuffed the camera back into its case, were shaking.

'That was close,' I said.

'*Ee*,' Ron laughed.

'Do you think we'll see any more?'

'Probably.'

'Oh.' I told myself I had been lucky, to see the first wild elephant I had ever seen in my life, but instead I dreaded seeing any more. What would happen next time? What if next time it were a real charge?

'Could you just beep?' I asked. 'I mean what would happen if you beeped at an elephant, would it just move off?' and I began to giggle at the strangeness of the situation.

'No, that's exactly what you shouldn't do,' said Ron seriously. 'If you beep you make it mad. And if it's a mother with a baby she'd probably kill you.'

I sat stiffly in the Land Rover, silenced by the idea that I was now travelling in a place where an animal could kill me.

We drove on, at last emerging from the bush and into a sudden flat expanse of land. I felt less claustrophobic; there were more places to drive or run to in the open like this. We were inside Chobe National Park now, the second largest in

Botswana, and all around us the land stretched out to the horizon. The only things of height were huge bald trees, their trunks silvery in the heat haze, their branches totally devoid of leaves. It made me think of a cemetery, as if the trees were dead monuments, as if something dreadful had happened and burnt away living things.

'Why are the trees like that?' I asked.

'It's the elephants, they eat everything they can find. Look, zebras.'

Just before us I saw a herd of stocky zebras about thirty strong. They were standing in a group to the right of the pathway, in the open, without shelter or nearby trees, quietly grazing. Then, suddenly, as we got nearer, a couple of the zebras lifted their heads, gave a sudden barking sound, and bolted to the left. The movement spurred all the others into motion and so they ran, zigzagging across the bush, a kaleidoscope of white and black and brown.

We arrived at Satau at dusk and I sat in the front of the Land Rover still a little rigid. We had passed whole groups of elephants, who had paid us no attention at all, but each time I tensed in case one should decide to charge us. I began to relax as Ron drove between the village compounds, round houses and reed walls. Everywhere children came running, shouting at the car, laughing, trying to jump in the back. Ron stopped the car by a reed fence that looked old and black in the dusk. I could see and smell the fire smoke from within the compound, and I could hear people talking.

Roy led the way through the gap in the reed

wall and into the compound where I could just make out a fire, and a group of people sitting on the sand. I knew how to behave now, and I followed Roy and Ron around, shaking hands, saying *Dumela*, until I was offered a chair. I could follow snatches of the conversation and I listened as an elderly man asked Roy if there had been rain in Maun, while another asked where the money was. An old woman began telling a child to go and get a chicken. My stomach growled, I had eaten nothing but hard-boiled eggs and chocolate. I had been a vegetarian for eight years but suddenly, thinking of chicken, my mouth watered. I was becoming tired of eating bread and battered fruit, of searching for fresh vegetables in the shops. I had tried *madila*, the sour milk that was so popular, and *dikgobe*, beans cooked to a mush, but I just couldn't persuade myself to like either of them. On its own the staple *bogobe* was tasteless and I had begun to long for meat. And eating meat was such an integral part of Setswana life, it was beginning to seem entirely natural that animals were reared, killed, cooked and eaten with relish. I swallowed hard, looking forward to supper.

We slept that night in the back of the Land Rover and it was pitch-black, the moon a tiny sliver in the sky, the stars obscured by rain clouds. I slept badly, dreaming of charging elephants, waking and lying in the car and wondering what would happen if an elephant came now.

In the morning the world looked more familiar, girls building fires or setting off to get water with buckets on their heads, the radio playing a Dollar Brand song, the cockerels crowing, women sweeping the sand in their yards. But I could see in daylight how poor our hosts were. Their houses were half fallen-down, they used the tiniest pieces of wood for their fire, and the smallest amount of tea leaves for their tea. I couldn't see any shop in the village, no school, no clinic, no post office, no phones. I wondered what people did for help when they needed it, about how it must be to be sent away from your home to live somewhere else once you were old enough to go to school. What would happen in drought when you couldn't gather rainwater, when you couldn't grow any food in the fields? But as I sat there, hugging a large metal cup of sweet tea, I saw the beauty in the place in which they lived. There were no tower blocks here, no roads or cars or pollution. The elderly couple had no rent to pay, no bills or bank accounts. There was something at once overwhelming and entirely natural about being in a place that was just land, sky and village. I sat and looked out at the vista before me; I had fallen in love with Botswana.

# 8

Botswana's tourist season was officially opened in April each year, when a party was held in Maun. Tickets for the party, organized by the national tourism association, were expensive, but other free parties were held on the same night. Ron and I had been invited to one, but first we went to the Duck Inn, the traditional watering-hole for the white people in Maun. The Duck Inn was situated just opposite the airport, with a low stone wall running round a modest outside eating area. The bar was owned by a glamorous white woman called Bernadette, known locally as Mother Duck. It was said with awe that she could drink the men under the table, and the bar was home from home for some of Maun's great white hunters.

That evening the outside area was nearly full and inside the bar was packed with white pilots and safari operators drinking beer. Behind Ron and me sat an elderly white man with a cowboy hat drinking whisky. He sat very solidly on his chair and when he wanted service all he had to do was nod, for he was one of the last great white hunters and well known in Maun. The Duck Inn was popular, even infamous, among those who still came to the Delta to hunt; mainly Americans who wanted a lion skin to take home with them. It was also a popular place for white tourists in general, for the Inn symbolized the

Wild West image the travellers had heard or read about and long drunken nights were common. Tourists rarely spent any time in Maun, except for getting supplies, and it was here that they could swap terrifying stories of near-misses with wildlife, plan the rest of their route, and even perhaps hire a guide.

Maun's great white hunters had been here for decades, their residence in Botswana going back to the 1930s. Some originated from German traders who had emigrated to what was then South West Africa and then moved east to Botswana before the outbreak of World War One. By the end of the Second World War, Maun was established as the gateway to a sport-hunter's paradise. A hunter only had to drive a few kilometres north to reach the huge herds of game on the fringes of the Delta. Game was aplenty, even in Maun itself, and just thirty years ago giraffe had been hunted where the secondary school now stood.

Ron and I sat and waited for our food. A little white girl out with her parents for the evening was staring at us. A waiter brought a bottle of white wine and a shiny metal bucket of ice to the family's table. Then he returned with the orders of beef, the meat so large it hung over the sides of the plates. The family was talking Afrikaans, which sounded a harsh, guttural language to me, and they took no notice at all of those who waited on them. Batswana, anyway, served in a rather cool, removed manner. They did not speak unless spoken to and they kept their eyes down; all signs of a respectful behaviour but infuriating to those who were used to the smiling servers in places such as the United States.

A man sitting to the left of our table lit a cigar and ordered a brandy. I could hear him going through a travel itinerary with his companion. 'One night Khwai, one night Third Bridge. Then straight to Linyanti, yar?'

'*Lekker*,' his companion replied as a waiter appeared with a giant plate of ribs.

From inside the bar I could hear Rod Stewart singing 'Do You Think I'm Sexy?' and the shouts as the pilots sang along.

It was such a completely different environment from Ron's family's compound which we had just left. There Madintwa and Eliah had been getting ready for bed. The fire was burning itself out and, with the onset of night, the day's visitors had left. We had delivered a pile of firewood, taken from the bush that afternoon, and placed it in a neat stack on the compound sand. Then we had drunk sweet tea, talked about whether there would be rain and received a shopping list of what Madintwa required which included pantaloons, a carton of Power and a new chamber-pot.

Inside the Duck Inn the pilots were getting frisky, their voices drunk and excited as one of them nailed a dartboard above the archway that led indoors to the bar. They began throwing darts, carelessly, without looking, as the Batswana waiters walked in and out, serving food and drinks. The head waiter was an elderly relative of Ron's and as he came out from the bar carrying two plates of veal schnitzel, a dart zipped over his head, just missing his face, grazing the white wall and landing on the floor. The man did nothing; his face showed no reaction at all, he just continued to serve. The pilots grew bolder now, darts flew this way and that as still the waiters continued to walk between the bar and the outdoor area. Ron watched, stony-faced.

'What do they think they're doing?' I hissed. 'They're going to stab someone with those darts.'

As I spoke a dart pinged off the roof and fell on to the tray one of the waiters was carrying.

Ron stood up. His relative, seeing this, gestured at him to sit down but Ron pretended he hadn't heard. 'Hey!' he said to one of the pilots. The man turned, his eyes a little bleary. 'Can you cut that out?' asked Ron.

The man looked shocked. 'Who the fuck are you?' he asked and two of the hunters in the bar stood up, walked forward and flanked the pilot.

I held my breath. Although I swore, I tried my best never to do it with anyone but Ron. I knew how strict Batswana were when it came to insulting language. I knew saying 'fuck' was considered so appalling that you could be sent to the Kgotla and thrashed — although I had not heard of a white person ever being thrashed at the Maun Kgotla. There was not even a Setswana version of the term, although I had asked about swear words as soon as I had arrived in Botswana with the British conviction that when travelling it was always useful to learn how to insult someone. Either swear words didn't exist, or no one would even speak them to me, and the worst I had ever heard was 'your father's arsehole'.

'Why?' said Ron very coldly, very deliberately to the pilot. 'Who the fuck are you?'

We were both standing now, facing the men. I wondered if they would hit us. I had never seen Ron violent, or showing any inclination towards violence, but looking at him now I saw that he could afford to be if he wanted. The hunters had beer bellies; the pilot was small and drunk. But Ron was young and fit and sober.

'Boys, boys,' said Bernadette making a sudden appearance, her lipstick shiny in the semi dark. Instantly the pilot and the hunters relaxed. One put his arm around Bernadette and she kissed him. 'Now, now,' she admonished. 'It's too early for this sort of behaviour. Roy,' she said to Ron, 'why don't you go and sit down?'

'It's Ron,' I said, 'not Roy.'

Bernadette ignored me and so did Ron. He walked up very close to the pilot and insulted him deeply in singsong Setswana, comparing the man's face to his father's arsehole. Two of the waiters stopped stock still, incredulous and then giggling.

'Now, now,' said Bernadette warningly to Ron, shaking out a manicured finger.

★　★　★

Ron was silent as he got into the Land Rover and we drove off to the party. An incident like this could drive him into silence for days. At last

131

he stopped before a large double gate which led on to a wide driveway bordered by giant leadwood trees. We passed two aluminum shelters which looked like the sort of construction road builders in London would take refuge in from the cold and rain. But outside one a small fire was burning and I realized someone was living there, perhaps a servant. The plot belonged to a prosperous white Zimbabwe couple who ran a number of safari enterprises based in Maun and who would be hosting the party.

Ron and I got out of the car and set off towards the house, a huge oval building with a thatched roof and massive glass windows and doors. The air smelt sweet, almost like honeysuckle, and I thought I heard the call of a nightjar. I stopped just behind Ron at the door, impressed by the size of the house. Two stone steps led into a mammoth kitchen area, its floor covered in thick red stone tiles, fully kitted out with worktops, a fridge freezer, washing machine, dishwasher and microwave. This was the most luxurious kitchen I had seen in Maun and I was quite dazzled by the sight. Where had all these things come from? None were sold in the shops in Maun, so they must have been imported from South Africa thousands of kilometres away. To the right of the kitchen I could see the living-room, its walls a creamy-beige colour, on the floor were two large zebra skins complete with heads and in the corner a stool made from an elephant's foot.

'Round the back,' a white man said as he saw

Ron walking up the steps. 'Where's your uniform?'

'We're invited,' Ron said.

The man stopped. He seemed unsure. 'Oh, okay then,' he said as his eyes flicked from mine to Ron's. At last he moved so that we could enter the house. I followed Ron out towards the back garden which rolled down to the edge of the Thamalakane River, the grass damp and springy underfoot. On the riverbank I could see the shiny glint of a speedboat and two canoes made from green fibreglass. All around the garden were dotted bamboo-cane lamps and the flames flickered from one side to the other in the light evening breeze. I looked to my left, drawn by the smell of meat cooking on a series of barbecues which stood on a large stone patio, larger than our entire kitchen. I could see the piles of meat — sausages and boerewors, slabs of beef and hunks of ribs, chicken legs and wings and breast, and other meat which I hadn't seen before. While I now ate meat, the sight of all the flesh on array made me queasy. Behind the barbecue was the bar, an oval thatched structure whose glass counter was lined with unopened bottles of every spirit imaginable. Behind the bar two black men stood to attention in white shirts. I turned at the sound of children's laughter and watched while two blond children came running out of the house, followed by a black woman in a starched green nanny's uniform with white apron and scarf. I thought I had wandered on to a filmset. The wealth of the house and the grounds, the excess of food and drink, was astounding. Now for the first time I saw how rich a country Botswana was, or at least its resources could make some people very rich indeed.

The garden was full of people and I stood by a stone wall and looked around for anyone I knew. The guests were all white safari people; there were no Indians, no Batswana except for those serving. I knew by now that the Maun tourism industry was dominated, controlled and owned by white people, but exactly why this was I couldn't quite understand. I thought perhaps it was because white people had been running safaris long before Botswana ever became independent and now they had the expertise and the client base to continue. Perhaps it was because you needed money to set up a safari company and all the white people in Maun had money. Perhaps it was because white people had the connections in South Africa and America and Europe needed to bring the tourists in. And perhaps it was because the white people did their best to make sure no Motswana managed to enter the industry at a high enough level to actually take any sort of control.

Maun was a place where, if you were white, you could probably succeed. I had heard of people who had arrived with two pairs of trousers and some loose change and who now had offices, houses with swimming pools and plenty of servants. Maun was also a place where you could disappear from anyone who was after you. I knew of one elderly American who, I had been told, was a notorious bank robber and on a wanted list at home. It was no wonder that the accused murderer Lord Lucan had been sighted more than once in Maun.

I watched the party guests as they chatted and drank and danced. The men in shorts and clean T-shirts, khaki socks rolled up to the knees, gold watches gleaming against tanned wrists. The women in flowing white skirts and little tops, ornate jewellery round their necks, ear-rings embedded with brightly coloured gems. I knew far more about these people than perhaps they were aware of, for Batswana endlessly gossiped about them. I knew that the woman in the short red dress dancing with her new boyfriend, a stocky man with a pony-tail, had last week left her husband of ten years who was now locked in an embrace with a tall woman in white shorts standing by the river's edge. I knew that the red-faced man smoking a pipe near the door to the house had recently divorced his wife and last week married her daughter. I knew who was suspected of offering bribes to the Land Board or the Department of Wildlife, who was trying to cosy up to which government minister, who had threatened to shoot who during a drunken argument.

And then I realized why I was feeling so uncomfortable; this was the first time I had been in a large group of white people since I had arrived in Botswana almost a year ago. For a moment I felt an outsider, as if I didn't know these people's language or how to behave. Their wealth intimidated me, and there was the same feeling in the air as there had been at the Duck Inn — these people wanted to party, they wanted to drink, they wanted to go a little wild.

'Everything okay?' I heard a man's voice and I turned to see a short, squat man with a pair of khaki shorts hitched up high on the crotch. I assumed this was Deon, the party's host. It was Deon who had invited Ron, for Ron had been installing computers at Deon's company and this had given Deon a competitive edge. He looked, from the back, a little like a hippo and as he turned to face me I saw his neck was like a hippo's as well. He had his arm around Ron's shoulder but now he ambled over to me.

'You're the girlfriend,' he said and he shook my hand, his fingers thick and clammy. 'Ronnie keeping you *happy* is he?' Deon asked with a leer.

'Where's the loo, the toilet?' I asked, feeling too close for comfort.

Deon pointed vaguely back to the house and I made my escape. Inside the house I found myself in what resembled a ladies' cloakroom at a cinema, only far cleaner and more ornate. The surfaces were so sparkling I wondered if the entire suite had just been installed. As I came out of the loo a woman was standing up close against a mirror inspecting her open mouth.

'I really need these teeth cleaned,' she said, her eyes flicking to mine in the mirror.

I smiled obligingly and washed my hands.

'Do you live here in Maun?' the woman asked.
'Yes.'

'And do you have a dentist?'

'Well, not really. I haven't been to a dentist yet. But I think there's one at the hospital.'

'A black, you mean? Is he *clean*?' The woman raised her eyebrows beseechingly.

I went back outside to find Ron tucking into a plate of ostrich meat. He had positioned himself behind the bar as if he were a waiter.

'What can I get you, madam?' he asked with a smile.

But I couldn't smile, I didn't fit in here. I was not a Motswana and I was convinced I was not an expatriate; I was somewhere in-between.

★　★　★

A week after the party my parents arrived from England and we took them to meet Ron's family. We drove to Madintwa's compound and, as on the day I had first met them, the yard was freshly swept, all the usual debris cleared away. Madintwa sat, her legs stretched out before her on a piece of old tarpaulin, flanked by Eliah on one side and her sister MaBoipelo on the other. The first time I had seen MaBoipelo she had been slumped against the wall of the house, and the few times I had seen her after that it had been the same. But then she had visited a new traditional doctor and made a sudden recovery from her long illness and joined family life again. Like Madintwa, she was a compulsive talker and once she started it was near impossible to make her stop. These days we called her MaB.

Ron led the way into the compound. My father accepted a white plastic chair, but then immediately stood up and began nosing his way around, picking up things, inspecting the reed wall, even peering into Eliah's house. My mother sat down on the sand and handed over presents. With each gift Madintwa clapped her hands and exclaimed in pleasure, then she wrapped the gifts up and put them very determinedly, reverently, to one side. These were special gifts, from England, and she wasn't going to leave them just lying around. I thought, as I watched her, that she would probably never use them at all.

Madintwa was sitting very upright today. It was almost as if she were preventing herself from smiling, or laughing, too much. She wore her best clothes and a yellow tasselled shawl, the sort a married woman would wear at a wedding. She was taking the visit very seriously. Madintwa called for some water, laid her hands on her lap, took a deep breath and began to speak in her preacher's voice. At one point my father tried to ask a question and I shushed him.

'She's not finished yet,' I hissed. 'It's a speech. It could take a while.'

At last Madintwa stopped and my mother looked to Ron for explanation.

'My grandmother is welcoming you to Botswana,' he said. 'She says Caitlin is her child now and she will look after her.'

'Tell her we can see that Caitlin is very, very happy here,' my mother said.

'*Ee!*' Madintwa said at once.

An hour later, wilting under the midday sun, we drove my parents out of Boyei ward. 'She's the matriarch of the family, isn't she?' my mother commented as we sat in the open back of the Land Rover.

'Who?'

'Ron's grandmother.'

'No, she's not,' I said. 'She's just trying to be all formal because you're here. Usually she's a laugh.'

Madintwa was my heroine now. The more I saw her, the more I learnt about her life, the more I admired her. I knew now that she had been married off as a very young girl, given by her family to an older man. Though still a child herself, she had quickly had three children, two of whom had died in infancy. Pregnant with the fourth child, Madintwa had decided to leave her husband because of what she called his bullying ways. She had not said to Ron or me what these were, only that she had been mistreated in shameful ways. And at this point a fight had broken out, with family members on both sides of the marriage called to Kgotla meetings. Madintwa was advised, by her family, by her husband's family, by the Bayei Chief, by the Batawana Chief, to return to her husband. But she refused. In the end she won and they were allowed to separate.

Then, many years later, when Madintwa's ex-husband became ill, he had sought her out and she had nursed him right up until his death. Today she lived just in front of one of her ex-husband's former girlfriends, and the two women were firm friends. Madintwa had gone against convention by demanding a separation from an abusive husband when such things were unheard of. And when he had needed her, she had shown herself too soft, too kind-hearted to turn him away.

# 9

The only thing missing from my life in Maun was a friend. Ron was my best friend and, unlike Batswana couples, we tended to do everything together, but I still missed having a woman friend. Then, one day in August, we set off to see a plot of land off the road in the village of Matlapaneng. As a Motswana, Ron was entitled to a plot of land for free which he would own on a ninety-nine-year lease. But it had taken us a long time to find a vacant plot, until finally we found one on a tongue of land which stretched along the Thamalakane from the old Matlapaneng Bridge.

The bridge was the oldest in Maun and it was bumpy and stony, its chalky surface covered with a thin layer of white sand which showed footprints from the endless passage of people and goats and donkeys. All along the edges of the bridge were wonky wooden poles, leaning this way and that, affording no protection at all from falling off the edge. The sides of the bridge, just below the surface of the pathway, were reinforced in places with strips of mophane poles which looked as if they were about to tumble down into the water. It was possible to drive across the bridge, but increasingly hazardous as drought and rain and traffic meant it was seriously wearing away.

Although there were houses, mainly large and

mainly owned by white people, on either side of the Thamalakane near the old bridge, this tongue of land was totally uninhabited. It began at one end of the bridge at a place people called the Hippo Pool. This was the deepest part of the river and even when the rest of the Thamalakane dried up there was always water here, which meant during drought hippos often found themselves restricted to a small area of water as the environment shrank around them.

A month ago, as the water levels dropped to their lowest, I had seen a hippo walking across the Matlapaneng Bridge in broad daylight, followed by a group of boys throwing stones. I wasn't keen on living anywhere near a hippo, especially as I had been told hippos caused more human deaths in southern Africa than any other animal. It was without doubt Botswana's most dangerous mammal and it seemed foolhardy to build a house in a hippo's territory. But then, the whole of the Delta, and at a pinch the whole of Maun, was hippo territory for they lived in and fed off the waterways of the Okavango and always had. And even though I had seen the hippo on the bridge and had been afraid, that couldn't take away from the beauty of the plot we had found on the end of the peninsula that snaked along the river from the Hippo Pool. The spot was unique for not only did it have the river on one side, but when the water was high it double-backed and formed a river on the other side as well. We would have our own little island.

When we arrived at the old bridge in order to mark out the corners of our plot, we found a party going on, for people were celebrating the fact that at last the river had arrived. For the past few weeks people had talked about nothing else in Maun, it was one thing that united everyone. Elders like Ron's grandmother were eager for the river to come, to know that the rains in Angola had been good that year, to know that when she went into Morutsa getting water for bathing or cooking wouldn't be a problem. Eliah was keen for a good flood too, as she had begun taking tourists out on a *mokoro* in the Delta, becoming the first woman to do so. White people wanted the river as well, for the tourism industry within Maun relied almost solely on the Thamalakane and once the water arrived then motorboats and canoes could set off on river safaris into the Delta.

So everywhere in the village people passed on what they had heard: the river up at Mohembo was flooding there was so much water this year, it had reached the Boro River and was moving so fast that it would be in the Thamalakane by next week, by tomorrow, by nightfall. The excitement was infectious.

A week before we had driven out to the Boro where a gush of water was seeping towards the Thamalakane, the sand of the riverbank becoming hard where the water had begun to force a channel. Further upstream the river was deep enough for Ron to borrow a *mokoro* and I had watched as he stood in the canoe, his body dipping and swooping to drive the boat along. He had looked both relaxed and triumphant, pleased not to have forgotten the skills of his

143

youth. For the past few days, every time we came anywhere near the Matlapaneng Bridge, there had been a swarm of tiny black biting flies. This, I was told, was the sign that the river really was coming, along with the appearance of the majestic fish eagle, a giant white-headed bird that sat on tree tops and telephone poles giving an occasional haunting cry which was so sharp that it seemed to leave echoes in the air long after the eagle had gone.

Ron stopped the Land Rover a little way from the bridge. There was nowhere to park for four-wheel-drive vehicles were everywhere, car doors and windows open, sound systems blasting out, in competition with each other. Men leaned on car bonnets, drinking beer. A group of church women were dancing in a shady spot under a wide acacia tree. Young children ran around their parents who were *braaiing* meat on steel drums. And it wasn't just Batswana, it was white people too. For the first time since I had been in Maun, people were actually mixing. Two large Afrikaner men were standing in the middle of the bridge, chatting with a local farmer. A white English safari operator was sharing a cigarette with a man from the Land Board. Children, white and black, were pushing out a canoe.

I set off along the bridge, walking slowly, having to almost squeeze my way around the people without either stumbling on the rocks or falling off the bridge altogether. When I got further along, and stopped under the spreading canopy of a huge wild sycamore fig tree which grew in the middle, I could see what all the fuss was about. Water was gushing under the bridge, hurtling and foaming, sticks and other debris shooting along with the strength of the flow. Before my eyes the Hippo Pool was filling up, the tree roots that had been exposed on the side of the banks were now being covered. As I turned to look the other way, it was to see that a river was forming, the grass and sand disappearing under a blue blanket of river, its surface like exploding sparklers.

'God, it's beautiful,' I murmured.

'*Ee*. It is *so* beautiful,' said a woman beside me.

I turned towards her, smiling. Everyone on the bridge was smiling. The arrival of the river was making people animated, keen to talk, even to strangers.

'I saw a hippo on this bridge just the other week,' I said.

'*Ijo!*' the woman exclaimed. 'I don't like hippos.'

'Nor me,' I laughed.

'But I have never seen one,' added the woman.

'What, never?' I assumed the woman couldn't be from Maun if she had never seen a hippo. 'Where are you from?'

'Mochudi,' said the woman, chewing on the word, pronouncing it as if it were an important place I must know.

'Are you working here then?'

'*Ee*. I have been transferred from Gaborone.' She looked glum.

'And what do you do?'

'I work in immigration.'

'That must keep you busy, in a place like Maun.'

The woman laughed.

'What do you think of Maun?'

'I think it is a very strange place. People here are very . . . ' The woman hesitated.

'Traditional?' I offered.

'No. They are backward.'

'Really?' I said, stepping back a little, offended and defensive. 'How do you mean, backward?'

'I mean they believe in these things like witchcraft and ritual murder.'

'They do?'

'*Ee*.' The woman dropped her voice a little and looked around the crowded bridge. 'When the river comes, it is said a child will die.'

'But why?' I asked. I had heard references to ritual murder; even before I arrived in Botswana I had heard about the practice. I thought it was just another stereotype, the idea of Africans sacrificing children. Yet in the time I had been in Maun I had heard of two specific cases of what was apparently ritual murder, complete with the identity of the murdered child, the traditional doctor who had advised the murder, and the man who had been responsible for having it carried out. It was a practice that went far, far back in history, but how often it really ever happened any more was hard to say. In the past a child could have been sacrificed, to bring rain perhaps or other good fortune. Today it was done for personal reasons, to bring wealth to a businessman or budding politician.

146

'Why?' the woman asked, echoing my question. 'Why do they do this? Hey, I can't say. I can't say how someone can kill their own child. What is happening to we Batswana these days?' She shifted then, arranging the tasselled ends of a blanket she had wrapped around her breasts, and I realized she had a toddler on her back.

'Sleeping?' I asked, peering at the child who was swaddled in layers of clothes.

'*Ee*. Her name is Bonny and she is sleeping. Where is Mozambia?'

I started, surprised. I still hadn't got used to how small Maun was, that with just twenty thousand people everyone really did seem to know everyone else.

'He's there.' I pointed to where Ron had joined Bashi and some other men *braaiing* meat on the riverbank.

'Hey, all he does is eat meat,' the woman said, laughing, and she punctuated her comment with a loud suck on her front teeth.

'Who, Ron?'

'No, my boyfriend Bashi.'

'Oh, my God, you're Bashi's girlfriend?'

'*Ee.*'

I shook her hand a little awkwardly, for we were standing very close together on the bridge.

'Pearl,' she said. 'My name is Pearl.'

I looked at her properly now. She was shorter than me, so that she had to tip her face up a little when she wanted to look me in the eyes. She wore a pale yellow T-shirt with a chunky white cardigan on top and, unusual for a Motswana woman, a pair of trousers. Her face was long and her top teeth protruded slightly which gave her mouth a heart-shaped look. Around her neck she had a red stone on a gold chain and in her ears were earrings in the shape of little black three-legged cooking pots.

'I'm Caitlin,' I said.

'I know,' said Pearl. 'You will have to teach me English, then I can talk with you.'

'But you already know English!'

'Ah, no I don't. I don't know it properly. I don't feel comfortable in it, *oa itse*?'

'*Ee*,' I agreed and, delighted, Pearl took my hand.

★ ★ ★

A month later we stood together in the kitchen at our house at the Tshwaragano school. Ron and I were having a party, but while he was outside *braaiing* meat I was inside being a waitress. I had not realized that inviting Batswana to your home meant working so hard. Each time I went outside to relax, I would be summoned across the plot.

'Castle times two!' a man would cry. 'And make them cold!'

'Get them yourself,' I muttered at last, seeking refuge with the women. But at once a woman patted me on the arm. 'I will take a Campari and soda,' she said firmly.

'Oh,' I said, a little surprised, 'we don't have any Campari.'

The woman looked at me, her eyes wide. 'Then I will take a Gordon's gin with tonic.'

'I'm sorry, there's no gin. We have wine, and beer.'

'I will take a Hunter's Gold.'

'Okay,' I said. I could see what the woman was thinking, she was thinking that if a white person was having a party then it should be a lot more lavish than this. I went into the kitchen where Pearl was breaking up hunks of ice and throwing them into a metal bath.

'This is getting to be hard work,' I mumbled. 'People just want me to wait on them hand and foot.'

'Shame,' Pearl said, hardly turning her head.

'And no one has brought *anything* with them, not even a bottle of beer!'

Pearl laughed.

'Where's your daughter tonight?' I asked.

'She is with Bashi's mother. And yours?'

'Mine?' I laughed, surely if Ron and I had a child then Pearl would have seen him or her by now. 'I don't have any kids. And no, before you say anything, I don't want any either. I've never wanted a baby. Though you know what, I wouldn't mind an older child, I like them once they start walking and talking. You can lend me Bonny when she gets bigger . . . '

Pearl smiled.

'Who knows,' I continued, 'maybe someday Alice could move in with us.'

'Alice?'

'Ron's daughter.'

'*Ijo!*' Pearl exclaimed.

'What?' I asked, thinking of Alice, of how I hadn't seen her since the night at Last Chance.

'What's wrong with that? She is Ron's child. He is her father. And I've told you how she's being passed from one family to another; you know she doesn't even go to school. She must be six years old at least. She can't read or write. She just sort of hangs around.'

Pearl sucked her teeth. It was a habit of hers, a way of signalling surprise or, sometimes, a disgust so deep there was no other way to express it.

'What?' I asked again, laughing.

'You want to take another woman's child into your house?'

'Why not? It would be best for her, wouldn't it?' and I bent and rummaged around among the blocks of ice, looking for a Hunter's Gold.

Back in the garden I stood by the fire, feeling romantic because standing by a fire was not something I had ever had to do in order to keep warm. I turned at the sound of a car outside and watched while Tiki drove in. Tiki was an old friend of Ron's, they had been at primary school together and now Tiki was trying to open a garage. He was a short, fast-walking man, given to long stories and explosions of laughter. Behind him came his girlfriend Beauty with their baby, Leonard, in her arms. She moved slowly, her body swaying a little, the smile on her face shy as if she hadn't been to a social gathering for a long time and was pleased to be going out. I had met Beauty twice in the past week and her face was one of the most beautiful I had ever seen, round with smooth, totally unblemished skin. I watched as she moved around the people at the fire, politely greeting each one.

'You smell nice,' I said as she finished the greetings and came to stand just a little in front of me.

'*Ee*,' she laughed. 'I have perfume tonight. But I have only put it here,' and she tapped at the small of her back, 'because I do not want to smell it myself, but other people might like to smell it.'

We stood companionably for a while, in the distance I could hear donkeys and, further away, the faint beat of drums. Then from inside the house someone changed the tape and 'Fight the Power' began blaring out, the song of the year, played at every party in Maun. I watched a man I didn't know doing a slow-motion dance, concentrating as if he were dancing with someone he deeply loved. He began to perform as others stopped to look, first stepping like a chicken on hot coals, then holding his pelvis with both hands, shimmying his hips from one side to another. Next to me I could hear both Pearl and Beauty laughing. I looked up at the night sky, feeling tiny, feeling that the people at the party were a speck in the universe, a gathering of laughter on a massive flat land.

# 10

Ron and I sat outside the office belonging to Maun's district commissioner. It was one of many council offices in an old, one-storey building with a concrete porch and thin, blue-painted pillars. In front of us was the DC's room, its door closed, and next to that an open door gave a glimpse into a small dim office in which five people were squeezed. A woman sat at an old wooden table, a tiny fan whirling uselessly away on a nearby shelf. She appeared to be a secretary for on the desk in front of her was a stack of large metal trays, each one full of pale-blue folders. Every now and again she sighed, picked up a folder, flicked through it, and put it back on the tray. The other people in the room looked like council workers, two of the men in faded green overalls splattered with white paint. I watched as a woman with two cups of tea and a paper bag of *magwinya*, little brown balls of freshly fried fat cakes, tried to fit herself sideways into the room.

It was 16 September 1992, and Ron and I were waiting to get married. Although still early in the morning, the sun was pounding down. I had been awake for hours, early starts no longer bothered me and it seemed natural to get up at sunrise. But the heat was hard to bear. Winter had once again faded away and now it was spring. Soon my favourite trees, the jacarandas, which lined the road where the Maun prison stood, would be in bloom. Overnight they would sprout delicate canopies of lilac petals which would last just days before blowing away.

I looked along the line of chairs on which we sat. Ron's uncle OT was crossing and re-crossing his legs as if he couldn't decide whether to get up and go to the courtyard for a smoke or not. Next to Ron sat his mother, Eliah, her expression serious, her headscarf tied tightly around her head. Her lips were pursed shut, but her eyes were bright and, if she had allowed herself, then I thought she would have been smiling. Marriage was a solemn and important occasion; today her first-born and only son was tying the knot and with that he would become, at last, an adult. Married people had more status than unmarried people; they were treated more seriously and with more respect. All the women I knew wanted to get married, yet none of them were. I had heard it said that men told prospective brides that they needed to prove themselves fruitful first. Then, when the woman had given birth once, perhaps twice, the man turned his attention elsewhere. There was no stigma to being unmarried and having a child, but still, women wanted to marry.

Suddenly the door to the district commissioner's room was flung open and a wedding party marched out led by three men in black suits, their heads newly shaved. On their hands they wore white gloves and each had a white carnation in their lapel. Next came five girls in blue party dresses, a riot of frills and bows, the dresses identical but because the girls were of such different sizes and heights not one had a dress that actually fitted her. I thought of Alice, how she would die to have a dress like the girls wore. We had spent the morning together the day before, Ron and I taking Alice and her cousin Kgakgamatso round the shops in the Maun mall, finally settling on new shoes and dresses for each of them. Alice had been paralytically shy, unable to lift her eyes off the ground even when addressed by Ron. The more I saw Alice the more I wanted to see her, and the more convinced I became that she needed security in her life. I watched as she crept around the clothing shop, her shoulders hunched as if she didn't want anyone to notice her. The only time she came to life was when she spied a pink dress with a little white apron sewn on the front and, stopping before it, she almost swooned.

Once the bridesmaids had left the DC's room, the elders of the wedding party began filing stiffly out. An old man came first, trilby hat on his head, a walking stick in his hand, followed by three old women walking carefully, with dignity, their own old wedding shawls around their shoulders. Then, finally, came the bride and groom, dressed like wedding-cake decorations come to life. The white train of the bride's dress dragged on the porch floor, gathering up sand and dust and debris like a broom.

Suddenly the silence was broken by the sound of ululations as the women in the wedding party began to cry and sing, sweeping their arms down to their knees, noisily leading the bride and groom along the cement porch and down to the sand where a black shiny car decked with white balloons awaited them. I saw Eliah watching the bride and groom as they got into the car, and I couldn't tell if she were watching with disapproval at the ostentatious display, or envy.

'Wow,' I said to Ron. 'That was quite a performance. Do you think we should be doing it properly as well?' and I laughed, a little hysterically, at the thought of wearing a white dress and being the centre of so much attention.

It had been my idea initially that we get married. Two months earlier the Tshwaragano headmaster had told me that as I was single and, as accommodation at the school was scarce, another teacher would be moving in with us. I told him I wasn't single, as he knew, but he just replied by asking me whether I was married or not.

We had recently moved from our original one-bedroom house into a slightly larger one, with two equally tiny rooms. The idea of having to share this with another teacher filled me with dread, and I had joked that perhaps we should get married, then at least we'd be allowed to keep the house to ourselves. Then we had forgotten the idea of marriage until Ron was offered a job in Sowa, a new town almost 400 kilometeres south-west from Maun, at a salt mine called Soda Ash Botswana. The town lay on the edge of the salt pans, the pans that I'd heard had featured in the film *The Gods Must Be Crazy*.

Ron would work in the IT department. Now,

if I wanted to, I could leave teaching, which was no longer the pleasure it had been at the beginning, and find something else to do. The behaviour of the Tshwaragano students had changed. They had begun to fight more amongst themselves and to challenge the teachers, especially those like me who refused to use the stick. And the school day never seemed to end; there were staff meetings that lasted for hours, school clubs to run, turns to be taken standing on duty at break and at lunch and during afternoon study, whole afternoons spent overseeing the weeding of the sports pitch. I lived on the school grounds; I felt I could never get away.

And then Ron began suggesting the idea of marriage. Legally, as I had come to Botswana as a teacher, if I left my job then I wouldn't be allowed to stay in the country. But if I was married, then I could. I knew, from Pearl, that plenty of white people stayed in Maun without proper paper work. Some came in with a work permit for a specific job that they quickly left. Others stayed on visitor permits which they renewed every three months and under which, in theory, they weren't allowed to work at all. Still others offered bribes to immigration officials — a cassette player, a cow, a wad of cash. But I wanted to do things properly. I wanted to stay in Botswana and be free to decide where and how to work. And when we were told that marriage to a Motswana meant instant citizenship, this seemed like the perfect thing to do. We would marry, I would then become a naturalized Motswana, and I would be free to stay and work as I wished. It would mean renouncing my British citizenship because Botswana, like most African countries, didn't believe in dual citizenship. At the last moment I rang my parents in England and told them the news, stressing it was just a legal formality. They didn't believe me. They sent a wedding present, as did other family members. My sister wrote to ask what I would wear. I said it was just a normal day.

Ron's grandmother, Madintwa, wanted a proper wedding with all the cultural mores observed. But Ron and I were wrapped up in ourselves; we didn't pay much heed to what anyone else wanted, the marriage was just something we had decided to do. We loved each other, I loved Botswana, and this was what we were going to do.

The wedding party drove away from the DC's office in a whirl of sand. I shifted on my chair, but beside me Eliah and Ron sat motionless, side by side. Batswana were good at waiting, they didn't fuss or moan, they just sat and waited. But I needed water. I needed to pee. I was getting too hot and too bored.

'Do you remember that dream you had?' I asked Ron. 'The one you had in America when your grandmother said she would find you a woman to marry?'

Ron smiled indulgently. 'We're next.'

'What?'

'We're next, they're calling us, come on.'

Ron, Eliah, OT and I stood up and walked towards the DC's office. The room was, as I had expected, very small. A shiny wooden desk took up most of the space and I couldn't believe how the previous large wedding party had possibly fitted in unless some had been sitting on each other's shoulders. At the desk sat a young man in a grey suit. He wore a thin, black tie, which looked impressive against his clean starched white shirt. But despite the status his clothing suggested, the chair he sat at was rather low and so, although he was sitting purposefully with one hand on the desk, scribbling away with a pen, he looked a little like a child pretending to be someone important. Beside me I felt Ron bristle. This was not in fact the district commissioner, this was the assistant district commissioner, and he was very young indeed. I didn't care who married me; but I sensed that Ron, Eliah and OT were insulted not to find a real elder in charge of the proceedings.

'You may sit,' said the assistant DC in English. I glanced at Eliah, this wasn't fair, for neither she nor OT would be able to follow what was going on if this were to be conducted in English.

Ron thanked the man, in very ornate, deliberate Setswana and the assistant DC relaxed slightly, the hint of a smile on his lips. I had thought that considering he was about to marry two people he would be at least a little friendly, some words of welcome perhaps, a joke here and there. But this was not the place for levity. And as I took my seat on a hard wooden chair I felt the urge to do something reckless and the more I felt it the more I realized I was suppressing the desire to giggle. I pulled my top lip into my mouth to control myself.

Ron and I sat next to each other, facing the assistant DC. Eliah stood on Ron's right, and OT to my left. The assistant DC pushed a form towards us.

'You can sign here,' he said.

I looked at Ron and he pushed the form over to me. I tried to read it, but my concentration level was low.

'You know the different types of marriage?' said the assistant DC, more as a statement than a question. 'Sign there.'

'No, actually,' I said, 'I don't.'

The assistant DC looked annoyed, as if I were delaying him. 'There is 'in community of property'. And 'out of community of property'.'

'Oh. And what does that mean?'

The assistant DC sighed. 'Most people take 'in community of property'. Sign there,' and he handed me a pen.

'But what does 'in community' mean?'

'It means,' said the assistant DC, 'that when you marry you both own everything. So it means if you divorce you split what you own.'

'Oh, okay,' I said dismissively, Ron and I would never divorce. 'And the other one?'

''Out of community of property' means you own what you take to the marriage. So if you have a car, you own that. And if you divorce, you leave the marriage with what you brought to it.'

'Okay, that one then,' I said. 'What do you think?' I asked Ron.

'I don't know,' he said, searching my face with his eyes.

'It sounds fairer,' I said, 'this 'out of community of property' business.'

'Let's do that one then,' agreed Ron.

I took the pen and was about to sign on the dotted line.

'But you need to think about the body,' said the assistant DC.

'Sorry?'

'You need to think who will own the body of your husband when he is late.'

'Late? He's always late!'

'He means when I'm dead,' said Ron and his voice was low because he was trying to stop himself from laughing.

'Yes,' said the assistant DC seriously. 'Who will own the body? His mother?' and he glanced at Eliah who stood next to her son like a rod of steel. 'Or you? Will you take the body back to the UK, as you are from . . . ' He swivelled round the form and looked at it. 'As you are from the UK?'

'Oh, this is nice,' I said, starting to giggle. 'We've come to get married and you're asking me about what happens when Ron dies!'

'I'm not getting buried in the UK,' said Ron in mock affront and we both collapsed.

The assistant DC drew himself upright on his low chair. He turned to Eliah and spoke to her in Setswana, asking her to control her children. Eliah frowned at Ron and I and, desperately, we tried to stop laughing, deliberately looking away from each other as at last we both signed the form.

'That will be two pula,' said the assistant DC

160

and he told his secretary to call the next couple in.

We emerged out of the DC's office and back into the sunlight.

'Do you feel any different?' I asked Ron, half expecting ululating women to be waiting for us on the porch.

'I feel happy,' Ron said, and he took my hand.

★  ★  ★

Ron left for his new job in Sowa straight away. For the next two months I invigilated school exams and, in the evenings, went to picnics with Pearl and Beauty. Shortly after Ron left, a newspaper was launched in Maun, the *Okavango Observer*. Botswana had only five national newspapers, all of which were weekly except for the government-owned *Daily News*, which came out every day. I went to visit the *Okavango Observer*'s editor, for with time on my hands I was looking for something interesting to do. The editor was a South African woman who said she wanted a community paper and encouraged me to set up a youth page to be written by students at local secondary schools. But a few weeks later, when some students wrote about racism, she accused me of being political and, in a rage, threw me out her office. Disheartened, I went back to invigilating exams.

Two months later, Ron returned to Maun and we packed all our belongings into the back of the Land Rover and prepared to leave. The last item to go in the back of the car was my bike, one of the first bikes to be sold at Maun's new sports shop. I had ordered a blue one, but had been given a pink one by the sales assistant who told me ladies' bikes only came in pink. I loved my bike. In the time since Ron had been in Sowa it had changed my life, allowing me to travel around Maun with a new freedom.

It was a brilliant December morning, the air sharp after a summer downpour the night before. Maun was green again, everywhere the grass was tall and thick, the leaves in the morula trees shiny and new.

We left the school by daybreak and I looked back to see the nightwatchman waving his unlit torch, a group of women setting up shop on the sand by the school fence ready to sell *magwinya* at teabreak, and columns of students in uniform jogging up the main pathway, trying to avoid a beating by not arriving late for school.

When we got to Eliah's compound we found the family getting ready for a trip to Morutsa. Alice was there, folding up blankets, putting out the fire, piling farming tools into an old canvas bag. I couldn't keep track of family arrangements, but it looked as if Alice no longer lived with Selina, Ron's stepmother, and for now was staying in Boyei ward with Eliah, although she still didn't go to school. She was wearing the pink dress we had bought before our wedding and it was already far too small. Alice stopped as we approached and stood still, her arms hanging loosely by her side, as we walked into the compound.

'*Dumela Mma*,' Ron greeted his daughter

politely. '*Oa re eng?*'

Alice looked bashful, but she smiled and answered softly, '*Ga ke re sepe*' — I'm not saying anything.

Ron asked if she were going to Morutsa, and asked her to take good care of his grandmother while she was there.

I was about to go into the house to see Eliah when a car pulled up on the sand pathway outside the compound. It was a low white vehicle with a speaker strapped to the roof. I wondered if this were the car that drove around the village making announcements, calling people to Kgotla meetings, informing villagers about clean-up campaigns or parliamentary visits. Normally announcements were made in the early evening and often I stopped what I was doing to listen. 'Batawana!' the speaker would cry in a rousing voice, 'Batawana! *Go na le puthego* . . . ' But then the vehicle would turn a corner, or the announcer would cough, and the rest of the words would be drowned out.

'That's my uncle,' said Ron as a large man hoisted himself out of the car. 'Rra Nama.'

'What, Mr Meat?' I smiled, translating his name into English. 'Is he the one that drives around making announcements then?'

'No.' Ron laughed. 'He's a politician.'

I looked more closely at the car and saw the letters BNF painted shakily on the side, the name of Botswana's main opposition party.

Rra Nama got out and headed straight towards me. '*Dumela Mma.* I am Mozambia's uncle. I have not met you before because I have

163

been travelling; we have had a very important rally in Kasane. Why weren't you there?' he asked, turning on Ron.

'Ah, politicians just like to help themselves,' said Ron.

'Not in the BNF,' said Rra Nama. 'It's time we had a change of government. Why don't we own this land or these animals any more?' and he held out his hands, palms up, in despair.

Ron nodded. 'The whites in Maun own everything.'

Rra Nama draped his arm around Ron, 'Ah, we blame the whites too much. It is always racism this, colonialism this. Look at you, Mozambia, you went to America, you got a degree. You can't complain that the whites have stopped you,' and Rra Nama delved through the car window, brought out a wad of biltong and waved it under Ron's nose. 'Ee, smell that. That is real biltong!' He tore off a strip of the dried meat and handed it to me.

'No thanks, I don't really eat meat.' I smiled in case Rra Nama would take offence. It wasn't true, I did eat meat, but never biltong. Wherever I went there was biltong, Ron kept piles of it in the car at all times, while at his mother's compound I often looked up at a tree or at the rafters of the kitchen to see fresh, red slivers of meat buzzing with flies, the older pieces hardened and black like salty stalagmites.

'You don't eat meat? That is why you are too thin,' said Rra Nama and he leant against the bonnet of the car, chewing contentedly. 'Hey, I am feeling fit these days,' he beamed, patting his stomach which hung several centimetres over his trouser belt.

I went into the house to say goodbye to Eliah. It was dark and cool inside, but for such a small structure the space was relatively large. I had very rarely been into Eliah's house, it was used for sleeping in and, on rare occasions, to shelter in from the rain, so there was usually no reason for anyone but Eliah to enter.

I found Eliah sitting on the double bed to the left of the room; she was folding clothes, quickly and efficiently, while calling out instructions to Alice and Kgakgamatso outside.

'*Ko ko!*' I called as I stood in the doorway.

'*Ee.*' Eliah turned to me and smiled.

I asked if she were going to Morutsa, for I had got used to opening remarks in Setswana that simply stated the obvious. She said there had been plenty of rain and that she had many tourists who wanted her to pole them.

'I am learning English,' she said softly in English, each word brought out after a lot of hesitation. 'My white people are teaching me.'

I laughed and said soon she would know more English than I knew Setswana. Then she ushered me to the foot of the bed where a glass-fronted cabinet stood. She reached up high to take a bag down from where it was hanging on the rafters. Then she folded the bag in half and handed it to me. I opened it and took out two suits, fashioned from brightly coloured printed cloth that Zimbabweans often sold in the village.

The suits had a traditional design, the sort of

165

outfit a married woman might wear to a wedding or other family affair, or even to church. The skirt was straight and a little rigid, and came halfway down to my ankles. The blouse had a square neckline and short puffed sleeves, and further down it was nipped in tightly at the waist and then flared out again stiffly for the cloth was new and not yet washed. I thanked Eliah profusely, it was not often that anyone gave me anything, they were usually demanding that I give them something — clothes or money or food. I thanked her again, folding up the clothes, knowing I probably wouldn't wear them for while the colours were beautiful and the pattern bright, the style was too fussy for me. But it was the thought that was important, and the fact that Eliah had had these clothes specially made for me. For a moment I wanted to hug her.

Outside in the compound Madintwa was ready to go. She sat on the sand, a tarpaulin sheet neatly folded beside her, her headscarf on, her fingers resting on the handle of a big old bag.

'Kate-a-lyn,' she called to me in the singsong way she pronounced my name.

'Oa tsamaya? O tsamaya ko Sowa?'

I told her that yes; we were on our way to Sowa.

'Ah, mama-we!' she said, beckoning me closer. She called out to Kgakgamatso to bring her a bowl of water.

I sat down on the sand, not even flinching when Madintwa took a cheekful of water and sprayed it all over my face. I had got so used to this procedure that it had come to symbolize good luck, as if the traditional form of farewell would protect me from whatever would come.

# PART THREE

# 11

I lay by the side of the swimming pool at the Sowa Sports Club, drying in the sun, staring up at the blue sky, drinking in the sound of silence. Forty-eight hours ago I had been in London, my first trip back to England in nearly two and a half years. Very little had changed at home, the shops were the same, the cars were the same, the people on the street looked the same, except now women wore odd tights called leggings. On the streets people passed each other with blank faces, only occasionally giving a tight grimace intended as a smile.

In London I couldn't even think about Botswana, the contrast was too great. The sounds of police and ambulance sirens replaced those of donkeys and cockerels, I smelt the fumes of cars instead of fire smoke and wild sage, I woke up at 5 a.m. to find the world dark and asleep. I was teased for having a South African lilt to my voice, and I annoyed people by complaining constantly about the cold. I had looked forward to rain and cold weather but I found it unbearable, my bones chilled to the core, forever shivering, having to venture out only after putting on layer upon layer of clothes.

I was unnerved by the traffic, the cars that drove through most of the night, the constant trail of aircraft leaving white pathways in the grey cloudy sky. I was so unused to walking on concrete after so long on the sand that my shins seized up, giving jolts of pain every time I took a step on the pavement. I couldn't believe I was finding things so difficult when this had been my home for twenty-five years. But I felt a glow about me, the glow of life in Botswana with its open landscape, its sun and its stars. Maun became a place I could hardly believe I had lived in, a small African village on the sand, hundreds of kilometres from anywhere. And it was Maun I wanted to return to, not Sowa.

I jumped in the pool again to swim. No one ever came to the Sowa pool during the day except for a pool attendant who halfheartedly attempted to scoop out water scorpions with a big net that looked designed to catch giant butterflies. The white people in Sowa mostly had their own swimming pools; few Batswana joined the club because the fees were constantly being hiked beyond their reach. But I was an expatriate now, a woman of leisure who could afford to join the club. I had virtually nothing to do all day, except write my Masters thesis which was still unfinished although I'd left Clark University years ago. I signed up for driving lessons, in order to learn how to drive a stick-shift, with a man called Jackson who had the longest fingernails of anyone I had ever met. He took good care of them, especially when opening and closing car doors, and they rapped impressively on the steering wheel when Jackson wanted to make a point. When I eventually sat the practical driving test in Sowa the examiner had a good look at me and then strapped on his seatbelt. 'I do not believe in women driving,' he said. 'You may begin.'

Apart from driving lessons, I attempted to be interested in cleaning the house which had a shiny fitted kitchen, three bedrooms and two toilets. The house was new, just like everything in Sowa was new: the roads, the council buildings, the Kgotla and the Sports Club swimming pool. Sowa town was just two years old and it had been built to house employees of Soda Ash Botswana, a mine 17 kilometres away. The population was hardly more than 2000 and there was virtually nothing to do in the town during the day, except go to the one shop and see if any food had arrived from Francistown. The place was clean, there were streetlights and shiny tar roads, the houses all had water and electricity. But it was a sterile place, a grid of green-roofed houses exposed to the winds and the sand of the Makgadikgadi. It was the most boring place I had ever lived and it was the most racist. Racism — and complaints about racism — was the very air that people breathed. In a business sense, the idea had been to mine the soda-ash deposits of the eastern Makgadikgadi Pans, sell the soda ash on the world market, and create a whole new industry for Botswana. The mine would also harvest salt. But while this was supposed to be a fact for national pride and was funded heavily by the Botswana government, the mine was managed by white South Africans who regarded the Batswana with derision and fear. When the South African communist leader and anti-apartheid activist Chris Hani was murdered, members of the Sowa Country Club held a *braai* to celebrate.

Because I had nothing to do, I began to write. I sent a feature on Sowa to a new newspaper in Francistown called the *Voice*. They published it and I tried to write more, fearing that without work I would turn into a frustrated housewife, my day built around Ron leaving in the morning and coming home at night. I stood at the door to the house the moment he arrived, eager for some human company, for someone to talk to, eager even to hear the tales of awful happenings at the mine. Two Afrikaner managers had called a black South African a monkey in the canteen at lunch and refused to eat at his table. Ron was constantly thwarted in his work by white superiors who weren't used to being challenged. On days when I took the Land Rover, Ron got a lift to the mine with a Motswana who would announce, grimly, every morning, 'Another day in paradise, my brother.'

Finding anything to write about in Sowa was hard. I wrote reports on kiosk licences, flamingos flying into power lines and clean-up campaigns. I wrote about a new ballroom dancing group who were keen to disprove the myth that ballroom dancing encouraged mischief and unwanted pregnancies.

Two months after I arrived in Sowa, I went to Francistown to visit the offices of the *Voice*. I found a cramped room on the top of a two-storey building. A man was glued to a computer, watching fish on a screen saver, while a woman sat beside him typing with one hand

174

and holding the phone with another. Eventually she put the phone down and beamed. 'Caitlin, our Sowa girl!' She laughed and the beads in her hair jangled as she gestured me over. 'Beata,' she said, offering her hand. 'We are so pleased you are writing for the *Voice*. This is going to be a wonderful paper, don't you think so?' and she shook my hand vigorously. 'Sadie, my darling,' she said to a woman hovering at the door, 'get some tea.'

I sat down, a little overwhelmed, Beata was too big a presence for this little dingy room. 'Caitlin, my darling, let me finish this, okay?' she said. 'And then we can talk. We can go for coffee, we can go for beer, and we can talk.' She turned as a tall white man walked in. 'Ah, Don, late again. This is Don Moore, the owner. And this is Caitlin, our Sowa girl.'

'Pleased to meet you,' Don said, sounding very British. He looked harassed and he stooped a little as if he were carrying a heavy weight.

'Sadie,' he said to the office cleaner, 'could we have some tea, please? Would you mind? Beata, can I use the computer for a moment. Is that okay?'

Don sat down, clearing piles of paper off a chair so I could sit as well. I looked around the desk, at the mess of notebooks and pens, folders and invoices. There was only one photo on the table and that was of an elderly bearded man in orange which Don adjusted with reverence.

'Thanks for your articles,' he said, with a hurried smile. 'Very nice, very good. But, now,

175

what we're after is a tabloid. What the *Voice* is going to be is Botswana's first tabloid newspaper . . .'

'Don!' yelled Beata, 'Printing and Publishing on the phone.'

Don groaned. He picked up the phone and began a long-winded explanation as to why he hadn't paid printing costs for the last issue of the *Voice*. Then he turned his attention back to me. 'I'm thinking along the lines of the *Mirror*. I'll give you some.' He searched around on the floor for a while. 'Beata! Where's that pile of *Mirrors*? Sadie! Have you seen . . . Okay, anyway, I'll find them later. So, what we're after is human-interest stories. People, photos, big headlines, lots of sport . . . '

'Page three?' I asked.

Don looked interested. 'Now that's an idea. Could we get away with that?'

'I was joking.'

'So, get back to Sowa and see what you can do. Go to the Kgotla, plenty of drama there. See who's suing who. Get some criminals . . . '

I left the *Voice* office with my overdue pay-cheque. I also clutched 200 hundred copies of the *Voice* because Don wanted them distributed in Sowa, a list of advertising rates because Don thought I could sell some advertising space as well, and a huge pile of the British *Mirror* held together with string.

Back in Sowa, there was still nothing to write about. So I began venturing out of the town, visiting the nearby village of Mosetse and interviewing a potter and a man making leather

176

goods. I went in the other direction towards Nata where a tourist lodge was offering specials for people who wanted to get married under the bird table. But within Sowa life was exceedingly quiet. Beauty and Tiki visited from Maun, disappointed to find such a soulless new town. The news was limited to the private primary school holding a fund raising and the chief complaining that people didn't attend public meetings. Life went on. Until the day I heard about a talking hippo in Nata.

A wife of one of the mine employees I had become friendly with told me about it one sunny morning as we stood chatting at her gate.

'Where is the hippo exactly?'

'Just go to Nata, drive right through and turn off towards the river and you'll find it.'

'Have you seen it?' I asked.

'No, but someone told me about it.'

'Who?'

'Oh, I can't remember. It may have been my maid. Here, I'll draw you a map.'

The next day I set off to find the hippo. It was a peaceful drive to Nata, the land stretching out flat on either side, interrupted by occasional shrub trees, no sign of life but for an ostrich darting across the hot tarmac. The village of Nata seemed familiar to me now, compared with the day in August 1990 when I had arrived on the back of a truck en route to Maun, a long time before the tarred road existed. I slowed down as I approached the village, passing Wild Beast Butchery and then crossing the riverbed which was dry. I continued on, past the small police station and then came to Sua Pan Lodge. Here the road forked, one way to Maun, the other way up to Kasane. I went the Kasane route, clutching the map the Sowa woman had made in my now sweaty hand. I turned off the road, as indicated on the map, and hurtled along a thick sand pathway. I wondered how far I would go before I admitted it was the wrong way. I had been in Botswana for almost three years and still my sense of direction was useless, each sand pathway, each clump of mophane trees all looked the same. Eventually I gave up and headed back to Sua Pan Lodge.

I pulled in at the courtyard where two men were sitting at a round plastic table drinking Coke and doing accounts. I greeted them and hesitated, then at the doorway to the bar I saw a familiar-looking man.

'Samson!' I said, recognizing Ron's relative who I had met up in Satau the day we were charged by an elephant. 'What are you doing here?' I asked.

'I work here.'

'Yeah?' I couldn't get over how people in Botswana moved around so much. One day they were working in one shop, the next day in another. You could meet someone farming a field in the bush hundreds of kilometres away from any real village, and then a week later see them sitting behind a desk in a council office wearing a suit.

Samson nodded. 'I am the barman.'

'Oh great, get us a drink, I'm dying.'

We went into the building and Samson

positioned himself behind the bar. 'Have you heard about this talking hippo?' I asked when we had finished our drinks.

'*Mma?*'

I smiled, feeling stupid. 'I heard there was a talking hippo around here.'

'Really?' Samson looked surprised.

'Well, that's what I've heard.'

'You could ask that man there,' he said, nodding outside.

'At the table?'

'Yes, he is the owner of this business.'

But just as I was getting down off my bar stool another man came up. Short and sweaty, his clothes looked a little bedraggled as if he had been herding cows across the pans.

'You want to see the talking hippo?' he asked, leaning on the bar.

'Yes.'

'Okay, but first buy me a drink.'

'Do you know where this hippo is?' I asked, ignoring the demand.

'Me?' He looked insulted. 'Of course I do and more especially I can take you there.'

'You can?' I looked at Samson to see what he thought of this.

He nodded. 'This man is a relative of the owner,' he said as if this were a reliable reference.

The man was really excited now and he led the way out, having forgotten about the drink. We stopped by the men at the table and explained our mission but they didn't seem interested. So my guide and I got in the Land Rover.

'Stop here,' my guide said a minute later as we passed a bar.

'I thought we were going to see the hippo?'

'Have you asked the chief?'

'Asked the chief what?'

He sighed. 'Asked the chief for permission to find this talking hippo.'

'Well, no, I haven't. So, where is the chief?'

'He is there.'

I stared through the window at the group of men sitting drinking on the porch of the bar.

'He is there,' my guide said again and then, as if just thinking of this for the first time, he brightened up and said, 'I can go and ask him for you.'

'Well, shouldn't I ask him myself?'

'No, don't worry, he is my relative.'

So my guide jumped out of the car and I waited and waited and just as I was about to leave he came back. 'It is fine,' he said getting in the car, a fresh can of beer in his hands. 'Let's go.'

I was feeling a little bit concerned about my passenger now, but I really wanted to see the talking hippo and, unable to admit defeat and just drive back to Sowa, I pressed on.

'This way,' said my guide and I drove off the tar road and along a sand pathway much like the one I had driven along an hour ago. After a while I decided it was the same one. We doubled back.

'This way,' said my guide and off we turned again. This happened about four times but the last turning seemed promising. We were heading towards the riverbed, I thought, for the trees were big and green so they must be getting their water from somewhere. But a while later I thought perhaps we were driving in circles.

'Where is it?' I asked getting annoyed.

My guide had slouched to one side and he stank of beer.

He opened his eyes and sat up.

'Where is this hippo? Where is the river from here? It must be at the river, right?'

'Oh, a river,' said my guide throwing up his arms. 'A river? A hippo? What is a river, what is a hippo compared with love?'

'Huh?'

'Do you believe in racism?'

'What?'

'Can black and white love each other? Myself I have no problem with that. A white woman, a black man . . . ' He slouched back against the passenger door. Feeling irritated, I drove back to Sua Pan Lodge, opened the Land Rover door and my guide fell out on to the sand.

I sat in the car sweating, trying to think what to do. I just couldn't give up now. I'd wasted the whole morning. I looked at the hand-drawn map again. Perhaps I should have turned off the tar road before entering Nata? I drove back through the village, stopping at a large wholesalers. Outside I saw a white man watching boxes being loaded into a truck.

'Hi,' I said.

The white man turned.

'Hi,' I said again. 'How are you?' I had got so used to lengthy greetings in Setswana that I had begun doing them in English as well. And it had started to seem very rude if someone couldn't at least try to ask how you were.

'*Lekker*,' said the man.

'Look, I know this sounds mad but I'm looking for a talking hippo.'

'Yes?' said the man.

As he didn't laugh I pressed on. 'Do you know where it is?'

'Yes, the kids were stoning him so he moved from the pool of water near here.'

Then he gave the name of a white woman and said the hippo had taken up residence by her chicken farm.

'So how do I get there?'

'Easy. Just cross the river and follow the riverbed to the right.'

The road was terrible and there were constant obstacles, deep sand, uprooted trees, thornbushes and anthills. I pushed on, wiping the sweat from my face with my shirt, as if this was an endurance test I had to pass. On and on I drove until finally and joyously I came to a small enclosure which sounded and smelt of chickens. I got out of the car and headed towards a tall, elderly man coming out of a small stone building.

'My name is Caitlin,' I said once the greetings were done. 'I am a journalist for the *Voice* newspaper in Francistown.' I tried to say this with conviction, but I still hadn't got used to the idea that I worked for a newspaper. 'I have come to see the talking hippo.' As I spoke I became conscious of how my way of speaking had changed, how I pronounced the English words slowly, as if they were foreign even to me.

'Edward Lebala,' the man said and we shook hands. He didn't seem at all surprised to see me; it was almost as if he'd been expecting a visit. 'Yes, it is a good hippo this one. I can take you.'

'You can?' I almost wept.

Lebala nodded and smiled and then took his time securing the fence of the chicken farm.

'Can you run fast?' he asked as we set off.

I followed Lebala through some dense bush and then into a slightly more open area. I wondered if the riverbed was far away for I had lost it during the last leg of my journey.

'There it is,' said Lebala.

'What?' I stopped abruptly.

Lebala was bending slightly from the waist, leaning forward and pointing towards a small morula tree just yards in front of us.

I took a step backwards expecting a hippo to come galloping towards me.

'It is a good hippo this one, don't be afraid, you take a nice picture,' Lebala said reassuringly.

'No,' I said, 'this is fine, I can see it from here.' For now I could see the head and shoulders of a hippo watching me from behind the tree. Its body was a deep dark grey, almost the colour of the tree trunk, its undersides a glittery pink. Its head was down but its eyes were raised and its tiny pointed ears were erect. Standing on the sandy riverbank, alone but for the morula trees, it seemed a monster.

As Lebala moved forward I felt forced to follow and we circled the hippo which stood motionless in the shade of the tree. It was midday and the sun was fierce, a band of heat levitating off the burning sand. Then the hippo turned its head and looked our way. My heart was beating so loudly that I couldn't make out what Lebala was saying. I was here in the bush just metres away from the most dangerous land mammal there was. If we angered it, if it decided to come after us, then there was absolutely nothing I could have done to escape. A charging hippo would catch me in minutes and then bite me in half with its teeth. A few months earlier I had interviewed a man at the Maun hospital who had miraculously survived a hippo attack in which two other people were killed. The attack had happened after two hippos had gone on the rampage through a crowded, residential section of Maun between the tar road and the river. Villagers said the hippos were male and were fighting, and those killed just happened to be in their way. Others said it was a case of witchcraft.

'Sorry?' I whispered. Lebala had just asked me something but I wasn't sure what.

'I am saying, don't you want to go nearer?'

'No, no, I'm fine.' My voice sounded trembly and I was viciously chewing my lip.

'Do you want to take a photo?' Lebala asked and I looked down at the camera hanging round my neck.

'It's got a good lens,' I said still in a whisper. 'I can just take it from here.'

Lebala shrugged.

'Shall we go?' I hissed as the hippo twitched one foot.

Lebala smiled and led me back out of the

bush. I turned every few moments to make sure the hippo wasn't coming after us.

We walked in silence back to the chicken farm where I sat down on the sand and took out my notebook.

'When did you first see this hippo?' I asked, trying to breathe deeply and get my heart to settle down.

Lebala leant against a tree and considered. 'It was some months back.'

I wrote this down.

'Weren't you afraid?'

Lebala shook his head. 'No, I saw this hippo and I was talking to myself, saying, 'You are here.' And then the hippo says, 'Yes. I am here. This is my water and as long as you don't come into the water you are fine.' '

I scribbled quickly. 'Was it speaking English or Setswana?'

'Setswana.'

'Have you ever heard of a talking hippo before?'

Lebala shook his head.

'Were you surprised when it answered you?'

Lebala nodded. He didn't seem to have much more to say, so I accepted an offer of water, packed up and left. It was only as I drove out of Nata that I realized I had been so scared that I hadn't tried to talk to the talking hippo.

When Ron came home, at last I had something interesting to tell him.

'I found that talking hippo!' I announced the moment he got in the door.

'Oh good,' Ron mumbled, looking tired.

'Bad day at the mine?'

Ron lay down on the sofa, pushed off his shoes and closed his eyes.

'I was this close!' I said excitedly, holding out my arms to illustrate. 'It took me all day. But I think it'll be a good piece. I picked up this bloke at the lodge, but he was wasted and we couldn't — '

Ron opened his eyes. 'What bloke?'

'Oh, I don't know. The point is — '

'You don't know him?'

'Well, he's a relative of the owner of the lodge. And I saw Samson there!'

'And he was drunk?'

I sat down on the arm of the sofa. I sensed a rebuke for going off with a strange man in a car. I wanted to show Ron it had been perfectly safe, but now that I was telling him the story I wondered if it had been.

'Do you think that was wise?' Ron sat up.

'He was small, he was drunk,' I said, exasperated. 'I could have pushed him out the car with one finger.'

'If you say so. I mean, I don't want you getting involved in nasty situations.'

'And you think I do?' I smiled and put my arm around his shoulder. 'I was just into getting the story.'

★ ★ ★

A week later I was standing outside a supermarket in Francistown loading up the car.

'Hey, you!' a white man began yelling and

waving his arms. 'Well, thanks a lot,' he spat as he came nearer.

I gave a blank smile.

'Don't you remember me?' he demanded. I recognized him now; it was the man who had given me the final directions to the talking hippo in Nata. 'Ever since you came round and wrote that bloody article I've had people trooping in and out of my house day and night looking for that hippo,' said the man. 'Bloody journalists.'

I smiled apologetically and drove back through Francistown, stopping to buy underwear at a large clothing shop.

'You want these *black* panties?' the check-out man asked, holding up the underwear. 'And these *red* ones?'

'*Ee*,' I said, shuddering at the word 'panties', annoyed that the man thought he could comment on what I was buying.

'You don't want *white* panties?' he asked.

'No,' I said, paying hurriedly and leaving. The check-out man watched me, as if buying anything but white underwear made me sexually suspect.

I drove back to Sowa in a rush, for Pearl and Bashi were arriving that night from Maun. When I got back they were already there, Bashi was outside at the fire with Ron drinking beer while Pearl was in the kitchen frying meat.

'You'll make someone a good wife,' I told her, lugging in all the shopping from Francistown. 'I can't remember the last time someone cooked for me.'

'But Mozambia is a good cook,' she laughed,

thumping a wooden spoon into a large pot of *phaletshe* on the stove. Although we hadn't known each other long, Pearl treated my home as if it was hers.

'Not any more he's not,' I said. 'He only cooks on the weekends now he's Mr Breadwinner. I suppose I should be grateful that he earns the money and I can do what I like.'

'*Ee*,' said Pearl with conviction.

'That meat smells good,' I said, packing away the supplies from Francistown. Pearl looked hot, the kitchen windows were steamed up with the cooking, but she was wearing a big long cardigan over her clothes. 'This house is very nice,' she said admiringly. 'This kitchen . . . I want one like this.'

'Has it been raining in Maun?' I asked, slipping into the sort of conversation Batswana always had.

'Hey, no.' Pearl's lips turned down in disgust. 'This heat is killing us.'

'And has the river arrived?'

'*Ee*. But it is too small.'

'What's all this about a street gang?' I asked. 'MaWestern or something? I read about them in the papers.'

'*Ee*, MaWestern. Hey, this gang is troubling us. At first it was just some small boys going around bothering people, now they are like an army. I can't even walk at night, I think I'm going to meet them.'

'They've been beating people up?'

'*Ee*.' Pearl shook her head in disgust.

I looked out through the kitchen door. I could

see Bashi wearing an expensive pair of sunglasses although it was nearly dark outside. 'But Maun is so small, people must know who they are, these MaWestern.'

'*Ee*,' Pearl said, 'they know.'

'So, how are things otherwise?' I asked as Pearl began pounding away at the *phaletshe* again.

She sucked her teeth.

'What?' I manoeuvred my way around her to get to the fridge.

Pearl took the wooden spoon out of the pot and waved it at the window, shaking it in the direction of Bashi and Ron outside. 'He has a girlfriend.'

'What?' My heart took a lurch. 'Who? What do you mean?'

'Him. Bashi. He has a girlfriend. She works at the furniture shop. She is very . . . ' and Pearl began to imitate a woman admiring herself in the window as if it were a mirror. She tossed her head and slapped the spoon back in the pot.

'Are you sure?'

'*Ee*. I found a condom. In the bathroom.'

'No!' I had been about to ask how Pearl knew; wanting to hear that it was just a suspicion, for I liked Bashi. Whatever his faults, he was a friend of Ron and therefore a friend of mine, and he was the first friend I'd made in Botswana. Now I wanted to go outside and his him. 'You found a *condom*? Where were you when this happened?'

Pearl sighed. 'I was at my mother's, in Mochudi. I wanted to bring my daughter to Maun. Bashi agreed she could live with us.'

'But Bonny already lives with you,' I said,

moving to the door and closing it slightly.

'No, my first-born. Naledi.'

'Your *first*-born?'

'*Ee.*'

'You mean, not Bonny, not your baby?'

'*Ee.*'

'You have another child? An older one? But I didn't know!' I felt disorientated. How could I think Pearl was my best friend and not even know that she had another child? 'How old is she? Is Bashi not the father, then?'

'Naledi is a big girl now, she is thirteen,' and Pearl's voice softened and her shoulders relaxed a little. 'I had her when I was too young. I myself was still at school. I didn't know anything then. I didn't even know what pregnant was. When I had that child, my mother took her while I went back to school.'

'And the father?'

Pearl hunched her shoulders. 'I don't know him.'

'He didn't help? Do you still see him?'

Pearl turned suddenly from where she stood against the stove. 'No,' she said. 'But when I have seen him, I just do this,' and she turned and mimed spitting on the floor. Then she turned back to the stove. I stood there for a few minutes and then I saw the conversation, as far as Pearl was concerned, was finished.

'So what will you do about Bashi?' I ventured.

Pearl's face, her whole body, was rigid with disappointment. 'Hey, these African men,' she muttered.

'It's not because he's an African, Pearl . . . ' I

sagged against one of the kitchen counters. I couldn't understand what Bashi was playing at. He must have wanted Pearl to know, if he had left a condom in the bathroom. I felt sick at the deliberateness of what he had done.

Pearl turned the gas off, the meal was done. 'I will leave him.'

I nodded, opening a cupboard, looking for plates.

'But,' and Pearl dropped her voice until it was very low, 'not now. I have nowhere to go. If I go back to Mochudi, my family are poor. How will I buy them meat? How will I buy the girls school uniform? No, in Maun I have a job. *Ee*,' she nodded, 'I am no longer at immigration. I have a job at a safari company . . . '

'You do?'

'*Ee*. And Bashi has a job. I have housekeeping from him. But I will open my own bank account and each month I will put a little money there until,' she slapped one arm against the other, 'I have enough.'

I opened the kitchen door a little; it was too hot in the kitchen. I looked out at Ron and Bashi outside. They were laughing, playing with the two dogs we had recently acquired, having a good time. I wondered what Ron would think when I told him what Bashi had done. He couldn't already know, I thought. He would not want to be friends with a man who could behave like this.

'I want to go to Emang Basadi,' said Pearl as she took the plates from me and began dishing out the food. 'How do I find them?'

'The women's group? They're in Gaborone aren't they? I think I interviewed someone from there once. But what about WAR? They'd know who you could go to.'

'WAR?' Pearl asked, placing pieces of meat next to the *phaletshe*.

'Women Against Rape, in Maun. They just started a few months ago. I don't know if they have an office yet, but . . . ' I was trying to remember if they had a telephone number, for I had written a piece for the *Voice* when the group had first formed, becoming the first rape crisis centre in Botswana. I had been interested in their work from the beginning because, years ago in the States, I had trained in the evenings as a rape crisis counsellor, working on a telephone help line. 'They started after that case with the Basarwa girls,' I continued. 'You remember, when those Afrikaners from Ghanzi raped three girls? And they got acquitted because the magistrate wouldn't take the girls' testimony as sufficient because there hadn't been any witnesses.'

Pearl dropped her head, dripping gravy over the food. 'You should be careful, writing about those things.'

'How do you mean?'

Pearl pursed her lips. 'Some things, people don't want to talk about them.'

'It's the same everywhere,' I objected, disappointed that Pearl seemed to be warning me away.

'Maybe. But here in Botswana . . . ' and then Pearl seemed to change her mind and she headed for the door with the plates.

'I met a talking hippo,' I said brightly as I followed her out.

Pearl looked quickly back at me, almost dropping the food.

'Yeah,' I laughed. 'In Nata.'

'Witchcraft,' said Pearl, arranging the food on the table outside.

'Oh, come on! I'll take Alice there to see it. She's coming for Christmas, did I tell you?'

'No,' said Pearl, frowning. I didn't know if she were frowning at the idea of Alice or at the sight of Bashi sitting there waiting for his food.

# 12

The night Alice arrived in Sowa there was a full moon. I was standing by the window in the living-room, watching the street. It was dead quiet outside. People rarely walked around in Sowa after dark; there was nowhere much to go. There were no street traders, as there were in Maun, selling last-minute essentials by the flickering flames of gas lamps, their stalls providing a place to stop and chat. On the other side of the street I watched while a sleek new Camry drove up at the gates belonging to one of the high-cost homes of the mine Boers. I could see the tall white wall that encircled the five-bedroom house, garage, servant's quarters and swimming pool. Over the top of the wall I could see the leaves of a giant pawpaw tree and the glint of a new satellite dish.

I stood in our living-room, waiting for Ron. He had left for Maun the morning before to collect Alice. She had spent Christmas with us, along with her cousin Kgakgamatso, and now she was going to try out a longer stay. Ron had wanted to make the round trip in a day but I'd urged him to leave earlier, for we had had word that his mother had malaria.

I heard the sound of the Land Rover long before I saw it. Then at last Ron pulled up outside our house. I watched while Alice got out of the passenger seat. She looked so small, so thin next to her father. I could see immediately, in the light of the full moon, that she was still wearing the dress we had brought her a year ago in Maun. It was far too small, the sleeves up round Alice's armpits, the little apron at the front faded and torn. She stood there silently, waiting for instructions from Ron, an old canvas bag balanced on the top of her head. I wanted to rush out and welcome her but I stopped myself. I wanted her to feel at home and I wasn't sure how.

'*Ko ko!*' Ron called as they reached the door to the kitchen.

I moved away from the window. '*Ee*,' I called back.

Ron came in, his face a wide smile, a bag in each of his hands.

'*Dumela Mma*,' he said, giving me a kiss.

Alice hung her head.

Ron asked whether she was going to greet me.

Alice stood rooted to the spot, her eyes on the floor.

'Oh, it doesn't matter,' I said. 'You must be exhausted. Have you eaten?' I busied myself in the kitchen, warming up some rice and chicken. I had made what I thought Alice would eat, for after Christmas I knew she didn't always like what I liked. She found pasta odd unless it was mixed with rice and cooked until it nearly became the consistency of yoghurt. She was mystified by pizza and scraped off all the toppings, eating only the base, and she vomited once when I made pea soup.

'Ready!' I called from the kitchen and Ron

and Alice came through to wash their hands. Alice took the plate she was offered and stood waiting in the kitchen.

'Through here,' I said, going back into the living-room. Ron and I sat on the sofa and began to eat, swapping stories of what we'd done in the past two days.

'So how's your mum? Was it malaria or not?'

'*Ee*. It was malaria. I found her in hospital . . . '

'No!'

'*Ee*. But she's fine now.'

Ron turned the TV on, for we had access to South African television in Sowa, and it was time for the news. I thought Alice might be interested in TV but she wasn't. She looked at the screen, because we were looking at the screen, but she seemed to be looking straight through it. Then I noticed how she was eating. She had sat on the floor, a little way from the sofa, and she was dropping bits of rice and chicken on the tiles. She ate with her hands and when she found a piece of rice stuck in her tooth, or had chewed her way through a bone, she just dropped it on the floor. I watched, fascinated, as a pile of food began forming on the floor around her plate.

'Alice,' I laughed.

She looked round.

I didn't want to tell her off. She had just arrived. This was her first night. She was used to eating sitting on the sand where it didn't matter if you dropped unwanted leftovers. Ron laughed and made a joke. Alice looked abashed and then smiled. She stood up and walked through to the kitchen, not walking straight across the room but following the wall as if she needed to be up against something solid. I heard her opening cupboards and then she came back with a broom and cleaned up her mess.

Ron and I looked at each other. We really didn't know much about children. For the past few weeks he had asked me repeatedly if I was sure I wanted Alice to stay with us. It was my idea, I reminded him. And I knew he wanted her, because more than anything he wanted to get to know his child, for her to have a father she could depend on and trust. But he worried about what it would do to me, and just as importantly what it would do to the both of us now we would have a child. But I didn't have any second thoughts. We had a big house, more than big enough to accommodate another person. I worked from home and had plenty of time on my hands, more than enough time to talk and play with a child. It seemed a waste having all these things when Alice, Ron's own child, had been brought up in poverty with a mother who was happy that someone else was able to provide for her daughter. I had not met Alice's mother, but I had heard stories about an abusive boyfriend and alcohol problems. I knew Alice had three sisters, from different fathers, and I knew that she had not lived with her mother for some time.

'Ron,' I whispered, 'she's falling asleep.'

Alice was sitting on the same spot on the floor again, but her eyes were closed and her head hung down on her chest.

'Alice, *we!*' Ron roused her gently with his hand.

Her body gave a start and her eyes opened, looking around with sleepy panic. Ron helped her up and led her to her bedroom. I followed. I had spent all weekend getting Alice's bedroom ready, cleaning it, installing a mattress and a sheet and a new red blanket. I had made her a little table out of sheets of wood and bricks, and placed two new books on top. But Alice was too tired to take anything in, I thought, for she ignored everything in the room and just lay down, fully clothed on the bed, and went back to sleep.

'My mother says she's difficult,' Ron said later as we sat out in the garden enjoying the light of the moon.

'Oh, I'm sure she'll be fine,' I said blithely. 'She's just moved around a lot. How do you mean, difficult?'

'Well, she takes things. She makes up stories . . .'

'She'll be fine,' I said.

★   ★   ★

The following months took on a pattern of their own. Ron enrolled Alice at the local primary school, and she trudged off there each morning in her new uniform. By lunchtime she was home again. We ate together and then she played with a neighbour's child in the back yard or on Sowa's quiet, empty streets. In the late afternoons we walked the dogs in the bush that surrounded the town, or went to the one shop for provisions.

'Is this your child?' people asked me in the shop and on the streets.

At first I hesitated. Alice wasn't actually my child, but then as she was living with me I supposed she was. 'Yes,' I replied.

The questioner would laugh. 'No she's not! You are different colours!'

Well, then, why did you ask me? I wanted to reply.

Other times people would ask Alice, 'Is this your mother?'

Normally she didn't reply, but after a couple of months she began to say 'Yes' as well. She started to put on weight. She learnt how to write her name, and she loved being read to in the evenings.

I looked at the kitchen clock. It was 2 p.m. School had long since finished for the day and still there was no sign of Alice. I was getting anxious. The primary school was a few minutes' walk away and I had been at the living-room window watching the children filing past on their way home. But all the children had passed now and I had not seen Alice. I knew she walked very slowly, but surely it couldn't have taken her this long. I wondered if she were playing some sort of trick. I knew now that she had in fact been sent to school in Maun but had absconded almost straight away and no one had ever taken her back. I heard a strange whirring noise and went into the smallest bedroom which I had turned into my office. I had just got a fax machine and there was

nothing more exciting than getting a fax. As I
tore off the paper I looked, once more, out of
the window. Alice was just walking past; she had
opened the gate and entered the yard so silently
I hadn't heard a thing. Sometimes living with
Alice was like living with a ghost. Now she was
walking painfully slowly around the sides of the
house, heading towards the kitchen door at the
back. Her head was hanging down and she was
struggling with a huge rucksack on her back,
full of schoolbooks.

Alice was doing well at school. She was shy
but seemed to fit in and the teachers said she
was well behaved. At the end of the first term she
had As in most of her subjects and Ron had
handed her the school report, saying she should
go and show it to her mother who would be so
proud. Now, all at once, she began to understand
how to read and how to write and she grew
proud of herself as well. I reached the kitchen
just as Alice got to the door. The kitchen had a
screen door that could be locked on the inside
and I always had it locked when I was alone in
the house. I felt safe in Sowa, but I never left
doors open if there was no one to go in and out
but me. I opened the bolt and the screen door
bounced back. Alice stood on the step, her head
down.

'Hi!' I said brightly.

Alice didn't move.

'How was school? Did you do singing today, is
that why you're late?' I spoke in Setswana which,
although badly pronounced, was grammatically
correct as I spent hours pouring over my

Setswana books and had started a correspondence course at a university in South Africa.

Alice shifted a little, inching her way into the house. She looked gawky in her school uniform and younger than her eight years. Her knees were knobbly under the skirt; her shoulders were hunched a little. When she smiled she was a beautiful child, with a long delicate face and big sharp eyes. But now she was frowning, the spitting image of her father in a sulk.

'Alice?' I asked, a little pointedly, still not getting any reply. I was itching to ask her to look at me, but I knew that for Batswana it was considered respectful for a child to avert their gaze when addressed by an adult. I wanted to do things the Setswana way but also to do things my way. I wanted Alice to be a polite child, to know how to behave appropriately around elders, but I didn't want her to obey an elder who asked her to do something inappropriate. I also didn't want a child who was simply there to fetch and carry. When I moaned that these days all the housework fell to me, Ron responded that Alice should be doing the housework now. But I still felt she was a visitor, someone whom it was my job to look after, not a child brought in to clean my home.

'Hello, anyone there?' I asked, attempting a joke.

Alice slowly dragged herself into the kitchen.

'Alice,' I said, 'you just need to say hello.' I was getting frustrated, for several months now I had been trying to get Alice to make some sort of greeting when she arrived home. I knew she was shy but surely she could manage a mumbled *Dumela* when she saw me, or anyone else. It had become a sort of war ground between us. I greeted her, she didn't respond. I tried again, she didn't respond. And then I would give up. Alice found it hard to respond to others as well, and if anyone came to the house and greeted her, she just hung her head and sidled up as close to a wall as she could get. With Ron, on the other hand, she always responded. It wasn't more than a mumbled *Ee*, but at least it was a response.

'Come and sit down,' I told her now. 'Look, I know my Setswana is not very good but I am trying to talk to you. You can be my teacher. You can teach me Setswana. And I can teach you English.'

Alice looked up, interested.

'But you need to say hello when you come home, okay?' Alice didn't reply. 'Is it your mother? Do you miss everyone? You know you can always see her, right? Every holiday you'll go there. And whenever you want to see her, and your sisters, you just tell us, right?'

'*Ee*,' Alice said at last.

'So, what shall we do this weekend? Shall we go to Francistown and buy you some clothes? What about going to the swimming pool? I can teach you to swim, then we can go for lunch at the country club.'

Alice smiled. 'That is too much doing,' she said and I burst out laughing. Alice often looked harassed with all my suggestions of things to do. What Alice liked to do was to dream. Sometimes I passed the open door to her room and caught sight of her sitting on the bed, dreaming. Other times she did it while washing up dishes in the kitchen, or while sitting in the shade of a tree outside. Like Ron, she could do a burst of hard work, like weeding the entire yard, washing clothes in a tub outside, loading the Land Rover full of firewood, and then she liked to do nothing at all. Like a lot of Batswana, both Alice and Ron had the ability for serious physical labour, but they also had the ability to sit and not speak and not to do anything at all. I admired this ability to just be, because it was something I was totally unable to do. And neither Alice nor Ron ever complained about physical ills. If Ron were sick he never mentioned it. I only knew he had a cold if I saw him drinking Lemsip with garlic. It was the same with Alice. One evening I found her lying in her bed, eyes closed.

'What's wrong?' I asked.

'I am sick.'

'Where does it hurt?' I came nearer to the bed. Alice looked surprised.

'Your throat?'

'Ee.'

'Anywhere else?'

'My head.'

'Well, why didn't you tell me, Alice? If you tell me you're sick then I can give you something, some medicine.'

Alice stared at me, as if no one had ever asked her where it hurt before.

Ron came home early that day, driving just ahead of a terrific storm.

'We've got to get a new car,' he said, rushing

into the house as thunder rumbled overhead and the sky went black. It was as impressive as a storm in Maun, but here there were sandstorms as well when the wind picked up the sand and salt from the pans and sprayed them over the town.

'What's wrong with the Land Rover?'

'Loads of things. I got these brochures of cars, look at this one!' Ron was excited, as he always was when he looked at pictures of new cars. Sometimes he spent whole evenings flipping through trade papers, circling the car he wanted. Unlike me, he wanted new, not second-hand, things.

'But I thought we were building your mum a house?'

'*Mma?*'

'You heard. I thought the reason she got that new plot in Maun was that we're building her a house. How can we do that if you buy a car?'

Ron looked crestfallen.

'It's not going to cost that much, once we have the bricks and cement, right? I thought you thought it was a good idea, and your mum seems really into it. And you're always saying she wants to move out of Boyei ward with all the gossiping and fighting going on.'

'You're right, you're right,' said Ron.

When the rains had at last stopped we went outside where a thick rainbow illuminated half the sky. Alice ran outside and exclaimed at all the water in our yard, then she hitched up her school uniform and began playing and laughing in the puddles. It was so rare to see her playful that I almost held my breath as I watched.

'You are soaking!' I laughed as she finally came in doors. 'Take everything off and have a bath.'

I followed Alice into the bathroom and put some scented bubble-bath under the running taps because it seemed luxurious and I thought she would like it.

'It's nice having you here,' I said, feeling the water, checking the temperature. Alice didn't answer. I turned from the taps, smiling, to see if she had perhaps left the room.

'You stole me from my mother,' she said, in perfect, vicious English.

I sat back from the bath, stunned. 'Oh, Alice . . . '

Alice stood at the doorway, her face expressionless. For a second I thought I had misheard her.

'I didn't *steal* you from your mother,' I said, trying to control the hurt in my voice. 'If you steal something you take what is not yours and you do it without asking. All we did is ask if you wanted to stay with us, and you agreed. And your mother agreed and . . . ' I was talking in English now, and I stopped, wondering if she understood. Alice suddenly seemed to know much more English than I had assumed, but now I was babbling away. Perhaps I should have said nothing, I thought, just walked away with dignity. Soon I would be begging her to say that she not only wanted to live with us but adored us too. And then, as Alice began silently undressing for her bath, I thought that my expectations had been too high. Somewhere, deep inside, I feared that perhaps I had actually wanted to be thanked for what I had done. But Alice hadn't asked to move in with us. And now I saw how hard it would be, adopting another woman's child.

* * *

Things were not going well at the mine. Soda Ash Botswana was losing money, not enough soda ash was being produced or sold, and the mine was not the economic miracle it had been expected to be. And, according to the Batswana, it was the Afrikaner managers who were to blame. SAB now stood for South African Bastards and stories of corruption and nepotism were constant. Shortly after Nelson Mandela was elected President in South Africa, Ron had been called to the general manager's office. There had been complaints, he was told, about the fact he had been wearing an ANC T-shirt. This was a political statement and there was no room for politics at a mine. By 1995 Ron had begun to wear the ANC T-shirt on a daily basis, his face stern as he set off for work in the morning. And now I got involved in the drama at the mine as well. Because people knew I worked for the *Voice*, they began ringing and visiting with stories of corruption and mismanagement. Day after day I found myself sitting in my yard listening while I was told what 'the whites' were doing wrong. Only once did someone stop and laugh, remembering that I was a white as well.

When a report I had written on the allegations

came out I was shunned in the street. Two white women who I had been on speaking terms with deliberately crossed the other side of the road when they saw Alice and I walking home.

'You're making matters much worse,' another white woman spat at me over a garden wall one evening.

The mine managers issued denials. There was no corruption, no mismanagement. They hired lawyers in Francistown to try and block reports before they came out. They threatened legal action. One day, while fixing a computer in the managing director's office, Ron was asked: 'Can't you control your wife?' The message was clear: if he couldn't control his wife then he would no longer have a job.

At the weekends Ron, Alice and I drove far out of Sowa, following riverbeds, picnicking in the bush, anything to get away from the pressures of the mine. Alice could greet people easily now, she smiled more than she frowned and she had not repeated the accusation that I had stolen her from her mother.

As winter arrived we built fires outside, told stories and roasted meat. Visitors from outside Sowa were rare. Ron's brother Roy arrived to take up a post as a mechanic, but Veronica was far away working at a primary school in Gumare. Pearl had not been back to Sowa, and when Bashi had sent word he was coming down Ron had told him not to bother. He was angry with Bashi for having an affair and so he shunned him without telling him the reason why.

In May 1995 Ron came home from work

early. 'We've been liquidated,' he said, almost skipping into the house.

'I know, I heard it on the radio. It proves it, doesn't it; it proves what everyone has been saying? They said on the radio it's the biggest liquidation in the history of southern Africa. Market problems were the official line. What will happen now?'

'God knows,' said Ron. 'But the Boers are out of here! People are saying they don't even care if they lose their jobs, as long as the corrupt managers are out.'

'You think it's a good thing?' As usual, I was more pessimistic than Ron.

'Of course it is.'

'But that's hundreds of people losing jobs, there's thousands of people who depend on them. What are they going to do, just close the place down?'

'The liquidators will sell it, then there will be new management. Why are you so cynical all the time?'

A week later one of the liquidators rang me up at home early on a Sunday morning. Negotiations were at a critical stage, he warned, it would not be a good idea to publish anything now. I didn't want to jeopardize something of national importance, did I? Shortly afterwards the riot police arrived. They set up road-blocks on the road to the mine, officers crammed inside armoured, military-looking vehicles clutching fibreglass shields. Some said they were there to prevent the Boers from leaving, others that they were there to prevent Batswana from looting the mine. Sowa's one shopping centre, which had never had more than a grocery shop, butcher's and chemist, was put up for auction and no one made a bid. Botswana's new town had turned into a white elephant.

# 13

A few weeks after the mine was liquidated, I got offered a job.

'Caitlin, I have something to ask you,' came the familiar, hurried voice of Anne Sandenbergh on the other end of the phone. Anne was an elderly white woman in Maun, who hated the term elderly, and who was a powerhouse of energy and zeal. Originally from Kenya, she had lived in Maun for decades, and she owned an aviation fuel company at the airport. Anne never introduced herself on the phone; she was usually in too much of a rush trying to fill me in on the details of various miscarriages of justice. Although busy with a business, children and grandchildren, she had found time to become the driving force behind the formation of WAR, Women Against Rape. An unpaid volunteer outraged by the increase in sexual abuse of schoolchildren, she was always tearing from one end of the district to the other, trying to offer counselling, investigating cases of abuse, lobbying for a change in the laws.

'Hi, Anne,' I said a little nervously, waiting for a tale of horror that needed coverage.

'The *Okavango Observer* is for sale,' she said, launching straight in. 'And I want to buy it. And I want you to be editor.'

'Wow.'

'So, what do you think?'

'Well, that's great . . . ' I was a bit hesitant. No one had ever offered me a job out of the blue before.

'And I'm going to give you a third of the shares.'

'Wow.' I sat back, thinking how the last time I had been in the *Okavango Observer* offices the editor had thrown me out.

'So, what do you think?'

'Well, I think it's brilliant. But I'm working for the *Voice* and . . . '

Anne breathed impatiently on the other end of the line. 'Look, I've got to go. It's only an idea, I just wanted to see what you think. I feel Maun must have a newspaper, do you know what I mean?' Anne always asked, 'Do you know what I mean?' She was usually talking so quickly there was no time to reply.

The original owner of the *Okavango Observer* had sold the paper a while back to a South African businesswoman and now she, too, wanted to sell. The *OO*, as it was now commonly known, had recently slowed down to two issues a month and, depending on advertising, sometimes not at all. Running a newspaper from a rural village wasn't proving easy.

'Do you really think she'll buy it?' I woke Ron up that night, unable to sleep.

'Mmm.'

'You do?'

'Mmm.'

'Do you think I should say yes to Anne? Ron? I'm going to say yes. Do you think I should?'

211

Ron groaned. 'Can we talk about it in the morning?'

'She says will I go up there and meet with her? And someone called Andrew, he's the lay-out man. If she offered enough then you could resign, right?'

Ron was wideawake now. 'How do you mean?'

'I mean, how long is your job at the mine going to last with all this liquidation business? And if I get a proper job then I can be the breadwinner. We can move back to Maun and you'd be free to start your own company.'

Ron started rubbing his chin anxiously. He had talked on and off for a long time about starting his own computer company but was nervous about whether or not he could do it. I had no such reservations; I couldn't see how he could fail.

★ ★ ★

When we arrived in Maun for my meeting with Anne it was as if we had entered a totally different village. Now, in fact, it was more like a town. For the past couple of years there had been a tar road from Nata, so Maun had finally become linked up to the rest of the country. I knew about the tar road, but on the road coming in to Maun I was amazed to see a row of brand-new streetlights. Now night time in the village would be electrified. And there were billboards for the first time, too, advertising tea, beer and washing powder. As we drove past the mall where Ron had worked I could see most of the sand had been concreted over. Everywhere the original village pathways were being pushed back into the bush as the concrete and tar expanded. Next to the roads were the upturned roots of giant, felled trees lying sprawled on the sand at the feet of big shiny bulldozers. And now, further along the main road, there was a new shopping centre. It began with an archway and led along a row of concrete buildings which so far housed a bottle store and an office. Opposite this was Maun's new restaurant, Le Bistrot, its outside eating area overhung with bougainvillea, the walls inside decorated with Paris street names.

Yet alongside the new developments, the old parts of the village stayed just as they were. So as we drove through, we saw people filling up at an impressive new petrol station in whose shadows stood traditional mud and thatched houses. Now people had a tarred road on their doorstep, and rubbish from the endless traffic was everywhere: burst tyres, bones, rusted food cans, old oil cans, even the rotting carcass of a dead dog. For the first time since I'd been in Botswana I saw graffiti, a shakily written 'u fuck' sprayed on the side of a brick structure that had never been finished.

We drove back and forth through Maun, marvelling at all the changes. On the streets young people were wearing new clothes, oversized denims and baseball caps on the wrong way. In the back of the Land Rover, Alice sat stiffly, her eyes wide as she stared at the people on the streets swaggering confidently, sweating in clothes that had been designed for a cold weather country. And as we drove through I wondered how I had changed since I'd first arrived in Maun five years ago, fresh off the back of a truck, knowing no Setswana, barely able to walk on the sand. I felt protective of the village now, quick to take offence if someone criticized it. And yet I couldn't tell what exactly it was about it that made me love Maun. I could see at once how through a visitor's eyes it was a rough, sprawling place full of litter and marauding donkeys and now, in winter, bare and dry. Yet it still touched something in me, made me almost homesick. It had changed so quickly that I felt the loss of the old village as sharply as if it had been my own home, and yet Maun was a place I had only lived in for two years. Now I was returning as a newspaper editor, the mother of a nine-year-old daughter, and, soon, I would become a Motswana citizen. I had applied for naturalization after our marriage three years ago and was constantly being told my application was just about to be processed. In the meantime I had been issued a residence permit and a work permit, so all I could do was wait.

We stopped to have a look at the *OO*'s office, one of two offices in a white, stone-washed building in the heart of what was now known as the old mall. It was Saturday and they were closed. I peered in the windows of the first office, to see that it belonged to an accountancy firm. Then I peered in the windows of the *OO*. I could see one room with two tables and two chairs, one computer and one phone. Outside, on the porch, I saw that the area was roughly cut in two in terms of dirt. On the accountancy firm's side of the porch it was clean, but on the *OO*'s side the floor was covered in hard pellets of goat shit.

When I stepped off the porch I landed straight back in the sand of the mall, for this area had not yet been tarred. In the middle of the sand was a small cleared area with a few plants dying from lack of water. The area had bright-green iron railings around it and I assumed the idea was to brighten up and beautify the mall. But it looked as if people were mistaking the area within the railings as a new rubbish bin and were throwing all their waste in there as they walked past. To the left of the *OO* office was a dry cleaners, while opposite was a new row of shops; a chemist, a hair salon and a shoeshop. Shoeshops belonging to South African chain stores had sprouted up everywhere in Maun, with several in both malls all selling the same shoes at the same price. But there were bigger shops too, standing impressively alone on the main road through the village. These were all furniture shops with window displays full of pale-blue brocade lounge suites, massive double beds covered in plastic sheets, display cabinets with jars of plastic pink flowers on top. I wondered who had the money to buy things at these new shops, who would be eating mussels in garlic at the French restaurant, and whether the expansion of Maun was following any real plan at all. Maun had changed from a sleepy Delta village into a hybrid township.

By the time we got to Ron's family's compound we were feeling overwhelmed. We passed Boyei ward, where Ron had been born and from where his mother had recently moved. Now she stayed in the house we had had built for her on the road leading to the village's old dumping site in a ward called Moeti. The road was still sand, and just as deep and hard to drive through as it had always been. On either side were well-spaced houses in empty yards, some built from mud and thatch, but many more from concrete bricks.

Ron drove slowly, idling as children and goats ran in and out of the pathway, until we reached the slight incline to the new plot. It was far larger than the one in Boyei, the yard cleared of vegetation so the place felt spacious. There were no immediate neighbours, except for a house being built on the plot at the back. The entire yard was encircled with a wire-mesh fence with a gate big enough to let a truck in. Alice got out of the Land Rover, fiddled with the gate, and we drove in. Before us was Eliah's new house, low and built from large grey bricks the colour of a wet elephant, the outside still unpainted. The front door was open and I could tell immediately that no one was inside. On the right of the new house, the women had built a square structure from reeds and this in turn was surrounded with a reed enclosure so that the structure was like a little house in its own yard. I wondered if anyone was really using the new house at all, or if it were just for show.

'*Ko, ko!*' Ron called as he headed off towards the reed wall.

'*Ee!*' Madintwa shouted back.

Alice ran forward with eagerness. '*Dumela mma*' she said to Madintwa, dropping down respectfully, her hand on one knee.

Madintwa beamed, reached out and held Alice close. In her right hand she held a long sharp knife; she was in the process of shredding a carcass. Then she looked around for Ron and I, her eyes wavering as she scanned the yard. I was standing close, greeting Eliah, yet Madintwa hadn't seemed to recognize me.

'It's me, Caitlin,' I told her, taking her hand.

Madintwa burst out laughing. '*Mama we!*' Then she pulled me close and examined my arms, patting me as if to make sure I were real.

'Her eyesight is going,' Ron said softly. He squatted down and joined his grandmother. She held the carcass while he began to pull off the flesh. They worked dispassionately, as if they couldn't see the blood and gore, as if they were shredding strips of cloth.

'God, it's awful, she can't even focus,' I whispered back. 'Can't she have an operation? It's cataracts, right?'

'She refuses,' said Ron. 'She won't even go near the hospital. She says she will die of a heart-attack if she has to as much go in there.'

I turned to Madintwa who was making space for me on the sheet of tarpaulin on the sand. 'You are from Sowa,' she smiled. 'And now you are back in Maun.'

'*Ee,*' I said with conviction.

Madintwa beamed again and called me her daughter-in-law. 'Hey, I am sick,' she said, shifting closer. 'My eyes,' she said, sweeping one hand across her face. 'My heart,' she said, holding her hand to her chest. 'My legs,' she said grasping her left shin and rubbing it.

I tutted sympathetically.

'My blood,' continued Madintwa. Then she sighed and looked up the heavens. 'I have AIDS.'

'No,' I said soothingly, 'I don't think it's AIDS.'

'Ee. It is AIDS.' Madintwa nodded her head determinedly.

I looked at Ron, wondering how appropriate it would be if I began to talk about how someone normally became infected with HIV. Madintwa was a single, uninvolved woman and the chances of her contracting HIV were near zero. But I knew she was an avid radio listener, and that these days there were so many radio announcements about AIDS that it wasn't surprising she had become convinced that she was infected too. I was about to say this when a vehicle drew up outside the gate. Madintwa struggled up and set off unsteadily for the toilet, her body leaning on a walking stick that I had not seen before.

Rra Nama, Ron's biltong-loving uncle, drove into the yard. On the passenger seat sat an adolescent boy, excitedly talking into a microphone, his words booming out of the loudspeaker on the roof of the car. Rra Nama got out, moving briskly, looking pleased with himself. He was standing in the local council elections and spent most of his time touring

Maun extorting people to support him.

'Are you back from Sowa?' Rra Nama asked, shaking my hand.

'Ee.'

'What is going on in that place?'

'Corruption, basically. Corrupt Boers and total mismanagement. You politicians should do something about it!'

'We will.' Rra Nama looked serious. 'We will.' But he knew that the year before the ruling party had once again won a landslide victory in the general elections and that support for the BNF was weak, especially in the rural areas. Botswana was a success story, the electorate was told, why change the status quo now? We left the family's compound shortly after, as the real reason for our visit to Maun was my meeting with Anne Sandenbergh. As we drove away from the yard it was with reluctance for I felt comfortable here now. I felt included in the family; I knew how to relate to its different members. With Eliah I was always polite, interested in her advice, quick to offer any help she might need. With Madintwa I could be more myself, telling stories and jokes, questioning her about life and Maun in the old days. And Ron softened in their presence, sinking down on to a chair with ease, proud of the new house he'd built, his salary that allowed him to buy them meat, the way his daughter, Alice, knew him as a father and was growing confident and loving.

We drove to Anne's house by crossing the river a few kilometres outside Maun and Ron dropped me off on the riverbank while he went to search for some of the family's missing goats. I opened the rickety little metal gate to Anne's plot and walked in, moving cautiously as a dog came tearing its way out of a clump of banana trees. I was entering from the back of the plot and before me was the main house, a handsome stone, peach-coloured building, with plenty of archways that made me think of the Mediterranean. I walked round to the front, passing a young woman pounding washing in a tin tub and an elderly man watering mango trees.

'Do you want some tea?' Anne asked, leading me into the house. It was cool inside and calm on the eye, with white walls and a tiled floor and the gentle hum of an old ceiling fan with wooden propellers. 'This is Andrew,' Anne said, depositing me in the living-room as she turned back to the kitchen.

I went to shake Andrew's hand. He sat on an old soft-looking sofa covered in delicate, faded blue flowers. He looked at once energetic and prepared. His white face was tanned and he wore a bright-green shirt which looked as if it had just come out of the wash. His legs were crossed and he was tapping one foot on the floor, while arranging a pad of paper and a pen on the coffee table in front of him.

Andrew leapt up as I came in and he brought his hands together in a soundless clap, rubbing the palms together. 'Pleased to meet you, girl,' he enthused, his Liverpudlian accent untouched by his years in South Africa and now Botswana.

'So you're the lay-out man?' I asked, as we both sat down.

'Lay-out man, coffee-maker, ad-seller, photo-grapher, bullshit-taker . . . '

I laughed.

'And what's it like trying to run a paper in Maun?'

'Fucking crap.'

I laughed again. This wasn't making me very keen on the job.

'No, really, Cait, it's good you know?' Andrew leaned back in his chair. 'The guys are great, they're really keen. We've got some great stories. There's a nice buzz.'

'Right,' said Anne, marching in with a tray of tea and biscuits. She sat the tray down, pushed it towards us, and then leant back in her armchair and lit a cigarette.

'They've agreed to a figure. It's a reasonable figure, considering I'm buying a newspaper. And that includes the computer and everything . . . '

I glanced at Andrew. He had given an odd little smile at the term 'everything' and I wondered whether this meant the paper had nothing at all, for I hadn't seen signs of much when I had peeked in through the office window earlier.

'What salary do you want?' Anne asked, getting straight to the point.

'Four grand a month,' I said quickly. Ron and I had decided that if Anne could offer me what Ron was getting at the mine then we could afford to leave Sowa at once.

'That sounds very reasonable,' said Anne.

I gulped my tea. Reasonable? It was eight times what I was getting at the *Voice*.

'Andrew?' Anne asked.

'Three is fine,' he said.

'Three?' Anne sounded outraged. 'I'll give you three and a half.'

'No, no,' Andrew protested, leaning forward. 'Three is fine.'

'No, four and three point five, that's decided.'

The phone rang and Anne got up with a sigh to answer it.

'Yes, yes,' she breathed heavily into the phone. '*Which* school? And where *is* that? Oh. Oh. And it's the maths teacher? He's what, British? American? Okay, British. And the mother's tried to lay a complaint with the police?' Anne's voice started rising. 'Well, he needs to have a little visit, do you know what I mean?'

Andrew and I left as Anne got involved in a mission for WAR.

★　★　★

When I met up with Ron again on the riverbank I was excited. 'I said yes,' I told him, clambering into the Land Rover. 'Four grand. We can leave Sowa!'

'Praise the Lord,' said Ron with a smile and a slap on the driving wheel, 'and pass the ammunition.'

That evening we went to Le Bistrot to celebrate. The clientele at Maun's new restaurant was less white than the Duck Inn, the hunters' bar that had now closed down. Its closure was being talked about as the end of an era among many expatriates, and I wondered if it were the

222

end of the era where Batswana could have darts thrown at their heads in their very own country. At Le Bistrot there were a handful of black people, prominent men in local government tucking down to beef served on thick wooden carving boards, the officer commander from the police station drinking red wine at the bar, the newly installed chief of the Batawana just entering with an entourage of men. Otherwise the restaurant was still dominated by white people: the safari operators who used to frequent the Duck Inn; a girls' night out for a group of wives; tourists still wearing the khaki they had worn in the bush. And then I saw Bashi, walking a few metres behind the chief's friends, moving leisurely, stopping to greet people sitting at the tables outside.

'There's Bashi,' I told Ron.

Ron nodded, unsurprised.

'Are you talking to him again, then?'

Ron shrugged.

'And did you ever tell him why you weren't talking to him, about Pearl and everything? About his girlfriend and all that?'

Ron looked bashful. But my attention was now on Pearl who was walking towards our table.

'Pearl!' I jumped up.

'Sorry we are late,' she said, pulling out a chair.

I looked at Ron. 'But I didn't even know you were coming.'

'Ao!' Pearl exclaimed, turning on Ron. 'Didn't you tell her we met today? Ee, in Shoprite. And we arranged to meet here at eight o'clock, didn't we?'

Ron was laughing and ducking away from me. 'Sorry, I forgot.'

'You look well,' I said to Pearl. She beamed and settled herself into her chair, arching her shoulders back until they were comfortable. And she did look well, her skin shone, her clothes clung to her, her eyes were flashing and bright. She wore a thick yellow cardigan with a brooch on the lapel that caught the light as she moved, and a flat multicoloured hat made from velvet on her head.

'*Dumela Mma*,' Bashi said, arriving at last at the table. He shook my hand smoothly. 'It is so nice that you two are coming back to Maun. And you will be running a newspaper, good.' He nodded his head. 'That is so good. We Africans believe in the freedom of the press. Do you mind if my wife and I join you, only do not attempt to ask me too many questions for my response will be, no comment.'

I smiled despite myself. If Pearl was still with Bashi then there wasn't much I could do. Perhaps Bashi had apologized for the affair; perhaps Pearl had believed his apology, I didn't yet know.

'*Rra*,' said Pearl with a smile that seemed a little coy, 'why don't you order the food?'

'You're not married, are you?' I asked suddenly. 'You just said, my wife and I . . .'

Pearl laughed a little loudly and Bashi put one strong arm around her shoulders and pulled her towards him. 'No, no,' he laughed as well, 'we are not married.'

The waiter came to the table and I asked for drinks. 'A white wine, a Malawi Shandy, a Hunter's Gold . . . '

'*Nnyaa!*' objected Pearl. 'I don't want a Hunter's Gold.'

'Oh, what do you want then?'

'I will have an orange juice.'

'An orange juice?'

'*Ee.*' And Pearl tapped the brooch on her lapel.

I looked closer. It was not a brooch but the star that symbolized membership of the ZCC, the Zionist Christian Church to which Ron's mother also belonged. 'You're in the ZCC?' I asked, amazed.

'*Ee,*' Pearl said proudly. 'We are not allowed alcohol.'

'Oh,' I said, feeling a little worried, trying to remember what else ZCC people weren't allowed to do.

On the long drive back to Sowa, Ron and I were mostly silent. I was thinking about my new job, he was thinking about resigning from his. It was the beginning of the winter holidays and we had left Alice in Maun. We had dropped her off at her mother's place a few days earlier in great excitement, her bags full of food she had chosen at the supermarket, copies of her school report, clothes for her three sisters. But the next day Ron had driven by to check if everything was okay, to see Alice rummaging through a rubbish heap, her youngest sister on her back, looking for bits of firewood. Her mother had gone to the cattle post; Alice had been left behind.

# PART FOUR

PART FOUR

# 14

I arrived early for my first meeting at the
*Okavango Observer*. I had thought about
nothing else for months and was both excited
and nervous, veering between optimism and
self-doubt. Ron and Alice were staying in Sowa
while Ron worked out his notice, and I had
rented a small, two-bedroom house in Maun, set
just off the tar road, which led down to a new
bridge that crossed the Thamalakane. I had
brought my pink bike up with me from Sowa
and I sped easily along the wide empty road,
passing schoolchildren and council workers,
donkeys and goats. As I turned left it was
downhill all the way to the bridge, and I coasted
past Maun's wildlife park, passing a large hairy
warthog sniffing around some rubbish left on the
roadside. It must have escaped from the park, I
thought, and I sped up, for warthogs had long
sharp tusks and I wasn't sure how fast they could
run. The sun was just rising as I reached the
bridge over the Thamalakane. This year, for the
first time this century, the floods hadn't made it
into the heart of the village and the river was
largely dry. Drought had been declared, with a
familiar tone of inevitability. As I crossed the
bridge I stopped to look at a small herd of
zebras, their necks bent, grazing on the riverbank
inside the wildlife park. I had never been in the
park, but I had heard the land had originally

been the district commissioner's golf course back in colonial days. Now it was a protected sanctuary for zebra, warthog, impala and baboons. Whatever the developments in Maun, however many tar roads were laid and shopping malls built, there were still wild animals living right in the heart of the village, as they had always been, only now their movements were restricted by a fence.

I arrived to find the *OO* office empty but for Andrew who was smoking a cigarette and playing a game on the computer. It was Saturday and the surrounding shops hadn't even opened yet.

'Morning,' I called, tying my bike up outside.

'Hey, girl,' Andrew replied cheerily.

'Where's the reporters then?'

'Haven't booked up yet,' said Andrew. 'Want some tea?'

He made tea in the small kitchen at the back, which was shared with the accountancy firm next door, while I poked around the office. I hadn't worked in an office for years and I felt a little at a loss, wondering how to get settled in. It would be just me and Andrew here on a daily basis, for the *OO*'s reporters were all freelancers, used to coming in, dropping their stories on the editor's desk, and disappearing until it was pay day.

'Here's Mogs,' said Andrew as a middle-aged man appeared on the porch outside, walking slowly, carefully wiping sand from his shoes before coming in.

'He's the sports reporter?'

'Yeah. Good man. He's a teacher in Shorobe, but he does football at the weekends. There's been a bit of trouble though, someone's told him he can't write for us any more 'cos he's a civil servant,' Andrew said, and laughed. 'Apparently he's breaking the law by having another job at the same time; mind you, the rate he gets paid here isn't enough to keep him in beer. Mogs! My man, how's it going?'

Andrew leapt up, rubbed his palms together, and the two men shook hands.

'*Dumela Mma*,' Mogorosi greeted me, his eyes averted a little. Then he turned as a young, stocky man came in.

'This is Cobrie,' said Andrew, giving the man a slap on the shoulder.

'Morning Mr Dooley,' Cobrie said politely.

'What's the news?' Andrew asked.

'Oh there is nothing.' Cobrie wrinkled his nose and chuckled good-naturedly. On his head he wore a baseball cap, the brim pushed rakishly to one side.

'Cobrie, this is Caitlin, the new editor.'

Cobrie shook my hand lightly, his eyes on the ground. 'Morning, madam,' he said. He reminded me of my students at Tshwaragano, boys who were playful and perhaps a little vain but who knew the hierarchy and who were respectful to their elders.

Mogorosi had sat down in the corner of the room and was slowly turning the pages of a newspaper, apparently lost in thought. 'So, Cobrie,' I said, 'how long have you been at the OO?'

231

Cobrie pushed back the baseball cap and ran his hands back and forth over his head. 'A year?' he offered, about to say more when another man entered the office, moving quickly, in a hurry.

'Lets,' said Andrew, 'Lets Open,' and he laughed. 'Wicked name, isn't it?'

I smiled. I had read many of the past *OO*s by now and there were two frequent bylines — Cobrie Kgaodi and Lets Open. They seemed to cover just about everything in the paper, from baseball results to court reports.

'Is it your pen name?' I asked the new arrival. He was taller, thinner than Cobrie, with uncombed hair and a slightly dishevelled air about him.

'*Ee*,' Lets said, although he hadn't seemed to have heard the question. He was busy moving round the office, picking things up, putting them down.

'What's your real name?'

Lets turned. 'I am Letswetswe Phaladi.'

He had an odd way of talking, I saw, speaking without really opening his mouth.

'And are you both from Maun?'

'*Ee*,' Cobrie and Lets said in unison. And now that Let's mouth was open I saw that he was missing his top front teeth.

Another freelancer, Sam, arrived and then we sat down together, only Mogorosi and Lets had to stand as there were not enough chairs.

'Right,' I said in what I hoped was an inspiring voice. 'We've got a while before our first issue and I think there's a lot of follow-ups to do . . . '

Cobrie took out a notebook and put it on his lap.

'The paper's been closed for a month, right? So when we do come out we have to show it's changed owners, that it's back and back for good. Now, I think the biggest issue at the moment has to be MaWestern.'

Cobrie shook his head. 'Ah this gang is really bothering people.'

'Yes,' I agreed. 'I heard about them even in Sowa. I've seen articles in the Gaborone papers as well, just last week. It's a gang of boys, right? Going around terrorizing people. So, they've beaten people up, forced an elderly man to eat the body of a decomposed dog?'

Mogorosi shuddered in disgust.

'What happened to that man, do you know?'

'*Ee*,' said Lets with authority. 'That man was hospitalized and now he is dead.

'For fuck's sake,' muttered Andrew, 'this is getting worse than Liverpool.'

'Have there been gangs like this before, in Maun?' I asked.

The reporters all shook their heads.

'So it's a sign of the times? A sign of how Maun is changing. It's bringing the village some notoriety, isn't it?'

'It was on the radio,' offered Cobrie. 'Last night.'

'But who are they? Maun's small enough, people must know who they are.'

'*Ee*, Lets knows,' said Cobrie with a grin.

'Do you, Lets?'

Lets looked around the office as if checking

who might be listening. He raised his eyebrows and gave a mysterious little smile, but the look he gave Cobrie wasn't friendly.

'So, what's being done about them? Have any been arrested?'

Mogorosi cleared his throat. 'The Kgosi called a Kgotla meeting last month, I believe Cobrie covered it, where people said how they had been attacked.'

'Kgosi Thlapi said the gang had threatened to cut open his stomach,' added Cobrie.

'It was agreed that these boys needed to be caught and soon,' continued Mogorosi seriously. 'A number of arrests were made.'

'But they're still around?'

The reporters all nodded.

'So we need a follow-up.'

'It is here,' said Lets, pulling out several pieces of lined paper from his pocket.

I quickly read through the two-page handwritten report. 'They dug up a coffin, at the graveyard?' I asked, appalled.

Lets nodded, his foot tapping impatiently on the floor.

'An elderly man witnessed the scene . . . do you have his name? Okay, here it is. You talked to him, right?'

'*Ee.*'

'They beat up a man on the street . . . people are saying the riot police should be brought in . . . ' I flipped the first page over and continued to read. 'They attacked a woman selling beer . . . she managed to stab one of them. Really? Wow, she's brave. When exactly did that happen? Oh, okay. So what do the police say? There's nothing in here about the cops, Lets?'

The reporters smiled, as if the police were a joke.

'Who usually deals with the police?'

'Me,' said Cobrie.

I looked around as the others agreed.

'Okay, then can you go to the station commander and ask him about everything in this story?'

'I will go on Monday.'

'Good, and ask if there have been any more arrests.'

'Okay,' Cobrie said good-naturedly.

'It's crucial that you get their response.'

'Okay,' Cobrie said again and he ambled out.

★   ★   ★

I spent most of that night sitting on the floor in my rented house going through the results of a crime survey I had earlier faxed to the jounalists from Sowa and asked them to hand out. Everyone was afraid of MaWestern. Women were locking themselves into their homes in fear; many said there were knocks on their doors in the small hours and men shouting that they should be let in. I got up just before dawn, it was getting light outside and I could hear the first cockerels. Otherwise it was silent, the hush before the sun rose and the day began. I wondered if MaWestern were really such a threat or if stories and rumours had been circulating

235

for so long that this anonymous gang had become far scarier than they really were. It was hard to imagine a small group of largely unarmed teenage boys had such a grip on the village that people no longer felt safe going out at night, let alone that they were responsible for a man's death. I thought about what I would do if the MaWestern threat were real, if I was woken up with someone pounding on my door. I didn't have a phone, I couldn't ring for help, but I did have neighbours in the house next door, I could always call them.

A few weeks later, I went with Andrew to pick up and distribute our first issue of the *OO*. We drove in his battered pick-up to the airport, waiting with anticipation for the Air Botswana flight to land. The paper had been sent to Gaborone for printing three days ago, and we were expecting it on the noon flight. We stood at the terminal's glass door, watching while the cargo was unloaded off the plane and then pushed in wire trolleys to an old green storage building.

'George!' Andrew yelled, cupping his hands, calling out to someone inside. The trolley with the *OO* had entered the building half an hour ago, but still the doors were locked.

'George!' Andrew yelled, pounding on the walls.

Eventually a tired-looking airport official with a bored expression on his face opened the doors, slowly, with much creaking.

Andrew and I rushed in, heading for the piles of freshly printed newspapers bound together with thick coils of string. Our first issue of the *OO* was beautiful. It was the first time the *OO* had been thick enough to light a fire or kill a scorpion with after it had been read. Andrew and I stood, flicking through the paper. The colour looked good. The photos weren't too blurred. The ads were in the right places. We beamed at each other, signed the cargo forms and jumped back in the car, Andrew driving like a maniac through Maun, leaping out to deposit thick piles of the *OO* at supermarkets and shops, at petrol stations and hotels, at bars and restaurants and hairdressing salons.

Then we rushed back to the office and I stood on the porch and watched as people began streaming in asking for the *OO*. On the front page was the MaWestern story. Cobrie hadn't had much luck with the station commander whose response to each alleged piece of violence was that the police could neither confirm nor deny it because it hadn't been reported to them.

★ ★ ★

Over the next few weeks I became so engrossed in the *OO* that Pearl started to complain. She was no longer working, for she was pregnant and the safari company had fired her. On the weekends, Bashi dropped her off at my house and she lay on the cool plastic-tiled floor, complaining that her legs had swollen, that her back hurt. She had never mentioned leaving Bashi since that evening in Sowa, she shrugged when I asked her about her savings account, and she and Bashi seemed happy again.

When Pearl wasn't lying on the floor or holed up in the toilet, she would suddenly revive.

'Let's go out. Let's go to Sedie. Let's go and visit my friend Charity. Have you seen the new lodge near Matlapaneng?'

'Pearl,' I grumbled from the desk where I sat. 'I've got to work. There was a power cut at the office yesterday, now I've got to get two days' worth of work into this morning. If there's a power cut tomorrow I've had it, because tomorrow is when I lay everything out.' I had become so obsessed with the *OO* that there was no time to relax between finishing one edition and beginning the next.

Pearl shifted on the floor. She bent up her legs, massaged the shins, and then stretched them out again. 'Are you drinking lots of milk?' I asked, eyeing her enormous belly.

Pearl shook her head.

'But it's good, milk's really good when you're pregnant.' I smiled reassuringly, although I wondered where I had received this piece of wisdom from.

'Nnyaa, we Batswana don't drink milk.'

'Oh, why?'

'It makes the baby . . . how do you say? When the baby is born and it is covered in . . . '

'Blood?' I offered helpfully.

'Nnyaa, it is covered in white.'

'It is? Yuk.'

Pearl laughed. 'If you drink too much milk then there is a lot of this white stuff, it is *all* over the baby.'

'Okay, fine, forget the milk. Look, I just have to do this. Have you seen this?' and I held up the page I was working on, a front-page report about AIDS.

Pearl hauled herself up from the floor and came to read over my shoulder. Then I wondered why I was showing her the piece, for according to the article one in three pregnant women in Maun were HIV positive.

I turned the page, trying to draw Pearl's attention to another article. 'I don't know where they get these figures from,' I said a little uselessly. Nowadays the threat of HIV was everywhere. The government regularly aired jingles that advised people to abstain, be faithful and condomize. There was even a billboard in the centre of the old mall, a huge wooden construction that dwarfed the buildings around it, which spelled out the message in large black print. But there was very little said about what HIV actually was, how you could get it and how you could not and on the whole people didn't really believe that they were at risk.

'I mean,' I said as Pearl lay back on the floor. 'They test people at the clinic, then they apply that to everyone. So if six men come to the clinic with some sexually transmitted disease and three test positive then, hey presto, half of all men in Botswana have HIV. It must be the same with women, if one in three pregnant women at the clinic are positive, then one in three of all pregnant women are. It seems a bit steep, doesn't it?' I wondered what I would do if I were pregnant, or if I suspected I had contracted HIV.

I didn't know if I would get tested or not, or even if it were possible to get tested in Maun, because once tested there was nothing that could be done, no drugs, no treatment.

Pearl sighed. 'Hey, the doctors just make these figures up to frighten us.'

'It's hard to take in, isn't it?' Anyway, I wanted to add, Bashi used a condom didn't he?

'I saw Thapelo yesterday,' Pearl said, referring to a woman who worked in one of the banks.

'Oh. How's she?'

'She is thin. She is very very thin . . . ' Pearl began massaging her shins again.

I knew what 'thin' meant, it meant someone had AIDS. It was what people said about each other, but quietly, in a hushed voice. Then the thin person would get fat again and the stories would begin about someone else. Because talking about sex was taboo, so talking about AIDS was taboo and so it became something to mutter and gossip about. AIDS was a little like MaWestern, an undercurrent of life in Maun that was so shrouded in rumours and fear that it was hard to work out what was true and what was not.

# 15

Alice was ten years old. She was sitting on the porch outside our new house in Maun, careful not to crumple her brand-new party dress. She and Ron had left Sowa a few weeks ago and returned home. 'Now that we are together we can laugh again,' Alice said on the first night in our new home, a small two-bedroom house near the Thamalakane River. The house had a musty smell and by Botswana standards it seemed old, its cracked walls sheltered by trees in a large rambling plot. From the river the house was totally obscured by foliage but from high up on the porch the view down to the Thamalakane was clear. In the mornings I walked the dogs in the direction of Maun, passing no one, just goats grazing on river grass and, high up in the trees, fish eagles waiting to pounce. Life along this section of the Thamalakane was as it had been for years, and yet in Maun the tar roads were growing longer and longer, new shops and businesses were opening every month offering fine wines and imported cheeses, satellite dishes and access to South African television channels.

This was Alice's first birthday party and she wasn't sure what to expect. She had been up since dawn, getting herself ready, combing her hair, tidying up her room. Then she had helped me make salads and open packets of crisps, blown up balloons. Now it was lunchtime and she was sitting on the porch, her face shiny with sweat, determined not to admit that the dress she had chosen was far too hot for a warm day in Maun.

'They are here,' Alice hissed at the sound of a car arriving in the lane at the back of the house. She looked panicked and got down from the porch and then stood there like an impala caught in a car's headlights.

'That's okay, Alice,' I laughed. 'You want people to come, it's your party, remember?'

'*Ee*. But I am too shy.'

'Look, it's probably only Veronica,' I tried to reassure her. 'And Kookaburra and the other kids. You won't be shy when it's started. And not too much cake, okay?'

Alice smiled in anticipation of her birthday cake.

'Why don't you go and help your dad?' I suggested, thinking she would feel easier if she had something to do. Ron was down at the bottom of the plot near the river clearing grass. Since he'd arrived back in Maun he had set about establishing his own computer company and already he had several repair jobs. The rest of the time he went into the bush, often just to track down missing goats, but twice in order to hunt buffalo.

He stopped work and wiped his forehead as Alice and I approached.

'Looks good,' I said. 'This garden could be amazing if someone had the time to do it.'

'Wait until we have our own house, Cait. I'll be working that garden every day. We'll have fruit trees everywhere. We'll have mangoes, jackleberries and limes. We'll have avocados by the score.'

'I can't wait,' I said, letting Ron's optimism convince me for once. It had been several years since we had secured the plot near the Hippo Pool, two years since Ron had cleared away the bush and erected a fence, and still we were no nearer to having a house of our own.

'And then I'll get the farm sorted out.' Ron slapped an axe on the ground and wiped his hands on his shorts.

'Mmm,' I said, a little unsure. Ron wanted to restore his grandmother's farm that lay about ten kilometres outside Maun and which had been dormant for years. It seemed a big job for one person, especially someone who was trying to set up a computer company at the same time.

'Cait,' Ron said in a confident voice, as if he were explaining something entirely logical that I had failed to quite grasp, 'if I can get the farm cleared and fenced then everyone can move there, I won't have to be running around all the time. My mum can stay there, and Madintwa and her sister. If they're all together then I just go there twice a week and deliver supplies. They can grow all their food there, enough to sell as well.' He smiled at the picture he was painting of a thriving family group living off the land.

'Why doesn't your grandma just move in with us?' I suggested. 'I don't mean here, I mean when we have our own place, she could build her own house there too, then you wouldn't have to be running all over the place.'

'And who would look after her?'

'I would.'

'Cait, you've got enough to do.'

'You mean you don't want her to move in with us?'

'Not really.' Ron looked at the ground. 'Anyway, it's my grandmother's dream to see that farm working again. I can get all the goats in one place, get some old man to look after them, and he can live there too. Alice can go there at the weekends, and Gabs can help out as well.'

'Gabs?'

'Gaomodimo. She's not doing anything. And she's a hard worker.'

'You mean Alice's big sister?' I frowned, trying to picture Gabs in my head. I had only seen her a couple of times. She was far taller and more mature-looking than Alice and I guessed she was about fifteen. 'Isn't she still at school?' I asked.

'Well, she was, but she took off to the bush. She was supposed to start secondary but then she got pissed off with her mum's boyfriend and left Maun for the cattle post.'

'What's the story with the mum's boyfriend, then?'

Ron shrugged. 'No idea.'

'Maybe she just doesn't want to go to school at all?'

'No, she really wants to go to school, it's just she can't take living at her mum's any more. She tried to find her dad, but he refused to acknowledge her, said she wasn't his.'

'That's terrible.' I scuffed at the sand with my feet. 'How do you know all this?'

'My mother told me.'

'And what's she got to do with it?' I laughed, to show I wasn't intending to insult Eliah.

'Gabs has been helping her out. They get on really well, my mother says Gabs is a real hard worker, and it's good for her, having a child around to help. Anyway, we're forgetting about big ears,' and Ron patted Alice on the head.

I was about to ask more but it didn't seem right discussing Gabs in front of Alice who had remained so still and so silent during our conversation I had quite forgotten she was there.

I came back up the slope to the house. Veronica and Roy had parked in the yard. In the back of their pick-up Kookaburra, Lloyd and the other children were shouting and laughing, eager for a party.

'You've got a pen in your hand,' Ron said coming up behind me.

'What?'

'Take the pen out of your hand, Cait. It's Sunday, you don't need to work.'

And then the children clambered out of the car and ran around the plot and I went to greet Veronica.

'You look nice,' Veronica said, hugging me roughly. Then she held me back by the shoulders and looked me over. 'This is a very nice dress. But you are too thin, you have no meat on your arms, look!' and she pinched my arms in her hands.

'It's just the stress of the job,' I said, pulling away.

Veronica smiled kindly. 'Once you have had a baby then you will look like a real mother.'

'Oh God, Veronica. First I'm too thin, then you want me to have babies.'

She laughed and called to the kids. 'Put the presents in the house,' she told them.

'No,' I said. 'Give them to Alice. It's her birthday, she can open them now.'

'*Nnyaa.* You put them in the house and then she opens them later.'

'Okay, okay.' I gave in. Veronica always knew how she wanted things done and I usually just went along with her.

'Now,' Veronica ordered the kids, 'go and play there.' She walked to a nearby tree and pulled off a branch. Then she brandished it at the children. 'Over there,' she shouted, swiping at their legs with the branch.

'We're not at school now,' I told her. 'Don't beat them, it's supposed to be a party.' I took the stick away from her but the kids let out a collective complaint at the game being spoiled.

'*Wena ke tla go betsa!*' Veronica shook her finger at Lloyd and, delighted, he laughed.

'Come in,' I urged. 'I've got some games. Pass the parcel and things. We've got prizes. I love kids' parties . . . '

Veronica clapped me on the shoulder. 'Where's the wine?'

She followed me into the house and went straight to the kitchen. 'Haven't you prepared the meat yet?' she asked, prodding a pile of beef Ron had left in a huge metal bowl. Veronica rolled her sleeves up. 'Where's the sauce? Do you have Tabasco?'

246

Another car pulled up in the driveway and I left Veronica at work in the kitchen. When I got outside Ron was standing with his uncle Rra Nama who was leaning on the bonnet of a dusty, blue pick-up truck. The truck had a megaphone on the roof and Rra Nama was driving around Maun urging people to come to a political rally. I had been woken by the megaphone at five that morning.

'MaAlice,' he nodded, shaking my hand.

I smiled; I found it ridiculous the way people referred to me as MaAlice, as if being a mother meant losing my own identity.

'Are you having a meeting?' I asked.

'*Ee*,' said Rra Nama. 'Two o'clock at freedom square. I am trying to get your husband here to attend.'

'I've told him I can't,' said Ron.

'Ao, a children's party!' laughed Rra Nama. 'The women can do that.'

Ron said something in Setswana and his uncle roared with laughter. Then he turned and got back in the car, the engine still running. And as he turned I saw him stumble a little, holding on to the open car door for support. He laughed as if the stumble had been nothing at all, but I suddenly noticed that his belly had shrunk quite noticeably.

'Is he ill?' I asked Ron as his uncle drove off.

'He was.'

'And he's not now?'

'He went to the traditional doctor. He sorted him out. My grandmother was really impressed.'

'I didn't know he'd been ill. I haven't seen him

247

for ages. What is it, do you think? What did the doctor say?'

'You worry too much,' Ron said, turning away from the driveway.

'Aunty Caitlin!' Kookaburra came running up, interrupting our conversation. 'Lloyd has just fallen from the tree. Are you coming to the wedding?'

'What?' I asked, confused, about to hurry off to find Lloyd. 'Whose wedding?'

'Uncle Roy's.'

'Really? Veronica!' I yelled, heading to the kitchen. I knocked on the window and Veronica opened it and leant out. 'You don't have any sharp knives,' she complained. 'I can't cut this meat.'

'Forget the meat, are you getting married?'

Veronica looked coy.

'You are! Why didn't you tell me? When? Soon? What do you want to get married for anyway?'

'You're already married,' said Veronica, her head still sticking out of the kitchen window. 'You know, Caitlin, many people said Roy and I, we would not last. They gave us a year, two years, five. Well, now we have been together for a very long time and now we are getting married!'

'Well, if you're happy . . . '

'Ee. I am happy. The marriage will show that our families have accepted us, both mine and the Ridges.'

I thought about the Ridges, about Ron's father and Selina, about Rita and Patricia and the rest of the family. I didn't see them nearly as much as

I did Eliah and Madintwa, but I knew that Veronica was trying hard to be a dutiful daughter-in-law. 'Do you think they *haven't* accepted you?'

Veronica attempted a smile. 'You're lucky with your in-laws, they respect you.'

I nodded, I knew I was lucky for I had heard terrible stories of women being abused by their mothers-in-law.

'You don't argue with them,' Veronica continued. 'I heard MaMozambia boasting about you at a funeral the other day . . . '

'Really?' I smiled, pleased to think I was being spoken of in this way.

★   ★   ★

The new *Okavango Observer* had been going for nearly two months when the police paid their first visit.

Cobrie and I had started work early that Monday, it took us hours to go over the weekend sports results and it was easier if the office were empty. At last we had things the way we wanted them and we stopped for tea.

'Did you hear Radio Botswana this morning?' Cobrie asked, spooning several sugars into his cup.

'No. Why? What was on the news?'

'They denied our report.'

'Our report?' I frowned. 'You mean a report in the *OO*?'

'*Ee.*'

'Well, don't keep me in suspense, Cobrie!

249

Which article was it?'

'On MaWestern.'

'MaWestern? We've had loads of stories on MaWestern; the last one was on all the arrests, right? Which MaWestern one was it?'

'The first one,' said Cobrie.

'What, the very first one since I've been here? The one about how they dug up the coffin at the graveyard?'

Cobrie nodded.

'But what do you mean they denied it? Who?'

'The police.'

'What, they've gone on radio to deny an OO story from ages ago?' I asked, bemused. 'But I don't see what exactly they could be denying. It was an allegation, how can they deny an allegation? You asked the police yourself about the coffin and all that and they said they couldn't deny or confirm anything!'

Cobrie shrugged and drank his tea. Then Lets came into the office, walking briskly, looking pleased with himself. He cleared a space and sat on top of one of the tables. 'Have you seen the *Daily News*?'

'No, why?'

'They are denying my story.'

'What?' I laughed. This was a joke. The government had better things to do than deny something that was long since over. But although I laughed, the sudden appearance of the denials took me by surprise. I hadn't even known that the original article had caused any controversy at all. If the police were denying that our report was true, then someone, somewhere, must have been discussing it for some time. And yet on the surface, our relations with the Maun police were as cordial as ever. 'Lets, this is the MaWestern one you're talking about? The *Daily News* are denying it, too?'

'Ee.'

Cobrie laughed and, ignoring an annoyed glance from Lets, he took out his notebook and began to write.

'What are you writing, Cobrie?' I asked.

'A story.'

'What story?'

'MaWestern,' he said, giving Lets a look. I realized then that there was an air of competitiveness between the two men. I had noticed a little friction between them, the way one tended to leave the office as the other came in, but I had thought it was just personal. Now I thought it might be professional, that they were in competition to get what they thought was the best story.

'So what's the story then?' I asked.

'I am from the police station,' Cobrie explained. 'This morning, even before I came here. I had heard on the weekend there were more arrests so I went to check my sources. There has also been more violence. Two people have been admitted to Maun General Hospital. And, again, the station commander says now things are spreading outside Maun. He says young thugs are calling themselves MaWestern in other villages.'

'I thought this whole MaWestern thing was over,' I said. 'We had loads of arrests last month.

What's going on now?'

A few days later I turned up to the office late, dragging my bike with a punctured tyre. I opened the office door and everyone turned my way, their faces expectant.

'What is it?' I asked, hurrying in, apologizing for being late. 'What's the excitement?'

Andrew lit a cigarette and moved to smoke it at the doorway to the porch. 'The cops were here, looking for Lets.'

'What do they want him for?'

'That MaWestern story.' Andrew kicked at some goat droppings.

'You're joking. Why would the cops want Lets?'

'Fuck knows,' said Andrew. 'But anyway, Lets wasn't here and I told them I didn't know where he was.'

The next day I was in the office bright and early when the police came in. They were two plain-clothed CID men and they acted like we had all offended them.

'We are looking for Lets Phaladi,' said the taller one with a sullen face and a peeling bottom lip that looked raw it was so red.

'*Dumelang Borra,*' I said pointedly, for the officers had not greeted us or announced their arrival, they'd just walked straight in.

'Where is he?' asked the sullen one, ignoring my greeting.

'I don't know,' I said. 'He's a freelancer. He's not here all the time.'

The CID looked round the room as if suspecting Lets was hiding somewhere.

252

'Well, tell him we are looking for him.'

'Okay,' I said. 'What do you want with him? Maybe I can help?'

Just then Lets appeared at the doorway and the CID men turned. They talked to him briefly on the porch and then all three left, Lets flanked by the cops and marched out across the old mall. Lets waved as he left, he didn't seem at all concerned.

Shortly afterwards a different group of CID arrived. They were led by an elderly man with whitened hair called Mr Radipudi, his face so long and with such high cheekbones that it made me think of a mournful goat. He greeted me morosely, shook my hand, took a seat and got out a file.

'We have investigated this report,' said Mr Radipudi getting out a battered copy of the first *OO* with the MaWestern story on the front page. His movements were slow and his manner almost reluctant as if he were on an errand he didn't have much enthusiasm for. 'And we have found it false.'

'You have?'

'*Ee*. These people in the report, we can't find them.'

'You can't?'

'*Ee*. This woman who was attacked while selling beer, we can't find her. Where does she live?'

'Well,' I slid the *OO* over to my side of the table, 'it says here Kgosing ward.'

'No, we have been there and we can't find her. There is no one selling beer in that ward.'

'Oh. Well, have you asked Lets?'

'*Ee*. We went with him there and there is no such woman.'

'Oh,' I said, realizing now what had happened after CID had marched Lets from the office.

'And again, this elderly man who found a body being eaten by dogs, we can't find him.'

I read the report again. 'You mean Rrakhei Rrakhei?'

'*Ee*. Our investigations have shown that none of these things have happened.'

Well, why didn't you say so earlier? I wanted to ask. Why wait over a month before coming and telling me this? And did he realize how unlikely it was that people would want to talk to the police anyway? In the few weeks since I'd been in Maun several people had come to the office to say they had been harassed or their family was being harassed by MaWestern. And when we asked, had they gone to the police they all said no. People thought they would get into trouble if they reported anything.

'Well, how can I help?' I asked Mr Radipudi. 'You want me to publish something saying you've investigated and haven't found any evidence?'

He looked past me and began tidying up his file.

'I could try and find the original story that Lets wrote — would that help? I don't think I cut anything out of it, but I could try and find it anyway,' I offered.

'*Ee*,' said Mr Radipudi.

'Okay, I'll look for it tonight and call you tomorrow.'

I searched high and low for the original story that evening but decided I must have thrown it away. So the next day I rang Mr Radipudi and explained this.

'Thank you, Davies,' said Mr Radipudi and he hung up.

★　★　★

As Christmas approached the issue of MaWestern appeared to die away again. December that year was the hottest I could remember. At night the air was damp but there was no sign of rain. I couldn't remember the last time I had even seen rain. It was beginning to seem like rain was something that happened in other countries, not Botswana.

'Are we off?' Ron put his head round the door to the OO office.

'Oh God, is it time already?' It was Saturday morning and I was catching up with work, almost forgetting that today was the day Roy and Veronica were getting married.

'Are you okay?' I asked, seeing how distracted Ron looked.

'Ee. I've just come from hospital. Rra Nama has been admitted with flu.'

'Oh.' I finished off the report I was working on, my attention on the screen.

'So where's Veronica, at the DC's already?'

'No, they're both at daddy's finishing things off.'

When we got to Ron's dad's house, a handsome but as yet unfinished oval house near the old Maun Bridge, the plot was full of cars. But despite the obvious presence of a lot of people, the place was silent. We walked cautiously round the sides of the house until we came to an outside courtyard, half enclosed with a low white concrete wall. Now I could hear a man's voice, low and serious but comforting, like someone reassuring an unnecessarily frightened child. I stopped as we reached the courtyard. Sitting in front of the wall I could see a row of people on reed mats. In the middle were Roy and Veronica. Roy wore a black suit and his eyes were closed, his head held awkwardly to one side as if he had been trying to stay awake and had just failed. He had one hand on his knee, his leg held as awkwardly as his head, as if he had been frozen in the middle of movement. There was a half smirk on his face and I thought he was about to let out a deep snore. Next to him Veronica slumped, her arms in the lap of her wedding dress. Her head was obscured by a long white veil, her chin rested on her neck, I could just see the bridge of her nose. She looked like a swan fast asleep.

'What's going on?' I whispered.

'The elders are advising them on marriage,' Ron said and he disappeared off back round the house. He didn't have much time for ceremonies. But for me it was different and I stood there, mesmerized by the meeting. It was scenes like this that reminded me just how much of a foreigner I was. I looked around at the people in the courtyard. Roy's mother, Selina, sat next to her son on the reed mat, her face long and gloomy, a yellow shawl round her shoulders, her feet bare. Next to her, her sister sat, her face solidly cupped in the palm of her right hand, the picture of depression. All round the courtyard the people sat in total stillness, listening as Roy's uncle spoke. No one seemed to have noticed I was there, or perhaps it was just not appropriate that anything interrupt the proceedings. I squatted down at the end of the row of women, listening hard, trying to follow what was being said. Roy's uncle was coming to the end of his speech, he was advising Veronica that a wife should never ask where her husband has been, and if Roy had any problems with his new wife he should come to his elders first.

Veronica shifted slightly and sniffed. I realized with a shock that she was awake and crying. I looked around the women sitting on the reed mats, waiting for someone to go and comfort the bride. But Roy's uncle looked satisfied, he glanced around the gathering and a few of the people nodded to him as if pleased things were going according to plan. Then everyone got up, shook themselves down, rearranging clothes, asking for water to drink. 'You okay?' I asked Veronica, sidling up, tugging on her white dress.

Veronica looked up, her face still obscured by the veil, her eyes wet. She took my hand in her hot dry one and squeezed it hard. Then Roy laughed and clasped me on the shoulder and I turned away to talk to the others.

# 16

The day the CID came again I was totally unprepared. It was a Friday morning in January and the heat was so strong it was becoming difficult to breathe. I was sitting very still at the computer, trying to move as little as possible. When I heard someone wiping their feet on the porch outside, I didn't even have the energy to turn round.

'*Ko ko!*' came a man's voice.

'*Ee*,' I said, swivelling slightly on the one proper office chair.

CID officer Mr Radipudi looked as weary as he had done on his first visit, but he also looked a little smarter today, a touch more confident.

'You're under arrest,' he said flatly, coming towards me.

I got up and laughed, shook his hand and invited him to sit down. 'And how are you? How was your Christmas?'

Mr Radipudi took a seat and put a file on the table. We sat without speaking until finally he gave a sigh. 'You almost made me lose my job.'

'I did?'

Mr Radipudi was not looking at all amused and I realized, with a jolt, that his visit was serious.

'I was meant to have finished this last year,' he said. 'I'm asking you to make a statement, and bring it with you to my office on Monday.'

'Okay,' I said, nodding as if this were perfectly normal. 'A statement about what, that MaWestern article?'

'*Ee.*'

'You mean what the article said, what the station commander said when we interviewed him, when we published it and so on?'

Mr Radipudi nodded and I jotted this down on a scrap of paper, assuming he was wrapping up his investigation, perhaps writing a final report.

'And Mr Andrew Dooley must come to the police station as well.'

'Andrew?' I was amazed. 'But he does the lay-out and ads. He's not a journalist. Or an editor.'

'Mr Andrew Dooley must come to the police station as well,' Mr Radipudi repeated.

'And do you want a statement from him?'

'No, just tell him to come to the police station on Monday.'

'And what happens then?'

'You will be charged with publishing a false article likely to cause alarm.'

'Excuse me?' I felt a stab of fear, as if I had missed something that had just suddenly caught up with me.

'Section 59 of the Penal Code,' said Mr Radipudi and he packed up his files and left.

I went home that afternoon and spent an hour reading the Penal Code, a small book with a soft blue cover outlining Botswana's criminal law. I had often referred to it to help define certain laws and to check possible punishments, but I had never noticed the alarming publications crime before, perhaps because no one in Botswana had ever been charged with it. I found it tucked away among lesser-known criminal offences such as telling fortunes and wounding ostriches. The Penal Code outlined the offence, and what an accused could argue in defence such as having taken enough steps to lead the accused to reasonably believe that the story they had published was true. I took some comfort from what I read, for I believed the MaWestern story was true. Then I read that if convicted, an accused could face up to two years in prison.

I worked quickly, writing down everything I could remember about the MaWestern article, attaching the questions Cobrie had asked the station commander along with the station commander's response. Once I had finished I sat at my desk, worried. I couldn't quite understand why I had to go to the police station on Monday or what they would do to me there. Would they take my statement and dismiss me, would they caution me, would they arrest me and lock me up? With another stab of anxiety I remembered that Mr Radipudi had already said I was under arrest. But then if I were, I couldn't understand what I was still doing sitting at home.

*　*　*

On Monday I went to the police station. 'If I'm not back in my office by nine come and bail me out,' I told Ron, trying to joke.

The Maun police station was a new glass and

concrete two-storey building set off the main Maun road, erected during the recent building boom in the village. It now served as police headquarters for the whole of the vast north-west district. I walked around the tall metal fence and entered the courtyard where a handful of plants were struggling to grow in the sandy soil. Two men in beige prison clothes were washing down a police car with a plastic bucket of water and some old rags, watched by a hefty man in full inspector's uniform.

I walked quickly into the building, heading up the stairs and along the corridor to where I knew the CID offices were. Mr Radipudi wasn't around. No one seemed to be around. The corridors were empty, all the office doors were open and the offices inside empty as well. So I walked up and down the corridor until Andrew showed up.

'All right, girl,' he said cheerily, clapping his hands together, unfazed by the depressing atmosphere of the police station. 'You look tired.'

'Yeah, I barely slept over the weekend.'

'Oh, it's all a load of crap,' said Andrew. 'Where's Mr Radipudi? Hey *Mma*!' he accosted a woman in a cleaner's uniform who had just begun shuffling down the corridor. 'Where's Radipudi?'

Finally someone directed us into an office where Mr Radipudi sat.

'Morning!' said Andrew taking a chair.

Mr Radipudi looked at us stony faced. He appeared far more officious here in his own office, sitting behind a desk which was empty but for an old phone, an out-of-date calendar advertising a local safari company, and a pile of blue folders.

'Do you have your statement?' asked Mr Radipudi.

'Yes.' I handed it over. He didn't even look at it, just added it to a file on his desk.

'We have finished the docket and we are sending it to the attorney general's chambers,' said Mr Radipudi in a flat voice as if he were reciting something he'd said many times before. Then he straightened up and adjusted his tie. 'You are to be charged with publishing an alarming publication, section 59 of the Penal Code.'

'So what happens now?' I asked, looking at Andrew who was jiggling his knees under the table.

'You will be informed,' said Mr Radipudi, 'when you are to appear in court.'

'You mean, *if* we are to appear in court.' I laughed nervously.

Mr Radipudi scowled and indicated that we could go.

★ ★ ★

The days went by and the weeks went by and nothing happened. Once or twice, as I drove past the police station or walked past the magistrates' court, I thought about going to Mr Radipudi and asking what was going on. But then I thought the attorney general must have read the docket and realized no crime had been

262

committed and that was that. The *Okavango Observer* was now growing into a proper newspaper. We came out weekly and distribution had been extended to local villages in the Delta. We had also weathered two libel threats, one from the white owner of a local bar after a report on a patron being assaulted and called a *kaffir*, and the other from a Francistown businessman who had the bizarre idea of building a sugar plantation in Kasane. Apart from the freelancers, including the paper's first women reporters, the *OO* now had its first full-time journalist, Enole Ditsheko. Enole was an earnest, God-loving young man from Maun who wore a suit every day, whatever the weather. He was punctual and charming and very ambitious. He wanted to be a journalist, he said, and was prepared to start at the bottom and work his way up. Enole was forever bringing people into the office, whether an ex-prisoner alleging abuse in the cells, or a girl without legs whose mother wanted money for food.

There were also stories of a more trivial nature to cover. One day a man rang to say the Duke of Edinburgh was arriving in Maun en route to a holiday in the Okavango Delta.

'What, the queen's husband?' I asked.

'That's right,' said the source. 'He'll arrive at about 4 p.m. today. But don't tell *anyone* I told you.'

Andrew and I rushed to the airport, which had become an impressive place to stroll around; the old Portakabin-type building had been replaced with a brand-new glass and concrete structure,

263

with fresh white walls and shiny floors. All hell had broken out during the official opening a month earlier with tents stolen, chairs broken and people assaulted during the scramble for free beer and food.

After waiting for a while, with our noses up against the glass, and Andrew looking forward to the day when the bar would finally open, we saw a smart-looking jet about to land. We ran down to the first floor and shot outside on to the tarmac. The airport manager tried to stop us.

'Hey, you can't go there. This is for the dignitaries,' he said, pointing to a small huddle of men in suits getting ready to say hello to the Duke.

'I'll take your picture,' said Andrew rushing past him. 'With the Duke right? I'll take your picture. We'll put it in the paper.' Andrew stopped and put his arm round the airport manager's shoulder. 'You and the Duke, eh?'

The airport manager was clearly torn and, as the jet had now landed, I ran forward, notebook in hand, thinking if I caught a glimpse of the Duke and if he was within shouting distance I'd ask him something, though I had no idea what. The jet came to a stop and the door opened. Out stepped the Duke. Looking suntanned and relaxed, a sporty straw boater in his hands, the Duke of Edinburgh was heading straight towards me. Say something, I said to myself, ask him something. This was the husband of the Queen of England. I was close enough to pick his nose. I could have asked him anything at all. Instead, slightly stunned at seeing a real life royal up close and stepping off a plane at Maun airport, I couldn't think of a single thing to say.

The Duke reached the bottom step, leaned forward, shook the airport manager's hand. 'What's the weather going to be like?' he asked in a bizarrely royal accent. 'It still rains a bit I suppose?'

The airport manager nodded, looking stunned too. The weather in Botswana was always fine and hot, except for a very few occasions when it rained. Naturally the Duke didn't want rain, and naturally every Motswana did.

The only one who wasn't looking stunned was Andrew. The Duke bid farewell to the dignitaries and then sauntered across the tarmac to a multicoloured helicopter. Andrew ran after him.

'Hey, Duke!' he yelled.

The Duke of Edinburgh kept on walking.

'Can I take a photo of you with your hat on?'

The Duke turned round, looked at Andrew for a second and said, 'Why?'

'Well it looks good,' said Andrew. But the Duke was now at the helicopter.

'Afternoon, your royal highness,' said the pilot, almost tugging his forelock, and in the Duke got.

★　★　★

As the months went on, the news — and tip offs — of news increased. But although on the outside it looked like the newspaper was doing well, moneywise things were beginning to get precarious. We needed more adverts and the pressure on Andrew was enormous. The safari

265

companies, where the real wealth was, said their market was overseas so why would they want to advertise in a local paper like the *OO*? The fact that we had reported on the fight at a local bar when a customer had been called a *kaffir* hadn't gone down well with some people. Snippets of conversations began coming back to me. The *OO*, I heard, was stirring racial tension. A common complaint was that 'it's just too *black*'. 'Who said that?' I would snap when Andrew passed on these tidbits. 'Why don't they come in here and say that? If the *OO* is too black then they must find Botswana really fucking black so why don't they fuck off back to where they come from?'

But then our money problems were put on hold as the paper became caught up in the threatened removal of the Basarwa — or Bushmen — from the Central Kalahari Game Reserve. Ever since the 1980s, the Botswana government had wanted to move the Basarwa out of the reserve, though it never really said why. The Basarwa didn't want to go and every time relocation plans were suggested the inhabitants of the reserve refused.

In March 1996 I had a strange phone call.

'Is this Caitlin at the *OO*?' a woman's voice asked. 'Ah, you don't know me but . . . It's about the Bushmen. They're about to be kicked out. The trucks are coming, they're going to bus them all out.'

'Where did you get this from?'

'Don't quote me!' the woman said in a panic.

'I'm not going to quote you,' I said trying to

calm her down. 'I'm just asking where you got this information from.'

'Oh, well, okay, I'll tell you, but don't tell him I told you.'

I rang the number I had just been given.

'Hi, this is Caitlin from the *OO*, I was wondering about the Basarwa in the Central Kalahari . . . '

'Who told you to come to me?' said the man sharply. 'I don't want to get PI'd.'

'Sorry?'

'PI'd, made a prohibited immigrant.'

'Oh.' I found it hard to believe that residency in Botswana was so tenuous that someone could be thrown out of the country just for talking about Basarwa in the Central Kalahari.

An hour later the man sidled in to the *OO* office. Without speaking, he surreptitiously handed me a fax from an American organization saying Basarwa in the Central Kalahari were to be forcibly moved within weeks.

'Don't tell *anyone* where you got this from,' warned the man.

I rolled my eyes at Andrew, who had been listening in on the exchange.

'Totally paranoid!' I laughed as the man left the office.

# 17

Botswana had never celebrated Worker's Day before, but this year the 1st of May had become a public holiday so we closed the *OO* office and everyone took a day off. I spent the morning in the garden, determined to clear the yard of grass which Madintwa had warned me was getting so high that it would be impossible to spot a snake before it spotted me. It was a cool, clear spring day and I had been raking at the grass since dawn without seeing any real improvement. When I heard a car at the gate I threw down the rake, relieved to take a break.

Veronica drove into the plot at high speed and parked the car on the sand, not even seeking out the shade of a tree.

'What is it?' I asked, poking my head through the driver's window. I had barely seen Veronica since her wedding and she didn't look at all happy today.

'Where's Mozambia?' she asked.

'At his mum's, I think.'

'Hey, he's never at home that one.'

'Well, he's got a lot to do,' I said. 'Gabs, his grandmother, the goats . . . '

'*Ee*. But this is where he lives, isn't it?'

'Yes, but it's not like anyone else can help, can they? There's only one of him.' I worried that Ron was spreading himself too thin, but I also knew I would think less of him if he didn't want

268

to help his family. 'Anyway, why do you look so glum?'

'Hey, Caitlin,' Veronica sighed heavily. 'It is this cattle lung disease. I am just now from the cattlepost. It is like the killing fields. Smell me, I smell of blood,' and she held out the sleeve of one arm.

Cattle lung disease was the only thing people in Maun talked about these days and it had dominated news reports for months. The year before there had been warnings that local cattle were infected with contagious bovine pleuro-pneumonia, commonly known as cattle lung disease, and people were terrified. I had lived long enough in Botswana to know the importance of cattle. It was not that everyone had cattle, and the percentage of cattle owners fell by the year, but that everyone wanted to own cattle. The animals conferred prestige and those who owned many were known as cattle barons. Cows were far more valuable than goats which were the only livestock Ron's family could afford to have. They could be used as dowry payments, were slaughtered to feed hundreds at weddings and funerals, they provided wealth in the form of a bank account for the future, and in the present they provided meat and milk. So the idea of a disease that would kill the cattle off was disastrous, it was far scarier to most people than the idea of HIV and AIDS.

Two months ago the vet officials had warned that the whole of the north-west district, already the most impoverished in the country, could be ravaged if farmers continued to trek livestock out of affected areas. Then, on Good Friday, President Ketumile Masire had flown in to Maun to announce that the entire northern cattle herd would be slaughtered.

Then things became secretive and confusing, no more public meetings were held, no one knew what exactly was going on. And so the killing began; in village after village government gunmen moved from kraal to kraal shooting cattle, and then women ran to slit the animals' throats. Sometimes cows that had already been shot staggered up again, hissing blood out of the nose, thrashing around the red-soaked sand of the kraal. Some cows were said to be protected by witchcraft and therefore wouldn't die however many times they were shot. It was rumoured that any vet officer who shot a cow that had been protected would himself die. And then I heard that in some places instead of shooting the cattle, the vet officers were driving them along trenches and into deep pits. A vehicle was then driven over the pit, packing the cattle in, some were killed by the machine, others by suffocation as they were crushed against each other, some were buried alive. Eventually the hole was filled and the killing moved to another area. One of the *OO* freelancers watched his family's cattle being killed in this manner, but when I asked him to write about it he would do so only anonymously.

It wasn't long before the story was denied. A seven o'clock news announcer on Radio Botswana informed the nation that a cattle slaughter report in the *Okavango Observer* was untrue.

After Veronica left, I gave up on the yard and sat stiffly in front of the computer working on the latest reports on cattle lung disease. But I worked half-heartedly, distracted by the tension in my back, the feeling that all my muscles had contracted into one.

By dusk I had given up working and I lay on the porch. My body seemed to have spasmed into a weird and new shape so that if I stood up I couldn't straighten further than my waist.

'Cait!' Ron called when he came home. 'Where are you?'

'Out here!'

'Good,' said Ron coming through the house and seeing me on the porch. 'You're resting.'

'I'm bloody not, I can't move my back.'

'Really?' Ron looked worried. 'What happened?'

'I've no idea. I was doing some weeding earlier . . . '

'I told you I'd do that,' Ron said, annoyed. 'I *told* you I'd do it.'

'Yes, you told me, but you haven't done it and I'm scared about snakes.'

'I told you I would do it, and I'll do it.'

'When?' I laughed. Now Ron was absorbed in his new business as well as constant trips to Morutsa, anything he said he'd do at home he never did. We barely saw each other in our separate efforts to make a success of our jobs, and the only time we relaxed was at our plot. There the foundations of our new house had finally been laid and each day Ron went and watered the concrete so it wouldn't crack.

271

'Let's not argue,' Ron pleaded. 'Maybe your back will ease up if you rest.'

I remained lying on the porch while Ron made supper. Alice was at Eliah's and wouldn't be coming back that night. It was cool on the porch, and it was relaxing to lie and watch the sun seeping down across the sky as dusk fell. I heard a car in the distance, its wheels churning in sand as a foolish driver tried to cross the dry riverbed.

Ron came out of the house carrying two plates. He set them down on the porch and we ate in silence.

'My mother was thinking . . . ' Ron said, laying down his plate.

'Yes?' I asked. When Ron began a conversation like this, it usually meant his mother had some plan involving goats.

'About Gabs.'

'Oh.' No mention had been made of Alice's eldest sister for some time, except that I knew she'd been staying in Morutsa with Eliah. 'What about her?'

'That she should be adopted.'

'Why?' I asked, surprised that Ron's mum wanted to adopt Alice's sister.

'Well, my mum and Gabs get on very well. She's really been working hard at Morutsa, and my mum needs some help. She's a hard worker, Gabs . . . '

'Yes, as you're always saying.'

'*Mma?*' Ron looked up, sensing criticism.

'No, no, go on.'

'You know Gabs doesn't want to live at her mum's any more, because of the boyfriend. Her own dad doesn't want her. But since she's being staying with my mum she's really getting on well. She could even go back to school, she really wants to do that.'

'So, your mum wants Gabs to live with her, at Moeti and at Morutsa?'

'Ee.'

'Well, fine. That sounds good.'

Ron beamed. 'Wonderful. So we can adopt her?'

'We?'

'Ee.'

'What do you mean, we?' I said. 'You mean you and me?'

Ron didn't answer and in the silence I felt an air of trouble.

'Why on earth would we want to adopt Gabs? How old is she? Sixteen? Seventeen? She's almost an adult. Why does she need to be adopted? And if she does, then your mum can go ahead and adopt her herself!'

Ron shifted around on his chair. When one of the dogs came up he slapped at it unnecessarily. 'There is going to be a family meeting. You remember I told you? The meeting so that we can properly adopt Alice?' I nodded. I had heard about this meeting many times but it was yet to materialize. Now that Alice had been living with us for a couple of years we had grown into a family. We balanced each other and we had fun together and Alice had begun to ask how long she was staying. Both Ron and I had thought we should adopt her in the traditional manner. This wouldn't mean any paperwork or going to court, but it would mean sitting down with Alice's mother and Ron's grandmother and other family members and discussing the matter. We would pay Alice's family some cattle, and Alice would formally become our child.

'So what about the family meeting?' I asked. I'd got used to how long it took for any meeting, public or private, to actually happen.

'Well, my mother thinks we could adopt Alice and Gabs together.'

'Why not the other girls as well?' I cried. 'Anyone else need adopting while we're at it?'

Ron scowled.

'Come on,' I said, 'we both want to adopt Alice, and she wants to live with us. She's been with us ages and she's only ten. And, she *is* your daughter. She'll be with us for many more years to come. But Gabs is almost an adult. I can't adopt a sixteen-year-old. When I was sixteen I was getting ready to leave home! I don't even know her.'

'I'm only asking what you think.' Ron got up and picked up the empty plates.

'Are you? Are you asking me what I think, or are you telling me what your mother thinks?' I bit my lip. I never criticized Ron's mother.

Ron stood at the doorway, a plate in each hand. His expression was stony. 'I'm asking you what you think.'

'I just don't get it,' I said, shifting in frustration. Ron and I had always been on the same side, now it felt as if we were on opposing teams, as if, for the first time, neither of us could see the other's point of view. 'You're making me feel mean saying no. But I just don't get why you would want to adopt someone, someone who's sixteen for God's sake, someone we don't even know that well.'

Ron hung his head. 'I just feel so bad for her,' he said at last. The scowl had gone from his face, his frown faded. 'Not having a father. Not going to school. I guess she reminds me a bit of me.'

'But you had a father, you went to school.'

'Yeah, I know, but I just really feel for her.'

I sighed. 'So what you're saying is, your mum wants Gabs adopted. Gabs will then live with your mum. She wouldn't live with us?'

'Of course not.'

'Gabs wants to live with your mother?'

'I've already said so.'

'Well, if your mum is so keen for the adoption, and it will make Gabs happier, then I suppose I can see the point. But I don't see why your mum doesn't adopt her herself. It's mad.'

That night my back was on fire; I couldn't move my legs without pain. I spent the next few days in bed and then, after several sessions with a chiropractor, I managed to start walking. Two months after my raking accident my back began to hurt again. The chiropractor had left Maun and there was nowhere to go for help. On some days the pain shot up and down my legs, other days it wasn't so bad and so I worked even harder to take my mind off things. At least, I thought, I wasn't ten months pregnant as Pearl now was, in a pregnancy that appeared to have gone on for ever. Several times I dreamt she had given birth, only to ring her and find that she

275

hadn't. Veronica was pregnant too, and so was Beauty, who had moved down to Mochudi to give birth at home. The only people I saw regularly now were Andrew and the *OO* reporters and the only thing I thought about was how to bring money into the *OO*.

Eventually I made an appointment with a back specialist in Gaborone. Madintwa's compound was busy the morning I left Maun. I had come to say goodbye, and to get the customary spray of water in the face. The family were getting ready for one of their many trips to Morutsa, piling supplies into the back of the Land Rover so Ron could take them there after he'd dropped me at the airport. Alice was there and she and her sister Gabs chatted happily as Eliah gave them instructions. Madintwa was in a particularly talkative mood, ecstatic because she'd just heard on the radio that all old people would now get a state pension. The only problem was a pensioner needed a birth certificate and Madintwa didn't have one.

'Ah Kate-a-lyn,' she sighed. 'Where am I going to get a birth certificate from?'

'Well, do you know where you were born?'

'*Ee.*'

'And do you know when you were born?'

'She has a rough idea,' offered Ron.

'I think you need a complete date. There must be records.'

Ron shook his head. 'People didn't write these things down.'

'Well, her passport,' I said brightly. 'What date does that have on it?'

Ron's mother Eliah in a characteristically regal pose. Madintwa is seated beside her. The picture was taken the year I arrived in Maun.

A youthful looking Madintwa sitting outside the family compound in Boyei ward bundling up reeds to sell. These were the days before she needed a walking stick, and before cataracts had ruined her eyesight.

Outside the house where Ron spent his childhood.

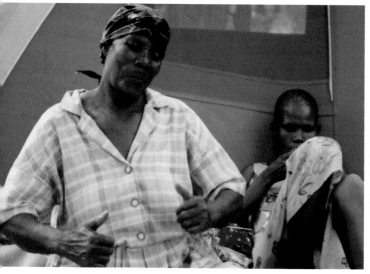

Madintwa giving the thumbs up. She's pictured at the farm, in front of the tent she slept in, with Gabs beside her.

Alice, just before she moved in with us at Sowa.

My sister-in-law Veronica, with Ruby and Lloyd. Ruby is wrapped up in several layers of clothing, as befitting a Motswana child, despite the fact it was a bright, sunny day.

Ron, mum and me in the grounds of the Tshwaragano school about a year after I moved to Maun.

A smiling Ron, with Chobe elephants in the distance.

The Old Matlapaneng Bridge over the Thamalakane River. The photograph was taken around 1991 when the bridge was still open to traffic.

Ron poling a *mokoro*, a traditional dug out canoe, in the Okavango Delta.

A typical compound in Maun where the more modern, square houses have begun to replace the traditional round structures.

The Thamalakane River in full flood outside our house in Matlapaneng. From a distance it was hard to believe that crocodiles and hippos actually lived here.

A family picture: Gabs and Alice are in the front, Ron is flanked by his mother and father. I'm crouched at the back next to Ron's youngest sister Rita, her daughter Kookaburra stands behind.

Ron, me, Ruby and Alice.

Just after Ruby was born…

Ruby whispering Alice a secret.

Ruby with her great grandmother Madintwa, moments before breaking her bead necklace.

Ruby and Robin (Veronica and Roy's son). This is one of the last pics I took of him.

Ruby and Eliah.

Gabs washing Ruby in our yard

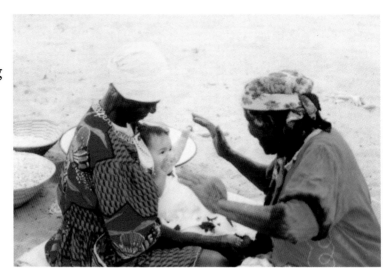

Ruby playing clapping games with Madintwa (right) and MaB (left).

Ruby at Eliah's new compound in Moeti.

Sheltered by reeds: Madintwa with Ruby at the farm.

Ron and
Ruby.

The three
of us.

Ruby, a
child of
Africa.

Ron laughed. 'She doesn't have a passport. When would my grandmother ever leave Botswana?'

'Jesus, it's hot.' I wiped my forehead and asked for some water. It was October. The floods had not made it far enough this year and most of the Thamalakane was dry. Maun was burning and yet another drought had been declared.

'You are going to hospital?' Madintwa said, spooning sugar into a cup of tea Gabs had just bought her.

'No, I'm just going to see a doctor, about my back.'

'*Ee*. You are going to hospital.'

I smiled. It was impossible to correct Madintwa once she had an idea in her head. 'It's just a check-up,' I said, 'just to find out what's wrong.'

'*Ee*,' said Madintwa. 'Eliah will come with you to Gaborone.'

'Oh, that's lovely, but I don't need her to, really. I'm just flying there and straight back.' I smiled at Madintwa to show her how simple the whole trip was going to be.

Madintwa shook her head sadly. 'Ah, we Batswana, we are horrible. See what we do to our children.'

I looked questioningly at Ron, feeling I'd missed something.

'She feels responsible,' he said, 'for your back problem . . . '

'Well, that's ridiculous. How is she responsible?'

'She feels you're her daughter now and

277

someone has injured your back.'

'Yeah, it was me, being an idiot and doing the gardening.' I laughed and winced at the same time. 'What?' I asked, seeing Ron's expression. 'You mean someone else did this to me?'

'That's what my grandmother says.'

'You mean someone bewitched me?'

'That is what my grandmother says.'

I looked down at the goosebumps on my arms. I had never really decided if I believed in witchcraft or not. But it was difficult not to believe in something everyone else believed in; I had seen people fall suddenly ill with no other explanation but witchcraft. Or perhaps there were plenty of other possible explanations and witchcraft was as good as any. Witchcraft was all to do with the power of suggestion, the power of the mind. To me, traditional doctors were a little like therapists. A client approached them to complain of various ailments that couldn't be explained or treated by a GP, the traditional doctor discussed the situation with the patient and perhaps offered treatment. It could mean herbal medicine, or it could mean helping the patient see the root of their illness, finding responsibility in a family member perhaps, or a neighbour. And so traditional doctors addressed the mind of their client, pointing to familiar faces in the client's life who could shoulder the blame or at least explain why things were the way they were.

Yet I had until now regarded the existence of witchcraft as an outsider, it was something that happened to other people. I had felt nervous at times, covering stories about witchcraft for the *OO*, but the nervousness hadn't lasted for long. Mostly bewitchment happened because of jealousy, someone saw someone else doing well and out of bitterness and jealousy they attempted to harm that person. I wondered if I were bewitched then who would have done it to me. And then I thought it was a ridiculous idea, I wasn't important enough to anyone that they would want to bewitch me. And bewitchment took away from my belief in responsibility; it could be too much of an easy answer. It wasn't because of poverty or government policies that you couldn't get proper medical care and were therefore seriously ill, it was because someone was jealous of you. It wasn't because of unprotected sex that you had HIV, it wasn't because of your own laziness that your business had failed, it was because someone didn't like you. A belief in bewitchment was almost like fate, and I didn't believe in fate. I had injured my back; no one was out to get me.

# 18

I returned to Maun strapped to a six-foot board, taking up most of the space in a four-seater Cessna. I had spent a night in intensive care and then two weeks in hospital after having a disc in my back removed. Now I was tied to a board with thick black belts, supposed to keep my body in place. As we hit turbulence a few hundred kilometres from Gaborone the board began to bounce and my nose grazed the ceiling of the plane. For six weeks I would not be allowed to sit, and for three months I needed to wear a white corset with metal bones tied tightly around my waist whenever I got up.

Back in Maun I spent the days lying in bed editing the paper and in the evenings, when it was cooler, I walked along the riverbank in my corset. Much of the time I was alone, with Alice at school, and Ron progressing from freelance computer work to setting up his own office. Pearl had had her baby, another girl, and she was at home, while Beauty who had had another son, was still down in Mochudi. I ate and I read and I convalesced and I told myself not to stress so much about my job. One day I received a letter requesting me to attend the citizenship selection board, but I sent Ron as I was still not allowed to sit. Another day Ron was informed that the family meeting to discuss Alice's adoption would be held that weekend and again I couldn't go.

He came back that Saturday evening with a smiling Alice.

'*Ko ko!*' she called politely at the door to our bedroom.

'Hey, Alice.' I hauled myself up on the bed. 'How did the meeting go?'

'It was fine,' she said shyly.

'And are you now Alice Ridge?' I asked.

'*Ee*,' she beamed. She had been writing Alice Ridge all over her schoolbooks for weeks, anticipating the adoption. Although Ron's mother and father had never married, Ron had always been given his father's surname and it was this surname that Alice wanted so badly.

'Shall we celebrate?' I asked. 'As soon as I'm up and about again we'll go out and celebrate, okay?'

'*Ee*. And perhaps I will need a new dress?'

'Perhaps you will.'

'Alice!' Ron called from outside. 'Help me unload the car!'

I lay on the bed waiting until they had finished.

'How's it going?' Ron put his head round the door.

'Fine. So Alice is adopted now? How did the meeting go?'

'Oh you know family meetings . . . ' Ron turned to go.

'Wait! Tell me about it. I don't get out much, tell me all the drama.'

But Ron seemed impatient to get on with supper.

'Okay, give me the highlights. How many cows

do we have to pay?'

'For Alice?'

'Of course for Alice!'

'Two, I think. Two each.'

'Two each?'

'Two for Alice and two for Gabs.'

'What?' I swung my body to one side and began strapping on the corset. 'What do you mean, two for Gabs?' But I knew immediately what he meant; he had adopted Alice and her sister as well. 'But I said no!' I cried. 'You asked me about adopting Gabs and I said no!'

Ron hesitated in the doorway, his body half-turned into the living-room. 'You didn't.'

'I did. I said it was mad.'

'But you said if my mother wanted it and Gabs wanted it then it was okay with you.'

'But I said *I* didn't want to adopt her.'

'You haven't,' Ron said, 'I have.'

I looked at him, unable to believe that he couldn't see the implication of what he'd just done. He'd just given me another child.

'But we're married, remember? If you have adopted two children then so have I. If you fell down dead tomorrow then I would be the legal guardian of both Alice and Gabs, right? Wouldn't I?' Now I was angry, Ron's family had gone ahead and done something I hadn't agreed to, which I hadn't wanted at all. 'What happened to the consultation you people are so proud of? Why did you bother asking me if you were then just going to go ahead and do what you wanted anyway?'

'Cait,' Ron said gently, coming properly into

the bedroom and closing the door behind him. 'I didn't realize. I thought you'd agreed.'

'But I didn't!'

Ron sat down on the bed and took my hand. 'You didn't say no.'

'I did, I did,' I insisted, but I was wracking my brain trying to remember. Perhaps I hadn't given an outright no, perhaps I should have been more explicit. 'So, you've gone ahead and done it,' I said bitterly, taking away my hand. 'Now I've got two kids have I? When's Gabs moving in then, are you going to build an extension?'

'She's not moving in,' Ron said patiently. 'Remember, you said if she lived with my mother then it was okay with you.'

'She's not moving in with us?' I relaxed slightly, fiddling with the corset.

'No.' Ron looked me in the eyes, searchingly. 'You said you didn't want that.'

'Too right I don't!' I snapped. Then I sighed. 'So, we've adopted her but she'll live with your mother?'

'As I have just said.'

'So, your mum's happy, Gabs is happy, you're happy?'

'I didn't think you'd be *un*happy . . . '

'Well I am. This is the first time you've done something without us both agreeing to it.' Ron looked crestfallen. 'If you don't watch it you're going to turn into a proper African patriarch,' I said, 'making decisions on your own and expecting to come back and find your food and wife waiting for you.'

'And what would you like for supper?' Ron asked.

'Oh, you know what I mean.'

'You're right. We should never do anything unless we have both agreed,' and Ron took the corset from my angry hands and began to do it up for me.

★ ★ ★

By early 1997 I was fully back at work with a lot of catching up to do. One morning I was sitting at my desk reading through a report about an Englishman going around Maun pretending to sell prawns imported from Mozambique. Cobrie was on the office computer typing in a football report, Enole was out on the porch drinking tea with an opposition member of parliament who'd come to prominence during the cattle lung saga. And Andrew was on the phone.

'It's Aaron,' Andrew called over to me, putting his hand over the receiver. 'Aaron from that Basarwa organization. He says the Bushmen are being moved out right now.'

For the past few months things had been quiet in terms of the feared forced removal of the Basarwa. No one had been moved from the Central Kalahari, let alone by cattle truck. Perhaps the international press coverage had forced the Botswana government to drop its plans. Perhaps there had never been plans for a forced removal in the first place, or perhaps the government was just biding its time.

'Let me speak to him,' I told Andrew, getting

up from my desk. 'Aaron? How are you? What's this about people moving out? Are people moving out?'

'Yes, people are being offered money to leave. One family has already moved out of Mothomelo. In Xade seven people have agreed to go. And a hundred people have signed up. People think they are being given big money, but this is not true. Most people, they don't want to move, but they are told that the army will shoot them if they don't go.'

On Monday I walked into the *OO* offices even earlier than usual. All the shops in the Old Mall were still closed; even the taxi rank was deserted. The only people on the street were a handful of school-children running, laughing, through a small puddle on the sand, for it had rained briefly in the night. Otherwise the mall was silent, even the goats huddled on the *OO*'s porch were quiet.

I went into the office, dropping my bag on the table, removing the dust cover from the computer, turning on the answering machine on Andrew's desk.

'Hi, it's Kerrin,' I heard a woman's voice. It was Andrew's wife. 'Andrew, you forgot to take the parcel. Can you call me when you get this?'

There was silence and then the next message began.

'Caitlin, I won't be in until approximately 2 p.m. as I have gone to meet a source at an undisclosed location.' It was Enole and I smiled as I moved over to my table, straightening a pile of *OO*s on the floor, bundled up and ready to go to Gumare. 'This is about the *so-called* forced removal of *Bushmen* written by this *Caitlin Davies* . . . ' came a man's voice and I stopped, suddenly, in the middle of the room. It was a stranger speaking and his voice was low and creepy. 'It is surprising really,' he continued, 'just why do *white* people come down from their countries and *mess up* other people's countries? Why can't she mess up her own country? I just find it a bit *sinister* if not subversive.' And the man rang off.

I walked a little nervously to Andrew's desk and played the message again. It was confusing, there was no introduction, the man didn't say who he was or why, really, he was ringing. But it was the fact that he used my name, that he was ringing to leave a message not for the paper, or for the editor, but for me, that I found unnerving. The message was sinister, the word the caller used himself, for it had an edge. How did he know I was white? Many people didn't even know I was a woman, most assumed because of my job I was a man. And very few could pronounce my name correctly. But the caller knew my name, he knew I was white and I was a woman and I was a foreigner. And to use the term subversive was worrying. Subversive suggested politically questionable, it suggested I had a hidden agenda. And subversives were dealt with accordingly, they were made prohibited immigrants.

I played the message for the third time, taking out my notebook and writing it down. I was still sitting and pondering the anonymous phone message when the others arrived at work.

'Listen to this,' I said to Cobrie, playing him the message.

Cobrie laughed, not because he thought it was funny but because he was nervous.

'Listen to this,' I said when the next freelancer came in.

The freelancer shook his head in disbelief.

'It is a government official,' said an elderly man at the doorway. I looked up to see a council health worker. 'The person on that message, it is a government official. No doubt about it.'

'Do you think so?' I asked worriedly. 'He doesn't say who he is.'

'No, that is the way they do it.'

Enole came in and threw some letters and a couple of Gaborone newspapers on the table.

'What do you think?' I asked, after playing the message again. 'Does it sound threatening to you?'

'*Ee*. It does.'

I picked up the letters Enole had put on the table and began opening them.

'Oh my God! I've just been awarded citizenship!' I showed the letter to Enole. I had been waiting years for this. I had recently renounced my British citizenship down at the embassy in Gaborone and since then I had been stateless, a citizen of nowhere at all. I held the letter, dancing around the room. 'I won't have to go to immigration any more! I'm legal!'

Cobrie and Enole shook my hand with great seriousness.

'You are a Motswana now,' said Enole and I

beamed. All thoughts of the phone call went out of my head. I was a Motswana now, an African citizen, and I could live and work as I liked. Legally, Botswana was my home.

★　★　★

That week the government-owned *Daily News* carried a half-page denial of the *OO* story about the Central Kalahari. It attacked me by name and said it was untrue to suggest that the government was coercing people to move by offering them cash. The denial coincided with a meeting with the *OO*'s owner Peter Sandenbergh, to whom Anne Sandenbergh had sold the paper the year before. We were up to our necks in debt for rent and printing costs, no one really had the time to manage the paper properly, and Andrew was calling it a day and leaving. Peter said we would have to close. I went back to the office, stricken, and spent the rest of the day tearing notices and front pages and photographs and cartoons and letters off the wall. If I hadn't been so depressed I would have been in tears. We were all given ten days' notice.

I spent the next few months hibernating. Getting up late, lying in bed, watching the rain. The house we were building was almost ready, the roof was on and we were waiting for the plasterers and plumbers to finish work. But until they had, we couldn't move in.

'I'm worried about you,' Ron said one morning. 'I don't usually see you like this.'

'I don't have a job,' I shrugged. 'I don't know

what to do with myself.'

'Make the most of it,' he urged. 'Get some rest. Relax. See your friends. Business is okay, you don't need to worry about money.'

'I know. But I was supposed to be the breadwinner, I wanted you to have the free time to do what you wanted.'

'You helped me set the company up, Cait. It's yours as well.'

'When will you be back tonight?' I asked.

'Usual time.'

'Which is?'

'Which is the usual time.'

I threw a pillow at him and he made for the door. I got up at last, no longer having to wear the corset any more. I wandered around our little house, poking my head into Alice's room, looking at a little pile of beauty products she had made on her bed; Vaseline, baby powder, hair straightener, face bleacher. I picked up the bleach, appalled at what she was putting on her skin, at the idea that she wanted to look whiter. It was a South African cream; it had no address, no list of ingredients, and what was in it was probably banned. I put it back on Alice's bed. I had been so wrapped up in the *OO* that now it seemed everyone had a secret life I didn't know about. Alice seemed happy enough, but alone in her room she was trying to change the colour of her skin. I assumed Gabs had settled down with Eliah, although Ron didn't mention her so really I didn't know. And Ron's business was so brisk that the other day I had gone into his office and seen a secretary I didn't even know he had.

I called the dogs and headed down to the river, walking for miles parallel with the dry riverbed. But then the dogs began harassing goats and I had to drag them home again. As I turned from the sand pathway and up to the house I almost fell over two young men sitting in the shade of an acacia tree right by the fence that ran around our plot.

'*Dumela Mma*,' said one of the men, politely.

'*Ee*,' I said noncommittally. I suspected they were about to ask for a job. These days people came round almost every week asking for work and sometimes they would sit for hours outside the house, waiting. Unemployment was new in Maun, but now so many people had moved here with the arrival of the tar road; then there was the financial crisis in Zimbabwe, and then the slaughter of all the cattle, so that there were more people than jobs. People could no longer rely on their relatives to give them work; they had to ask strangers as well.

'I love you,' the man said.

I stumbled a little, pulling on the dogs. Then the man leered at me and his friend laughed. 'I want to make love to you.'

I made a show of reining in the dogs as if the men were in danger of being mauled. Then I opened the gate in the fence and walked quickly into the yard. Twice recently we had had an attempted break-in, but both times we had arrived home and scared off the would-be intruders. The first time someone had tried to force the lock on the front door, the second time it was the lock on the back door. I wondered if the attempted break-ins were connected with the two men waiting by the fence.

When I reached the house and went inside, I locked the door from habit. I walked around, cleaning up the dishes, sweeping the floor, wanting to look out of the window to see if the men were still there but not wanting them to see me. At one point I peeked from between a curtain in the bedroom, they were still there and they remained there for a further hour, once waving in my direction although I couldn't be sure if they had actually seen me.

I'm getting paranoid, I told myself. I'm not going to cower in my house. I called the dogs and strode defiantly outside, to see that the men had gone.

'These two blokes really freaked me out today,' I told Ron when he came home.

'Really?' He looked worried.

'Yeah, they were sitting outside the yard. One said, 'I want to make love to you' . . . '

Ron looked shocked.

'Then they sat out there for ages. What are you looking for?' I asked as Ron bent down and began reaching under the bed.

'The gun.'

'You've got a *gun* under the bed?'

'I'm not going to be able to hunt buffalo without a gun.'

I stood back and watched while Ron slid a shotgun on to the floor. 'Anyway, why are you so late?'

Ron sighed. 'I had to take my grandmother to a funeral. Then on the way this imbecile crashed into me, so we had to go to the police. You know how long that takes.'

'Was everyone okay?'

'Yeah, fine, but the brake lights have gone. And when we got to the funeral, my grandmother expected me to wait for her and then drive her home again. Then she wanted to visit my uncle . . . '

'Rra Nama?'

'*Ee*. He's bedridden.'

'He is? I thought the traditional doctor had sorted everything out?'

'So did my grandmother.'

'So he's not even getting up any more?'

Ron shook his head.

I took a deep breath. 'It's AIDS, isn't it?'

Ron stared at the floor for a while, then he nodded.

'But no one is saying it's AIDS?'

'No. Someone's been coming round from the hospital to wash him and everything.'

'Will he go back to hospital?'

'No, they discharged him.'

'What about those new drugs, anti-retrovirals. Has he tried them?'

'How much are they?' Ron asked.

'I don't really know, perhaps a few thousand a month,' I said helplessly. 'I don't see how anyone could afford them, really.'

I watched Ron. I could see he was doing sums in his head, working out how to get money to treat his uncle. But I didn't even know if it were possible to get anti-retrovirals in Maun, whether the hospital or any of the private doctors had them, or even what exactly the drugs were and how they worked. Ron and I looked at each other in despair. I knew it had only been a matter of time before a family member or friend contracted HIV, but now that it had happened it was too late to help. People died quickly from AIDS in Botswana.

★   ★   ★

By the end of 1997 I was getting increasingly worried about what to do. I was also feeling isolated, without an office to go to every day. Enole was now studying in America, another freelancer, Tebogo, had gone to the UK, while a third, Thato, had gone to Australia. Cobrie was working at a garage and Andrew had a new job. Pearl was living on the other side of Maun, stranded without a car and with a new baby to look after. And Veronica was now in Francistown where she had just given birth to a boy, Linus.

'Guess what?' Ron said when he and Alice came home one December lunchtime.

'You're late?'

'Ha ha. I had to wait hours for Alice. I waited outside the school until every single child had come out, except for her. Anyway, guess what?'

'What?' I asked, expecting to be told a joke.

'CID were at my office this morning . . . '

'Why?'

Ron took an apple from off the top of the fridge. 'They said, 'Your wife should report to us at 1.45', and I said, 'No way' . . . '

'What do you mean *report* to them?' I walked into the kitchen.

'I told them it was too short notice and that I wasn't going to see you until this evening.'

'But what did they want?'

'Oh, something about an alarming publication.'

'But that was a *year* ago!'

At exactly 1.45 p.m. we headed to the police station, hurrying up the stairs to the CID offices. The corridor was empty; the office doors were open, revealing the usual empty rooms. Finally we found a man alone in an office at the end of the corridor. He looked like he was about to go on safari for he was wearing a khaki outfit with the name of a Maun safari company embroidered just above his chest. I wondered if he'd been working undercover, perhaps following up reports of illegal employees, or whether a safari company had given him the outfit as a present and he had decided to wear it to work.

'*Dumela*,' Ron and I said at the same time.

The man looked up. '*Dumela. Le kae?*'

'*Re teng*,' said Ron. 'She's been told to report to CID.' He looked and sounded perfectly relaxed. Ron was never intimidated by people in authority.

'Where is the charge sheet?' said the man, bored.

'They didn't give us one,' said Ron.

'Who called you here?'

'You people,' snapped Ron. 'They came to my office.'

'Which one?'

'I only have one office.'

'I mean, who called you here?'

'I don't know.'

'Was he big?'

'Not really.'

'Was he dark-skinned?'

'No.'

'Was he old?'

'A little.'

Then as they were still talking a man came in and stood in one corner.

'He's the one,' said Ron turning around. I looked as well; it was the head of CID, Gilbert Goitse. I couldn't believe he had personally gone to Ron's office to get me.

Gilbert Goitse gestured that we should follow him, so obediently we trailed behind him along the corridor and into a room that had been empty a few minutes ago. I sat down and Ron followed suit. Goitse said nothing. He was a sturdily built man in his forties and he looked a little big for the chair. I knew his face well. We had had a photo of him in the *Okavango Observer* a few months earlier after he had been nominated for a Good Samaritan Award. We had launched the award, sponsored by a local supermarket, to reward people spotted around Maun doing good deeds. Goitse had been nominated for putting out a fire with a bottle of milk. An excited reader had rung the *Okavango Observer*'s office to say he had been coming out of the bank in the Old Mall when he saw flames burst from the bonnet of his car. Luckily CID chief Gilbert Goitse, who had been hanging around outside the magistrates' court, walked over with the milk he was drinking and doused the fire.

'What's your interest in this?' Goitse said as another officer entered the room and tried to usher Ron out.

'I'm the husband,' said Ron flatly, refusing to budge.

Goitse sighed and pushed a file across his desk. Then he looked at me. 'You will be appearing for mention at 9 a.m. tomorrow morning. The charge is publishing a false report likely to cause fear and alarm to the public.'

'Tomorrow?' I squeaked. I was trying to get my notebook and pen out of my bag but it was so full of rubbish I was having trouble finding what I wanted.

Goitse paused. 'Tomorrow, December 10th, at nine o'clock.'

'But I don't have a lawyer.'

'You don't need a lawyer,' Goitse said sounding bored. 'You are just pleading.'

'You're saying I don't need a lawyer?' I tried to sound incredulous but I had just slipped my notebook under the table so Goitse couldn't see that I was having a hard time trying to write.

'If you intend to engage a lawyer it is up to you,' shrugged Goitse as if he couldn't care less. 'It's just guilty or not guilty. If it's not guilty you don't need a lawyer.'

I raised my eyebrows as far as they would go at Ron and he raised his back at me.

'The trial will be next year, next February,' said Goitse. 'Any questions?'

I tried to think of a question. I needed a question that would help explain the whole thing clearly, because right now it was totally bizarre. If I was to be in court tomorrow then how could I possibly prepare myself? How could I possibly appear without a lawyer? And if the government could really take me to court over an article that was almost two years old, an article that I personally had not written, and charge me with breaking a law I had not broken, then perhaps they could lock me up as well. I thought of the anonymous caller to the OO office and wondered if it were in any way related.

'Can I look in that docket there?' I said after a few minutes.

Goitse looked at the file protectively and even laid one hand across it. 'No, you can't look at the docket. It is a police docket.'

The man at the door began to usher us out.

# 19

The courtroom smelt, it was a tight, hot smell of sweat mingled with fear and anxiety. Ron and I had arrived on time, pushing our way through the crowd on the steps outside where people sought the shade of the court building, a strange grey structure which reminded me of a butterfly cake. Now we sat inside a small, dingy room where fifty people were crammed on four wooden benches, sitting thigh to thigh. It was 100 degrees pure Botswana sunshine outside and not much cooler inside. On the way in, a clerk had told me that the air-conditioning was working today, but I couldn't see any sign of it.

On a bench at the front of the room sat three lawyers, including Carl Anderson, a neighbour of ours, and a handful of uniformed police and plain-clothes officers. I was the only woman in the room. The men at the front appeared relaxed, as if they had all had a good night's sleep. One was leafing through a newspaper; another was doodling on some paper.

Ron and I sat there not talking, waiting. In front of us were two elderly men who had been brought from Gumare, charged with killing and eating an antelope. Suddenly a young woman entered through the door at the back of the courtroom wearing a very white shirt and a very dark-blue skirt. We all looked up. She held a pile of pale-blue paper files in her arms and I wondered if she were the magistrate. Then I recognized her; she was a volleyball enthusiast doing her one-year community national service as a court translator. We once profiled her in the newspaper beaming and clutching a volleyball.

The woman sat down next to the empty magistrates' table and we all continued to wait. I looked through the window to my right which was covered in strips of plastic blinds angled in such a way that I could look out but, I suddenly realized, no one could see in. That was why, I thought, all the people I could see outside were going about their daily business without wondering what was going on in here, the district's sole magistrates' court. I could see two women waiting to cross by Maun's first zebra crossing, painted on the road just last week.

'All rise!' a man's voice instructed from somewhere at the front of the courtroom and immediately everyone stood up. By the time we had all sat down again, the magistrate had appeared and was heading towards his table, identical to the one I had used as a teacher at the Tshwaragano school. I couldn't believe that the young man now taking a seat had the power to send me to jail for two years, that my fate and everyone else's was in his hands, for there was no jury system in Botswana as the population was said to be too small. I wondered if I went to jail which one it would be. There was Boro Farm Prison a few kilometres outside Maun in the bush, renowned for the sign on the sandy pathway that read: 'Home of the Vegetables'. And there was the main Maun jail next to the primary school in the centre of the village where I often passed prisoners watering their small plots of spinach and cabbage.

I still hadn't been given a charge sheet and I felt that I should be holding something to tell me why exactly I was here and what would happen next. Then I heard my name and I squeezed myself from the back of the room and walked towards the bench. In front of me I saw Lets Phaladi, the *OO* freelancer, also heading to the bench. I had not seen him for months; while the case against Andrew had apparently been dropped, because he had not been summoned to court, I had no idea that Lets had now been charged. I stood obediently by the bench, the backs of my bare legs resting against the solid wood for a second before we both sat down. Next to me Lets looked casual, he even had a pair of sunglasses on his face. I thought about hissing to him to take the glasses off. I remembered that a few years ago a new law had been suggested that would make it illegal for young people to wear sunglasses while addressing an elder.

I scanned the courtroom, looking at the faces to my right, trying to calm myself down. I could see Ron at the back, bending his neck from one side to the other, trying to get a good view. Then the volleyball enthusiast read something out and my stomach lurched, for I hadn't caught what she said. Carl Anderson stood up at the front bench. I had chatted to him the night before and he had said he would fill me in on court procedure in the morning. When I turned up at his office he had volunteered to help me out in court today, waving away my repeated assertions that I didn't have any money with which to hire a lawyer.

I watched while Carl stood up and said he was doing something or other in Latin and he would tell the court why I couldn't plead. Then he sat down.

The volleyball enthusiast began waving at me and I almost waved back until I realized she was telling us to stand. Lets and I got up, and he finally removed his sunglasses.

'Name, Caitlin Davies?' asked the translator in English, although I was the only person in the room whose first language was English. She wasn't looking at me, she was looking somewhere over my shoulder.

'Yes,' I said, as clearly as possible.

'Age thirty-one?'

'No.'

'Place of residence: Disanang?'

I hesitated, hadn't she just heard me say no?

'Place of residence: Disanang?'

'Yes.'

'Job: editor?'

'Yes.' I looked around, did anyone notice I had said no or shouldn't I make a fuss?

'Publishing a false statement likely to cause fear and alarm to the public, contrary to section 59 of the Penal Code. Do you understand?'

I was tempted to say no, I didn't. But instead I heard both Lets and I say yes.

'What do you plead?'

I was about to speak when Carl leapt up again.

'My client is very concerned that she has not been given adequate time,' he said smoothly, placing some papers on the table before him. 'I want this objection noted, and she wants a new date to be set.'

The magistrate had his pen midway from his book and he looked nonplussed. He raised his eyebrow at a CID officer who was about to get up.

'Accused number one will be going to the Media Institute of Southern Africa to get a lawyer,' continued Carl. 'This will not necessarily be myself. It might be a lawyer from South Africa and this will take time.'

I relaxed slightly. It sounded impressive, the idea of getting a lawyer from South Africa, as if they should know about these things down there. And it was particularly impressive because I was unemployed and as yet didn't know how I would get a lawyer at all.

The magistrate turned to his left and looked directly over my head for some time. I turned to see he was looking at a wall calendar.

'What date do you suggest?' he asked. I was about to speak when I realized he was addressing himself to Carl and the CID officer and I waited while the men decided on 16 February. Then the volleyball enthusiast made a shooing motion with her hands and Lets and I left. But just two steps from the bench I realized Carl was asking whether we were being released on our own recognizance until the mention date. Lets and I stopped in our tracks. Did this mean jail versus bail? I could see the magistrate busy writing

302

something. We waited.

'Yes,' mumbled the magistrate at last.

I walked back through the courtroom, quickly in case the magistrate changed his mind.

I spent the afternoon at Ron's office on the phone to a woman at Ditshwanelo, the Botswana Human Rights Centre, who advised me to get hold of the sworn statements the state's witnesses had made to the police. I would need to know who these witnesses were. However, she warned me against contacting any of them or I could be put in custody for interference.

I left Ron's office feeling miserable. It was boiling outside, and I put my umbrella up, both to give some shade and to cover my head so I could avoid looking at or talking to anyone else. I felt I was living in a parallel universe and while everyone else got on with their lives all I could think about was the trial. I walked back to the Old Mall and wandered into a clothing shop, aimless, not sure what to do with myself. I had been in the shop for a couple of minutes when my co-accused, Lets Phaladi, strolled in with a friend.

'Let's go outside,' I said, hurrying him into a little alleyway next to the shop. 'I just spoke to someone at Ditshwanelo. Lets, these people named in your story, do you know where they are now?'

'*Ee*,' said Lets totally unconcerned.

'Well, don't *whatever you do* contact them, because that would mean interfering with state witnesses or something, but I just need to know that they are still around.'

'Yes, they are still around,' said Lets.

'In Maun?'

'*Ee*. This one, he lives in Botshabelo ward . . .'

'Good, good . . .'

'And this other one, she is at the cattle post.'

'Okay,' I said straightening up. 'Well, I suppose we are going to need them at the trial, to know what they said to you about MaWestern, so that's good if you still know where they all are.'

'No problem, Cait,' said Lets cheerfully. 'Only most of them have now passed away.'

'You what?'

'*Ee*,' Lets said and he shook his head sadly.

'You mean they're dead?'

'*Ee*.'

'But you just said . . . Well, that's great, that's just great.'

'Listen, Cait,' said Lets. 'I will ask the state to drop its charges against you because I am the one who wrote the story . . .'

'It's too late!' I yelled. 'I'm the editor, I'm responsible for what you wrote.'

'Relax, Cait,' said Lets. 'Don't worry,' he said, and he and his friend walked off.

'Don't worry?' I yelled after him. 'I'm about to stand trial for a story I didn't write, most of my potential witnesses are *dead* and I shouldn't worry?'

★ ★ ★

The next day I spent the morning in the post office. Normally I liked the post office, for the queues moved slowly and it was a good place to chat and hear news. But today it was busy and I was distracted and impatient. Pensioners sat on the hot concrete floor waiting to be called forward, forming groups that everyone else stepped over. The queues were even more haphazard than usual and it was an hour before I reached the counter. In my hand I had a letter to my parents in England, explaining the upcoming trial.

'Three one-pula stamps, please,' I asked the counter woman. I hadn't greeted her; I was in too much of a rush.

'There are none,' said the woman flatly.

'How do you mean there are none?' I snapped.

The woman looked at me and rolled her eyes as if indicating to the other people waiting that I was a difficult customer.

'How do you mean, no stamps?' I repeated. I wasn't usually a complainer, I hated the way expatriates always complained, but I had waited over an hour just to get some stamps.

The woman sighed. 'We have no one-pula stamps.'

'Well, does anyone else have any?' I asked, gesturing along the line of counter staff.

'No,' said the woman immediately.

'Do you have fifty thebe stamps?' I asked.

'Nnyaa.' She shook her head.

'Well, what about twenty-five thebe?'

Again she shook her head.

'Okay, ten thebe?'

'Yes, I have ten thebe.'

'Okay, then why don't you give me ten times

ten thebe stamps?' I asked.

'Nnyaa,' said the woman. 'They will not fit on your envelope.'

I looked down at the letter in my hand. It was true.

'So, when will you be getting more stamps?' I asked.

'Soon,' the woman said easily.

Inside my head a voice was shouting, aren't you a post office? How can you not have any stamps? Couldn't you put a sign up saying this? I've spent two hours in here! All I want is some stamps! What's wrong with this effing country?

★ ★ ★

On Christmas Eve we were at last ready to move into our new home. The walls had finally been plastered and painted, the floor tiles laid, the power connected. It had taken so long to build the house that I had been beginning to think it would never happen. But now we packed up the Land Rover, tied the dogs in the back, and were ready to move.

We drove through Maun and turned off right over the new Matlapana Bridge, a two-lane bridge built parallel to the old bridge which was now a protected monument and closed to traffic. We passed the Hippo Pool which still had water, but the level had fallen dramatically and would fall even further unless it rained soon. I had seen people fetching water from the pool last week, young girls dipping in plastic containers, their hands only metres from the two crocodiles and

306

one hippo which had taken up residence in the water.

From the pool we turned left again, immediately entering the bush, trees on one side and the flood plain on the other. The pathway turned a corner then, so that we arrived suddenly at our yard, its short, wire-mesh fence not visible until you were right up close. Ron leapt out and opened the gate and then with a roar we drove in. I got out and stood on the sand, breathing in the smell of rain clouds. It was windy now and I could hear the branches of the leadwood tree scraping on the tiled roof of the house. Above me the sky was dark. When the wind stopped there was silence. There were no lights, no signs of other humans, just an empty house on a wild peninsula at night.

I walked towards our new home, my arms laden with boxes and bags. Some of the bags had never been properly unpacked since I'd arrived in Botswana seven yeas ago. We had moved so many times that I had never really emptied out everything. I still had the orientation notes I'd been given at Farnham, my name-tag and a complimentary packet of unopened syringes. I still had lesson plans for classes I'd taught at Tshwaragano, old copies of the *Voice*, and a hard lump of crystallized salt from Sowa Pan.

I came round the house on the side facing the river, along a pathway that led on to a wide concrete porch, big enough to sit and eat on, to play on, to lie and watch the river or the sun set. This door was the back door for it couldn't be seen from the gate, but I knew at once it would become our front door. It led straight into a long rectangular room, on the right of which was the kitchen, which led via an archway into a cool pantry area and storeroom.

The large chunky tiles on the floor were of a reddish-brown colour and they gleamed in their newness and smoothness so that at once I had to take off my shoes and walk barefoot on them. We had painted the walls yellow and, with red blinds on all the windows, I could imagine the light in the house when the sun rose the next day. Even now, in the dark, it was airy and spacious. As we spoke to each other our voices seemed huge, patterns of sound echoing off the ceiling.

'It's yours!' I told Alice, taking her by the hand and leading her to where her bedroom was. 'This is your room. You can do anything in it! It's yours. You can draw on the walls, whatever you want!'

Alice inspected the room seriously and then carefully laid her possessions on the bed.

I hurried off back through the living-room, to our bedroom and, opposite, the bathroom. In the bedroom the walls were also yellow and here there were two windows, one facing the yard and main gate, the other giving a view over the Thamalakane River. On the ceiling hung a fan, with long wooden hands that made me think I was in an old, hot country airport waiting for a flight somewhere, for a journey to begin.

'I can't believe it,' I told Ron, sitting down on the bed. 'I can't believe we finally have a house. No more rent! No more keeping other people's places clean!'

Ron leaned in the doorway, beaming. He had taken time off work so we could settle down in our new home, his hair was uncombed and already a light beard had grown on his chin. He wore his old T-shirt from Clark University, the sleeves torn, the picture on the front so faded that it was impossible to see what it had once been.

I went back outside, I couldn't keep still. The dogs were lined up on the sand, their noses twitching feverishly.

'They can smell the hippo,' Ron said, coming on to the porch.

I watched the dogs; their whole bodies were taken up with the smelling.

'What was that?' I hissed.

'That is the hippo,' said Ron.

I stopped, stiffening, listening. Down on the riverbank I could just make out a shape, a huge dark bulk, silent except for a vague munching noise. The munching noise came nearer, the dogs began to bark, and I stepped back quickly on the porch. Ron came out with a torch and shone it around. For a second I saw the hippo, just by the fence. Then Ron switched the torch off and the night was dark and silent again.

# 20

The Thamalakane River was dying. Despite the rains over Christmas and the beginning of the new year, the level of the river had barely risen at all. The only part that was still deep with water was the Hippo Pool which was now home to three hippos. I sat on a large stone in the middle of the bridge, looking down at the water below. I had just returned from Gaborone where I'd met a lawyer who would represent me at my trial. My case had been taken up by the Media Institute of Southern Africa, and now at least I had proper legal defence.

A herd of goats were stumbling down the riverbank, rushing for a drink. At the edge of the water a young girl was filling huge plastic containers which an elderly man then piled on the back of a donkey cart. I knocked a pebble down into the water and watched it plop against the surface. I was waiting to see a hippo appear. I could already see the crocodiles, the dark jagged lines of their bodies like strips of corrugated iron on the sandbank, basking in the sun.

Suddenly I saw a ripple on the surface to my right. The ripples grew bigger, enlarging and multiplying and, in the centre of the movement, I could just see two tiny ears. And then, although I was waiting for its appearance, the violence of the hippo's head bursting up through the river threw me backwards in surprise. The hippo looked around, then it silently opened its mouth, displaying a pink inside and great tusks of teeth. It looked like a yawn but I knew it was a sign of aggression, a marking out of territory, a warning away to intruders.

★　★　★

The day of my mention, 16 February 1998, dawned at last. As I got up at 5 a.m., having slept badly, I found myself wondering what to wear. I didn't usually give it much thought but today I did. In the end I chose a black dress with little white flowers. I looked as if I was going to a funeral. At 6 a.m. it was still dark outside but within half an hour it had developed into a cool, brisk morning with the promise of rain in the air.

We drove to Maun and stopped first at Ron's grandmother's where we sat and drank tea and listened to the news on the radio. This was what Ron always did in the morning, checked on his grandmother and Gabs to see what they needed for the day, and caught up with his mother in between her trips into the bush. As the news finished Madintwa began to struggle up from where she sat near the fire.

'Where are you going?' Ron asked.

'I am coming with you,' Madintwa said, wobbling as she stood.

'There's no time,' I hissed to Ron. 'There's only half an hour before we have to be at court. I don't think she should come, what's it going to do to her blood pressure?'

At last I persuaded Madintwa that she should stay and we set off for court. But when I opened the door to courtroom number one I held back in dismay; this was nothing like the courtroom where I'd appeared for mention in December. This was the sort of courtroom I had seen in films; a shiny floor and a high ceiling, a central walkway lined with benches on both sides packed with people, the magistrate up at the front, a real wooden dock on the left with space enough to hold three people.

I squeezed on to one of the benches and no sooner had I sat down than a woman at the front stood up holding a file and declared: 'The State versus Caitlin Davies.' I walked along the shiny floor, my flip-flops making a pattering noise. Then I stepped up to the dock and stood there, waiting. The prosecutor was saying something to the magistrate, and I saw now that it was not the young man I had appeared before last year, but the chief Maun magistrate. I turned to my right to look at Ron who was doing a 'what's going on?' expression with his eyebrows. I was worried, it was only a few months ago that we had written about this magistrate in the *OO*.

One morning, a local lawyer had come hurrying into the *OO* offices to whisper a story about witchcraft in court. He said the court staff had come to work to find a white, powdery substance sprinkled all round the walls of courtroom number one and in the chambers of the chief magistrate. Intimidation of magistrates wasn't new and it sounded as if someone was dropping a not so subtle hint of what might happen if they were to be convicted. But it turned out that the magistrate himself had sprinkled the powder because, the night before while working late, an owl had appeared at his window. The magistrate took this as a bad sign, ordered the owl to be killed, and then, for extra protection, had sprinkled his chambers and the courtroom with powder.

'Does accused number one want to say anything?' the magistrate asked. I looked across at him, he had said it like a statement not a question and he wasn't looking at me but writing in a book on his table. With a stab of horror I realized that the magistrate was himself going to write down everything that happened in court. I scanned the room, there was no one else taking notes. No court secretary, nothing. Then I saw that everyone was waiting for something, and I realized that I was accused number one.

'Sorry?' I said in a wobbly voice.

'Does accused number one have anything to say?' asked the magistrate again, glancing at me quickly before writing again. He was older than me, short and tired-looking.

'Yes, your honour, your worship,' I stumbled, not knowing how to address him. I spoke loudly because it seemed the only way to drown out the beating of my heart. 'I do have a lawyer, he was going to communicate with you . . . ?' I bit my lip. The lawyer I had met with in Gaborone had assured me he had written to the Maun court outlining the reason why he wouldn't be making an appearance today.

The magistrate continued writing. 'Anything else to say?' he asked, his pen poised in mid-air.

I shook my head, looking for Ron in the courtroom crowd and suddenly realizing that he had chosen to wear a black-and-white spotted waistcoat that my mother had bought him from Marks and Sparks in London. He looked as if he was attending a circus.

\* \* \*

Two weeks later I turned up for my third court appearance with a new lawyer, Dingaan Gumede, a smart young man with a neatly trimmed moustache, his shirt sleeves and collar so crisp they looked as if they were held in place by cardboard. But when we got to court the state prosecutor was absent and the mention was postponed. A week later I was back in court, and again the prosecutor was absent. When I arrived for my fifth court appearance the trial was finally set for May.

\* \* \*

Every morning I started the day with a visit to the Hippo Pool. It was my favourite time of year, the time when summer was melting away and the mornings were finally becoming cool. The pool had a surreal quality about it in the early morning light, with no sound but for the giant lehututu birds which marched along the riverbank. The large black birds had red heads like turkeys and long sharp beaks and they were as tall as a child. As they strutted around they made a sound like someone blowing down the mouth of a big glass bottle.

I walked along the bridge, unhurried, enjoying the tranquillity. But while the place and the morning were beautiful, I saw that the pool was beginning to have a look and a smell of decay. The level of the water had shrunk significantly in recent weeks and now there was a brackish quality about it.

I scanned the surface, looking for ears. Within minutes I had counted four hippos; the pool was getting crowded. On the bank opposite lay another two, their bodies like smooth grey stones, their pink jowls squashed on the sand. Six hippos were too many, and perhaps others would join them as well. And then, from the water just below me, I saw something else emerging from the pool, a small wet body shaped like a comma. The creature dragged out a pink bottom, so pink it looked bloody, and then finally its head. At first I had thought it was a pig; now I saw it was a baby hippo. The moment it emerged fully from the water, an adult hippo got out and followed. I watched as the two of them began to root around the bushes on the bank, the baby's body wobbling slightly as it moved. 'It's ever so sweet, isn't it?' A white woman walking her dogs stopped on the bridge beside me. 'I don't think I've seen a baby hippo before.'

'Nor me,' I agreed.

As we stood on the bridge a huge green Department of Wildlife truck drove up, moving slowly along the riverbank to take up position where the slope was least steep. The hippos were going to be relocated. The pool would be ringed with shade cloth to restrict the animals' movement and eventually hunger would drive them into the open back of the truck where hay laced with molasses was waiting for them.

★　★　★

A week later and the Hippo Pool was deserted. The sign at the entrance of the bridge, warning people to stay away during the relocation exercise, was gone. All that remained were the marks on the sand where the truck had stood. The pool felt empty now and, in the heat of the day, the air was hot and silent. I walked on to the bridge, looking around. The hippos were gone, but I could see the crocodiles still there, lying on the riverbank right next to the water, slapping their tails. I was about to leave when I saw ripples on the surface of the pool. The water broke and a baby hippo popped its pink head into the air. I waited for hours, watching to see whether the mother hippo was in the pool as well. But the Department of Wildlife had taken the adults and left the baby behind. Feeling unusually sad, I left the Hippo Pool and set off for Maun. Although the trial had been set for May, I was due back in court for another mention. But I was the only one.

'Can't you just ask that the case be dismissed?' I hissed at Dingaan. 'The prosecutor isn't here, Lets isn't here, his lawyer isn't here . . .'

Dingaan smiled sympathetically and adjusted his cuff links.

★ ★ ★

When I visited the Hippo Pool two days later the bridge was busy with people. They were all looking in one direction, across the pool and to the opposite bank. There I could see the baby hippo, and, right next to it, its mother. They were munching patches of grass, seemingly oblivious to all the humans standing and watching nearby. I stood there silently. The mother hippo must have walked for days, propelled by the desire to return to her child and in my mind her journey began to seem epic. I went home hugging myself, pleased with the happy ending.

★ ★ ★

The day of my trial finally dawned. I walked through Maun, a cardigan wrapped around me it was so cold. The village was quiet today and I passed just a handful of people going to work, walking slowly, skirting donkeys and chickens on the road. In my bag I had faxes of support from friends in England. I patted it protectively as I reached court.

'Aren't you wearing a black suit?' asked Dingaan as he came walking down the courthouse steps.

'Why, should I be?' I asked anxiously.

'No,' Dingaan laughed. 'I have been told court will begin at 9 a.m. prompt. And I have some

317

interesting news for you today, a message from the attorney general.' I took the fax he handed me and scanned down it, trying to make sense of what it said.

'Sit!' instructed the magistrate as we walked in to the courtroom. Lets and I promptly sat down on the wooden bench, my heart fluttering in excitement. Dingaan handed over the fax from the attorney general and the magistrate read it, his expression puzzled. At last he looked at a CID officer for explanation. 'Is this an acquittal or a dismissal?'

'What?' asked the CID man.

'Is this an acquittal or a dismissal?'

'It is a dismissal,' Dingaan said.

I suppressed an urge to jump up and shout. The attorney general had decided it was not worth proceeding with the case. It had been dropped due to insufficient police evidence.

'You may go.' The magistrate waved at Lets and me.

I stood up, expecting more, expecting an explanation, an apology. But the court translator was already calling the next accused to come forward.

When I got outside I looked at the fax again. I saw it had been written on 8 May but had not been faxed until 22 May. For the last three weeks the case had been dropped and I had not known this, I had thought I was still on trial. As people began to congratulate me I started to feel cheated. Why hadn't the attorney general read my docket three years back and realized there was not enough evidence with which to prosecute? For six months I had dreaded my trial, but now I wanted it. I wanted to know what the police had against me, to see and hear their witnesses, to be asked and to respond to questions. And I wanted to be found totally innocent.

I left Ron's office and passed by a photographic shop where his dad now worked to give him the news. Ron's dad thought it over for a while and then he put his hands on the counter top and shrugged.

'Don't worry,' he said, 'they'll find some other way to get you.'

'You think so?'

'Well,' said Ron's dad, 'it depends on whom you have offended.'

I got a combi home, flagging one down at the Old Mall. When I'd first arrived in Botswana there had been no combis in Maun, the only transport apart from private vehicles were the long-distance buses. But now the small white combi vans were everywhere, with sliding doors and bucket seats inside. There were no such things as combi stops, passengers just yelled at the driver when they wanted to get off. The drivers were all young men, while adolescent boys acted as conductors, swinging themselves in and out of the vehicle, wearing cheap sunglasses, putting the coins into fake-leather hip bags. Most of the drivers drove like maniacs, swerving to avoid livestock and people, racing with each other, often blowing tyres on the tar roads that had begun to crack in the heat. They put up posters of naked white women on the back screens of their vehicles. They cussed and swore at other motorists. A week ago I had almost been knocked off the road by a combi driver. When I had held my hands up, palms up in a display of frustration, the driver drove back up close to me and leaned out of his window.

'Fuck your arse!' he shouted, laughed and drove off. I was left standing open-mouthed on the sand by the side of the road. No one had sworn at me like this in years.

I sat squashed against the combi window as we hurtled along the tar road. I looked out anxiously; ready to push myself to the front, to yell that this was where I wanted to stop. I wanted to get home, to get away from Maun and the magistrates' court as quickly as possible. I was no longer on trial, I was supposed to just get on with my life. But now I would have the feeling that someone was watching over my shoulder, watching what I wrote. I knew that whatever was said about democracy, about freedom of speech and open debate, criticism wasn't something that was encouraged in Botswana. But because Batswana were polite, and spent so much time agreeing with you, you didn't necessarily know when you had displeased someone or why, until the day the police came for you. And if they could come for me once, then, I thought, they could come again.

* * *

The next morning, I woke to find Alice up early, sitting outside our bedroom window washing.

She wore her mustard-yellow school tunic and she was bent over a tin tub. I could see she was happy for her tongue was sticking out of her mouth, the way it did when she was concentrating on something she enjoyed.

I went outside with my coffee and sat beside her. 'You're up early.'

'*Ee*. I am washing.'

'You think you're going to get that clean and dried before school?'

Alice began to sing a church song, her voice sweet and high. Then she stopped and picked the school shirt from the tub, rubbed at it, and placed it back in the water.

'What do you want to do when you leave school?' I asked. It had been a long time since I'd had a conversation with Alice that didn't centre on my trial.

Alice looked up, sucking on her tongue. 'Work.'

'You want to work?'

'*Ee*.'

'Where would you like to work?'

Alice's head flopped back over the tub and she began rubbing at the shirt again. 'Anywhere,' she said at last.

'Doing what?'

Alice stared at me until, exasperated, I stood up and threw away the dregs from my coffee cup.

As we left home that morning, we drove past the Hippo Pool.

'Let's stop,' I told Ron. 'Alice, you have to see this baby hippo, it's really sweet.'

Ron mumbled that he had to be at work, but I

had already opened the car door. Alice followed me on to the bridge, eager for anything that would delay her going to school. She didn't like school any more; she was totally uninterested in any of the lessons, the only thing she put any effort into was keeping her uniform clean. Two days ago Ron had been called to the school to be shown exercise books that Alice had quite literally torn apart.

I turned to watch Alice following me. She was dragging her feet on the sand, feigning disinterest in the baby hippo. But then she stood on the bridge and looked around. 'Where is it?' she asked.

'I don't know, I'm looking. There's the mother. She's the one that walked back from the Delta to get her baby.' I pointed to the adult hippo, its ears and forehead just out of the water.

Then Alice started to smile and point as well. I looked over to the riverbank where two men were squatting on the white sand. I saw a glint of metal as one of the men took out a large, long knife. He leant over and thrust the knife forward, cutting away methodically while his companion looked on. As the man with the knife paused and leant backwards for a moment, I saw what Alice had already seen, the dead baby hippo. 'Oh, no.' I let out a wail.

Alice looked at me oddly as I moved further down the bridge. I never normally worried about animals, but I felt involved in the fate of this one. I kept walking until I was opposite the men on the riverbank. The one with the knife looked up. I felt nervous suddenly, wondering if the men had killed the hippo and, if they had, whether they wanted anyone to see them cutting it up. But the man waved his knife and smiled. He greeted Alice and me and then returned to his work.

'How did it die?' I called down.

The man shrugged. 'Perhaps it was run over by a car.'

'Aren't you worried about the mother?' I asked.

The men laughed.

I walked back along the bridge towards Ron waiting in the car. He had a matchstick in his mouth and was totting up sums on a scrap of paper which he had pressed up against the steering wheel. I reached the car just as the mother hippo let out a thick wet chuckle that made my flesh crawl.

# 21

Alice and Gabs sat on the sofa in the living-room surrounded by wrapping paper and just-opened presents. I sat next to them, perched on the sofa's wooden arm. Ron's mother had given us the sofa, when she had bought a new one on hire purchase from one of Maun's many furniture stores. The sofas were so expensive that I had heard of two people who had committed suicide when they couldn't meet their monthly payments and their lounge suites had been repossessed.

It was Alice's fourteenth birthday. Gabs's birthday had been a few months ago, and we were having a joint birthday party for them. I worried, ever since we had formally adopted Gabs, that although she didn't live with us and was not our child in the way Alice was, that she was somehow losing out. If I bought Alice a new dress or schoolbag, then I made sure I bought a new dress and schoolbag for Gabs as well. I didn't want there to be any jealousy between them.

And yet, although I wanted them treated equally, I had begun to resent the time Ron spent helping Gabs. The idea had been that Gabs live with Eliah, but Eliah was rarely in Maun and so now Gabs was to look after Madintwa. But in practice Ron looked after both of them. In the morning, before work, he checked on his grandmother and Gabs at Moeti. Often he went there at lunchtime, too, for it was close to his office and meant he could quickly return to work. On the weekends he drove Gabs to her new school and helped her water her agricultural plot. After work he shopped for Gabs and Madintwa, perhaps taking his grandmother to a doctor's appointment or to visit relatives, Gabs to the dentist or to her mother's. Gabs was doing well at school and Ron helped her with her homework, the way he had helped Alice when we lived in Sowa, spending hours explaining maths problems or measuring out wood for her carpentry lessons. Ron returned home most days when it was dark, exhausted from both running a business and looking after his grandmother. He no longer cooked at home, he no longer cleaned. He barely had time to inspect the garden.

★  ★  ★

Alice and Gabs tried on the ear-rings I had given them. 'You can wear them at school,' I told Alice. 'They're so small, I don't think they'd mind.'

Alice scowled at the mention of school. She was failing every subject but for English. In the evenings she lay on her bed pretending to read her schoolbooks, but really she was inspecting her face in a slice of mirror which she kept hidden between the pages of her book.

'Thank you,' said Gabs, wrapping up her ear-rings carefully in pink tissue paper.

I smiled, trying to look cheery. It was their

birthday party; I wanted them to have a good time. But there was something I took to be slyness about Gabs, something about the way she spoke out of the side of her mouth while walking past me, that created a distance between us.

'Jesus!' I said. 'It's half past two. Where is everyone?'

Alice turned her head and looked out of the window in the direction of the gate. Above her the large living-room window was covered in burglar bars. The bars had become common in Maun with the increase in house break-ins and now every new concrete house, however small, had a row of black iron bars in the windows. But the bars in our windows were fashioned into flamingos and other, imaginary, birds and in the corners was a setting sun, the burglar bars reaching out like sunrays towards the ceiling. At first I hadn't wanted burglar bars, it worried me that if there was a fire, and if we couldn't get to the doors, then we wouldn't be able to get out of the house. And I didn't want to live as if I were in a prison. But now that the bars were in place they were subtle enough that I hardly even noticed they were there.

I got off the sofa and went to stand by the window. It was my favourite place to stand for it looked down on to the flood plain and the dry riverbed. In the mornings I watched herds of goats scattering across the grass followed by thin herding dogs. Then a group of women arrived, crossing the riverbed and heading for the big houses on the opposite bank where they worked as maids and nannies. At the same time lone men who worked as nightwatchmen crossed the riverbed in the other direction, passing our house as they headed home after a night spent freezing in a sentry-box or out in the open by a fire. And it was here, when the river was high, that I watched guides from nearby safari lodges poling tourists along the water, the clients dreamily trailing their hands on the river, touching water lilies, making ripples.

'It's two thirty,' I said again. 'Where do you think everyone is?' Ron had gone to pick up family members: his grandmother, Alice's two younger sisters, at least one cousin, possibly more. I knew Ron's sister Rita would come, but Veronica was in Sowa now, with a new baby I hadn't even seen. Pearl would come too, and Beauty, but they were always late. I expected Ron to be late too, for he had also gone to the farm. Now that the paperwork and title deed had been arranged, he was finally free to set to work. He wanted the whole farm cleared and fenced before the rains fell. Then he would hire a tractor and his mother and he would plant. I had been only once to the farm, and to me it was a nondescript place, a huge overgrown plot of bush. I couldn't see how one person could possibly tame and transform it.

'Who did you invite?' I asked Alice. 'From your school?'

Alice shrugged and crumpled some wrapping paper in her hand.

'Kgomotso?' I asked. 'Kgomotso and Dineo, yes? You invited them. And Mpho? Any boys?'

327

Alice sucked her teeth.

'Gabs, who did you invite?' I asked but Gabs just gave a mysterious smile.

'So apart, from Kgomotso, Dineo and Mpho,' I turned back to Alice, 'who did you invite?'

'I didn't,' said Alice.

'You didn't what?'

'I didn't invite.'

'What do you mean? You didn't invite *anyone* from your school?'

'*Ee.*'

'You didn't invite anyone at all?'

'*Ee.* I didn't invite anyone at all.'

'But what about all of this ... ?' I asked, gesturing to the kitchen, to the piles of food, to the bowls of potato salad and coleslaw we had made, to the meat marinating in the sink, to the bottles of fizzy orange Fanta. 'I asked you how many people you were going to invite and you said ten, Alice. You and Gabs were inviting ten each, remember?'

Alice smiled. I couldn't be sure if she were embarrassed or pleased. These days she often seemed to be pleased when I was angry.

★ ★ ★

A few months after the party Ron came home one evening and dropped a pile of faxes and letters for me on the kitchen table. I was cooking and didn't pay the pile much attention, mainly because I wasn't expecting any cheques.

'Just a little for me,' Ron called out from where he sat on the sofa in the living-room. He

328

had a laptop on the table in front of him and he was staring at the screen in concentration, his finger drawing circles on his chin.

'What?' I stopped where I was, the spoon in my hand.

'Just a little for me,' Ron said mildly, looking up for a second and then returning to the screen.

'What d'you mean, just a little?'

'Alice and I have eaten.'

'Where?'

Ron sighed. 'At Moeti.'

'Well, couldn't you have told me?'

'How?'

'I don't know. Maybe you're going to have to get one of those cellphone things.'

'I'm going to,' Ron nodded. 'I've got a brochure. Nokia have this really expensive one.'

I snorted. I had only been joking. 'But you knew I was cooking. Couldn't you have waited to eat until you came home?'

Ron frowned at the screen.

'If I'd known Alice and you weren't eating then I wouldn't have made this. I would have made something else. But perhaps you've forgotten what it's even like to cook, now you can run to Moeti and get the fold-out tray and the hands on the knees and the whole treatment from Gabs.'

'Here we go,' muttered Ron.

'Here we go what? Ron! You don't do a thing around here.'

'When am I going to cook?' Ron stood up and flapped his hands impatiently. Then he opened the front door and stood on the step looking out.

I turned round and saw the door to Alice's room was open a crack and I could just see the edge of her shoulders as she stood behind it, listening.

'And you're always doing this,' I said to Ron's back.

'Doing what?'

'Eating at Moeti.'

'Is that a problem?'

'Yes, it is a problem. We're supposed to be a family. We used to eat together. We used to sit together and talk, and eat, and everything.'

'I only started eating there because of you.'

'Really?'

'*Ee*. You're always saying you're fed up with cooking, so if I eat at Moeti you won't have to cook for me.'

'I'm not *always* saying that. And, anyway, that doesn't solve the problem. The problem is you used to take your share of the cooking and now you don't. Going to eat food someone else has made doesn't mean you're taking any more responsibility, does it?'

'I don't do it to upset you,' Ron said, and he walked off the back step. A few months ago I wouldn't have complained, but now I was working again, too, freelancing for *Mmegi* in Gaborone. And perhaps it wasn't so much that Ron didn't cook any more, it was that that part of his life didn't exist any more. He was no longer a student with time enough to make tuna melt, time enough to sit down and eat from the same plate. I resented him helping so many other people, but then I felt guilty, for who else could help them?

That night as we sat out on the porch, Alice and Ron determinedly eating the food I had made, I felt depressed. I always seemed to be on at Ron about something. I brought the mail outside to the porch and flicked through it, guessing what was what but not really looking at anything carefully. I saw one of the faxes had the Republic of Botswana crest on the top and I assumed it was an answer to one of the many questionnaires I was always sending off to government departments. Then I saw it was from the High Court in Lobatse. In scribbled handwriting it said at the bottom of the first page: 'Attached hereto please find a summons served to you by fax in the above matter.'

'What the hell is this?' I asked out loud, unrolling the rest of the fax and reading it. 'You're commanded to appear before Justice I. P. Aboagye on Friday 11th day of December 1998 at 9.30 a.m. to show cause why you should not be held in contempt of court . . . Ron!' I yelled. He was in the kitchen doing the washing-up, his face glum. 'Ron!'

He came outside, hands dripping, looking around as if expecting to see a snake on the porch or a hippo strolling by past the fence.

'What?'

'It's a bloody summons! This thing, here, this fax, it's a summons.'

'A summons for what?'

'Oh these people!' I spat, furious. 'If they think I'm going to fall apart this time they're mad.' I went inside, crumpled up the fax and threw it on the table. Ron picked it up.

331

'What story are they referring to?' he asked, smoothing out the fax.

'That murder one. The one where they're pleading battered women's syndrome.'

The article had been published in *Mmegi* the week before. A woman called Sephonono Harvey stood accused of murdering her husband and lawyers from Metlhaetsile Women's Information Centre in Mochudi were to argue before the Lobatse High Court that Harvey was a victim of battered women's syndrome and therefore shouldn't be held criminally responsible for her acts. Battered women's syndrome was not recognized by any judiciary in southern Africa, and it had never even been argued in a Botswana court before. It seemed unlikely such a defence would go down well. The majority of police officers, lawyers and judges in Botswana regarded cases involving women battered by their partners as a joke. They were domestic affairs, and under customary law, men were legally allowed to 'chastise' their wives. The Harvey case would make legal history, whether or not the defence was accepted. If it was not accepted then it was quite possible that Harvey would hang. I sat watching Ron as he uncrumpled the summons and read it. 'I don't get it,' he sighed.

'Nor do I,' I agreed. 'I only wrote about battered woman's syndrome as a defence. And look at this, they fax this summons last thing on a Wednesday afternoon, to *your* office, and expect me to get down to Lobatse first thing Friday morning. That's a thousand kilometres away!' I stood up, feeling anxious. Perhaps the summons was proof that Ron's dad was right, that I had offended someone in power who had found a new way to intimidate me. The MaWestern case had been thrown out of court, now they were trying something else. Someone was out to get me and they knew how to find me, they knew who I was married to, they knew where my husband worked, they even knew his fax number.

I was about to go to bed when I decided to ring the *Mmegi* editor, Sechele Sechele. I found him still in the office.

'Have you been summoned?' I asked.

'Summoned?' Sechele sounded busy. 'By whom?'

'The Lobatse High Court. I've just got a summons. I'm being done for contempt of court over that murder case, the battered women's syndrome.'

'The police have issued you with a summons?' Sechele was giving me all his attention now.

'No, that's the funny thing, the court just faxed it to Ron, my husband's, office.'

'That's odd,' said Sechele.

'Isn't it? So, you haven't been summoned?'

'No.'

'But how can they summon a reporter and not her editor?'

'I have no idea,' said Sechele. 'Look, our lawyers are on leave at the moment. I'll try and get help but I can't promise anything right now. Just try and get it put off until the new year.'

'Okay.'

'Okay, fine,' said Sechele. 'Don't worry, chin up.'

'Oh, I'm not worried,' I said breezily, 'I've been through this before, right?'

In the middle of the night I woke up, my pulse racing. If I didn't get to Lobatse by Friday morning what would happen? I guessed they would issue a warrant for my arrest. Could I even get to Lobatse tomorrow? I would have to fly. That would cost too much. I was scared of flying. And anyway the plane would probably be full already. Also, I wasn't going into any courtroom without a lawyer. I would contact Dingaan first thing in the morning. He would tell me what to do. What if he wasn't around? And if he was around, how was I going to pay him? I would have to apply to MISA's legal defence fund again.

Right, I thought, turning over and over in the bed until it grew light outside, this was the plan. I would rush to Dingaan, hire him myself, although I didn't have any money, and get him to tell the court down in Lobatse that I couldn't come on Friday. I sat up; I was leaving for the UK on Monday, for my brother was getting married in five days' time. For the first time in four years I would celebrate Christmas in London. Would I be allowed out of the country if I had been summoned and failed to appear, if there was a warrant for my arrest?

When I rushed into Dingaan's office the next morning he smiled.

'Oh Caitlin,' he said leaning back at his desk. 'What have you done now?'

'I haven't done anything,' I bristled. I had gone through the Penal Code the moment I had got up and found that contempt of court carried a three year jail sentence. 'Read this,' I said and I handed over my summons.

Dingaan read it and began chuckling. 'Oh, you do lead an interesting life,' he said.

'Yeah, really interesting, do you want to swap?'

'Sit down, sit down,' Dingaan said. 'Can we get you some tea?'

I sat, my bag on my lap as if I were about to leave.

Dingaan read the summons again and then read the offending newspaper article which I had brought with me.

'This is very strange,' he said thoughtfully.

'So, is it contemptuous?'

'No, no, not at all.'

'Can you get this date postponed or adjourned or whatever you legal people call it?'

'Leave it with me,' said Dingaan and I did.

★　★　★

I arrived at Heathrow airport and joined the wrong queue. It was only as I neared the passport desk that I remembered I was no longer a British citizen. I was a foreigner now and my place was in the long, slow-moving queue to the left. I joined at the end; waiting for ages until I reached a white-faced immigration officer and handed over my Botswana passport.

'Hmmm, Botswana?' queried the immigration officer.

'In Southern Africa,' I said. 'Next to Zimbabwe.'

The immigration officer inspected the back and the front of my passport.

'And why are you coming to the UK?' the officer asked a little suspiciously.

'To see my family,' I said. 'My brother's getting married.' It felt odd, to have to explain why I was coming to the place where I had been born.

'Oh, you're from here?' asked the officer.

'Yes.'

'What made you go to Botswana?'

This seemed a little personal to me. 'Oh, lots of things,' I shrugged.

'And how long will you be staying?'

'Just two weeks,' I said reassuringly, getting out my return tickets.

'So, you'll be going home on . . . ?' The officer checked the dates.

I frowned, confused. I had just arrived home, I wasn't going home. But then I realized that as I was a Motswana, England was no longer my home.

# 22

I came back to Botswana to find Ron's uncle Rra Nama seriously ill. The day after I arrived in Maun I picked up Madintwa and we went to pay our respects. I got lost twice on the way and Madintwa started panicking, her eyesight was so poor now that she couldn't give me any directions.

'Is there anything I can bring him?' I asked her.

She sighed heavily and shook her head.

'Is he eating?'

'*Nnyaa*, he is not eating. But!' and she brightened up, 'he has been asking for watermelon.'

I stopped by the side of the road where a young girl was selling watermelons, the dark-green fruits piled like cannonballs on the sand.

Eventually we found the family's compound, which appeared empty. Rra Nama's five children were not around, and I guessed they were at the cattle post. We stopped at the open door to the house and Madintwa leaned heavily on her walking stick. '*Ko ko!*' she called in a wavery voice. Rra Nama's illness had affected her deeply. He was half her age; he should be visiting her on her sick bed, not the other way round.

'*Ee,*' a woman's voice came from inside, flat and sad.

I followed Madintwa in and stood on the

smooth mud floor. The room was empty but for a thin mattress and an old wooden cabinet with two bottles of disinfectant on top. Rra Nama lay on the mattress, his body covered with a crisp white sheet. His wife sat on the floor, struggling to put on a pair of plastic gloves. She looked up, startled, when we came in as if she'd forgotten that we were out there. Then she hurriedly stood up and went outside, her hands almost hidden behind her back as if to draw attention away from the gloves.

Madintwa collapsed on to the floor by Rra Nama's mattress, landing heavily.

'*Dumela Rra*,' she said, struggling to reach over and take Rra Nama by the hand.

But his struggle was far worse than hers. He was lying on his side, and the arm that propped him up was as thin as my wrist. 'Hey, I am sick,' he said. His face had sunken so that it looked skeletal, but his voice was lucid and his eyes were bright.

I came forward and shook his hand, squatting down next to the mattress. This was the first time he had said he was sick. Since I'd been in the UK, Rra Nama had been taken to Namibia to visit a famous traditional doctor. It looked as if that trip had been the last straw. His career in politics was long since over. Although President Masire had retired, it looked likely that the BDP would win this year's general elections as usual. While there were now more opposition parties and they were growing in popularity in the urban centres, any opposition to the BDP was far too fragmented to win power.

'I've brought you a watermelon,' I said uselessly.

Rra Nama smiled. He tried to look around for a knife, and as he shifted on the mattress the white sheet fell off and I almost gasped to see his stomach which was concave like an empty cooking pot. I felt ashamed to see him like this. There were drugs he could have taken but even if he could have afforded them, it was too late now and his body could no longer digest anything.

I found the knife and sliced open the watermelon the Setswana way, chopping it in half horizontally. I placed one of the halves near Rra Nama, the oval fruit gleaming with red flesh and white pips. Rra Nama struggled up again and managed to scoop some of the fruit into his hand. I looked away. I couldn't bear to see him lift the fruit to his mouth.

'Hey, I am sick,' he said again, leaning back on the mattress. 'And how is Mozambia?'

'He is fine,' I said.

'And Alice?'

'She is fine.'

Rra Nama chuckled. Then he closed his eyes. I looked at Madintwa, not sure whether we were to leave or not. But she had closed her eyes as well.

★   ★   ★

On 23 February 1999 I sat with Sechele, the *Mmegi* editor, on the way to the Lobatse High Court. It was hot, but not nearly as hot as it was back in Maun. Sechele was dressed like a businessman, in a yellow diamond-patterned tie. He appeared cool but impatient. We were about 50 kilometres from Gaborone and the scenery was green, soothing, and totally unlike what I was used to. We joked about what we knew about Justice Isaac Aboagye, the judge I was to appear before. Sechele said he was known as the hanging judge because of the number of people he had sentenced to death.

I looked at the car clock. It was 9.10. I was due to appear at 9.30. Dingaan had managed to get the initial December date postponed, but at the last moment I was told that Dingaan wouldn't be accompanying me to court as Carl Anderson, his partner, was on his way to the Lobatse High Court anyway. Things had come a strange full circle for it was Carl who had represented me at my very first court appearance during the MaWestern case.

I looked at the clock again.

'It's nine twenty,' I said worriedly.

Sechele laughed. 'The last thing you want to do when charged with contempt of court is to arrive late.'

'Why, would that be really bad?'

Sechele smiled. 'It would be rather contemptuous.'

'Are we nearly there?'

'Lobatse is just past that mountain there. Okay, fine. Put up the window, I'm taking off.'

I gritted my teeth as we sped towards Lobatse, convinced we weren't going to make it in time. I tried to distract myself. I thought about Rra

Nama's funeral in Maun a few days ago. I thought about how the funeral programme had said he had died from malaria, how no one had even whispered the words HIV or AIDS.

He had died the day I had seen him last, and just a few hours after Ron had arrived to visit. He had told Ron he was about to die, and he had asked Ron to be guardian of his five children. I sat in the car, looking at the bush land outside, hoping for a sign of Lobatse. I didn't see how we could be the guardians of five children when we already had two of our own. So many people were dying from AIDS that it had become almost inevitable; it had lost its surprise. Nine years ago HIV figures had been dry statistics, now everyone had a family member who was sick. But no one could say why it was spreading so fast.

At 9.27 we screeched off to the right at what appeared to be the beginning of a town. Sechele parked and we leapt out of the car, rushing to court number six.

I walked into the courtroom a little gingerly, expecting something similar to the courtroom in Maun. But this was totally different. Wooden panelling covered each of the four walls and as I walked in my shoes echoed impressively. Inside, the room was split into several levels. It was like being in a squashed-up basketball court.

I turned as two women walked in. They both wore black robes and they both wore trousers. Apart from Pearl, it had been a long time since I'd seen a Motswana woman in trousers. It was the Metlhaetsile attorneys who I had talked to so

341

often on the phone but never actually met. I stood up to greet them.

'How are you doing?' Maame Baffour Awuah said, shaking my hand.

'Fine, how are you doing?'

We both nodded and smiled at each other; clearly neither of us was doing very well. It was Maame I had quoted in my article on the Harvey murder trial and she too had been charged with contempt of court. Unlike me, Maame had appeared on the first date set back in December.

Behind Maame came Monica, the lawyer who was actually defending Harvey, and they both sat down next to Carl and the state prosecutor. I stood with my back against the wall, in front of me the black robes of the four attorneys billowing out like roosting crows.

There was movement to my left then, and I turned as a woman came quietly in and walked towards a wooden bench behind a short glass wall. She looked terrified, her body standing stiffly to attention. I couldn't think who she was. Then I realized she was Harvey, the woman who had killed her husband.

Suddenly a door opened on the top level of the courtroom and a police officer put his face around it. 'Judge coming,' he hissed.

Everyone stood up and we watched while an elderly man entered the courtroom wearing a fetching red gown. Justice Aboagye shifted some papers on his desk, the spectators in the gallery sat down, and we all waited. 'Is the person who wrote this here?' he suddenly barked. He waved a copy of *Mmegi* in the air.

'Yes,' I said. 'It's me.'

Carl got up, said he was defending me and then immediately sat down again.

'You wrote this?' the judge demanded, peering down at me.

'Yes,' I said, worriedly.

'So,' said the judge, 'you are Ca . . . Ca . . . ' he stumbled over my name. 'You are Davies?'

'Yes.'

'Are you Miss or Mrs?'

I almost laughed. But the judge, and everyone else, was waiting for my answer.

'Mrs,' I said.

'So you are married?' snapped the judge.

I nodded.

'So, *Mrs* Davies, did you write this?'

'Yes, I did.' I lifted my finger to my mouth and shredded off a bit of skin. I waited for the judge to tell me how the article was contemptuous.

'So you wrote this story in, Meg, Meg, what do you call this thing?'

'*Mmegi*, my lord,' said Carl.

'Yes, you wrote this in *Mmegi* and did you think these were the facts as you wrote them?'

'Yes.' I looked panic-strickenly over to Carl. Wasn't my lawyer supposed to be talking on my behalf? I didn't know what the crime was, so how would I know how to defend myself?

'Were you there in the courtroom?' snarled the judge.

'No.'

The judge started scribbling. Suddenly he waved the copy of *Mmegi* in the air again. 'Where is the editor of this?' he demanded.

343

I stood still, my arms stiffly by my side. I could sense the people beside me turning round. Behind me Sechele must have stood up in the spectator's gallery and now I heard him say, 'Here I am.'

'You are the editor?' said the judge.

'Yes.'

'Well, come down here then,' snapped the judge.

There was a rustle behind me, the sound of someone walking down the rows of wooden benches.

'And put down those things!' snarled the judge.

I turned to see Sechele, still unsure which way to go but now bending to hand a file and a briefcase to a colleague. A moment later he was standing next to me.

'I said put down those things,' said the judge.

Sechele put down his notebook and pen.

'You are the editor of this,' said the judge for the third time.

'Yes,' said Sechele. 'Your lord.'

'And you published this, this article?'

'Yes, I did.'

'And did you believe the contents to be fact?'

'Yes, your lord.'

The judge began writing again. Then he looked up and snarled at Maame, 'What are you doing sitting down? It is you who is the accused.'

Maame quickly stood up and shuffled backwards to join Sechele and I.

'Sorry, my lord,' she said.

'You gave Mrs, Mrs, uh, Davies, the interview

that is quoted in this article?'

'I did, my lord,' said Maame. She looked as if she wanted to add something else but was unsure whether it was wise or not.

'Are you the defending attorney?'

'No, my lord.'

'You are not the defending attorney?' the judge raised his eye-brows and his voice came crashing down. 'Yet you took it upon yourself to present so-called facts to the press?'

Maame hung her head.

My body was rigid now. When would this cross-examining end and when would he tell us what law we had broken?

'You allow this to be put in the paper, for everyone in Botswana, everyone in South Africa, in the whole world, to read!'

Some ten minutes later the judge finished with Maame and turned on me again.

'And what is your relationship with this Metla, this Metlhaetsile group?'

To my relief Carl leapt to his feet. 'My lord, I need to talk to my client.'

'I have just talked to your client and she has answered me,' said the judge, irritated. 'I don't see why you have to talk to her.'

Carl mentioned something about establishing something in Latin and the judge relented, allowing us to talk privately in a small room which felt padded though it wasn't. It was just small and white and windowless with a short wooden bench like a sauna room.

We walked back into the courtroom and Carl stood before the judge, adjusted his frilly white shirt and black cape, and began. Beads of sweat were gathering on his face but he looked in control. As he began speaking, to my surprise, the judge's demeanour began to soften.

'Yes, go on,' he said after every statement Carl made.

I began to relax.

Carl was handling things nicely. I began to tune out as the two men had their exchange. I had been standing now for an hour, my back was aching. In the silence between the two men's exchange my tummy began rumbling. It was hot. The air was oppressive. I kept on slipping away into other, vague thoughts and then pulling myself back to where I was.

'Yes,' the judge was nodding, 'go on.'

Carl went on. He drew the judge's attention to the first four paragraphs of the story. He said it was clearly using the future tense to show that this was the defence that would be argued, not facts already agreed on in the court. He said I was a layperson not an attorney. He said I had a long relationship with Metlhaetsile because I was concerned with women's empowerment.

'What?' the judge barked.

'My client is interested in women's empowerment,' said Carl.

I bit my lip.

'And so are the attorneys at Metlhaetsile,' continued Carl.

We all stood there for another ten minutes while the judge wrote at length. Then he turned on Sechele.

'Is she a reporter with your paper?' he asked.

'Your lord,' Sechele said carefully, 'I came here to offer moral support, I was not aware I would end up the accused and . . . '

The judge burst out laughing. The women sitting below him typing away smiled. The police officers grinned.

Finally it seemed the judge had heard enough. I looked at the clock, it was 11 a.m. Then I looked to my left. The woman on trial, Harvey, was still standing. No one had said she could sit down.

The judge wrote on and on. I wondered why he was making so many notes. Then he looked down at us. With a shiver I realized he was about to pass judgement, that this was the same procedure he used when he told someone they were condemned to hang.

'Having heard Mrs Davies and upon the explanation given by Mr Anderson, I find that Mrs Caitlin Davies . . . '

I held my breath.

' . . . had no intention to prejudice the proceedings at this trial in any way when she interviewed Ms Baffour Awuah and sent her report to the *Mmegi* newspaper.'

I smiled, this sounded positive.

'She had good reason to believe that she was talking to the right person, as Ms Awuah's firm was engaged in the defence of the accused, and that the facts given to her by Ms Awuah were the true facts of the case. I accordingly find her not guilty of contempt of court and discharge her.'

I let out a big sigh of relief. Carl shifted together a few papers, Sechele looked at his watch, Monica turned round and gave me a smile.

The judge paused and went on. 'Ms Baffour Awuah has admitted having given the published facts to Mrs Davies . . . '

I stood up straighter; the judge's tone was not conciliatory now.

' . . . She was not the attorney directly defending the accused and she had never attended the trial. She therefore had no justification in telling the press her own version of the facts in the case as if those facts had either been found by the court or were not in issue . . . '

I looked to my left to see Maame slumped, her head down.

'I find her conduct grossly irresponsible and contemptuous and I reject her half-hearted apology,' said the judge. 'She is to go to prison for seven days.'

Someone gave a sharp gasp of alarm. Prison? He was sending her to prison? I looked at Maame. She looked like she had been slapped in the face. She shakily took off her glasses and wiped at the edges of her eyes. Then we all rushed outside, the black capes of the lawyers flying into the midday sunshine.

★ ★ ★

Five months later Aboagye's ruling against Maame was overturned in an eighteen-page judgement issued by the court of appeal. The appeal judges drew attention to the 'summary manner' in which the case had been taken and noted that the power of courts in terms of charging people with contempt should be 'exercised sparingly and with great caution'. The court found that Maame, Sechele and I had been brought before court without specifically knowing what the charge against us was and that Judge Aboagye had adopted a procedure of 'question and answer long after the event'. Maame's sentence was deemed unduly severe and her conviction quashed. But by then the damage had been done. Maame had spent forty-eight hours in jail. I had returned immediately to journalism after my appearance in Lobatse but now I had a new reason to take a break. I was three months pregnant and I wanted some peace and quiet for the unborn.

# PART FIVE

# 23

The day I found out I was pregnant I was alone at home. I had just bought a cheap plastic table from a wholesalers and set it out on the sand in front of the porch. Here I could sit and watch the daily life of the river, from people crossing in the early morning, to women washing clothes at midday, to people walking their dogs at sunset. Each morning three lehututu birds came strutting past the fence giving their glass-bottle call and sometimes, in the distance, I would see an impala escaped from the Maun wildlife park. As the heat of the day rose the riverbanks became crowded with goats and donkeys, and then in the afternoon when the day began to cool herds of milk-white Brahmin cattle headed past our plot. Just before dusk, planes began swooping overhead as the pilots raced and dived towards Maun airport. By the time it was dark the livestock were gone and the river became hippo territory again.

I sat at the table outside, a pregnancy testing kit before me. I had never thought things would happen so quickly. I had never wanted to become pregnant and then suddenly I had. At the age of thirty-five, I had become convinced that I wanted a baby. After years of agreeing that he didn't want children, Ron suddenly admitted that he did as well. Yet no sooner had we decided to try for a baby, than we succeeded. I went inside to tell Ron about the little red line on the pregnancy testing kit, to call him on the phone we had had installed just a few months ago, a job which had taken five men and a fork-lift truck. Ron arrived home minutes later and we looked at each other and giggled, we had a secret that no one else knew about.

An hour later I walked through the door of a new Maun clinic run by Dr Patrick Akhiwu, a beaming Nigerian man with dimples in his cheeks. I expected to be examined, to be tested, to be measured and to be advised. But the midwife, MaKupaza, just smiled. A short, friendly Malawian woman, she merely asked me what shoe size I wore, in case my feet swelled during pregnancy, and then told me to come back in six weeks. As I stepped out of the clinic I saw the day had become overcast and there was smoke in the air as if we were downwind of a tremendous bush fire. I still couldn't quite believe I was pregnant.

When we told Madintwa the news she lifted her arms into the air and thanked the ancestors. When I told my parents, my mother was speechless with surprise. When we told Alice, she refused to believe us, pointing out that I didn't look pregnant at all.

By the time I returned to Dr Patrick's I knew that I now carried something whose face was fully formed, which even had nails on its fingers and toes. I had no morning sickness, no moodiness, no fatigue. Instead I felt the strongest I had ever felt. Before, pregnancy had seemed to me an unnatural state. I had watched in sympathy while pregnant women waddled the streets of Maun, labouring under the size of their bellies. But now that I was pregnant, it felt right.

When I was a few months into my pregnancy, Madintwa offered to give me massages. Once or twice a week I went to the family compound in Moeti to be admired by Ron's grandmother. The massages were playful affairs; Madintwa rubbed around my tummy with some cream, stopped to chat, and then rubbed around my tummy some more. But as I neared five months, and the baby's movements became clearly visible, Ron's mother started to give me the massages herself, in order to keep the baby in the right position for birth. Eliah was no longer going to Morutsa, she had moved back to Maun until the baby was born. Each morning Ron dropped me off at Moeti and I waited in the yard while Eliah washed, a laborious process that took hours and involved scrubbing every square inch of her body. Once Eliah had washed she would emerge from behind the reed wall and march sedately towards her concrete house. Madintwa was already inside the house waiting. These days it took her a long time to get up in the morning but if I were arriving for a massage then she rose earlier and took her place in Eliah's bedroom, sitting with her legs outstretched on the bare cement floor, a headscarf tied askew around her head. Her face wobbled slightly as she peered forward, trying to follow the proceedings. Eliah had been quietly overjoyed when we'd told her the news and had gone straight to church to pray.

'I want to make you happy,' she told me one day, in broken English, smiling shyly much as Alice used to do. But as I reached five and then six months of pregnancy we began disagreeing over where I was to give birth. I wanted to go to the private hospital in Gaborone because I had medical aid, but it was 1,000 kilometres away and I would have to move there well before my due date. I also wanted to have a Caesarean, which one doctor had recommended in order not to damage my back again. But Eliah was against both ideas. She wanted me to give birth in Maun. We never actually discussed these things face to face; rather Ron came home from work and passed on a thought from his mother.

Once I was positioned a little nervously on my mother-in-law's double bed, Eliah picked up a bottle of runny pink cream labelled 'Happy Event' and slapped it carefully all over her hands. Then I lifted up my shirt and she slapped the cream all over my stomach as well. And then I closed my eyes and hoped for the best.

At first I had liked the idea of massages and the idea of being cared for in this traditional manner. There were no antenatal classes in Maun, very few pregnancy books in the local library, and I discovered that the attitude of most people was that pregnancy was something that happened to you and you simply sat back and waited until it was over.

There were virtually no tests available at Dr Patrick's surgery; nothing to either reassure me or to worry me about the baby's well-being. So the idea of the massages gave me comfort, made me feel like someone was keeping an eye on the baby and me. Dr Patrick had now become the proud owner of a scan machine but the images of the screen seemed to be far removed from what was actually happening. Still, he and Ron got a lot of enjoyment out of them.

'See! Look, the head!' Dr Patrick said.

'Yeah, amazing,' I replied, unable to identify anything at all on the fuzzy screen.

'What a shame the printer's not working,' said Dr Patrick. 'Then we could print out a copy for you.'

'And what about any other tests?' I asked. 'You know, amnio what-sit? I mean, I *am* thirty-five . . .'

Dr Patrick burst out laughing. 'You won't be able to get anything like that done in Botswana. Relax, you should be happy, you're going to have a wonderful child.'

So I had turned to the Internet. Sometimes, in the evening, I rather secretively looked up pregnancy sites to read of another thing I should not do, eat or drink. I read updated health alerts, I read the bulletin boards, I read adverts for top-brand cribs and strollers and car seats, none of which were for sale in Maun. I read about the things I didn't suffer from like stretch marks and constipation. And I read postings from women determined to give birth the natural way, without drugs or surgical intervention. I read about courses on which you could learn breathing techniques, about aromatherapy oils not available in Botswana, of how giving birth was like running a marathon and just needed stamina

357

and a positive state of mind. And I began to decide against travelling all the way to Gaborone, to decide against having an operation, but to give birth at home in Maun.

Neither Pearl nor Veronica gave me much in the way of advice except to say in a matter-of-fact way that childbirth was agony. During the birth of her third daughter Pearl had lain in hospital in Mochudi giving birth on her own while the nurses had their tea-break. By then, of course, she was a member of the ZCC and had plenty of people to pray for her.

'You will have to get a maid,' Pearl told me one day. She was having her hair done and every few seconds the hairdresser yanked her head backwards. We sat on the porch outside Pearl's new house, built with the proceeds of Bashi's thriving real-estate business. The outside was as yet unpainted and the building loomed up large from the sand.

'Don't be ridiculous,' I said, 'I'm not getting a maid.'

'You will!' Pearl laughed. 'When you move around with a child there are so many things you have to carry with you. You will need help.'

'That's where the extended family comes in,' I told her, listing on my fingers all the family members who would help; Madintwa, MaB, Eliah, Alice, Gabs. I saw our child as a family child, with a grandmother and great-grandmother, with two uncles and three aunts, with hordes of cousins, and with two sisters already. In the Setswana way, the child would belong to everyone and everyone would care for the child. It would have a family — my family — in England, but it would also be an African child, as familiar with computers as it would be with surviving in the bush. My child wouldn't be afraid of elephants.

Madintwa handed out bits and pieces of advice when they came to her. She advised me to avoid lying on my back for then the baby would split and become twins, and she reminded me it was very bad luck to see a snake while pregnant. But in general no one told me much about pregnancy or childbirth at all.

★   ★   ★

I had always known Eliah was a physically strong woman. I had seen her carry bags of cement and logs of wood. I had seen her poling a *moroko*, weeding a field, building a house. I had watched her recently thatch the roof of my office which we had built on the plot at home. But this was the first time I actually felt how strong she was as her well-muscled arms pummelled away on my pregnant stomach. When she decided that the baby inside me had to be in a certain position then she threw herself into ensuring that it was so. As I lay on her bed, peering down to see what she was doing, I could see the outline of my baby's buttocks rising up like bread to the right of my stomach. Then, quick as anything, Eliah lunged for the buttocks, squeezing and pushing until an elbow, or a knee perhaps, pushed up from under my skin in another part of the bump. I had thought the idea of something growing inside me would be repulsive but it was not. Now wherever I went I was accompanied by someone else, someone getting ready to be born.

One day I shouted out as Eliah tried her usual adjustments.

'What is it?' asked Ron, appearing in the doorway to the bedroom. It was lunchtime and he had come to Moeti to eat.

I laughed to try to cover the alarm my shout had caused. Ron regarded my pregnancy with bewilderment and awe. He had put on more weight than I had; he had bought running shoes intending to begin regular jogging along the river in the early mornings, with some notion that becoming a father involved becoming fit.

'She is not good with pain,' Eliah told Ron over her shoulder.

I smiled nicely, determined that I could show her that indeed I *could* deal with pain. I knew Eliah had given birth to Ron under a tree and, a few hours later, returned to work in the field.

'I had a dream,' said Eliah, putting the lid back on the bottle of Happy Event. The massage was over; everything was progressing as it should.

I sat up, interested. 'What did you dream?' I asked, pulling my shirt back into place.

'I dreamt the baby's name,' she said, her face visibly softening.

Ron, Eliah, Madintwa and I all beamed at each other, held together in anticipation of the baby to come.

'What was the name?' I urged.

Eliah straightened up. 'Lethonogolo.'

'Letogo . . . ' I echoed.

'Nnyaa, Lethonogolo,' said my mother-in-law, stringing out each syllable.

'Lovely,' I said brightly. I looked at Ron, willing him not to approve the name. I wanted the baby to belong to the family, but ultimately I wanted him to belong to Ron and me and that included choosing a name. We knew by now that the baby would be a boy, a scan had suggested it was a boy, people told me I would have a boy because I carried so high up. I dreamt it would be a boy. I wanted to name him after my father, but somewhere along the line we began to call him Rocky. Ron would lie on the bed waving a rattle over my tummy and Rocky would jump round inside. By the time he was born he would be familiar with Ron's voice, and the sound of dogs and the sound of hippos too.

\* \* \*

As I neared six months of pregnancy, and as Rocky moved all the time, day and night, never keeping still for more than half an hour, I got a new job. Women Against Rape received funding to produce a report on violence against women in the north-west district. My task was to research the current services available for women who had been raped or otherwise abused, to collate data from the courts and hospitals, and to find out what services were most needed.

I spent the mornings at the Maun magistrates' court, begging for access to records from a clerk of court who said women deserved to be raped because they asked for it. They wore modern fashions like short skirts, he said, it was their own fault. I tried to ignore him, keeping my eyes on the records in front of me. I was amazed at the number of people being arrested and charged with rape, with attempted rape, with defilement. I examined the charges, the women's testimony, the police and medical evidence, the comments of the magistrate, the final sentencing. I noted the age of the accused, and I took in their names, too, my stomach sickening as I followed the arrest, trial and dismissal of first a former OO free-lancer, then a man who worked at the Maun museum, and then a relative in Sedie ward. It was because Maun was so small, I told myself. It was because groups like WAR were making it easier to report a rape in the first place.

I attended public meetings where a local chief said the idea of marital rape was laughable because a man couldn't rape what he owned. The work was depressing, but no more depressing than when I had trained as a rape crisis counsellor ten years ago in Massachusetts. It was an academic exercise and I approached it as a journalist trying to establish the basic facts. I interviewed council representatives and social workers. I attended Kgotla meetings in small villages outside Maun, shaking with nerves as I got up to speak in Setswana. But with all the interviews and meetings and statistics, it was impossible to find a woman who would actually talk about being raped. And because rape was such a taboo, I found it nearly impossible to ask any woman to talk about it anyway.

362

By now WAR had a proper three-room office, a secretary and two employees, a phone and a vehicle. And the better equipped the group grew, the more cases they helped take to court, the more the backlash intensified. Anne Sandenbergh had got used to coming out of court to find the tyres on her car had been let down. One night she had an anonymous phone call from a distressed woman. Anne drove out to a remote meeting place in the bush, only to find she had been set up. Instead of the distressed woman she met three men who warned her against pursuing a case involving a traditional doctor and the rape of young girls.

While I worked for WAR and dreamt of the baby to come, Ron threw himself into work on the farm. Soon the rains would come and it would be time to plough and plant. He single-handedly cleared the farm of trees and stumps, made a demarcation line and built a fence from thornbushes. He wanted the place sorted before Rocky was born. One Saturday I went with him to the farm and was amazed at what he had achieved. The large expanse of overgrown wilderness was now ordered. Entering the farm from the main pathway, there was a large field on the left in which would grow watermelon, mealie and beans. On the right was a flat, cleared area of sand with a tent and a simple reed house, a cooking area and a place to hang clothes to dry. And behind that was a kraal for the goats. But as I walked around admiringly, I still found it hard to understand Ron and everyone else's attachment to the place. It was hot and dry; there was no water supply. At night there were lions nearby, in the mornings there were baboons. There was little for me to do but sit in the shade and watch while everyone else went about their tasks. But for Ron, and for Alice and Madintwa and the others, the farm was where they came alive. Ron stripped off to his shorts and worked until the muscles in his arms contracted into cement. Madintwa sat on the sand, shushing away the chickens, making predictions about the weather, hobbling around with her walking stick inspecting the progress. And Alice didn't even have to be asked to build a fire or prepare food; she just did it straight away. And then she sat on a log to rest while Gabs plaited her hair.

As my pregnancy reached eight months I began to feel the strain. My WAR report was almost finished, I was ready to give birth. But instead I found myself wandering around aimlessly at home, too hot and too tired to do anything useful. One evening we went out for dinner, the WAR coordinator MaPhefo was leaving for a degree course in England and this was a farewell supper. I sat awkwardly at the table, my stomach now large enough to serve as a shelf, watching a little enviously as the others tucked into their meals, refilling their glasses of wine. I had lost my appetite now; I just wanted the baby to be born. I could no longer lie on my back any more, and when I got up my centre of balance had shifted so that it took a while to feel properly upright. Several times a day I experienced violent electric shocks down my legs that left me gasping.

'Have some wine,' said Stef, a young Italian woman with whom I'd written the report for WAR.

'I can't.'

'Oh, a little is good for you,' she insisted, filling a glass.

'Is that what they say in Italy?'

'Oh, shut up,' Stef said good-naturedly.

'So when are you going to Gaborone?' one of the other women at the table asked, an elderly white woman and a former nurse.

'I'm not.' I smiled, flicking a fork around my pasta. I knew what would come next.

'Don't tell me you're having the baby in Maun?' the woman asked in horror.

'Yup.'

'Oh, Caitlin,' she leaned forward, touching me on my arm, 'you can't!'

'Well, I am,' I said, defensively.

'But Maun hospital is a dreadful place,' said another woman, a young Motswana who had recently spent a week there with malaria.

'Go to England,' said MaPhefo.

'It's a bit late for that,' I muttered.

'Well, make sure you take your own blood supply with you,' said Anne Sandenbergh.

'What?'

Next to me Ron put his knife down.

'Take your own blood with you,' repeated Anne. 'You don't want a transfusion from there.'

I gritted my teeth. The idea of a blood transfusion hadn't even occurred to me.

'You're freaking her out. Stop it,' said Stef.

Across the table Ruth, a young Englishwoman who did fund-raising for WAR, smiled sympathetically.

'You know your blood group right?' asked Anne.

'No.'

'Well, find out what it is, if Ronnie's the same then tell them at the hospital if you need any blood it *has* to come from your husband. I'm telling you, Caitlin, you have to think about AIDS.'

★   ★   ★

Outside the restaurant I hauled myself into the car. 'I think we should go and look around Maun hospital,' I said.

Ron started the car.

'What do you think? I mean, we'd made up our minds up to have the baby here, right? Now I don't know what to do. What should I do? Have it here or go to Gaborone?'

'I don't know,' sighed Ron. 'Whatever you want.'

'But what do *you* want?'

'Whatever you do.'

'Then let's go and look around, then we can decide once and for all.'

Ron drove along on the road home.

'You are going to be with me, aren't you?' I asked.

'*Mma?*'

'When I give birth.'

Ron was silent.

'Ron?'

'My mother can come.'

'Your *mother*?' my voice rose in dismay. 'I don't want your mother!'

Ron sped up as we crossed the bridge.

'You're kidding, right?' I watched his face worriedly. 'How could you not want to be there?'

'I wouldn't know what to do,' Ron mumbled.

'You don't have to *do* anything!'

'But it's women who do these things. Traditionally . . .'

'I don't care about traditionally!' I snapped, furious that we hadn't had this discussion earlier, that I had never actually asked Ron whether he wanted to be at the birth or not, that I had simply assumed he would be and that now I was just weeks away from my due date.

★　★　★

The next day, Ron and I had blood tests and found we had the same blood type. Then we arranged to meet at Maun hospital. I drove there alone, parking outside the metal gates on the sand and walking in. I looked around carefully. On the right I passed the original hospital building erected prior to independence by foreign missionaries. It looked church-like, with white-washed stone walls. But now the building was empty and other low, one-storey wards had been built around it. I walked on, passing piles of junk on the sand, old filing cabinets, trays and needles. Then I turned left towards the maternity ward, towards the long building with dirty white walls and blue doors and window-frames. It resembled a narrow Portakabin and had an air of impermanence about it, although by local standards it was old.

I stopped by the maternity ward. Behind me I could hear the familiar sound of the Land Rover roaring in. I knew Ron would drive right through the hospital gate and park where he liked. I turned as he pulled to a stop and leapt out, looking cheery. Then the back door opened and Gabs got out. Her face was sulky, as it often was these days. She was no longer doing well at school and, like Alice, she was often sullen.

I stiffened. 'What's she doing here?' I asked Ron, my voice low.

'Who?'

'Gabs. What's she doing here?'

'Well, she was alone at Moeti.'

'So? We've come to look round where I'm going to give birth! This isn't a family outing. This is you and me.'

Ron's face grew stony, but he spoke quickly to Gabs and she got silently back into the car, throwing me a glance that was hard to read. We walked without speaking up to the entrance to the maternity ward. I couldn't believe that Ron thought it appropriate that Gabs come with us for this visit.

The midwife on duty appeared surprised when we asked if we could have a look around. I had the feeling no one had ever asked her this before.

'I'm going to have the baby here,' I explained. 'Can we just have a look round the ward and everything?'

The midwife looked from me to Ron.

'Men are not allowed in here,' she said.

Ron made a joke and she relented. 'Wait here,' she said a little reluctantly, 'I will call a nurse.'

Eventually an efficient-looking nurse came hurrying out. 'Ah my dear,' she said kindly, taking me by my arm. 'Come and see. Yes, come and see, everything here is very nice. See?' she asked, leading us down a corridor. 'This is the private ward,' she said, opening a door. Inside was a small clean room that smelled of disinfectant, a bed with a flowery cover, a jar of plastic flowers and a bottle of water on a cabinet in the corner, curtains at the one narrow window. The nurse took me by the arm again and led me back along the corridor. 'And this is the delivery room.' Again she opened a door. 'We have everything here you need . . . We had a white woman giving birth just last week!'

I looked around: at the bed in the middle of the room so high it looked like a table, at a white porcelain sink in the corner, and at a machine standing unused against one wall. Then I looked at, and looked away from, a pair of stirrups attached to either side of the bed like something a horse might be strapped into during a major veterinary procedure. I won't be using those, I thought to myself, a little unnerved.

But I left the hospital quite cheerful. I had made the right decision, I would give birth in Maun.

★　★　★

By the time Christmas arrived that year I had given up any sort of work at all. Every waking hour I spent expecting the baby to arrive. I had been given several possible due dates by MaKupaza at Dr Patrick's clinic, who said the baby would probably come in January. But I knew the baby would come early, Rocky would be born at Christmas, or possibly on New Year's Day. In the meantime I sat at the plastic table on the sand in front of the porch and watched the river. I ate mangoes and pawpaws from our trees, the juice seeping down my chin. I eyed the banana trees hungrily, willing them to bear fruit too. I had rarely eaten fruit before, now I was ravenous.

One weekend both Alice and Gabs stayed with us as Madintwa and Eliah were in the bush. The girls and I no longer got on well. I was distracted by the impending birth; they were both in sulky moods. If I asked either of them to do anything, to sweep the house, or help in the garden, they dragged their feet as if it physically hurt them to do so.

'Are you jealous?' I had asked Alice a week ago.

'*Ee.*'

'You are?' I was surprised she'd answered so readily. 'But Alice, me and Ron love you. You're our child now. Just as this child . . . '

'You will love the baby more,' Alice said, her eyes seeking mine as if wanting a confrontation. 'And he will be cleverer at school than me.'

On Sunday morning Ron left for Maun to shop. When he came back several hours later his expression was stiff. He called gently to the girls, telling them to pack their things and get in the car.

'What is it?' I asked, as he stood waiting for Alice and Gabs on the porch.

'Nothing.'

'Ron?'

He shifted where he stood. Then I saw he had tears in his eyes.

'What is it? Tell me.'

Ron gestured that I move away from the house. 'I don't want you to get upset,' he said, taking my hand. 'Not while you're like this.'

We both looked down at my stomach.

'But?'

'But. It's Alice's mother.'

'Yes?'

'She's dead.'

★   ★   ★

The following morning I had a routine check-up at Dr Patrick's clinic. I sat in the packed waiting-room. In the corner Brenda Fassie was belting out a song on the TV screen. On the table in the middle of the room sat a tray of hot water, cups and tea bags. Every sitting space was filled. Next to me a young police officer sat stiffly, the top of her hat leaning against a poster for home-based care. I squeezed myself down on the end of one of the sofas. People in Maun made few allowances for pregnant women, and countless times I had been beaten to vacant chairs in offices and banks by elderly men who believed it was their prerogative to sit, not a woman however pregnant and sweating she might be. But this time I was ruthless, and I had sat down even though the space on the sofa was small.

I sat thinking of Alice and Gabs and their two small sisters. Their mother had just died. I couldn't imagine their pain; I couldn't imagine what I could do to help. No one seemed to know how or why she had died, although it was nothing to do with AIDS. She had been sick, she had complained of stomach pains, a neighbour had walked several kilometres to someone who was said to have a phone. The ambulance had been called but it had never come. I asked questions, but it didn't seem to matter to anyone else how or why it had happened, only that it had happened. Now the funeral arrangements were beginning. Alice and Gabs had moved to their late mother's compound. They had had their heads shaved. They were waiting for all the relatives to arrive before the burial could take place. Ron was in demand. He was one of the only people the family knew who had a car. He would have to fetch the firewood, he would have to donate some goats for the funeral food, he would have to dig the grave and buy the coffin just as he'd done when his uncle Rra Nama had died. And he had done it several times since then as well, even carrying bodies from the mortuary, as the number of people dying from AIDS increased. The original village cemetery, next to the school where I had taught ten years ago, was full. A new cemetery had now been built and that was getting full too. In banks and in the post office many of the tellers were absent from their posts having signed off for sick leave or for a hospital visit.

I looked up as the clinic door opened and Veronica walked in. 'Veronica!' I cried, about to get up but not wanting to lose my place on the sofa.

Veronica turned and gave me a blank smile. I waited while the receptionist tended to her and then she came over.

'You look rough,' I said, trying to push my bottom along the sofa to create some space.

She sighed. I had not seen her for ages and her face looked blotchy, her eyes tired.

'What's wrong?' I asked, immediately wishing I hadn't. People didn't ask what was wrong with someone who needed to see a doctor. 'You okay?'

'*Ee*. It is malaria.'

'Poor you,' I said. I had had malaria for the first time at the beginning of the year and I knew how terrible it was. By the time I had seen Dr Patrick I had been hallucinating, and I had spent most of the night on a drip.

Veronica glanced away from me, as if she didn't want to discuss things further. And then midwife MaKupaza called me in. She took her time with my check-up as she always did, chatting and smiling, leisurely weighing me, taking my blood pressure. I loved my check-ups with MaKupaza, she was willing to spend as much time as I wanted, willing to allay any fears, to talk about anything at all that I suggested. When I had told her I had drunk red wine before

I'd known I was pregnant, she'd laughed and said, 'Well you're not an alcoholic, are you, my dear?' When I'd rushed into the clinic one morning saying I had backache and demanding to know if I were about to miscarry, she'd patted me on the stomach and told me to go home and get a good night's rest. When I'd told her that in England people could give birth in pools of water she laughed so much she'd almost dropped a urine sample.

I lay on the clinic bed in my usual position. 'I think it's coming soon,' I said.

MaKupaza smiled. 'First babies are usually overdue.'

'Oh Rocky won't be, he's going to be born this week, I'm sure about it. And he hasn't been moving at all today, he must be tired.'

Again MaKupaza smiled. She gently lifted my shirt and put a cone to my stomach. I stopped talking while she listened to the heartbeat. MaKupaza moved the cone to another spot on my stomach, listened intently, and then moved it again. 'You haven't felt movements today?'

'No, not at all, and you know how this baby likes to move!'

MaKupaza nodded. She wasn't smiling now. Again she travelled across my stomach with the cone.

'What is it?' I asked. 'Can't you hear anything? You can't hear a heartbeat?' I tried to sit up, panic shooting through my body.

'It's okay, my dear, it's okay,' MaKupaza soothed, but she wasn't looking at me, she was looking away.

# 24

At the beginning of 2000 the rains came. The baby was fine, Dr Patrick had given me a scan, we'd all seen Rocky's heartbeat. Veronica was fine as well, she did not have malaria, she was pregnant again. And Maun, and Botswana, and the whole of southern Africa, was suddenly on flood alert. Each afternoon I sat on the porch watching as blue-grey clouds moved swiftly across the sky. As the clouds arrived overhead, the light would suddenly dim and all at once the birds stopped singing. Then I would know that a power cut was seconds away, as the winds started gushing through the trees, flicking sand into the air, breaking branches, knocking down power cables. I sat and watched as bolts of lightning broke vertically across the sky while rumbles of thunder exploded in the air. Then, finally, the rain began crashing on the tiled roof, forming a curtain of water at the entrance of the porch and soaking the sand in the yard. On the banks of the Thamalakane River children ran for shelter and wet donkeys stood stock-still in the open.

In January 2000 it rained like this every day. It rained like this the day my contractions began. I was three weeks past my due date and ten months pregnant. It was early evening and I was lying on our bed dozing. The contractions were mild, just a tightening sensation in my stomach, but I sat up at once. In the living-room I could hear Ron and Alice watching the Discovery Channel on our brand-new television. Outside there was the sudden, echoing sound of a hippo in the river. I listened to its splashes, waiting for the moment when it would give its great booming chuckle, wondering how many hippos had now made their way down the Okavango Delta and back to Maun. Above the splashing noise I could hear the bouncing sound of the frogs, out in their thousands after two weeks of rain. And then I could smell that rain was coming again and I got up and moved to the window, pushing aside the red blinds.

As I peered between the burglar bars and into the evening it was in time to see a shaft of lightning slice across the sky. This was the rainiest year I had ever experienced in Botswana; floods had closed roads down in the capital where homes had been washed away. Throughout southern Africa the rain was causing havoc. I watched the news on our new TV and saw a report about a woman in Mozambique who had given birth in a tree. For a drought-stricken country like Botswana, despite the damage the floods were causing, rain was always good news. At night the land around us appeared to seethe; below the sound of the frogs and the bats, it sounded as if the river itself were breathing in and out.

★ ★ ★

The next morning, disappointingly, the contractions had gone. I had started to time them and then I had fallen asleep. I woke to find our yard awash with water, birds singing in every tree, rustles of life in every clump of grass. I walked to Sedie Hotel and swam in the pool, trying to ignore the disapproving looks of the lodge's cleaners.

'Your baby will get cold,' one of the women complained as I got out, my enormous stomach leading the way, straining against the maternity swimming-suit my mother had sent from England.

By lunchtime the contractions were back, slightly more intense, even painful. I willed them on in terms of frequency, dying for labour to begin. I even cheated a little, convincing myself that they were now coming just ten minutes apart. A little while later I rang MaKupaza and described what had just happened.

'You've lost a plug,' she said. 'The blood you describe. It means labour is starting.'

'So, what should I do?' I asked.

'I think you should go to the hospital.'

I put the phone down. The contractions were coming every ten minutes. So I rang Ron and then I packed a bag. Packing a bag was described on all the Internet pregnancy sites. I packed a magazine to read, a tiny little doll-sized nappy, and a bright-orange sleep-suit my sister had sent from England.

'What are you grinning about?' Ron asked, parking the car outside the fence, the engine still running.

I almost ran along the sand, carrying my bag. Now that MaKupaza had said labour had started, I was keen to get into my hospital bed.

Ron drove like a maniac through the streets of Maun. It was a Monday afternoon and bank employees and shop workers were strolling home, hand in hand. The sun was already setting and there was a hot, heavy feeling in the air. The rain during the night had left a gassy smell. Along the sides of the roads the grass was luminous.

We drove past a grumpy security guard at the hospital gate and parked near the maternity wing. To our right the out-patients area was packed with people sitting, crouching, or lying on the concrete floor. Three dogs were angrily pulling rubbish out of a bin, rooting among the syringes. When I entered the maternity wing the corridor was empty and sour smelling as if it had not been cleaned for days. I felt disorientated; this didn't feel like the maternity wing I had looked around with Ron a few months ago. There was no one to meet me, no indication of what should happen next. I sat on a tiny bench in the corridor waiting for someone to come and help. Ron stood beside me, sniffing occasionally as he had begun to do when he was nervous.

'What happens now?' he asked.

At last a nurse appeared and took me into a small room leaving Ron very definitely outside. The nurse began questioning me — When did the contractions start? How frequent were they? — and then she shoved her hands inside me without comment.

The nurse snapped her gloves off.

'How much?' I asked.

The nurse looked down at me, not used to having a patient that asked questions. 'One centimetre,' she said.

'*One* centimetre dilated?'

The nurse nodded.

'Right, so I'll go home and come back later.'

'Oh no,' said the nurse. 'We are admitting you. You're in the early stages of labour and you won't be leaving until you have your baby.'

It sounded like a threat. She scowled at me before heading off to have a chat with a sour-faced doctor, the two discussing trivialities across the balloon stomach of a silent teenage girl on another table in the corner of the room. I got up and was directed to the first of three wards, narrow rooms with eight beds in each. Ron had asked for the private ward, the single bedroom we had seen when we had visited the hospital last year, but it was already booked. 'There is an *Indian* in there,' one of the nurses said, with an air of great significance.

'*Dumelang,*' I said, mumbling a greeting to the six women in the public ward.

None replied.

The scowling nurse pointed to one of the two free beds.

'Stay here,' she said. 'Someone will come and change the sheet.'

A cleaner came eventually and whipped off the sheet to reveal the mangiest mattress I had ever seen, stained with what looked like centuries of women giving birth. I sat on the edge of the bed, feeling panicky. The room was still silent. The women around me lay on their beds in their pink hospital dresses, some with babies under the blankets next to them, some presumably waiting for labour to begin or to continue or whatever indeed they were waiting for. There was no chatting. No sound but for a woman turning over and a baby, unseen beneath the covers, bleating.

I lay down on the bed, fully clothed. Ron had gone, for men were not allowed into the ward, but I thought I heard his car outside. He had given me his new mobile phone to use. I clutched it now in my hand. Someone had told me hospital patients in England were not allowed to use mobile phones as they interfere with machines. I had the worrying thought that there might not be any machines in this hospital to interfere with.

As I lay there a very young woman, in fact a girl, staggered up from the bed next to me. As she moved I caught sight of a tiny scrumpled baby face left behind on the mattress. The girl clutched at a bag which I guessed contained washing gear and then she attempted to head off to the toilet. She took two steps and then looked down. Blood was pouring down her legs on to the floor. She watched the flow, stunned for a while, then bent down and weakly patted at it with a face cloth. After a few minutes she gave up and hauled herself back on to the bed which I now saw was completely and utterly soaked in blood. Oh Jesus, I thought, clutching the mobile phone.

As night fell and the ward got dark and the doctor who was supposed to come and examine me had instead gone home, I tried to sleep. But as soon as I closed my eyes I heard a scurrying from somewhere above my head. I opened my eyes. A row of fat, jet-black cockroaches were marching down the wall, spreading out like a stain on the paint. I sat up and grabbed the magazine I had brought with me in my hospital bag. I rolled it up and then lunged at the wall, splatting at the cockroaches that were nearest. Some of the other women in the ward moved, disturbed, on their beds.

'Cockroaches,' I said, in case they wondered what I was doing. I bashed some more. Then I closed my eyes. More scurrying. More cockroaches. I moved on the bed so I lay as far away from the wall as possible and as I did so I saw a real posse of cockroaches gathered round a cup on the metal bedside table, scurrying determinedly up the sides and into the inches of gunge inside.

I leapt up out of bed and headed a little unsteadily down the corridor, holding the cup out before me. I passed the other two wards and then saw three midwives in faded blue uniforms huddled around a small table.

'Look!' I said, holding the cup out with a flourish.

They did not seem interested.

'I just found this cup next to the bed. Look!.'

One of the midwives took the cup from me, inspected it and pulled a face. 'Some patients . . . ' she said, 'are like that'.

Patients? I thought, what about the person who is supposed to clean the place up? I left the

381

cup on the table and, defeated, went back to the ward. The midwives seemed to think I was creating a fuss about nothing and, for a moment, as I passed the women in the wards, I was filled with fury that Batswana put up with so much.

Just as I was finally falling into some sort of sleep, huddled as far from the cockroach-infested wall as possible, I saw something white and blurry at the corner of my vision. Shaken, I sat up. I looked around in the gloom of the ward, wondering if I was beginning to see things. Just then another white shape appeared, shooting out from under my bed. I leapt up as a long, thin cat ran down the middle of the ward.

'A cat!' I yelled, following after it as it hid under another bed. 'There's a cat!' I said to the other women. 'It was under my bed!'

A couple of them agreed, yes, there was a cat. I stood in the ward, unsure what to do. Then the cat shot out from under my neighbour's bed and ran past with another ghostly white companion. I set off down the corridor to the midwives again.

'I've just seen a cat,' I said. 'It was *under my bed*!'

One of the midwives sighed. 'Oh, these cats,' she said. 'There are *so* many of them. You can even fall asleep and wake to find one right by your eyes!'

Oh, well, that's fine then, I thought, stunned, and headed off once again to bed. I must have eventually slept for at one point I woke to see a midwife laying a little bundle on the now empty bed beside me. I had liked the look of this midwife earlier, she was gentle and from her accent I guessed she was a Zambian.

'Someone,' said the midwife in a hushed, tender voice, 'has had a baby.'

She left the bundle tightly swaddled and went off.

Oh, my God, I thought, there's a baby on the bed! What shall I do? Where is its mother? What if it falls off the bed?

I dozed again and then woke to find two midwives had arrived to check my tummy. One bent forward and I assumed she was going to put her little metal cone to the bump to check the heartbeat when instead she bent to my face. I looked at my watch by the bed. It was 3 a.m.

'I've been reading your card,' whispered the midwife very close to my face.

I waited.

'I see you're a journalist.'

I wanted to tell her this wasn't the right time. I was off-duty; I didn't have my notebook.

'It's my son,' said the midwife, urgently. She was now close enough that I could see a piece of apple skin caught between her front teeth.

'Yes?' I asked.

'He really wants to be a journalist.'

'Does he?' I asked weakly.

'Yes. You see, he's doing a course. Hey, he is very hard working, my son.'

'That's nice.'

The midwife leant even closer. 'Can I get your address so he can contact you for help with his studies?'

At 6 a.m. another midwife had a good shove

inside me to find I was now two centimetres dilated.

'You're kidding,' I said. 'You mean after *twelve* hours I'm *two* centimetres?'

The midwife nodded.

The ward was livelier now, it was daylight and a woman had appeared with a metal trolley of food. She began slopping soft *phaletshe* into battered metal bowls and then barking at the women to come up and take the food. She progressed slowly down the ward and paused when she came to me. Now the other women in the room grew interested. Would the white woman eat soft *phaletshe*? The food woman decided not to bother finding out, turned her trolley and pushed it to the next ward. Despite myself, I felt tears prickling at the corner of my eyes.

'I'm going home,' I said to the midwife who still stood beside me.

'You can't,' she said.

The head of the hospital, a Norwegian doctor, came on his rounds an hour later. He agreed I could leave and not return until the contractions were five minutes apart. I went outside, walking as quickly as I could. The light was bright, the sand so soft and reassuring under foot. Patients and staff moved sluggishly around, but compared with the gloom in the maternity ward this seemed like a party. I sat on a little stone wall next to a bright-purple bougainvillea tree and waited for Ron. The second I sat down the contractions intensified. I stood up to see if that was more comfortable and realized I could barely stand. I began counting seconds in my head. Another one came. They were five minutes apart. This was no longer an even remotely pleasant experience. It was pain and it was scary. But there was no way I was going back into the maternity ward until the very last moment.

I went home and the day wore on. MaKupaza advised me to walk around so I went a little unsurely out of our plot and down to the Thamalakane River. After all the rains the river was full, fuller than I had ever seen it. The surface was covered with the white flowers of water-lilies like a field of daisies. Each day the water crept closer up the slope to our house, spreading by the hour, turning the sand wet. The Thamalakane seemed alive now, as if the riverbanks held a thick, muscular creature rather than mere water. Along the riverbank, on the opposite side from our plot, I could see a woman with an umbrella so big and so low only her legs were visible. Near her I could see a group of children splashing around, playing. I thought about warning them about the crocodile I had seen in this exact area two days earlier. But I knew they would just laugh and say they had powerful medicine that would protect them. I watched while two women, naked from the waist up, began to fish. They were using traditional cone-shaped nets which they slapped quickly into the water, trapping any fish underneath.

By lunchtime I could no longer sit or stand and I was getting desperate. Every five minutes I was overtaken by a wash of agony that couldn't be described or located, it was something that was everywhere. The minutes in-between were pure bliss and then a contraction hit again. Twenty, then forty, then sixty seconds long. But the pain didn't feel like a *contraction*, which I had naively imagined would resemble a tightening sensation. I had seen a cat give birth not long ago and somewhere in the stupidity of my mind I had thought it would be the same with me; the stomach contracting a few times and pushing the baby out. In fact, I had never really considered how my baby *was* to come out and now I wondered why women's bodies hadn't evolved to make things easier.

Beginning to panic I lunged for the sheets I'd printed out from the Internet, searching for the sections on labour pain. 'Fucking load of crap!' I yelled, reading how I should *picture* the pain as flowers opening, as hot sunlight entering my uterus.

By nightfall I had had enough. I couldn't keep still. One second I was lying on the bed, the next walking up and down, the next sitting on the floor. Nothing helped. I was trying to fight the pain and I was losing miserably.

'Ron,' I groaned from where I was in the bedroom.

Ron came and stood by the doorway. He had just come back from the farm where an old man he had hired to look after the goats had disappeared, along with the goats.

'I'm going to the hospital. I'm going to have to go back.' At least, I thought, there would be something for the pain. At least there someone could do something. Alice was asleep by now, so we left, locking the house behind us. She would sleep undisturbed, for Alice always slept through every single noise imaginable. Once in the car I slammed my palms on to the windscreen and pushed at the glass every time the pain came. I was unaware of anything outside but that it was night, it was dark but there were no clouds, no obstruction to the stars. As we neared the hospital I opened the window and breathed in the familiar smell of hundreds of fires in hundreds of compounds burning throughout Maun.

'You've got Mum and Dad's number?' I asked, in between contractions.

'Yes, yes,' said Ron, gritting his teeth and looking terrified.

My parents were not the only ones who had given instructions that Ron contact them the moment anything happened. Back in Eliah's compound, Madintwa was waiting for news.

★ ★ ★

'Yes, now things are happening!' said the midwife who admitted me back into the maternity ward, sounding very pleased. 'You are eight centimetres.'

I groaned. It was Tuesday night, the contractions had begun on Sunday, I had been in labour for nearly three days. I was nearly out of my mind with the pain. But I was less concerned about the hospital now; I couldn't have cared less about cockroaches or cats, I could have given birth in a shopping mall or a car park, it no longer mattered. I knew the room where I now lay; I recognized a couple of the nurses, including the kindly Zambian woman looking after me now.

'Oh, you're brave,' she crooned, 'much braver than I was. Scream if you want, it's no problem.'

I obliged.

'Drugs,' I said. 'Give me something.'

The midwife smiled.

'Drugs,' I said again. 'What can you give me?'

'There's nothing,' the midwife said, amused.

'What, *nothing*?'

She nodded.

I pushed myself up on the bed. There was now barely breathing space between the rounds of pain. I had no idea if or when this was ever going to stop. 'There must be *something*.'

The midwife shook her head.

'Do something,' I pleaded. 'I've had enough! I can't take it!'

The midwife didn't reply. She just broke my waters and wheeled me on a wheelchair out of the examining room.

'Do you want me to come with you?' asked Ron, shuffling his boots out of the way of the wheelchair. I looked down and noticed his boots were wet with mud from the farm. I was being pushed so quickly I didn't have the chance to reply.

In the delivery-room I found myself on the bed. The Zambian had gone and now another blue-uniformed woman was there. It was the scowling midwife from the day before.

'What's a man doing in here?' she grumbled to herself.

I looked at her, and at the room, and I began to scream.

Ron took my hand and I squeezed his finger-bones together until I thought they would crack.

'Please!' said the midwife in my ear. 'Deal with the pain, you're disturbing the other patients.' She turned as the Zambian came in. 'White women,' she said in exasperation, nodding towards me on the bed.

Time went on. Someone was doing an awful lot of groaning and panting.

'Don't scream!' said the grumpy midwife as she shut the door with a slam.

Still I lay on the table, still the pain went on. What on earth was I doing in this place? I looked around in the brief seconds when the pain lessened. The room smelt. I looked down at the bed. I had no idea a person could lose so much blood and still be conscious. It was like a goat had been slaughtered. I looked around again, increasingly annoyed at the sign on the door because the word 'delivery' had been misspelled. 'It's spelt wrong,' I tried to say, several times, but the words just didn't come out. I wondered if it was raining again outside, the blinds were closed and I'd lost track of time and place.

'Do you want to push?' asked the grumpy midwife. She was standing at the end of the bed but her voice, her entire presence, seemed to be coming from somewhere far, far away.

'Yes,' I said. Why hadn't she asked me that

hours ago? I had never even thought of pushing until she mentioned it and now it seemed the most glaringly obvious thing to do.

'When was the last time she ate?' the Zambian midwife asked Ron.

'When did you last eat?' Ron said into my right ear.

I groaned.

'I don't think she's eaten for a long time. She doesn't seem to have much energy left,' said the Zambian turning on Ron. 'Why didn't you make sure she ate?'

'I'll do a drip,' said the grumpy midwife. She came round the bed and held my left hand up while she tried to get a needle in. 'Keep your arm still,' she said, annoyed.

The moment the plastic sack of liquid began dripping into my hand I knocked out the entire apparatus with one blow. I just couldn't deal with another form of pain, and at least this one I could get rid of. Outside I heard cockerels calling furiously and I wondered whether it was morning now.

The grumpy midwife clicked out of the delivery-room in her white clogs and came back.

'Push,' said everyone in the room.

I tried to do as I was told but I didn't know exactly what I should be pushing or how. I could feel a weight but I didn't know what it was. I didn't for a moment consider that it was a baby.

The stirrups hanging on either side of the bed came into focus. Oh, my God, I realized, they actually use these things on people.

'Get this fucking thing out of me!' I screamed.

Ron looked at me in shock, as did the two women. Even childbirth wasn't a good enough excuse for abusive language.

'Close your mouth!' snapped the grumpy midwife. 'Bend your head.'

What? I was totally confused.

The midwife came over, closed my mouth and forced my head forward.

'Get an ankle,' she said, manoeuvring my body because I seemed incapable of following any sort of instruction. 'Get an ankle with each hand.'

What? I had now discovered that if I stuffed my hand in my mouth and bit down on my knuckles it really helped. There was no way I was taking my hand out of my mouth in order to grab my ankle.

'She's not cooperating,' said the midwife. 'Go and call . . . '

Still I was on the bed, still I was in pain, but things had shifted slightly.

'You're doing it,' encouraged Ron. 'You're doing brilliantly.'

Then I realized I wasn't screaming any more.

Another woman entered the room, a large, friendly-looking midwife who loomed over the end of the bed. A moment later she had moved to where the drip had been. She quickly rolled up her sleeves and before I knew it she was pushing down on my stomach with both hands, her arms straight at the elbows, little drips of sweat on her forehead.

*She* was going to push this baby out of me? I was outraged. After ten months of protecting my stomach the idea that someone could just push down on it was unbelievable. I began to fight her violently, reaching up and clawing. The woman howled as I scratched my nails right the way down her arm.

'She's exhausted,' said the Zambian.

'She's not pushing,' complained the grumpy midwife.

'I am!' I protested. 'I'm trying.'

'What are you *doing!*' I heard Ron say from beside me, appalled.

I peered down the bed to see the glint of metal and the midwife wiping a large pair of scissors.

'This is normal,' said the midwife, irritated at Ronald's outburst.

Suddenly I was bombarded with instructions. Close your mouth! Push! Put your head down! Try! Push!

I felt as if blood was going to burst from my veins all over my face.

'If you don't push . . . ' said the grumpy midwife very deliberately and very slowly, moving so that her face was inches away from mine, 'your baby *is going to die.*'

How could she say such a thing? How could she say that? In absolute terror that I would give birth to a dead baby, I pushed again.

'The head is out!' said Ron from somewhere close by.

The next thing I knew there was a fantastic sudden gush and then a shocking gap, a calm. I had just dropped a cannonball. Was that it? My legs started trembling. I willed someone to tell me what was going on.

'It's a girl,' said Ron.

'Is it okay?' I asked.

'Yes.'

'Is it okay?' I asked again.

'Of course it is,' said Ron, smiling. 'It's a girl.'

And then I realized what he was saying, it was not a boy, it was a girl. And I knew that it had always been a girl, that we were meant to have a girl, that a part of me had been expecting a girl all along. A week ago I'd dreamt I had a girl and I woke to tell Ron we had to choose a girl's name just in case.

I looked down and saw a large, pale, naked body and a thick glutinous jellyfish umbilical cord. I couldn't take it in. I lay there still waiting for more pain, for the next contraction. I simply could not take it in that it was over. That a child had been born.

The grumpy midwife suddenly smiled. 'In Africa,' she said, speaking softly and peeling the gloves off her fingers, 'we believe that a person appreciates something that they have suffered for.'

I stared at her, unable to speak. Now everyone was busy and I was not doing a thing.

'Can I put my legs down?' I asked, unsure.

The midwife shook her head. 'Placenta.'

I mentally rifled back through the Internet sites to remember what this bit was about. The woman who had tried to push the baby out of me, whose arms I scratched so badly, moved closer and held my hand. I turned to face her, trying to apologize, and as she moved a finger slightly I saw deep-red blood come pumping out of the hole in my arm where the drip had been.

Then my baby was crying and Ron laid her on me and I thought: it's a little me. I knew her at once; she was completely and utterly recognizable. We had chosen her name. She would be Ruby in English and Yarubi in Seyei. Yarubi means one who is born during difficult times.

Ruby took to my breast immediately, without a second's thought or confusion. When she had finished sucking she was put into Ron's arms while I was taken to wash. The cleaner led me into a bathroom that must have been private it was so clean. She helped me climb, naked, into the bath and sponged off most of the blood. You should be using gloves, I thought, scared suddenly of all the blood I had seen in the maternity ward, of all the blood I had shed myself.

'Would you like a cup of tea?' asked the midwife when I staggered back into the delivery-room.

'Oh, God, yes,' I sighed.

'Well, your husband can go home and get you one.'

'Can't you give me one here?'

'No, my dear, your husband will get it for you.'

'And bring *food*,' I called as Ron kissed Ruby all over one more time before heading for the door.

After Ron had gone I settled myself back on the bed and fed Ruby again. When she appeared to have finished, I sat up a little, worriedly cradling her wobbly neck, and a shoot of hot yellow liquid came flooding out of her nose. She scrunched up her little black eyes and howled.

Oh, God, I thought, what have I done? What am I supposed to do?

'*Mma*!' I called out to the cleaner I could see sweeping the floor in the corridor.

The cleaner came in.

'*O a bona*,' I said, indicating the yellow mess and my screaming baby. '*Mathata ke eng?*'

'Take her to the midwife,' advised the cleaner.

'I'm too afraid,' I said, for the moment I even thought about standing up I realized I was terrified that I would drop the baby. 'You carry her!' I implored.

The cleaner chuckled and expertly lifted Ruby from me. Then I trudged after her down the hallway.

'Did you burp baby?' asked one of the midwives.

'No,' I said. I wanted to say that no one had told me to but it sounded so feeble. The Internet sites hadn't said anything about *after* the birth, about feeding or burping — or maybe they had and I had just not looked that far.

The midwife laughed. 'Ah, these new mothers,' she said, swinging Ruby over her shoulder. 'Look, baby is sleeping now. You must wrap her up,' and she began to swaddle Ruby tightly in cloth. 'And you must lay her on her stomach.'

'Oh,' I said. 'I thought you were supposed to lay them on their back.'

'No,' said the midwife, 'on the front.'

'But,' I said, 'in England they're laid on the back, so they won't choke.'

'I was *trained* in England, my dear,' said the midwife.

★ ★ ★

In the car on the way home I looked around Maun, slowly, as if I were swimming underwater. I couldn't believe that most of the women I saw going about their daily tasks — roadside vendors, women gathering water and firewood, women driving to work, running businesses — had gone through what I had gone through the night before. I wanted to ask other women about their experiences, most of all I wanted to know if they had screamed. The hospital midwife had told me I could scream; when I had I had been told to shut up. And I couldn't remember hearing any of the other women in the hospital scream. I wondered if I were a freak. I wondered why any woman could want to give birth without pain relief. Was it a test of something? Of courage? Pain threshold? Madness?

But once at home I was on the most natural high I had ever experienced in my life. It was a feeling of both immense relief and immense excitement. I crouched on the tiled floor in the living-room and studied Ruby in her little travel cot I had bought in Gaborone. I could not get over how fully formed she was. She had come out perfect. Her head was covered in thick black hair. Her face was pink and round and as smooth as a pot. She had a little pugdog nose and red, almost bruised-looking, lips. My mother-in-law would be pleased for Ruby's top lip had a little dip in it, exactly like her own.

Ruby's arms and legs looked long and strong, the fingers clasped into fists and the toes curled.

Everywhere she had deep creases of fat. How on earth had this human being been squashed up in my stomach for so long? 'She is *white*,' said Alice a little accusingly when she returned home from school to find the baby had arrived.

I spent that night watching Ruby in her cot, shining a torch on her face every now and again to make sure she was still breathing. She had a red strawberry patch on one eye that I hoped would go away, and plenty of hair lining her ears which seemed a bit wolf-like. I wished someone would come and weigh her and measure her and do all the things I had read about on the Internet, but I had discharged myself from hospital a few hours after birth and now Ruby was all mine.

# 25

The morning after Ruby was born, Ron drove back into Maun. He had had several messages from the office, and he wanted to tell his grandmother the news. But a few hours later he was back.

'What about the business?' I teased as he lay on the bed looking at his daughter. Ruby's fists were clenched and she held them up above her head like a triumphant boxer. 'What about the farm?'

Ron shrugged at the irrelevance of the questions; he couldn't take his eyes off his baby. I looked at the food he had brought home with him, devouring a slab of just-cooked beef as if I were a lioness.

'Is it okay if my mother comes?' Ron asked as at last he stood to go. Barclays Bank's network had crashed and he had an emergency call-out.

'Definitely,' I said, dying to show Ruby off, intensely proud of myself. If I could survive childbirth, I thought, then I could survive anything. I was far stronger than I had ever imagined. I had not given birth like Eliah under a tree, but I had done my best. 'You mean to visit or to stay?'

'Whatever you want,' Ron said. 'I'll bring her later.'

I lay back, happy at the idea of Eliah coming,

happy at the idea that someone was coming to help. I knew that, traditionally, women in Maun spent three months in confinement after the birth of their firstborn, usually staying at their mother's house. And while the term confinement sounded imprisoning, I knew the tradition had its benefits. New mothers stayed indoors and were waited on and fattened up and spoilt the way they had never been during pregnancy. I knew that in theory men, even the baby's father, were not allowed into the house. But things had changed in recent years, women with paid jobs couldn't simply be confined for three months, and nowadays more men were keen to stay with their babies as well. But I hadn't thought about confinement myself. I hadn't thought it would apply to me.

When Eliah arrived I was standing at the bedroom window. Ruby was lying happily in her cot. She had barely slept since she had been born, but my energy felt boundless as well. I watched as Eliah got out of the back of the Land Rover and headed towards our house, a tin bath balanced on her head. Since I had given birth everything around me had taken on a new sharpness so that every detail in my surroundings was bright and clear. I could see Eliah wore a pure-white poncho with gold buttons, her ZCC badge glinting in the sun, a red-and-gold-patterned wrap around her head. She looked expectant, happy even. When she reached the side of the house she put the bath down for a moment. Inside I could see a large box of washing powder, another of tea-leaves, a big bag of mealie meal, an industrial-sized jar of talcum powder and enough baby blankets to cover the First World.

'*Ko ko! Dumela,*' she said softly at the bedroom door.

'*Ee!*' I said and beamed. Madintwa had already been to visit, along with her neighbour. The two women had sat on the floor by the bed, every now and again hauling themselves up to lean over, pat and admire the baby. Then Madintwa had given both Ruby and me a good-luck spray of spit in the face and sat back, satisfied, her legs sticking out, her hands in her lap.

'*O montle,*' Mma Dintwa said — she is beautiful. '*O montle tota.*'

Now I sat up as Eliah appeared a little hesitantly in the doorway to the bedroom.

'*Tsena!*' I cried eagerly, inviting her in.

Eliah headed straight for Ruby in her cot. Then she stood and looked down at Ruby who was asleep at last, her jowls sagging, her eyelids heavy, a smell of milk in the air.

★ ★ ★

The next morning, a little after sunrise, Eliah came into our bedroom with a plastic baby's bath and assorted supplies. Ron was up already and making coffee in the kitchen. Alice was getting ready for school. I was bending over Ruby who was fussing in the cot.

'She is hungry,' said Eliah behind me.

I laughed. 'I've just fed her.'

400

'She is hungry,' Eliah repeated, gesturing at her own breast.

I hesitated. I had just fed Ruby. But perhaps my mother-in-law was right. I picked Ruby up and carried her to our bed, lying down on my side to feed her again. I looked up to see Eliah was frowning. 'You can't feed lying down,' she said.

'Yes, I can,' I said, smiling back at her. 'It's better that way, it's better for my back.' I settled down and Ruby continued to feed. When I looked up a few moments later Eliah had bought a plastic chair in from the porch and was positioning it near the bed, facing where I lay. She sat down, and then immediately stood up and came over. Without speaking she leant over and, with her cold hands, rearranged my breasts. Then she returned to the chair. I smiled down at Ruby, at the way she pulled greedily three times and then sucked and then sighed. But I was unnerved by what Eliah had just done. And I didn't like being watched.

A little while later Eliah announced it was time for the baby to be bathed. She poured a little water into the plastic bath, felt the temperature carefully with her fingers, and then indicated that I pass Ruby to her. Although Ruby looked big and strong, her vulnerability worried me. The idea of bathing this wobbly creature who couldn't even hold her own head up, was scary. So I sat back on the floor to watch Eliah do the job.

Eliah peeled off Ruby's nappy and, cradling her along the length of one arm, she put her in the bath. At once Ruby opened her mouth and screamed. Eliah ignored the noise; she began to clean the baby from head to toe. Ruby thrashed and splashed and her face turned red with screams. I got up from the floor, hovering, not quite confident enough to demand my baby back, to demand that Eliah stop washing her. Just when I was about to object, Eliah decided the bath was done. Effortlessly she lifted Ruby out, liberally sprinkled talcum powder all over her, put on a fresh nappy, then a sleep suit, and then swaddled her entirely in a thick white blanket.

'It's a bit hot,' I murmured.

'She is hungry,' Eliah replied, handing my baby back to me.

At midday she bathed Ruby again. And when the sun set she did it for the third time. 'She's crying a lot,' I said, standing with my arms folded, watching. 'I don't think she likes it.'

Eliah rested an elbow on the floor for a moment and looked up. Her expression said that babies weren't supposed to enjoy this; they were to be washed because that was what had to be done.

'I want Ruby to love water,' I said, kneeling down so that I could take over. 'She isn't liking this.'

Eliah sat back a little from the bath. She muttered something and her tone seemed ominous.

'Sorry,' I said. 'But I want her to like it.' I looked up then to see that Alice had come quietly into the room, and was standing there looking from her stepmother to grandmother with interest. I wasn't sure if I were now feeling the effects of lack of sleep, or if Alice really was enjoying the sense of confrontation in the air.

★   ★   ★

Over the next two days Eliah continued to wash Ruby at sunrise, midday and sunset. In between she urged me to feed her. When she was not either washing Ruby or watching me feed her, she cooked up meals intended to strengthen and fatten me up. But they were foods I didn't like: great masses of *phaletshe*, tin bowls of goat meat shiny with oil, frothy fish-heads that left the house reeking and made me want to retch. Eliah knew I didn't like these foods, that the only traditional food I really loved was *leketa*, a type of wild spinach, yet still she continued to cook them. I didn't know if this were because they were the only foods she knew how to make, or if she were determined I would eventually eat them. One afternoon I came staggering out of the bedroom, my stitches causing me pain, to have a look round the kitchen for food. I stopped, surprised, by the pantry area. I hadn't known Eliah had brought so much with her, I couldn't remember seeing all these supplies arriving in the house. But there were sacks now of mealie meal, a tub of white cooking fat, enormous bottles of sunflower oil.

'Hi, hon,' Ron said as he came into the house and I turned surprised, for I hadn't heard him come in. My senses seemed to be dimming, I couldn't remember seeing Ron leave the house that morning, or what our last conversation had been.

'Is she staying a while then?' I asked, pointing at the pantry.

Ron shrugged. 'Just while you need her.'

I took a deep breath, willing myself to think before I spoke. 'It's just . . .'

'Where's Yarubi?' Ron smiled. 'Where's my little *phuthumphi*?'

'In the bedroom, practising her boxing moves.'

Ron took a step towards the bedroom and then turned. 'Have you eaten? My mother says you need to eat more.'

'The thing is,' I said, 'I really fancy some, you know, English food.'

'You didn't like the fish?'

'What fish?'

'I gave my mother some fish last night. I told her you only like it fried.'

'Oh, the fish, yes, well, she cooked that. She boiled it and boiled it . . .'

Then Ruby gave a cry from the bedroom and like a shot Ron was off down the hallway.

'Here comes the rain,' I said the next morning, hopefully, as I watched Eliah prepare Ruby's bath. But the rains had stopped now and the heat was unbearable. Eliah walked around in an old pink bra and skirt.

I had said it was fine that Eliah move in, but I had totally forgotten that in the ten years we had known each other we had never actually been alone for more than half an hour. And now we had opportunities for confrontation several times a day. On the third morning I came back to the bedroom from washing to see Eliah feeding Ruby from a bottle of gripe water.

'No!' I said, too loudly.

Eliah turned, a scowl on her face.

I took the bottle and turned it around. 'See, it's alcohol. It's eighty per cent alcohol. You know, like beer. Or wine.'

Eliah looked past me. 'You give it to the baby when she cries, when she cannot sleep.'

'Sorry,' I said, 'but I just don't want to.' I tried to smile. I knew Eliah was trying to help but she never made suggestions, she never asked, she just told me what to do or did it unasked herself. I bent down to scoop Ruby up, willing my mother-in-law to leave us alone. I had always been a little intimidated by Eliah, but now I realized with a feeling of both guilt and dismay that it was quite possible that I actually didn't like her. She was too stern, too self-controlled, she never offered, she just took charge. And now she was spoiling things, she was spoiling the birth of my baby and I wanted Ron to stop her. I took Ruby from Eliah and laid down with her on the bed, peeling away her swaddling until she was naked but for her nappy.

'*Ao!*' Eliah objected.

I looked up.

'She will get cold.'

I wanted to say it was summer, it was ninety degrees outside. But Ruby was fussing again. Eliah marched over and began to re-tie the swaddling. Incensed, I got up from the bed. 'She mustn't get too hot,' I said a little desperately. 'In

England, people don't let their babies get too hot. It's dangerous.'

'She is a Motswana,' said Eliah flatly.

'Yes. But I'm not. And I'm her mother.' I walked to the window and fiddled uselessly with the blinds.

★  ★  ★

'How long does this confinement last?' I asked Ron that night. We were sitting in the living-room, together on the sofa, Ruby in my arms between us. It was late. Alice was in her room admiring herself in her slice of mirror. Eliah was in the spare room resting.

'*Mma?*' Ron was holding his finger in Ruby's hands, marvelling at the strength of her grasp.

'This confinement thing, how long does it last? I mean, at what point is it over?'

'When the umbilical cord is healed, I think. Why?'

'Why? Because,' I lowered my voice, 'your mum is driving me mad. It's like a battle zone in here, honestly Ron. We're not getting on at all. I'm afraid to even come out of our room.'

'Oh, come on.'

'It's true.

Ron hung his head, looking miserable. At last he nodded. 'My grandmother agrees. She says my mother has to move out before she drives you mad.'

'Exactly!' I smiled, relieved. At least I had an ally in Madintwa. 'The umbilical cord is fine, look. We can take this plastic thing off now, see, it's almost healed up.'

Ron bent his head to inspect.

'You tell her,' I urged.

Ron looked miserable again. 'I can't.'

'Yes, you can. You don't have to be horrible, just say it nicely. Say the cord is healed, thanks for all your help, and take her back home.'

We sat in silence for a while, watching our daughter. Then I heard a soft but urgent knocking on the door. 'Who's that?' I asked, getting up. I went to the back door, the knocking increasing, becoming louder now. It was pitch-black outside, I couldn't think who it could be.

'Who is it?' I asked at the door.

'It is me.'

'What?'

'It is me,' came my mother-in-law's voice.

'It's your mum!' I told Ron, laughing. 'What's she doing outside?' I opened the door to see Eliah in her bra and skirt. Her hair was wet and by her feet, on the porch, I saw her metal bath upturned, suds seeping out. She had been having a bath.

'I didn't know you were outside!' I said smiling.

Eliah pushed past me, her face thunderous.

★   ★   ★

On the fifth day I began to feel weak. Ruby still woke every hour during the night and I fed her and then I couldn't get back to sleep. I checked her compulsively, while next to us Ron slept soundly. In the morning I opened my eyes before either of them, overcome with excitement that I had a baby. Sometimes I wondered where she had come from.

Each day she seemed to change, to grow stronger, to begin to be aware of her surroundings. But I felt my energy sagging now. I went out of the room when Eliah washed Ruby, unable to bear the sight. I saw the bottle of gripe water was half-empty, though I had not seen Ruby drinking it. I peeled off the swaddling at every opportunity and then guiltily re-tied it when Eliah came into the room. Eliah's presence was everywhere. She no longer said '*ko ko*', when she came into the bedroom, but slid silently in. I had offended her, I thought, by not wanting to do things her way. But she wasn't going to give in or compromise, she was determined whereas I was exhausted, confused and hadn't slept for days.

That evening a car drew up outside and I went to the bedroom window to watch. As I stood holding back the red blinds I saw Selina, Ron's stepmother, get out of an old white Land Rover with her daughter Rita. It had been a long time since I'd seen either of them and I was pleased they had come to see the baby. I let the blind fall back into place and went to pick Ruby up, wiping milk off her face, getting her ready for visitors. Ron's father had been to visit the day before, a short polite visit during which he took photographs of his latest grandchild. Now she would meet more of the family. I settled Ruby on my lap and waited. I could hear Selina and Rita's footsteps outside on the porch, then the voices of Kookaburra and her cousins playing on the tree which overlooked the river.

'*Ko ko!*' I heard Selina say at the back door.

'*Ee,*' Eliah replied.

Then there was an exchange that I couldn't make out. I looked up as Alice came into the room. 'Who's here?' I asked, although I already knew.

'It is Mrs Ridge and Rita.'

'And the kids?'

'*Ee.* But MaMozambia says the children can't come in.'

'Oh?'

Alice nodded.

'Children aren't allowed in when there's a newborn?'

'*Ee.* They can make the baby ill.'

'Oh, okay. So is Selina coming in?'

Alice didn't reply, for Eliah now had joined her at the doorway. 'Mrs Ridge is here,' she said rather loudly. 'Can she come in?'

'Of course!' I laughed.

Selina had already followed Eliah down the corridor and now she too squeezed herself into the doorway.

'Stay there!' Eliah ordered.

Selina froze, one foot in the door. 'Ah, Caitlin, my daughter. I have come to see the baby.'

'Here she is!' I beamed, holding Ruby up.

But as Selina took another step into the room Eliah again warned her back. Then suddenly the two women were back in the living-room, their voices raised.

'What's going on?' I asked Alice.

'They are fighting,' she said, her eyes round.

'I can hear that. What are they arguing about?'

Alice put her eyes to the ground, a smile creeping around her lips. 'MaMozambia says Mrs Ridge can't come in because . . . she is dirty.'

'What?' Ruby began to cry and I jiggled her on my lap.

'*Ee*. She has boyfriends. So she can't come in. MaMozambia says you don't know who she is sleeping with.'

I was struggling now both to keep hold of Ruby and to understand what was going on. I could see why children weren't allowed in; perhaps they had a cold or other infection they might pass on. But then Ron's grandmother, and her neighbour, were just as likely to have a cold and they had seen Ruby when she was barely a day old. And Madintwa had spat in her face. And if Selina did have a lover, then what about Ron's dad, who was he sleeping with? And what of Eliah herself? Until recently she had had a boyfriend too. Eliah seemed to be taking advantage of the situation; relishing the power she now had to decide who could come in and who couldn't. At last the women's voices stopped and I heard the back door slam and then the car start up and drive off. Half an hour later another car drove up and I could see through the window that it was Pearl. I opened the top window and waved. I was dying for Pearl to come in so I could tell her about my confinement and ask her what I could do. As I stood waving, Ron came into the bedroom behind me. He had missed the drama with Selina and Rita, and had just returned from work.

'Come in!' I called to Pearl and, standing outside on the sand, she waved back.

I lay down on the bed and waited. But at once I could hear Eliah's voice at the back door. Ron went out of the room and then came back.

'What's going on now?' I asked.

'Pearl wants to come in.'

'Obviously,' I said. 'She wants to see the baby.'

'My mother doesn't think it's a good idea.'

'Why not?'

Ron picked Ruby up from where she lay and walked with her to the window. Then he lifted her up so Pearl, now standing back outside, could see.

'This is mad,' I objected. 'She's my friend, I want her to come in.'

'Not yet,' said Ron, not turning round, not looking at me.

'Look,' I said, going over to the window and touching Ruby's tummy. 'The cord is healed, hasn't it? The confinement can be over now.'

Ron determinedly shook his head. Outside Pearl pulled a face, gave me the thumbs up, and went back to her car.

'She's so small,' Ron said softly, holding Ruby against his chest. 'I don't want anything to happen to her.'

I looked at him and I suddenly remembered that he was an only child, an only child in a place where people usually had many children. And

411

Eliah was the mother of an only child. But perhaps she *had* had other children, I thought with a flash of realization, perhaps something had happened to them just as something had happened to two of Madintwa's babies. And maybe that was why both Eliah and Ron wanted to take such extra special care of the baby we had now.

'I don't want anything to happen to her either,' I said, my voice softening. 'But she has to meet people. She can't be held captive in a house for months on end. She needs to go outside. She needs to see new faces. Look, I know your mum's worried about infection and so on, but you can't keep Ruby wrapped up in blankets for ever. And it's not like Pearl, or Selina or anyone, is going to make Ruby ill just by looking at her.'

'You don't think?' Ron looked worried.

'No, I don't. The cord is healed. Your mum can go now.'

★   ★   ★

But still Eliah stayed. Still she cooked *phaletshe* and boiled fish-heads. Still she washed Ruby three times a day. Now when the phone rang Eliah would answer it herself. Then she would come into the bedroom and tell me I was wanted. But when I got to the phone in the spare room Eliah had always put the receiver down and the line was always dead. One morning I looked out of the window to see that my friends from WAR, Stef and Ruth, had come to visit. Stef knocked loudly on the window. 'Cait!' she

412

yelled. 'I've been ringing you and ringing you! What's wrong with your phone?' She held up a six-pack of Guinness. Beside her Ruth brandished a tiny pair of baby shoes.

'Come round the back!' I hissed through the window. 'Ruby's asleep. She never sleeps. For God's sake don't wake her up!'

I rushed to the back door before my mother-in-law had a chance. But Eliah was already on the porch.

'*Dumela Mma*,' Stef and Ruth greeted her.

'*Ee*.' Eliah looked worried.

'These are my friends,' I said calmly. 'They're from England,' I explained, although Stef was not. 'In England we visit when a baby is born. Are they allowed to come in?'

Eliah shifted on the porch step. She didn't reply.

I took a deep breath. I didn't want Ruby woken up. I didn't want a fight with my mother-in-law. But these were my friends. I had not stood up to Eliah when she barred Pearl, and later Beauty, from coming in and I had regretted it ever since, although I knew they would understand because they were Batswana themselves. This was different.

'Ron's mum is worried about the baby,' I said.

Behind me Eliah picked up a broom and began to sweep.

'She's got it into her head the baby needs to be confined.'

'What?' Stef raised her eyebrows.

'It's tradition,' I said a little defensively. 'It's just to protect the baby.'

'Shall we come back later?' Ruth offered.

'No, no, come in,' I insisted, leading the way to the door. 'Don't laugh but I've made a video of Ruby, shall I show you? Is that okay?' I asked Eliah, explaining now in Setswana.

Eliah shrugged as if she couldn't care but her body was stiff as if, at any moment, she would fly to the door and bar entry herself.

'This is a bit much,' said Stef as we sat down in the living-room to watch a video of Ruby who was sleeping, unseen, a few metres way.

'Don't start,' I said. 'Just don't get me started. Oh, to hell with it, just come in and see her.'

Stef and Ruth followed me into the bedroom, bent down over Ruby and cooed and aahed. She was huge, they said, and she was gorgeous.

\* \* \*

'Your mum has to go,' I told Ron that night. 'I can't take it. She's totally taken over. If you don't talk to her then I'm going to.'

Ron got up, as if to physically escape what I was saying, and stood by the front door.

'She wouldn't even let Stef and Ruth in!' I said as I got up to follow.

'Ao!' Eliah objected, appearing from around the corner of the house.

I turned, surprised. 'It's true.' I eyed her. 'You wouldn't let them in.' My heart began thumping. For weeks we had paced around each other without actually fighting, now I was taking things a step further.

Eliah shook her head vehemently. 'I didn't say that.'

'You didn't want them to come in,' I insisted.

'Feed her,' Eliah said, taking a step forward towards me. I flinched and clasped Ruby to my chest as if Eliah were going to take her away from me.

# 26

And still Eliah stayed. Now she skirted around me, less insistent on the rituals of bathing and feeding, but the house was filled with an atmosphere of suppressed fury. I couldn't see how Eliah and I could ever go back to the relationship we once had. And now I wasn't sure what that relationship had been. I had never forgotten how, shortly after we first met, she had told Ron she approved of me but that people change. But I thought I hadn't changed, it was Eliah who had. At first she had not seemed to expect too much from me. I was a foreigner and I didn't know the ways of the Batswana. She had been friendly, in a rather cool way, and had never pressured me into being a dutiful Motswana daughter-in-law. She had accepted that Ron and I lived apart from the rest of the family, and she had never demanded my presence at weddings or funerals. She had given me gifts and she had rarely made any requests in return, never asking me for money the way other family members did. She had seemed to take it for granted that we would build her house, but it was not something she had ever asked for. But then slowly, over the past few years, she had begun to exert her pressure on our lives, first suggesting that Ron and I adopt Gabs, and then that I should give birth naturally in Maun. Now she was telling me how to look after my child.

It was open now that we didn't like each other, but it wasn't open enough. Our limits of language, our differences of culture, meant we could never really be open. I could talk to Eliah, but I could never really express myself. And I realized that it wasn't just Eliah who had changed but me as well. I was no longer so eager to fit in, to be liked, or to compromise.

As the days went by I began to try to establish my own rituals of looking after a new-born baby and, at last, Eliah began to go out. In the mornings she washed and dressed and went to church, where she had been promoted into a senior position. Now she wore a blue dress with the collar up, a green tie tucked tightly into her waistband, and military-style green epaulettes on her shoulders. On her head she wore a green beret puffed up like a tea cosy. She never announced either her departure or return so that sometimes I just felt that she had gone, the air in the house felt lighter.

Eventually I decided I had to return to some sort of normality. But at first I was too afraid to take Ruby outside. For the first few weeks of her life she had not left the house. The first time I went outside with her I shook with nervousness in case I dropped her. So I put her in a travel cot and carried her out in that, laying her on the grass, showing her the world around her. I wondered how long it would be before she would focus, before she could put her head up and really look around. I imagined that one day she would simply stand up and begin to walk, open her mouth and begin to talk. But I never left

Ruby alone in the garden, not even if Eliah were there, for I feared the snakes. Since we had moved into our plot I had seen several snakes a month, including a gigantic, shiny, green boomslang with emerald eyes which I had stumbled upon one morning, its head poking up from a pile of grass.

★　★　★

One day, without warning, Eliah left. I woke to hear Ron loading his mother's supplies on the back of the car. Ruby was sleeping and I went to the window, lifting the blinds a little to peer out. The sun was rising and the garden was aglow. I could see the morning light flickering on the fronds of the two palm trees to the left of the window, and, further down the plot, casting shadows on the walls of my office.

I walked into the living-room in time to see Eliah leaving through the back door with a large hessian bag on her head.

'What's happening?' I asked as Ron came back into the house for his bag of tools. 'Is your mum going?'

'*Ee.*'

'Oh. When was that decided?' I felt hurt that no one had discussed this with me, even though it was I who had wanted Eliah to leave.

'Last night. She says it's time for her to return to Morutsa.'

'Oh. Well, I guess that's good then?'

'Yup.' Ron smiled briefly and kissed me goodbye.

'I wanted . . . ' I said, following him to the door.

Ron turned round.

'I wanted, you know, to thank her. For all her help . . . '

Ron raised his eyebrows.

'No, really. I mean she meant well, didn't she? Don't you think we should say goodbye properly?'

'She's in the car.'

'What, already?'

'*Ee.*'

'You watch Ruby for a second . . . '

Ron sighed; he was going to be late for work.

I hurried outside, turning the corner of the porch and walking barefooted on the sand towards the car. I could see Eliah sitting in the passenger seat, her back rigid, her face stern.

'*Go siame,*' I said, bending down a little to speak through the open window.

'*Ee,*' Eliah continued looking straight ahead.

'Thank you,' I said, 'for all your help.'

Her eyes flickered to mine and for a moment I thought she would speak, that she would express some regret for the misunderstandings we had had. That she would accept my thanks for her help. That she would wish me luck. But she remained sitting, staring wordlessly ahead until Ron came out and got into the car. As I stood there watching them drive off, I realized that Ron was in the middle, he was caught between his mother and his wife and if he ever had to decide between the two I didn't know whose side he would take.

A few weeks later my parents arrived and at last I could relax. Each morning my parents took Ruby off in the pram, along with a new dog Ron had bought from Gaborone. Our old dogs had long since died and we had named the new one Rocky. My parents went exploring, finding new paths along the river, discovering how to distinguish a pile of hippo dung from that left by a cow, designing inventive ways to keep the river flies off Ruby's face. And at home they laid Ruby out on a swinging chair Ron had hung from the largest leadwood tree, pushing her and laughing as she shook her boxer's fists in the air. And I was indulged as well, encouraged to rest or to hide in my office and work. My mother did her best not to interfere, although she worried about the amount of time I devoted to breastfeeding. 'I think Ruby's full,' she said one evening as milk spurted convulsively first out of Ruby's mouth and then her nose.

Ron was largely absent during their visit. He had the company to look after and he had the farm to tend. He was not only the breadwinner in our small family, but the sole breadwinner in an ever-increasing extended family. He still checked on Madintwa and Gabs several times a day and now I discovered that he was providing for Alice's two younger sisters, Gosegomang and Ene, since their mother was no longer alive. He came home one evening to say Eliah had suggested we adopt them. But I said no. We already had Alice, we already had Gabs, and we were trying to provide for Rra Nama's five children as well.

The day my parents left I drove home from the airport with Ruby snuggled next to me in a car seat I had borrowed from Beauty. I drove slowly along the path from the Hippo Pool to our plot, turning to follow the road home, the edges of the path lined with tall green grass. And when I parked the car on the sand in front of the house I had a sudden sense of dread. There was no reason for it, the house looked as it always did, there was no one around, nothing to disturb the peace. But still, as I picked Ruby up and walked round the house to the porch, I had a feeling that something wasn't quite right. I tried to ignore the feeling, to concentrate on happy things such as the fact that my sister was arriving for a visit in just a few weeks.

She was to stay for a month, and now instead of praying for rain I prayed that the weather would hold and Flora would have the sun she craved. I couldn't wait for her to arrive.

★   ★   ★

'Babe!' Flora cried as she emerged from the arrivals hall at Maun airport. She rushed towards Ruby who hung in a sling around my neck. I had tried to carry her the way Batswana women did on my back but the act of doubling over to tie her on was too uncomfortable.

Ruby opened her eyes and beamed at her English aunty, perhaps sensing that Flora's

421

suitcase was packed with coordinated outfits for her niece to wear.

★ ★ ★

A month later and I was alone again. The house and garden became the boundaries of my world and I felt safe and secure, away from the demands of the real world. I no longer shopped, but gave Ron lists of what we needed for the house. My days revolved around Ruby from the moment I opened my eyes in the morning. And still Ruby never slept for more than two hours at a stretch. In the mornings I pushed her to the Hippo Pool, and in the late afternoons I lay on the bed with Ruby naked beside me, her body a soft cushion of flesh, creases of fat in her legs and arms, little deposits of grime in the folds of her neck. The strawberry patch above her eye had faded, the thin layer of hair on her ears had gone. She could focus now; she could lay her fingers splayed on my face, her eyes on mine. Sometimes she would laugh, her mouth open like a little bird, her arms and legs jerking away happily in different, uncoordinated, directions. Other times she looked like her father, or Alice, her mouth turned down in a stony stare, her eyebrows raised as if disputing a point someone had just made. Sometimes she looked as if she were already forty years old.

There were days when I wondered if I would ever return to my old life. I could no longer work, and I couldn't find anyone to help me. Eliah was back in Morutsa, Madintwa was too ill, Gabs was looking after Madintwa. Ron spent even longer hours at the farm where the work was never-ending. As each crucial project was finished — the farm cleared, the farm fenced, the goats moved, the soil turned, the seeds planted, the farm weeded, the harvest gathered — the cycle began again. At home our plot had become totally over-grown. Some mornings I struggled with the lawnmower I had bought Ron one birthday, but Ruby howled when I turned it on. I managed to clear a small area around the porch, to keep it sandy and free from undergrowth, but even here the original bush was inching its way back up to the walls of the house.

I never seemed to have time to clean or to wash or to cook or to garden, yet all I was doing was looking after a baby. I saw Pearl often; she came round with her daughters and helped where she could, as did Beauty. I had not seen Veronica because she had just had her third child, another boy, called Robin, and she was far away in Sowa recovering. I couldn't ask Alice to help for she was at school. And now she had become reluctant again, coming home later and later each day. One afternoon I caught sight of her far off along the riverbank, walking with a boy. I watched as they walked along the path to our house. And then, once on the flood plain and in view of the house, the boy turned and walked away. I told Ron about this, annoyed and suspicious that the boy hadn't wanted to be seen, that he hadn't had the nerve to come near the house where Alice lived. But Ron said this was proper, the boy was being respectful by keeping a distance.

One morning, pushing Ruby in her pram towards the Hippo Pool, I stopped to see a thin white man walking quickly across the flood plain. 'All right, girl?' he cried, his hands swinging together, palms clasped. It was Andrew, my old colleague from the *Okavango Observer*. He and Kerrin had left Africa to travel around South America but now they were back, and they had a five-month-old baby girl, Isabella. Kerrin and I had never known each other that well before, but now I was amazed at how interesting it was to have long conversations about breast-feeding, about machines that helped you express milk, about dummies, about whether or not to let a baby cry at night.

★　★　★

When Ruby was six months old I drove her to the chemist to have her second round of immunizations. I was worried; she had had a bad reaction the first time, with a fever and screaming. This time I dosed her with painkillers before the jab and drove home fearfully, checking her temperature, hoping this time it would be different. That afternoon Madintwa and Gabs came round and Ron decided to cut the lawn. I was lying down in the bedroom when Ruby woke up and yelled. Her face was flushed and her eyes were screwed up tight. Her yells turned to screams and the screams got more and more desperate. I couldn't see how she was even managing to breathe.

'Ron!' I knocked on the window.

He stopped and turned off the lawnmower. 'What?'

'It's Ruby. Help. I don't know what's wrong with her. She won't stop screaming.'

Ron wiped the sweat off his face and came inside.

'See!' I said in a panic. 'Feel how hot she is. And look how red it is where the injection was, this lump is huge!'

'She'll be fine,' Ron said, though he didn't look convinced.

'But how do you know?'

'She just needs to sleep it off.'

'But she's in pain! I can't stand this,' and I picked Ruby up and hurried outside, with some vague idea that being outside would help her, would calm her down. I began to walk around the perimeter of the house, jiggling Ruby up and down, and still she screamed.

'Here, let me do that,' said Ron, taking his daughter and holding her up against his chest. He sang to her and rocked her and then he too began to walk round the house. Still panicking I followed him. 'Do you think we should go to the clinic? Should we call Dr Patrick?'

Then Madintwa appeared, upset by the noise, hobbling on to the porch clutching her walking stick. 'Mozambia *we*!' she called as Ron shot past. 'What's wrong?'

'Ruby had an injection this morning,' I said. 'She won't stop crying. And she's got a fever.'

'*A ka ka*,' Madintwa said, and she hobbled off

after Ron. Now all three of us were walking around the house and still Ruby screamed.

'Stop following me,' Ron said on his fourth trip around the house. 'She's going to sleep, see?'

I stopped where I was and Madintwa stopped beside me. We stood there, our ears straining to listen. The screams were growing less intense now, we could hear hiccups and then, at last, silence. Ron reappeared on the porch, his face triumphant. He went inside and laid Ruby in her cot and then he returned to mowing the lawn.

I dragged a chair outside and sat in the shade of the pawpaw tree, Madintwa next to me on the sand. Gabs and Alice were washing clothes down by the river. The plot was peaceful now.

'He's working too hard,' I said as I watched Ron begin to hack around a tree stump.

'*Ee.*' Beside me Madintwa shaded her eyes with her hand. 'He is too thin.'

'He works too hard,' I said again. 'I hardly ever see him.' I shifted on the chair. I hadn't meant to start this conversation, but seeing Ron at home for once, working on our garden, soothing Ruby to sleep, I wanted it always to be like this. And I realized it never was. 'He spends all his time at the farm,' I said, 'when he's not at the office. He doesn't even see Ruby . . . '

Madintwa straightened up.

I looked at her, expecting to see a smile of sympathy, of agreement, on her face. But her expression, I realized in confusion, was offended.

'What?' I asked.

Madintwa threw her hands into the air. 'What will we eat? What will we eat if Mozambia

426

doesn't work at the farm?' She looked at me, her eyes wavering as if I had just threatened to steal her pension.

'Well,' I said hesitantly, 'we can buy you food.' I wanted to add that the farm didn't bring anything to the family anyway; it was hard labour with virtually nothing in return. The rains had been good at the beginning of the year, but still the only crop worth selling had been water-melons. We bought most of the food the family needed from a shop. And as for the goats, the precious goats that everyone always worried about, many of them had wandered off or died.

Madintwa spat on the sand. 'That is our family's farm, Mozambia knows that. He is trying to help the family. That farm is the way we will eat.'

'I didn't mean . . . ' I started but Madintwa shushed me.

'You don't want him to help us?' she asked.

'Of course I do,' I protested, 'but he has a family here as well, he has . . . '

Madintwa grabbed at her stick and propelled herself up on the sand. 'Mozambia is helping the family.'

I sat silently on the chair. I had never fallen out with Madintwa. We had always been friends; she had always been on my side. I found it hard to see why she thought Ron should put the farm above everything else, that he should put his grandmother, his mother, his daughter, his adopted daughter, his aunts, his uncles, before his own wife and daughter. And my thoughts shocked me because I had never before thought of myself as a wife. Now I knew I didn't want an extended family, I wanted my own small family at home — Ron and Ruby and Alice. I couldn't even see the benefits of the extended family; they demanded and they begged and they gossiped and they fought. They wanted food, they wanted firewood, they wanted clothes. But when I wanted help from them, they were nowhere to be seen.

★  ★  ★

By the winter of 2000 I was increasingly isolated. Ron and I had always done things together; we had always been best friends. Now we operated like a Batswana couple, with distinct family and social roles. He went out to work, he farmed, he earned the money, he was the head of the house. I cooked and I cleaned and I looked after Ruby. I had what so many women wanted: a responsible husband who never went to bars, who never had affairs, and who repeatedly told me I didn't have to work because he would provide for me. But this wasn't what I wanted.

Now when Ron came home I was full of resentment.

'You're never here,' I said the day Ruby turned eight months old. She had spent the morning crawling solidly around the house, every now and again stopping to inspect her knees. When she got tired of crawling she tried scratching — first on the covers of books, then along my arms, then the surface of the sofa — and then, with two new teeth, she tried chewing.

'What do you mean?' Ron said from where he

lay on the floor. Ruby sat before him, inspecting his belt-buckle. 'Da!' she cried. 'Guh!'

'Just that.' I moved into the living-room. 'You're never here.'

'Well, I'm here now, aren't I?'

I sighed impatiently. 'I know you have to help your family, I know you're the only child, but you have to draw the line somewhere.'

Ron began to take Ruby's nappy off.

'What are you doing?'

'My grandmother says she shouldn't wear nappies all the time.'

'Oh?'

'*Ee*. They will flatten her buttocks.'

I laughed. Madintwa adored Ruby's buttocks, she said they were just like hers.

Ron looked up, offended. Ruby beamed and began singing, her tongue flicking back and forth as if she were ululating at a wedding.

'Anyway . . . ' I began again. 'You don't have to help your family every single minute of the day. You can say no. You're the one who is *choosing* to do all this. Why are you never here?'

But Ron had nothing to say. I asked and I talked, I ranted and I yelled. But whatever I did, he had nothing to say.

In October that year I flew back to England. I wanted to take Ruby to meet my brother, to see my parents and my sister again. But I also wanted to know if life would be better in England. I didn't seem to be able to see things in perspective any more. I couldn't tell what was wrong or how to put it right. So I bought an open ticket and I left.

# PART SIX

# 27

'I've made a New Year's resolution,' Ron said softly as we sat on the porch, watching the last of the day's sun sinking down behind the trees on the riverbank opposite. It had been a long journey back to Botswana, we had been travelling for almost two days, and Ruby was sleeping on my lap. I had only lasted three months in the UK. I had felt homesick for Maun, for my own home, and for Ron. Ruby was nearly a year old now, things were becoming easier. I could sleep at night, my mind felt clearer. And Ruby needed her father; she needed to be where she belonged.

Ron spoke quietly, careful not to wake Ruby. 'I'm going to spend more time at home.'

'Yes?' I asked, pleased to hear this, not quite believing it.

'*Ee*. My family are driving me nuts. You're right; I can't do everything for them. And you're my family too. That's my New Year's resolution.'

Ruby smiled in her sleep and I cuddled her closer. Our plot was magical in this light, overgrown but lush, the trees and the grass encircling the entire house. The sinking sun lit the fronds of the banana tree and the air was full of the sound of cicadas. Our dog Rocky sat by the fence watching two stray dogs running along the river's edge. I watched as Ron got up from the chair. His head was freshly shaved, making him look older, and he had worry lines on his forehead.

'I washed the bath. It's so clean you won't believe it.'

I laughed. 'You've been busy.'

'And I'm sorry about the garden.' He stood on the edge of the porch, his hand resting on one of the pillars. 'I really tried to keep the grass cut. I didn't want you to come back and find everything overgrown like this. I'm going to clear all the front and build a deck. What do you think?'

The next morning I rose early. I was back in Africa now, the sun was up, and the first urge I had was to open all the windows. The sky was clear. There would be no clouds, no rain, no drizzle. Down by the river I could hear the call of the lehututu birds as they strutted along in single file, the manic honk of a donkey running along the grass, a host of cockerels announcing that day was here.

Ron left for work and I took off Ruby's clothes and left her to stagger around naked, slipping a little on the smooth tiled floor for her steps were still unsteady.

'Mama!' she said and I ran to help her upright again. In the months since we'd been in England Ruby had learnt to walk and she loved to cruise around a room holding on to the wall, stopping to point and say 'Car!' each time she saw a beetle or a fly. She walked with her tummy thrust out, taking her new role seriously.

That morning I wiped the dust from all the

surfaces of the house, the place seemed unused, as if it had stood unoccupied for the whole three months we had been gone. I wondered where Ron had been staying all this time. There were spiders' webs in the kitchen sink and sandy dust on the red blinds. I took pride in my work; this was my house. I wanted it clean, I wanted to make a fresh start. Things would be different now. Ron would spend more time at home. I wouldn't complain. And now I would be able to work again, too, for a local nursery school had a place for Ruby.

Ten days after I returned from England, I picked Ruby up from the nursery along with Editor. I had met Editor that morning, she had been working as a cleaner but she wanted a job with children. She was young with a shy, wide smile, her hair scraped back into a bun, her finger-nails freshly painted a pale pink. Editor would go to nursery with Ruby, and she would look after her at home while I worked in the office.

It was a bright sunny Friday morning as I drove through Maun on my way home, Ruby in her car seat, Editor sitting in the back. The tar roads were busy; there were so many vehicles now that people had begun to demand that traffic-lights be installed. I glanced to my left where, in the distance, a third new shopping mall had been built. Security guards had been hired to patrol inside the shops, and outside on the pavements small boys had begun to beg aggressively. We passed a man in bedraggled clothes gesturing in the middle of the road as cars swerved around him. Then I looked at Ruby.

'She's asleep,' I called back to Editor. 'There's no point me showing you where we live if she's asleep. I'll take her home and she'll probably sleep for a couple of hours. Let's do this tomorrow instead. Can you be at the school at eight tomorrow?'

'*Ee*,' said Editor.

'Okay, show me where to drop you off.' I stopped the car not far from Matlapaneng, leaving Editor to walk the sand pathway to her home. Then I drove off towards the Hippo Pool, checking every now and again that Ruby was still asleep.

As I neared home I sped up, hurtling along the road, the grass on either side was the tallest I had ever seen it and the sand was soft and deep. There was no one around today, no boys on donkeys, no women down at the river washing or fishing. I turned the corner quickly and saw a man standing at the gate to our plot. My stomach tensed with irritation, he probably wanted a job, I would have to stop and talk with him when I really wanted to get Ruby indoors. I put my head out of the car window.

'*Dumela Mma*,' said the man. He looked young and fit as if he was used to manual work and he wore khaki shorts and a cream-and-brown patterned shirt. For a second I wondered if I had met him before, perhaps he was a relative whose face I had forgotten.

'*Ee*,' I said.

'Sorry,' said the man in English, fiddling with

the gate. 'I didn't hear you coming up.'

I frowned, not knowing what he was talking about.

'I am looking for Mr Brown,' he said.

'There's no Mr Brown,' I said, feeling hurried. I'd forgotten to buy dog food. I would have to go back to Maun once Ruby had had her nap and lunch. I felt rushed, it was mid-morning already.

'Where does he live?' asked the man.

I thought about it. There was one man I knew whose surname was Brown but it would be hard to give directions. 'I have no idea,' I said.

'Who lives here?' asked the man, gesturing at the house.

'I do.'

'Shall I open the gate?'

'Okay,' I said, 'thanks.'

I waited in the car, the engine still running, while the man tried to open the gate. But he was having trouble with the latch, as most people did. 'Don't bother,' I said after a few minutes, 'I'll do it.' I got out of the car and unlatched the gate, seeing as I did so that the latch had been bent to one side, the way it did when someone who didn't know how to work it had forced it.

I drove into the yard, glancing in the rear-view mirror to see that the man had now walked in through the gate behind me. I wondered where Rocky was, but our dog had recently developed the habit of jumping over the fence and disappearing until it was food time.

'You can close the gate after you,' I called, my head hanging out of the window. Still the man continued walking towards me. He held something in his hands and he was turning it over and over, looking down at it. Now I was a little worried, I didn't want this exchange to go on, I just wanted to get into the house. I reversed the car.

'What is it?' I asked.

'No,' said the man, 'I am asking for water.'

'First you want Mr Brown and now you want water,' I muttered to myself. 'Now you're bothering me,' I said a little louder. 'Just go, and close the gate after you.' My voice sounded a little rude and the man stopped where he was, standing on the sand halfway to the car.

'Just go and close the gate after you,' I repeated.

Slowly the man turned to go. He walked through the gate, down the sand pathway and disappeared into the green bush.

I got out of the car, gently picked up Ruby and headed to the porch. I opened the back door and from habit put the keys in the lock on the inside and locked the door. Then I walked hurriedly down the corridor to the bedroom where Ruby tumbled into the cot still asleep. Relieved that she hadn't woken, I went back into the kitchen, throwing down my bag, that day's newspaper, my car keys. The back of the car was full of food shopping; it would take me ten minutes to get it all indoors. I put some water on to boil; I would make Ruby some pasta for lunch. Then I went back outside to the car. And as I stepped off the porch and rounded the corner of the house the man I had just met at the gate was right there. It was if he had appeared from nowhere, as if he had dropped down from outer space. I sensed him rather than saw him, a feeling that someone was standing where they shouldn't be. I ran, immediately, my heart thumping. Part of me was thinking, how on earth did he get in here? I hadn't heard the gate; I hadn't looked out of any of the windows to see whether he'd reappeared from the bush.

The second I began to run the man ran too. He was right behind me. I reached the back door, swung it open and leapt inside but already the man had one hand and one foot in the door and was trying to push it open to get in. I was using all my strength to push him out but he was far bigger than me, bigger even than Ron. And his face was wild. In the few minutes since I'd seen him at the gate he had become a different person. He was towering over me, his jaw clenched, his eyes a little bloodshot in the corners. Neither of us spoke. It was as if we were in a silent, slow-motion film. And all colour seemed to have drained from my surroundings, the door, the man, the sun outside, had all faded into light and dark. He was intent on shoving me backwards through the partly open door, determined to get in the house. I threw up my hands, trying to block him but he just pushed me off. I tried again, reaching high up for his eyes. Out of nowhere I remembered someone once telling me that to disable a crocodile you must get it in the eyes. The man's eyes seemed to me the most vulnerable part of him, I wanted to gouge them; I wanted to stick my fingers right in his eyeballs.

But he held his head back, far out of my reach.

'I'll stab you,' he rasped. 'I'll stab you.' And now I saw that in his left hand he had a knife. The second I realized this the man got into the house. The moment he did so he turned the keys that were still in the lock where I'd left them, and he put the keys in his pocket. I was amazed at how quickly he did this, as if he already had a plan, as if he knew where the keys would be and where to put them. And I knew now that I was dead. There were burglar bars on every single window in the house. The bars were iron and they were thick. A newspaper report flew into my head. A man in Francistown had broken into a woman's house and she had escaped by jumping through the window. But I wouldn't be able to do this. And the door opposite me, the front door, was locked and the key was on the ring of keys the man now had in his pocket. There was no way out unless I managed to get the keys back and the only way I could do that was if I killed him and how was I going to kill him? I felt I had stumbled into a horror movie. A stranger was in my house saying he was going to stab me and there was nothing I could do. So this is how it happens, I thought, this is what it feels like.

Panic prickled up and down my skin, I could hear my heart booming as if it were in my ears. I glanced at the pan of water boiling furiously on the stove, I would throw it over him, I would scald him in the face. But the man sensed what I wanted to do and he grabbed hold of my wrist before I could move towards the stove. I walked backwards into the kitchen.

'Where's the money, where's the money?' he spat, holding my wrist hard with one hand and grabbing a bag off the kitchen table. I could feel the adrenaline in his body, his hand was rough and his grasp was like iron. And I could feel his excitement, feel him thinking: this is a white woman, she has to have money.

'That's not money, that's a camera,' I said as calmly as I could. 'Let go of me and I'll get the money.' I tried to steady my voice. He was inside my house but I didn't want him to see my terror. He began pulling me around all over the place.

'Let me get my purse,' I said, 'just let me get the purse.'

A part of me felt relief. He wanted to rob me, that was all. This was a robbery. An armed robbery. I would give him whatever he wanted and he would leave. But the house was locked and I was inside it and I knew with a sickening feeling that robbery wasn't going to be enough for him.

I got the purse and handed it over. He began riffling through it, apparently angry it contained perhaps a hundred pula and that was all. And then I noticed that the knife, his knife, was on the table. My vision closed in on the knife, everything else in my sight became black but for the shine of the blade. I grabbed it and began to fight again. Irritated, the man pulled out a screwdriver and began stabbing me on the hands and arms. I let go of the knife and it dropped with a clatter on the floor before the man bent and picked it up again.

'Here! Take the car!' I cried, trying to walk

towards the car keys.

'I don't want a car!' he spat, furious. He reached out one arm and pointed. 'I want vagina.'

'No!' I recoiled, struggling to move backwards. 'No, come on, don't do this.'

'I want vagina,' he demanded, grabbing at me.

'Look,' I said, 'don't do this. We are two people. You don't have to do this.' I began talking like mad, as if my life depended on it, as if by talking I could prevent what was going to happen until help arrived. But I knew there was no help. I was miles from any other house. Even if someone were passing our plot right now they would never be able to see what was going on inside. I could scream but there would be no one to hear me. Another newspaper report flew into my head. Three Englishwomen had been car-jacked in South Africa. Two had been raped, but one had managed to talk her attacker out of it. I kept on talking, all the time walking backwards, trying to keep a distance between us.

'You'll get caught! If you do this you'll get caught!'

The man laughed, walking towards me.

'You'll die if you do this! Do you believe in God?'

'No.'

'You don't believe in God?' I tried to sound incredulous. I didn't believe in God, but Batswana were a Christian people; I didn't know anyone who didn't believe in God. I thought that there must be some way to reach him, to stop him from what he was threatening to do, to reason with him. 'You don't believe in God?' I asked as he grabbed my arm again. And then I stopped. Ruby had woken up and she was crying, a cry that said she hadn't had enough sleep, that she had been disturbed. At once I tried to break out of the man's grasp. I had forgotten about Ruby. I had forgotten that my child was sleeping in her cot in the bedroom. It was inconceivable that she was going to have to wake up to this. But as I struggled the man's grasp increased until I was almost pulling him into the bedroom. I had to get to Ruby. Perhaps I thought that if I had a baby in my arms that would stop him. But most of all I had to get to her.

I got to the doorway of the bedroom and he slapped me. But still I moved backwards, until I reached the cot. Ruby was standing up, her little white T-shirt crinkled, her fat brown hands clasping the yellow bars of the cot. I picked Ruby up and held her tight, resting her on my right hip. 'It's okay,' I crooned, 'it's okay.' Her face was flushed; her hair was plastered on to her scalp with sweat. But she stopped crying and she sighed, her head falling on to my shoulder. 'It's okay,' I said, again, smoothing down her hair. But how could it be okay when she had woken to see her mother in the doorway and a strange man attacking her?

'I'll kill you,' the man rasped. I bent Ruby's head, pushing her face into my chest. Then he started hitting me. A blow to both sides of the head. I heard the crack of his fist on my temple and I staggered.

'Please,' I implored, 'the baby.'

'I'll kill her too,' he said and I saw his hand land on Ruby's back. I couldn't see the knife. I couldn't see if he had just stabbed her.

The man lashed out with another blow, hard, on my breastbone. This was the first time he'd really used his strength and it was enough to throw me backwards on to the bed. Then I saw the knife was in his hand again. As I lay on the bed, my feet dangling on the floor, he hauled up my skirt and efficiently cut away with the knife, slicing off my underwear. I suddenly knew he had done this before, he knew exactly what he was doing. I couldn't feel any pain and I looked down to see whether there was blood, whether he had just cut off my clothing or whether he had also sliced me. There was no blood. But now I saw he was undoing his thick leather belt, and then he dropped his shorts. I forced myself to keep looking, I wanted to know what he was going to put inside me. It could be the knife, it could be anything. I saw the tip of his penis, swollen and a gory shiny red. He was diseased.

I turned my face to my right, holding Ruby close, kissing her while he attempted to rape me. How could he do this with a baby on the bed, with a baby in my very arms? But he wasn't hard enough and this made him furious. 'Open,' he rasped, 'open.' He tried to force my legs up high and I pushed against him. It was inhuman; my body couldn't bend up like this. I wasn't going to cooperate. I wasn't a carcass of meat; my limbs couldn't be yanked up from my body like this. Then he began stabbing me along the inside of my thighs. One, two, three, he stabbed on the right leg. One, two three, he stabbed on the left. I could see the knife going in but couldn't feel a thing. I thought that when it came to killing me it would take a long time and be very messy. He would have to stab me millions of times.

'I've got AIDS!' I yelled. 'I've got AIDS! I've got AIDS!'

'I don't care,' he panted. At last he managed to penetrate and I went back to soothing Ruby, her body burrowed against mine. The man's face came down close on top of me and there was spittle at the corners of his mouth. For one appalling moment I thought he would force me to kiss him. I could sense that he was furious and desperate. 'You're done,' I told him after a few moments. 'You've finished.'

He stood up.

'What a man you are,' I said. 'Hey you're a *real* man, eh?' I lay on the bed with Ruby attached to me, liquid seeping down my legs.

But he wasn't listening, he didn't hear the sarcasm, he was looking around, deciding what to do next.

'Go and wash,' he ordered, pulling me up from the bed and dragging me out of the bedroom.

I had a sudden image of a pair of keys in the lock on the inside of the bathroom door. 'Let me wash alone,' I said. 'You've just raped me, at least let me wash on my own.' My voice was trembling. I sounded as if I were crying; I wanted to sound as if I were crying, as if I had been defeated. But I was far too scared to cry. It seemed like this was the only chance I had. I had to appear weak if he was going to let go of me. I pushed my way into the bathroom and, as I tried to shut the door, he suddenly realized what was going on. He threw himself at the door but I had shut it now and turned the keys.

I stood, petrified, in the bathroom, Ruby still on my hip. Her eyes were open, she was awake but she wasn't crying. I could hear the man storming around the house. I thought I heard him try the front door. I thought I heard keys. I decided he was trying to find the right key on the unfamiliar bunch in his pocket to get out. Then there was more noise. He wasn't going to leave, he was going to keep me prisoner in the house. Definitely now he would kill me. He had raped me. It was broad daylight and I had seen him. He could not possibly afford to let me go. I heard footsteps coming down the hall, the handle of the bathroom door being rattled up and down, and I began to scream.

'My husband's coming! My husband's coming!' It had to be nearly lunchtime now. The man might just believe it; he might just believe that Ron was on his way home.

The banging and the noise went on. It sounded like the man was turning the house upside down. Then I heard the sound of a door slamming and then silence. I stood in the bath, slipping a little on the shiny surface, and peered out through the small window at the top of the wall. 'It's all right,' I told Ruby who had begun to whimper. 'It's all right.' Then I saw the man coming round the side of the house pushing my pink bicycle, my camera bag over his shoulder. The bike had a flat tyre. It was impossible to ride. I watched, my whole body rigid with concentration. I couldn't believe that he was actually leaving. He got to the gate. He opened the gate. He wheeled out the bike. He took the sand pathway and disappeared into the green bush. He was gone.

I couldn't decide what to do. My feet were aching from where I stood on tiptoe in the bath. Then I opened the bathroom door and looked down the hallway. I could see the keys back in their usual place in the back door. I ran to the door, as fast as I had run when I tried to escape the man outside, and locked it. But perhaps he was still inside the house? Perhaps I had just locked us both inside. He had disappeared the first time and then he had come back. Perhaps, just now, I hadn't seen him leave at all. There was a buzzing in my head that was making it hard to think. I ran to the spare bedroom, locked the door, and picked up the phone. I called Ron. His cell-phone was engaged. I rang again. Still engaged. I put down the phone. Then it rang. It was Ron. 'I've just been raped and stabbed and he left on my bike!' I cried. Then I ran back to the bathroom and locked myself in again.

I stood in the bath scanning the window, scanning the yard and the bush and the path outside. The man had gone. He was nowhere to be seen. He had actually left. I'm alive, I thought, my entire body suddenly overwhelmed with euphoria. I could have danced up and down on the spot. He's gone and I'm alive. I wasn't killed. Relief flooded through me like warm milk.

Then I was terrified again. Where was Ron? He had said he was coming, so where was he? I ran back to the spare room and rang him again. 'Where are you?' I cried, my voice juddery as if I were suddenly freezing cold.

'I've got him,' he said.

'You've caught him? You've got him?'

'Yes.' Ron was breathing heavily, there was noise in the background.

A few minutes later a Med Rescue vehicle pulled up outside the house. Ron had rung a private ambulance service for help and I watched as two white men got out of the vehicle.

'Where were you stabbed?' asked the taller one.

'My baby,' I said, feeling unable to speak in whole sentences. 'Stabbed her. The back.'

The man gently inspected Ruby. 'She seems fine,' he said. 'Really, she seems fine.'

I sighed in relief.

'And your stab wounds?'

'Here,' I said, lifting up my skirt, 'and here. What about AIDS? Have you got drugs? Are there any in Maun? Can you get me the drugs?'

Both men looked at me, confused. They began talking about stab wounds and blood and HIV.

'But he *raped* me,' I said.

'Shit,' said the taller man. His hands fell by his side and he looked at the ground.

'What about drugs? What are my chances?' I heard my voice, it was totally hysterical.

The shorter man mumbled something about it being fifty-fifty.

'We need to get to the police first,' said the taller man gently. 'Then to the hospital.'

'Fine, fine,' I said, climbing into the vehicle. My thighs felt like wood and I could see yellow marks spreading across my skin, bruising before my eyes. And then I began shaking so badly I thought I would dissolve.

# 28

We drove into Maun, a siren attached to the top of the vehicle screaming as we went. I sat with Ruby on my lap, feeling precarious. We were driving fast and I felt I was escaping something. At the police station we were shown into a small dirty room on the ground floor and I sat down on a dusty wooden chair, waiting. It seemed someone was looking for a woman police officer and couldn't find one.

Eventually I was taken upstairs and into a larger room. I walked in, Ruby attached to my hip, to find a woman typing at a desk and two men standing in the corner chatting. I turned as another male officer came into the room, had a look around and left. Then two more men came in. I didn't know where the Med Rescue men were now. I was standing in the middle of the room and no one was talking to me. I could feel my clothes were dishevelled, and my thighs were so stiff I could barely move.

Two more officers came in, both of whom I knew. I felt that word was going around the police station: a white woman has been raped, come and have a look. And it wasn't just because I was white that people were interested, for many of the Maun police officers knew me. They knew I had written on the mistreatment of rape survivors at the hands of Maun police, and that I had written reports in which officers in this very station had allegedly tortured detainees in other cases. And it was Maun CID officers who, three years back, had arrested me and charged me with causing fear and alarm, only to see the case dismissed.

'I should be alone with a woman officer,' I said to the room in general. One of the men smirked. 'What are you smirking at?' I exploded. The man shrugged and walked out.

Then a woman officer came in and took me back to the dirty room downstairs.

'You need to make a statement,' she said, her voice flat. I looked around the room, at the broken grey blinds, at the remains of a takeaway meal on a greasy polystyrene container, at the scuffmarks of mud on the floor.

'Yes,' I said, trying to focus. 'A statement. But can I go to the hospital? Please . . . '

The woman looked down at a sheaf of papers on the desk. 'First we will write a statement then you can go to the hospital.' She looked up at me again. She was young, her face could have been soft but her expression was officious.

I knew a medical exam was crucial and the quicker the better. I knew the evidence needed in court. I knew the procedure from my time spent researching violence against women in the north-west for WAR. I had not washed. The rape had been barely thirty minutes ago. All I had done was put on fresh underwear. I wanted a medical exam and I wanted drugs.

'Please,' I said again. 'I need to get AIDS drugs, please.'

The woman nodded reluctantly and I sat and

451

waited while someone went to look for a vehicle. Then I sensed someone at the door and I turned to see Ron. He rushed in and knelt down beside Ruby and me.

'Are you okay?'

'Yes. Did you get him?' I asked. My voice sounded strange, as if it wasn't me speaking.

'*Ee*. The army helped.'

'So where is he now?'

'The cops have taken him. Are you okay? Where were you stabbed?'

I shrugged off the question. 'I was raped, Ron.'

Ron's head snapped back.

'I told you, on the phone, I told you.'

'I didn't hear . . . ' Ron shook his head. 'Oh, my God.' He laid one hand on mine and with the other began stroking Ruby up and down her back the way he did when he wanted her to sleep.

The woman officer reappeared at the door. 'We can go.'

'I'll take Ruby,' Ron said, standing up.

'No!' I sat backwards on the chair, holding Ruby tight.

'Cait. I'll take her. You're exhausted. You go to Dr Patrick's. We'll meet you there.'

I walked outside and got into the police car. 'I want to go to Dr Patrick's, not the hospital,' I said, fumbling around for a seat-belt. The woman officer sat crammed in the front seat, in-between the driver and me. I leaned forward and searched the driver's face. 'Please. I need to go to Dr Patrick's. It's just down there. They'll have the drugs.' I knew at the government

452

hospital I would have to wait for hours. I felt time was of the essence although I didn't know what drugs I wanted, nor how quickly they had to be taken, nor what their effect would be.

The woman officer nodded that this was okay. Then I began to cry, to shake and convulse. The officer patted me twice on the shoulder.

We arrived at the clinic and walked in through the sliding glass doors. Dr Patrick had recently moved to new premises and inside the building was plush. On the left was a desk that looked like the reception area of a smart hotel. In the middle of the waiting-room was a glass-topped coffee table, with three fake-leather sofas arranged around it. Original framed paintings of wildlife were on the wall alongside a large TV screen.

I walked stiffly towards the woman waiting at the desk.

'Dumela Mma,' said the police officer behind me.

'Ee.' The receptionist sounded bored. Then she looked at me. She knew me; I was one of the clinic's oldest patients. I had known her since her job had been to make tea and sort files.

The police officer leant forward, her voice low. 'She needs to . . . ' the officer hesitated. 'See a doctor.'

We were shown into Dr Patrick's office where we found him in his white coat sorting through paperwork. 'Caitlin!' he beamed, standing up. Then he saw the police officer and he hesitated.

'I've been raped,' I said, stopping in the doorway.

Dr Patrick slammed his fist on the table. 'No!'

453

'I need an exam. For court. He's been caught. I need drugs.'

For the next hour things were blurred. At one point I caught sight of myself in one of the waiting-room's mirrors and thought: I will never be able to look at myself in a mirror again. I could not bear to look at the woman in the mirror, especially her eyes. She was separate from me, a detached image that I knew was mine but which could have been that of a stranger, a stranger I didn't want to look at too closely. 'What about AIDS?' I asked Dr Patrick. 'What are the drugs you take? Have you got any?'

'Anti-retrovirals,' he said. 'If you get on to anti-retrovirals in time then the chances of infection are low.'

I stared at him.

'Caitlin, the risk is small.'

I turned my head suddenly; convinced I could hear the sound of Ruby crying.

'Do you believe me?' Dr Patrick asked, looking at me closely.

'No,' I said, 'I don't.'

I was taken to another room to see the gynaecologist. He sat behind a desk, while the police officer sat a little behind me, her hands folded on her lap.

'I'm going to test her for HIV,' the gynaecologist told the police officer. 'I'll test her first and then . . . '

'Talk to me!' I exploded. 'Why are you talking to her?'

The gynaecologist stared at me for a moment. 'Okay. Okay. Calm down. I'm going to test you for AIDS,' he said very slowly, as if talking to a child.

'But why?'

The gynaecologist sighed and glanced at the police officer.

'You test the rapist, not me. It doesn't matter what I am. That's what the new rape laws said, that's what the amendments were all about. The accused is tested. Not the survivor.'

The gynaecologist tapped on the desktop with a pen. 'If you are HIV negative now, and later you become HIV positive, then that would show it was the rapist who infected you.'

'Take the blood,' I said, giving up, holding out my arm.

'I'll examine you first,' the gynaecologist said, gesturing to the raised bed in the corner of the room.

I climbed stiffly up, my legs shaking as the gynaecologist moved nearer.

Wordlessly he took a swab and then he began scribbling on a form the police officer had given him.

'Can you see I was raped?' I asked.

The gynaecologist mumbled something about sexually active, child-bearing women of my age. 'There is some bruising,' he said at last.

My old midwife MaKupaza came in then and she took the blood quickly and without pain. Then we went into a separate room for a douche. MaKupaza closed the door. 'It's okay, my dear,' she said, as she washed her hands.

'What about AIDS?' I asked. 'What are my chances?'

'It is in God's hands now,' said MaKupaza. I stared at her, incredulous, as she handed me a small jar of pills wrapped tightly in a wad of yellow toilet paper. I unwound the paper. The label on the jar said anti-retrovirals. I was to take three a day. Immediately I took one, swallowed it and began to leave the room.

'Wait!' said MaKupaza. She offered the toilet paper so I could wrap up the jar again.

I shook my head.

'People will see,' she said.

'I haven't done anything wrong,' I objected.

'But they will *talk*,' she said. I stuffed the jar of pills into the douche packet and walked out. I waited by the lab-room door. I was given two folded pieces of paper. One said there were no traces of semen on the swab the gynaecologist had taken. My first reaction was relief. My second was worry; if there was no semen then what evidence would I have in court? I knew how many rape cases never made it to court because of a lack of medical evidence, and how many accused rapists walked free because a doctor couldn't testify convincingly. The other piece of paper said I was HIV negative. I folded it up and held it tightly in my hand. All it told me was that I was HIV negative now, it didn't tell me whether I had just become infected; it didn't tell me whether the rapist had AIDS when I knew he had.

★　★　★

The police officer and I returned to the police station, while Ron took Ruby to Moeti. Again I sat in the ground-floor room while the woman police officer took down my statement, writing painstakingly slowly. People came in and out. But no one offered any sympathy; there were no expressions of concern, of gentleness or comfort. The room grew hotter and my lips became dry.

'Can I have some water?'

The police officer frowned.

'Water? My mouth is too dry . . . ' I tailed off.

'There is a tap outside,' the officer said, laying down her pen.

'Outside?'

'In the yard.'

'Do you have a cup?'

The officer shook her head.

I stood up shakily and went outside, blinded by the glare of the sun. I found the tap, the water pipe wrapped with a dirty sodden cloth. I struggled to turn it on and then bent my head, my mouth open, trying to gulp the water.

'Can I use the toilet?' I asked, returning to the room. The police officer pointed upstairs. I went up the stairs to the second floor, searching for a toilet. But when I found one it was so filthy I backed out in disgust. As I started walking down the stairs again I almost walked into a CID officer I knew from my work with the *Okavango Observer*. Gently she took my hand and squeezed it.

'Did you hear what happened?' I asked. 'Did you hear what's happened to me?'

'*Ee*,' the officer nodded.

I waited for her to say more.

'Shame,' she said at last and turned to go. Then she added something over her shoulder, 'He's told the boss he didn't rape you . . . because you have AIDS.'

'What?' I held out my hand to steady myself. 'That's what the rapist said?'

'*Ee*. First he said you are his girlfriend.'

'No!'

'And he has a record, this one.'

'For what?' I looked around the empty stairway, my voice low.

'Armed robbery. He just came out of prison.'

Once the statement was written I found myself sitting outside the police station on a low concrete wall. I had been told to sit there but I couldn't remember by whom. Ron was next to me, he had returned with Ruby who was fretful.

'What are we waiting for now?' I asked.

Ron sniffed. 'They're looking for a vehicle.'

'For what?'

'To go to the house.'

I wiped the sweat from my eyes and shifted Ruby on my lap. My body was overcome with exhaustion and I had my head in my hands when something made me look up. There, heading towards me, was the man who had raped me a few hours ago. He was naked but for a pair of undone shorts. He had leg irons around his ankles. He looked dirty. But he strutted on, the leg irons clinking. Then he stopped to leer at me, flicking his tongue suggestively from side to side like a grotesque chameleon.

'Let's go,' said a CID officer coming up

458

behind me. He was a tall man and he walked with his shoulders slung back as if he were a senior officer and was used to giving orders.

'What?' I was beginning to cry. I was trying to turn away, to hide my face from the man who had raped me. In a minute he would be right next to me.

'Let's go to your house,' said the CID officer, 'and you can both tell us your stories.'

'You're kidding?' I blurted out. This is not a story, I wanted to say. There is no *story* here; I've just been raped.

The CID officer looked annoyed.

'I'm not going anywhere with that man,' I said shakily. 'I'm not going to my house with that . . . '

'So you are refusing?' The CID officer was standing over me now, his bulky body blocking out the sun.

'I'm not going anywhere with him,' I repeated.

'Well, so you are refusing to go to the scene of the crime.'

'No,' I wailed, 'I'll go there, fine, but not with him. I'm not going into my house with him.'

Ron stood up, moving so he stood in front of the rapist, shielding me from his view. 'She's right. Why does she have to go there with him?'

I sat while the men argued. I put my head down again. I jiggled Ruby on my lap. At last we were taken back into the police station and to a room upstairs. Still Ron and the CID man were arguing. More officers came in, more men joined the argument. The Setswana washed over me and I made no attempt to keep up.

459

'What's going on?' I asked as at last the room fell quiet.

'They've agreed you don't have to go,' Ron said, his face furious. 'I'm going.'

*　*　*

I sat in the upstairs room at the police station, waiting. Ruby had at last fallen asleep in my arms. For forty-five minutes I sat in the room while the bulky CID officer lectured me.

'You are being very uncooperative,' he began. He stood by the desk, his legs apart. 'Very uncooperative. Do you realize this case will be thrown out of court because you are refusing to go to the scene of the crime?'

I moved on the seat, my legs sticky on the hot plastic. 'I'm not refusing, I just don't see why I have to go *with* the rapist . . . '

The CID officer sighed impatiently. 'You need to get used to seeing the accused because he will be cross-examining you at the trial.'

My mouth snapped shut. I hadn't thought about this, that I would face a cross-examination by the man who had raped me.

'But I don't get why I have to go to the house with him. Can't you see that? Why are you doing this to me?' I bit my lip; I was going to cry.

'These are the laws in Botswana,' said the officer ominously. 'And they apply to everyone. It was the same with Bosch.'

I looked up, shocked. He was referring to Mariette Bosch, a woman recently arrested for murder and sentenced to death by Justice

Aboagye. The only similarity between her and me was that we were both white. 'But she was done for murder,' I protested. 'I'm reporting a crime, I'm a victim.' I knew rape counsellors didn't use the term victim, they used the term survivor. But I felt like a victim and I wanted to be treated like a victim by the police.

The CID officer picked disinterestedly at his finger-nails.

'I need to go home. I need to wash. I need to feed my baby.'

'There is no vehicle. So just calm down.'

But although I was desperate to get home, when we did eventually get to the house I suddenly didn't want to be there at all. I showed the woman police officer around, she picked up my slashed underwear from the bed and wrapped it in a plastic bag. No fingerprints were taken, no photographs. The police and CID left and Ron and I were alone.

'What happened?' I asked. We were sitting in the living-room. It was dark outside but we hadn't put on any lights. In the bedroom Ruby was asleep. 'Did you have to come into the house with that bastard?'

Ron hung his head. 'He didn't want to. He told the cops I was going to shoot him. I had my gun, he saw me pick it up from the back of the car. I could have just shot him.'

'And then you'd be done for murder.'

'*Ee*. It would have been worth it.'

'No, it wouldn't,' I sighed. 'What did he say, when you came in here?'

'He said he'd been bewitched.'

461

I felt frozen, unable to co-ordinate my body into doing anything at all but sit on the sofa.

'You're brave,' Ron said, stroking my face. 'You're really really brave.'

⋆ ⋆ ⋆

That night we slept in the bed where I had been raped. It didn't bother me where I slept; I was past caring. But I wondered when the nightmares would start, when I would begin to get flashbacks. I knew from my work as a rape crisis counsellor that there were stages survivors went through. There would be denial, anger, this I knew. But I had known it all in a theoretical way and now it was going to happen to me.

I wondered how Ruby would get through the trauma. What had she actually seen and what would she remember? Would she be scared of strangers now, would she cling to me?

Despite the questions I fell asleep at once and I slept soundly until woken by the sun seeping in through the red blinds the next morning. I looked around, knowing something terrible had happened but struggling for a second to think what it was. The day before seemed to have gone on for ever. Then I lay down and went over the rape, trying to piece it all together, to remember what exactly had happened and when. I wished it were all over but it wasn't. The police would be coming round this morning; they wanted to draw a sketch of the house. The rapist would be put on trial. And I would have to live with the fact that I now had HIV. Then how would I be able to be a mother and look after my child?

'Where are you going?' I asked in a panic when Ron appeared in the doorway fully dressed.

'I've got to open the office. I didn't go to the farm yesterday, they don't have any food . . . '

'I'm coming with you!' I shot up. Wherever Ron was going I was going to go too, I couldn't bear the idea of being alone at home. I sat in the car, in the back next to Ruby in her car seat. I flinched when Ron put the radio on. I couldn't bear to have any music playing. I needed silence, I needed to be alert. I looked anxiously out of the window, scanning the bush as we drove along the pathway to the Hippo Pool. The fear that had been with me during the rape, the fear that I was going to die, was constant.

Ron stopped the car at Maun Fresh Produce. When I'd first arrived in Botswana eleven years ago, Maun Fresh Produce had been a small concrete building, hot and gloomy inside. It had sold basic groceries but on many days there would be no eggs, or no cheese, or no apples. Today it was a huge building, large and airy like an aircraft hangar with neon strip-lights and trolleys and cashiers working behind computer- ized check-out screens. Batswana shopped for onions and mealie meal, for Vaseline and cooking oil, meat pies and Coke. Expatriates shopped for imported cheeses, for lasagne and ice-cream, for hair dye and gardening tools.

The moment I entered the supermarket I was overwhelmed. It was too big and too bright. Everyone was looking at me. It was as if a space were clearing around my feet. They looked, and then they hurriedly, surreptitiously, looked away. I wanted someone to come up to me, to ask me how I was, to say out loud that they had heard I had been raped, that I had almost been murdered. If it had been another crime, if I had just been stabbed, or robbed, or if I had sustained terrible injuries in a car crash, then people would approach me. But the people around me didn't know what to say, rape was too unmentionable.

As I turned and began to walk unsurely along a brightly lit aisle, I knew logically that everyone couldn't be looking at me. But I also knew that many people were. While there were now hundreds of white people in Maun, we were still a tiny minority. If a white woman had been raped then it would be easy to know which one she was. And I felt when people looked at me that they expected to see a wreck and yet here I was operating as normal. Here I was shopping on a Saturday morning, my husband next to me, my child in the trolley, her little legs poking through the wire holes.

Then I told myself that people were only looking at me because I was looking at them. And I was looking at them because although I knew the man who raped me was in custody, I was looking for him everywhere. Outside the shop I had searched the people sitting in cars, standing and eating take-aways, chatting with friends in the shade. Now I searched the customers in the check-out lines and I scanned the faces of the cashiers. And I realized that it wasn't people I was looking at, it was just men. And it wasn't just men, I admitted to myself, it was black men. This realization unnerved me; it took the ground from under my feet. Suddenly young black men were a threat, my heart started pounding every time a black man looked my way; their eyes bored into me and adrenaline began pouring through my limbs.

I stopped in the middle of one of the supermarket aisles, gazing at a shelf of nappies. When I looked round Ron and Ruby had gone and I started to panic, feeling exposed.

'Dumela Mma,' came a woman's voice from behind me.

I turned round. It was a woman I knew from one of the safari companies.

'How are you?' she asked.

'Fine,' I said and smiled. 'Actually, I'm not fine . . . '

'I know.' The woman laid a hand on my arm. 'It happened to me.'

'What?' I asked. I searched her eyes. And I could see at once and without any shadow of a doubt that she was talking about rape. Her eyes had a sort of film about them, as if she were present here in the supermarket, enacting day-to-day routines, but in reality, in real life, she had been terrorized and she had faced and escaped death.

'When?' I asked.

'Last year. A man broke into my bedroom. He came through the window.'

Around me the sounds of the supermarket seemed to fade, the noise of people talking, of

465

the tannoy system, of children's cries, all became muted.

'The army caught him.'

'That was you?' I asked, stepping back. I had heard about the case. I had heard about it the way people in Maun heard about any crime, by word of mouth. I had heard how a woman had been held in her home and raped for hours, how she had been stabbed repeatedly, how she had jumped naked out of a window. I had heard about it the way people were now hearing about what had happened to me.

Outside the supermarket we got back into the car. Ron had picked up supplies for those at the farm. He handed me some take-away fried chicken. I shook my head. Food disgusted me. I could not imagine ever liking food, I could not remember ever liking food.

'You have to eat, Cait,' he said, his eyes catching mine in the rearview mirror.

Outside a police car drove by. 'Bastards,' I said as it passed.

Ron unlocked the office, letting the secretary in, and then we drove in silence to the farm, bumping on the thick sand pathways, hurtling through remaining pools of rainwater. Ron always drove fast but today the way he drove was aggressive. I didn't want to go to the farm, I wanted to go home. But I couldn't stay home on my own. I looked out the window, seeing the familiar landmarks, clumps of mophane tees, one or two houses made from reeds, a fork in the road.

We turned left on the final pathway to the

farm and then Ron sped up and drew to a halt in a clearing to the right of the field. And at last I felt safe, miles from anywhere, surrounded by family, everyone going about their normal tasks. Alice was cooking, her head bent over a three-legged pot, her arm wafting away smoke from the fire. Her younger sisters Gosegomang and Ene appeared from a pathway deep in the bush, piles of firewood on their heads. I noted their presence with muted surprise; I hadn't known they came to the farm. Had Ron's mother or grandmother somehow adopted them while I had been in England? Did Ron bring them here every week-end now? Gosegomang rushed forward, opened the car door and playfully grabbed Ruby. Expertly she swung Ruby on to her back and with a wide smile she set off towards the goat kraal.

In the field I could see the dark, stick-like figures of Gabs and Eliah, they were walking nearer, they had heard and then seen the car. I hadn't seen Eliah for a long time; even before I had gone to England I had seen her only infrequently since Ruby had been born, since she had tried for a time to confine me. But although she never visited, never came to our home, I had taken Ruby to see her as often as I could. Eliah might not like me, but she loved her granddaughter. And Ruby loved her.

I got out of the car and headed towards Madintwa who sat on the sand in the shade of a tree. I had been back in Botswana for less than two weeks so I hadn't seen much of her recently either. But although we had fallen out the day

467

Ruby had her immunizations, we were still friends. Since that day, Madintwa had behaved to me as she had always had, as if there had been no falling-out at all. She was as affectionate as ever, she patted my arms, she joked with me and called me her daughter. It had got to the point when I thought I had imagined that she had ever been angry.

Slowly the family gathered around where Madintwa sat. Gabs brought a plastic chair for me to sit on; Alice shuffled along with some tea. I looked at Ron as he sat stiffly on a fallen log. I knew he had seen Eliah and Alice in Moeti the day before, had told them a little of what had happened, that I had been attacked. But then they had hitched out to the farm and there had not been time to speak about anything else. I wanted Ron to tell them now, to tell my in-laws exactly what had happened.

Ron began to speak. Then he paused and sent the girls away. Alice and Gabs moved off, their eyes down, their expressions sullen. In the distance I could hear Ruby howling with laughter as Gosegomang pushed her along, naked, in an old wheelbarrow, bumping up and down on the sandy path. Ron continued to speak. I sat intently, listening, making sure he was getting the details right. It seemed important to me that Eliah and Madintwa knew everything. When he finally said that I had been raped I held my breath. I anticipated the shock and horror on their faces. I thought Eliah might have some words of comfort or advice. And I knew Madintwa would pull me to her and pray.

Ron finished speaking and still I sat, waiting. Eliah's eyes flicked to mine and then flicked away. Madintwa sighed and wrapped a shawl around her. Then Eliah rose and headed back into the field and Madintwa turned to Ron. 'Where is the meat?' she asked. 'We have no meat.'

# 29

Two days after the rape I woke again with a terrible sense of dread and foreboding, as if something unspeakable were about to happen. The dread was located in my breastbone, precisely where the man had hit me. As I lay in bed, willing Ruby not to wake, I felt sick to my stomach. I still hadn't eaten. I wondered if AZT, the anti-retroviral pills, were making me feel sick. I got up and took the pills from the wardrobe, opening out and reading the packet insert. There was information about various trials and various outcomes but no mention of taking AZT after rape. I scanned the tiny black print, the words jumbling on the page. Why I had been given them if they weren't for use after rape? I read the impressive list of side-effects. They included anxiety and I was already feeling anxious, very very anxious indeed.

I lay down again, waiting for the day to begin. I could hear Ron in the kitchen making coffee and outside a donkey braying right next to the fence. The day before at the farm had left me numb. My in-laws had offered no help and I could see Ron withdrawing into himself with the horror of what had happened. He didn't know what to do or what to say. And he looked at me worriedly, sometimes calling out 'Cait!' when he saw I was far, far away, when my mind was not in the present at all. I hadn't yet told my family in England. The phone line at home had been dead since Friday, as if saving me from the call I had to make.

The night before, late, Bashi had come round and talked with Ron outside. Now I expected Pearl would come and, an hour later, I heard her car pull up at the gate. I watched from the bedroom window as she walked towards the house, her youngest child in her arms. I could see Pearl was on her way to church. She wore a white flowery hat and a shawl around her shoulders. I went to the back door to meet her and, as she came round the side of the house and stepped on the porch, she almost tripped.

'*Dumela Mma*,' she said, regaining her balance, her grasp on her child tightening.

I smiled at hearing her so formal and I turned round, looking for a clean chair to offer her. Pearl took my hand and then she hugged me.

'Hey, Caitlin, this place . . . ' her voice faltered. 'This place . . . '

'So you heard?' I asked. 'You heard what happened?'

'*Ee*. I sent Bashi here last night to find out if it was true. Your phone's not working.'

'I know.'

Pearl sat down and looked at the floor of the porch. She didn't know what to say. Then two male relatives came round, an uncle and a cousin of Ron's. They stayed only a little while, and, like Pearl, they hardly spoke. They had just come because they had heard the news and they wanted to offer condolences, the way people did when someone in a family had died. And, as

471

when someone had died, the Setswana way was to visit the bereaved not in any way to cheer them but to sit silently and share in the heartache. And other people came too. A white woman who lived opposite arrived with flowers and bubblebath. Anne Sandenbergh came with a chicken casserole. Stef came and Ruth came and they told me to call them whenever I needed anything.

In the afternoon Kerrin and Andrew came round; a maid had told their babysitter that a white woman in the house on the peninsula had been attacked. I told them what had happened, I sat on the porch and went through the whole ordeal detail by detail, because I wanted to, not because they had asked. It was becoming compulsive. It was all I did, go over and over the attack in my mind. What I had said, what the rapist had said, what I had done, what he had done. And I wondered why, when I related it now to Kerrin and Andrew, I appeared so calm. Why isn't it worse, I asked myself, why do I seem to be coping with this? And then, the rest of the time, I couldn't believe it had even happened. The wounds on my legs were almost a relief. The fact that I couldn't walk without pain made me know that what had happened really had happened. My life had changed in a split-second; it had changed and I didn't know how to get it back.

★ ★ ★

On Monday morning I woke late, opening my eyes to find Ron handing me a cup of coffee. He was dressed for work and he had his car keys in his hands. In the bathroom I could hear Alice brushing her teeth. I had noticed with surprise the evening before that the bathroom door no longer locked. When anyone pulled it closed it simply swung open again. And yet I couldn't remember having a fight with the rapist at the bathroom door, I could only remember getting in and locking it.

'Where are you going?' I asked Ron, reaching for my AZT pills.

'To work. I'm taking Alice to school.'

'Wait!' I said, panic-stricken. 'I'm coming too.'

'Cait, you're not even dressed. Ruby's asleep.'

'But don't leave me here!' I cried, hurrying out of bed. 'Why didn't you wake me? Just wait, okay, just wait.'

'What do you want me to do?'

'I don't know, I don't know.' I began rummaging through my clothes. 'But I'm scared. I can't stay here . . . I don't know how I'm going to leave the house . . . I don't know how I'm going to get to the car.'

'What if I come back?'

'Yes?'

'I'll take Alice, open the office, and then I'll come back.'

'Okay. Lock the door after you.'

The moment Ron left, the moment I heard the key turn in the back door to lock it, I was absolutely, overwhelmingly terrified. Ron would

473

be back in perhaps half an hour. It wasn't soon enough. It wasn't safe, being here on my own. Shaking convulsively, I woke Ruby, grabbed a bottle of milk and ran in my nightgown to the car. I left the engine on as I went to open the gate, scanning every bush, every tree, making sure no one was there, that no one would suddenly appear. Then I drove wildly across the flood plain to Kerrin and Andrew's house. I stopped when I got there, appalled. How was I going to live if I was too scared to stay in my house but equally terrified of leaving it? I sat in the car, trying to compose myself. But I was petrified, petrified that something was coming after me, that I had to escape from something that was about to happen.

Since Friday I had gone over and over the rape thinking what I could have done, at what point things could have turned out differently. I knew the rape wasn't my fault, but this didn't stop me thinking about what I could have done. If I had never dropped Editor off at her home, if I had brought her back with me the way I had planned, then the rape would never have happened. The man would have seen there were two of us and left us alone. And if I had stayed inside the house, if I hadn't come out to the car to get the shopping, then the man would never have caught me. But now I began to fast-forward and to think about what could have happened. If I hadn't locked myself in the bathroom, if the rapist hadn't left, what would have happened then? Would he have raped me again before killing me? Would he have kidnapped me, made me take the car? What would have happened to Ruby?

★ ★ ★

On Tuesday the man who raped me appeared in court for mention. Anne Sandenbergh came round to tell me. WAR was involved in the case now, as it was with nearly every rape case in Maun. Anne came to see me at Ron's office. As I couldn't stay at home alone I had come to work with Ron and then sat aimlessly in the office. I wanted him to drop everything, to close up the office, to let the farm look after itself, to stay at home and care for me and be my bodyguard. But he couldn't. Too many other people depended on him as well.

'He appeared about an hour ago,' Anne said.

'Where? Which courtroom are they using?'

Anne looked angry. 'They took him to Maun senior secondary . . . '

'What? They took him to the *school?*' I imagined the rapist walking into the school grounds, his legs shackled, flanked by police officers, as children came out of their classrooms to stare.

'Apparently there is no other building to use. The bank has taken back the magistrates' court building. So they're using a room at the school.'

'So what happened?' I shifted backwards so I was up against the hard office wall. Now that Anne was here, now that the court process was beginning, the whole rape suddenly became real again. It was a real person who had done this to

475

me. I had thought a lot about the rapist in the past few days. I had wondered who he was, what had driven him to try to kill me. Why raping a woman with her baby in her arms had seemed, to him, like a good idea. But now that I was talking with Anne I didn't want to know anything about him. I didn't want to know his name, or where he was from, or any details at all that would make him real.

'The police say they've finished their investigations. They'll set a trial date . . . Are you okay?'

I nodded, unable to speak.

'Caitlin, sometimes people want to know every detail of their case, but sometimes they don't. I don't know if you do, if you'd rather I just . . . '

'No, no. I want to know everything that happens. Did he plead?' I asked anxiously. If he said he was guilty then perhaps I wouldn't have to go to court, perhaps I wouldn't have to be cross-examined.

'He pleaded not guilty,' said Anne. 'I'm sorry. But at least he didn't get bail. The magistrate said no.'

After Anne left I went to the police station, leaving Ruby in Ron's office. I parked by the fence and then sat in the car for a moment, trying to find the energy to get out. Inside the building I went upstairs to the CID offices and put my head round an open door.

'*Dumela*,' I said, trying to sound confident.

The officer looked up.

'I was wondering . . . I'm wondering about . . . the things that were stolen from me. On Friday.'

'Case number?'

'I don't know. It was on Friday. I was raped. At my home.'

The officer went out and came back with a colleague. He was a short, square-faced man who had come to the house to draw a sketch of our home. He had seemed polite, even gentle.

'Has anyone found any of the things that . . . man took? The camera?'

The CID officer shook his head.

'No? The bike? My purse? The money?'

'Nothing. Everything was stolen . . . by people in the bush.' The officer looked sad.

'Which prison is he in?'

'Boro Farm.'

'Oh, God. That's an easy one to get out of.'

The first CID officer agreed. 'People are always breaking out of Boro.'

'Oh, God,' I mumbled. 'You will keep him in there won't you?'

'*Ee*,' the first officer laughed. 'We will keep him.'

'But you say break-outs are common?'

'*Ee*.' The officer nodded enthusiastically, 'and he will come straight back to you.'

★　★　★

Now I became obsessed with AIDS information. I went to the Maun public library where there were just two books on rape. I flicked through them, looking for something particular; I was looking for something that said I wouldn't get AIDS. I knew I had to keep taking the pills for another two weeks, but that I wouldn't be tested for HIV again until at least six weeks after the rape. Six weeks seemed like a very long time, but under Botswana law a rapist is only tested upon conviction, for to test an accused rapist before conviction was regarded as a violation of his human rights.

I drove home that day with Editor in the back of the car. I travelled everywhere with her, yet until a few weeks ago I had never hired someone to work for me at all. I felt awkward around her; awkward about being someone's employer, but I increasingly relied on her to look after Ruby when I couldn't. Sometimes, as I worked in my office, I could hear the two of them laughing and I would look out of the window to see Editor lifting Ruby high up in the air, or carrying her giggling down to the river on her back, or sitting quietly on the sand braiding Ruby's hair. As we drove along the road to the Hippo Pool we passed new houses on the right, buildings that had gone up in a matter of weeks, modern homes with satellite dishes on poles in the gardens, burglar bars on all the windows. A white woman waved as I went past and I slowed down, wondering if she needed help.

'Hi!' she called.

I stopped and wound down my window.

'Do you live around here?' the woman asked.

'Yes,' I said cautiously.

'Well, my dog's disappeared. The big Dobermann with the red collar?'

I nodded; I had seen the dog around. 'I'll let you know if I see it.'

478

The woman smiled. She wore a white summer dress and her hands were dusty with flour. 'So, where do you live?'

I pointed in the direction of the peninsula that led to our house.

'Oh,' said the woman, frowning, 'I heard . . .'

'Yes,' I said quickly. 'That was me.'

The woman shivered. 'They're like animals aren't they?'

'Who?' My vision began to blur, I knew what the woman was about to say.

'The locals, the Batswana men. They're *like* that, aren't they?' The woman wasn't really looking at me, she wasn't really looking for agreement, she just took it for granted. I saw her glance at Editor sitting in the back of the car and then her eyes moved on.

'I'm married to one,' I said, beginning to wind the window up.

'Sorry?' The woman looked confused.

'I'm married to a Motswana.' I drove off, wondering how people saw my case, knowing that among the white people in Maun this was, to them, evidence of the intrinsic dangers of African men. I would be used as an example of what could happen to white women.

I put a year calendar up on the wall in my office, marking in my next HIV test. But then I took the calendar down. All those days to get through, I thought, I can't face all those days to get through. And if people were talking about me now because I had been raped, I could imagine what would happen if I had HIV. People with HIV were shunned. A few weeks earlier, at a

479

public meeting in Maun, a woman had got up and said she had HIV. It was the first time anyone in northern Botswana had done this, yet it was sixteen years since the first AIDS-related death had been recorded. A few days later, the commerce and industry minister told the press: 'Rapists expose victims to high risk of contacting HIV/AIDS. Since we all know that HIV/AIDS has no cure, being raped is akin to being sentenced to death.' I read her statement and I felt sick. People were supposed to be being encouraged to find out their status, to access what help and drugs were available, to de-stigmatize the whole disease. And now I was supposedly being sentenced to death. I was appalled at the level of my own fear. I thought I was educated, I thought I knew that HIV was just an infection, that people with HIV should be treated the same as everyone else. And yet I now so desperately didn't want to be HIV positive myself.

★　★　★

A few weeks after the rape I was beginning to feel stronger. I slept at night. I had no nightmares. I dealt with what I had to do in the morning. I accepted a couple of work offers. I marked deadlines in my diary. I was alone for only an hour each morning, after Ron went to work and before Ruby woke and I too was ready to leave the house. In the evening, after I came home but before Ron did, friends came and stayed with me. But it was the first hour upon waking that was the hardest. As Ruby slept I paced the house, alert to every noise outside, checking and re-checking the view through every window. I left bottles of Rescue Remedy on shelves around the house, gulping it down, knowing it wasn't helping. I borrowed two dogs off Stef and her partner Bryn, anxious to have some security in the yard. I had an alarm system fitted with sensors in each room. If the alarm went then men from Coin Botswana, the security company, would, in theory, arrive within minutes. Ron bought me a mobile phone. I bought a spray gun. I did all this without any thought of logic. I was preparing myself to prevent something that had already happened.

★   ★   ★

On the morning of my thirty-seventh birthday I was feeding Ruby breakfast in the living-room. She had just woken and her hair stuck in long ringlets around her head. She sat on the cool tiled floor, her eyes busy, her hands pointing everywhere. 'Mama!' She pointed at the window. 'Cheese!' She beamed as I handed her a bottle of milk. But the milk quickly bored her, for now all she wanted to do was to climb, putting great effort into getting a chunky leg up on the sofa and then stopping, stuck, unable to haul her bottom up as well. She began to howl in frustration and, outside, the dogs started to bark. I leapt up. If the dogs were barking then there was someone outside. I was still on edge. I still scanned the windows all the time. I had to have silence. If Ruby cried I tried to quieten her as

481

quickly as possible, I had to be able to hear what was going on around me. I looked out the front window and saw the dogs had rushed to the gate. Then I could see the figure of a man trying to open the gate. I began to shake.

'Shush,' I urged Ruby, picking her up from the sofa. I put her on my hip and stood unsurely by the window. I couldn't decide whether to hide somewhere in the house so the man thought no one was home, or whether I should show him I was here, that the house was occupied.

'What?' I yelled, throwing open the front door. I was not a polite person any more. I wasn't going to say *Dumela*; I wasn't going to engage in conversation. The man heard me and he began working his way along the fence around the plot.

'What?' I yelled again, terrified, holding on to the doorframe, about to vomit.

The man said something. I couldn't make it out. I thought perhaps he was asking for a job, or that someone had sent him to see me.

'No!' I yelled. 'Just go. Leave!' The man left, reluctantly, walking slowly. I watched him walk down the sand pathway and into the green bush. He was going to come back. He knew I was alone and frightened. I ran to the spare room and locked Ruby and me in, cowering, waiting for the inevitable.

A month after the rape I had my first nightmare. It came after talking with a woman called Beata, a Polish psychologist who was staying in Maun. She had little experience of counselling, or of rape, but she offered to help. I woke up from the nightmare in a sweat. I had dreamt a group of men were outside by the gate. They were sitting on the sand, waiting for me to come out of the house so they could kill me. And then I realized that since the rape I had not entered our yard or the house alone. I had always been with someone else, or I knew a friend was there waiting for me. On three occasions when I arrived home to find no one there I simply turned the car round and drove off. I could not even sit in the car at the gate. Even if the car was locked. Even with a cell-phone. Even with a spray gun.

When I was at home, when Ron or someone else was there, I went into my office and tried to work. But the only thing I could think about was the rape. I flipped through the WAR report on violence in northern Botswana that I had written the year before. I had estimated that a woman was raped in Botswana every twelve minutes. Most were committed by a man the woman knew, but in recent years the number of rapes committed by strangers had risen dramatically and the weapon of choice was always a knife. I looked down at the report in my hands. I had become a figure in my own report, I had become a statistic.

And now everyone around me seemed to be acting suspiciously. I hadn't suspected the man who raped me of murderous intentions, now I had to look at people with more care. I mustn't be so gullible. And now there seemed to be signs of potential danger all around me. In the first five years I had lived in Botswana I could count the number of times men had accosted me on the streets on one hand. Now it was happening daily. On the way to meet Beata one morning I passed a middle-aged man masturbating on the roadside. On the way back I had to swerve to avoid two men peeing on the road, both of whom stopped to wave and grin at me. The next day, when I went to pick up Beata because her vehicle had broken down, it was in time to save her from a group of four men who were 'proposing marriage'. In the past such men could have been reported to the chief, but reporting such things to the chief didn't even occur to most people any more. Instead, the police and the courts and the media advised women not to walk alone at night, not to visit bars, not to wear short, Western-style clothes. Women had to change the way they behaved, they had to police themselves, they were to take care outside the home. But I had been stabbed and raped in my home and so now nowhere was safe.

As the day of the rape trial neared, I began to suffer repeated bouts of dizziness. I had no idea who was to prosecute my case nor what stage the investigation had reached, nor what evidence there was. What I did know was that under the current laws I would have to prove penetration, I would have to provide corroboration of the rape, and I would be cross-examined by the man who raped me because, like all accused criminals except murderers, he was afforded no legal aid.

Four days before the trial I went for my second HIV test. It took several hours before I had the results. I was HIV negative. I scrumpled up the lab report. I felt no reassurance at all. I would have my third test in another six weeks. If that were negative I would face another one six months from the rape and a final one a year from the rape. The fact that two tests had proved I was negative didn't comfort me. What if there had been a mix-up in the lab? What if I had been given someone else's results by mistake? Nothing now was certain, nothing could give me back any sense of certainty.

I drove home, stopping to pick Alice up from school. We had barely spoken in the past few weeks. I felt I should talk to her about the rape, about what had happened, but I wasn't sure how. I was okay, I told her, she could ask me anything she wanted but, as yet, she had nothing to say. And if I asked her to do anything for me, to boil water for tea, to keep an eye on Ruby in the bath for a moment, she scowled and dragged her feet as if I were being unreasonable. And she had started to come home from school later and later each day, sometimes not until dusk.

A few days before the trial the police arrived at my house one evening to deliver the subpoenas.

'This is about the rape case,' said one of the officers. 'Do you still remember it?'

I smiled blankly. As if I could have possibly forgotten it. But I reminded myself I was lucky. The man had been caught. Less than seven weeks from the attack and the trial was set, but not without constant pressure on the police. One morning I went to meet a lawyer who was to help with the prosecution. I didn't know him, he was new in town, but he knew me.

'I was almost the one who prosecuted you for that *Okavango Observer* case!' he said beaming, setting his cell-phone on the desk, pushing aside a half-read cowboy novel.

'You were?'

'*Ee.* I was working for the attorney general's office at the time.'

I smiled politely, I wasn't interested. I just wanted reassurance about the upcoming rape trial. I asked whether the case would be heard in camera, rather than in open court and at once the lawyer was on the phone.

'I've got a white lady here . . . ' he said into the receiver, giving me a friendly smile as he spoke. 'Caitlin Davies. You've heard of her? Yes. Yes. She's been raped by a black thug.'

I stared at the lawyer, open-mouthed. I had no intention of hiding what had happened to me, but he had not even asked my permission. The identity of rape survivors was, in theory, not supposed to be public knowledge. Newspapers were not supposed to name or otherwise identify people who had been raped, although they often did. I remembered how the *Voice* had once printed the photo of a little girl who had just been raped, along with the photo of her rapist.

'So,' the lawyer said, 'it looks like you can give evidence in camera. I've just been to the prison, by the way, so I saw the accused.'

'You did?'

'*Ee.* He's very well known. He's got that gun tattooed across his chest.'

'That must be new,' I said, my heart thumping uncomfortably. 'He didn't have that before, I'm

486

sure he didn't.' I began biting my finger-nails. What if, when the case came to court, I failed to identify the man? What if he had a tattoo and I said he didn't?

'Yes, he asked me to represent him!' and the lawyer roared with laughter. 'I said no, of course. So he accused me of only working for whites!'

The afternoon before the trial I went to the police station. Finally I had been given the name of the officer prosecuting the case. We met downstairs in a bright and airy room with a large cleared table and freshly dusted filing cabinets. The prosecutor looked a little like Mr Radipudi, the man who had arrested me years ago. He was tall and thin and a little elderly. But his face was relaxed and smooth, as if he were well cared for at home, as if the stresses of the job couldn't take away from his basic pleasantness.

'*Dumela Mma,*' he said, holding out his hand as I came into the room. His hand was soft and his gaze was held down a little out of respect.

'Caitlin!' said the lawyer, sitting on a chair to my left. 'We thought you were never going to get here!'

I nodded distractedly. I had left Ruby at home with Editor and Mactracy, a gardener I had hired a few weeks ago, and I was worried. What if Mactracy turned out not to be the dependable sort of person he appeared to be? And what about Editor? What did I really know about her except that she was not, as she had first said, a Motswana at all but a Zimbabwean.

'Here is your testimony,' smiled the prosecutor in a calm, unhurried fashion. 'Perhaps you can read it? And then we can go over it.'

I took the paper he handed me. I skimmed over what I had written almost two months ago. It was a police statement. It seemed accurate, but it was devoid of emotion. I put the paper down and nodded. 'That seems all right. Is that what I will say in court?'

The lawyer leaned forward. 'Caitlin, you need to be as specific as possible.'

I bristled slightly. 'How do you mean?'

'Well, it's not good enough to just say, 'and then he raped me'.'

'It isn't?'

The lawyer smiled. 'No.'

'Okay, he penetrated me.'

'No,' the lawyer said again.

I threw him an angry look.

'You need to say, 'He put his penis in my vagina and moved up and down'.'

'I don't see why,' I snapped. 'If I say I was raped, I was raped. If I say I was penetrated, then I was raped. Why do I have to say what you're saying?' I looked at my cell-phone. It was mid-afternoon already. Ron was supposed to be here.

'This is the way it needs to be done in court,' said the lawyer with a sigh.

'Fine,' I said, furious. 'He put his penis in my vagina and moved up and down. Okay? Happy now?'

The lawyer smirked.

'And afterwards, after the rape, did you see any semen?'

'What?'

The lawyer waited.

'Well,' I said hesitantly, 'there was some liquid, on my leg, but I can't say if it was . . . '

'Oh, come on, Caitlin,' the lawyer slapped his thigh, 'you're a big girl. What do you think it was!'

I left the police station an hour later. Ron had arrived with Gabs, ready to go over their statements, because she had been in the car when Ron caught the rapist. But I had needed help and Ron hadn't been there and now I was furious with him as well. I drove home fast, breaking the speed limit, rushing back to Ruby. Tomorrow I would be at court. I would see the rapist again for the first time since the rape and I didn't know what I would do.

# 30

On Tuesday 10 April 2001, I walked into my in-laws compound in Moeti with Ruby in my arms. Ron's mother would look after Ruby while Ron and I went to court. I walked into the yard feeling stiff. I had not slept much the night before and in the morning I hadn't known what clothes to wear. I still had the clothes I had been raped in; they were stuffed at the back of the wardrobe. I didn't seem to be able to get rid of them, but I also couldn't bear to see them. I had been raped while wearing a skirt. Now I couldn't wear skirts any more, I only wore shorts or trousers. But I knew I had to play a certain role on the witness stand, that I needed to wear a skirt or a dress. This is what the lawyer had advised me. 'And not a red one!' he had laughed. His final piece of advice for me the afternoon before was not to become emotional. 'But won't the magistrate *want* to see I'm emotional?' I asked. 'No,' said the lawyer, 'because if you are emotional then you will be seen as an unreliable witness.' I was desperate to keep my mind clear, to be able to take the stand and recall every last detail of what had happened. I had to ensure my voice didn't break, that I didn't dissolve into tears.

As I walked further into my in-laws compound, I began to feel undressed, the sway of the dress around my legs feeling strange. Eliah had just finished bathing; she was hanging out her face-cloth on the reed wall. Madintwa was sitting by the fire drinking tea. The women looked up as I walked in, but they only had eyes for Ruby. I put Ruby down on the sand and she toddled off, rushing to her great-grandmother, looking forward to a morning of play. Her favourite thing to do was to clamber on Madintwa's back and then Madintwa would pretend to be a donkey.

'Go siame,' I said, preparing to leave.

'Ee,' Eliah said.

I waited a second, to see if either woman had anything to say. But Eliah had walked off into the house and Madintwa was busy admiring Ruby's buttocks. The trial was to be held in a room at Maun's old council buildings, the place where I had queued for most of the day waiting to get my O Mang, my national identity card after I had become a Botswana citizen. As we pulled up at the council car park I could see the place was deserted. No one stood in the sand courtyard. It was empty but for three chickens pecking on the ground. I walked around nervously, stepping up on to a low cement porch, peering in through a row of windows. Inside a small room I could see rows of wooden benches, and then a higher bench behind which the magistrate's chair was covered in a white cloth as if it were a museum exhibit. Then I saw two small wooden docks where the rapist and I would face each other.

We waited outside the courtroom for an hour, standing among the purple flowering bougainvillea trees, shading ourselves from the sun. At last

491

the magistrate arrived, entering through a back door. We were called in and I turned, to take one last look around. I had not stopped scanning the area for the rapist since I had arrived.

We walked in and took a seat on an empty bench on the right. Beata the psychologist arrived; she had offered to be present during my testimony.

'Have you seen him?' she asked.

I shook my head, not able to speak. And then, from out of the window, I saw a group of men being taken from the back of a police car and walked across the sand. I craned my neck, I just couldn't see if the rapist was there or not. What if I didn't recognize him, what if I failed to identify him? And when I did see him I expected to shake, to vomit, to collapse. Or perhaps, I thought, I would simply get up and run.

And then he entered the courtroom and I heard a noise come out of my mouth. It was the sound of utter contempt. I felt like spitting to one side, like Pearl did when she passed the father of her first-born on the village pathways of Mochudi. The rapist was led to the front, handcuffs around his wrists, and sat down. I stared at the back of him. I bored my eyes into the back of his head. For weeks I had dreamt of revenge. I wanted to find him and I wanted to torture him. I wanted nothing more in the world than to see him suffer. I had always opposed the death penalty but now, given the chance, I would have clapped to see him hang.

He looked more presentable than the last time I had seen him outside the police station. He had clothes on now. He looked clean and well dressed. He was bigger, fitter, than I had remembered. He looked a little fatter; perhaps prison was being good to him. But there was absolutely no doubt that this was the rapist. I didn't know why I had ever doubted that I would be able to identify him. He shifted in his seat a little so I saw the side of his face and the square set of the jaw. He looked strong. I couldn't believe I had fought against someone who was so strong. I had believed that he was going to kill me and I saw it was true, he could have killed me.

I studied the other people in the courtroom, wondering whether any relatives of the rapist were here, perhaps his mother or an uncle, perhaps he was even married. But he appeared to be alone.

Ron and I shifted down the bench as Anne Sandenbergh and then Stef arrived. I kept looking around for Pearl, wondering why she hadn't come. We sat while a few cases were heard for mention. And then the rapist was called and stood in the dock. I watched him take the stand and I realized with dismay that he was enjoying himself. There was a lopsided swagger to his gait, an awareness that everyone in the courtroom was looking at him. I opened my bag and took out some pills Dr Patrick had given me, homeopathic pills designed especially for victims of sexual abuse. I had been taking them all morning but they didn't seem to be doing much good. I wanted a shot of something, something that would give me the strength to take the stand, but

I knew there was nothing I could take that wouldn't alter the clarity of my mind as well. I had to keep myself together, I had to be so convincing in my testimony that the rapist would be convicted. Because if he weren't, if he were released like most accused rapists were, then I couldn't see how I could continue to live in Maun.

'I want to take notes,' the rapist told the magistrate in Setswana. I flinched at the sound of his voice. I had forgotten his voice. I hadn't described it in my police statement and yet it was so distinctive, a low rasp filled with aggression.

The magistrate nodded that this was allowed.

'I want paper.'

The magistrate ordered someone to provide paper.

The rapist laid the paper and pen down, looking satisfied.

'Anything else?' the magistrate asked with a note of sarcasm. I looked at the magistrate intently. He was a short man in his thirties and he looked very tired and very ill. He seemed to be slumped behind his desk.

'Ee,' said the rapist. 'I want to complain that the police aren't looking after my property properly . . . ' he spoke on, a catalogue of complaints which the magistrate noted down.

The magistrate asked that the court be cleared and the police prosecutor gestured at Ron. I sat up in alarm. I had thought Ron would be with me when I gave evidence, but now I realized that he couldn't because he was a witness too. Then I

494

was called to the stand. Shakily I took the Bible I was offered and I swore to tell the truth. The rapist was directly opposite me, but I was determined not to look at him. The police prosecutor had told me to address myself to the magistrate so I watched the magistrate now, waiting to be told to begin.

'It was Friday afternoon,' I said, my hands clasped on the sides of the wooden box. 'February the twenty-third. It was around ten-thirty a.m. and I was coming back from Maun with . . . ' I paused, the police prosecutor on my left had just gestured that I stop. I looked at the magistrate, he was writing slowly on a sheaf of paper. I realized in alarm that he was going to write down what I said in longhand himself. I had completely forgotten that this was what the magistrate had done during my OO trial. I wondered how he would be able to listen to what I said, write down what I said, and make notes of anything he needed to ask, anything he would need for his eventual judgement.

I waited until the magistrate glanced up, indicating that I could continue. 'I was coming home from Maun with my one-year-old daughter in the car.' I tried to speak clearly, but the very thought of Ruby made my voice weak. I took a deep breath. 'I arrived at my home and there was a man at the gate . . . ' Again the police prosecutor gestured at me and again I stopped. But I didn't want to stop, I wanted to get to the part of the rape, I wanted to get that part over with.

'Why didn't you just leave then?' the magistrate asked.

'Sorry?'

'When you saw him, why didn't you just leave then, or call your husband?'

I stared at the magistrate. Why didn't he understand? 'I didn't think anything was wrong,' I stumbled, 'I thought he wanted a job or something. I didn't know him but I thought he could have been a relative asking for help or something.'

The magistrate wrote on his pad of paper, then he gestured that I could continue. But his question had unsettled me, made me feel that I was to blame. And as I continued to talk, as I continued to pause after every sentence, my mind began to drift. I felt as if I were lifting out of my body and floating somewhere. As my evidence went on I began to fight an encroaching sense of panic that I wouldn't remember what I had just said, that I wouldn't know what to say next. To make matters even slower the court translator was translating every word of what I said into Setswana for the benefit of the rapist who was also busy writing.

I continued giving evidence. Twice I felt my voice choke. The rapist sat opposite me, staring. A few times I looked at him but then I turned my head away, addressing myself to the magistrate. I wanted the magistrate to believe me; I wanted to tell him that this had happened, that he had to convict this man because otherwise he would rape again.

'He got into the house,' I said, 'and he was

shouting, 'I'll stab you, I'll stab you' . . . ' I stopped as the courtroom door creaked open. Lets, the former *Okavango Observer* reporter with whom I'd been charged with causing fear and alarm, walked in. I had heard he was now working for Maun's new newspaper, the *Ngami Times*. I couldn't believe he thought he was allowed to be present during my evidence.

'He's a reporter,' I said, breaking off from my testimony.

The magistrate was still writing and he didn't appear to have heard me. I watched while Lets strolled into the courtroom and looked round for a seat. 'He's a reporter,' I repeated. 'He's a journalist.'

The magistrate ignored me.

'The media isn't allowed in here,' I said as firmly as I could, but I could hear I sounded hysterical.

The magistrate sighed, apparently annoyed at my outburst, and waved Lets out with his hand.

I went back to giving evidence, my voice speeding up, eager to get to the actual attack, to pass that hurdle. 'He got into the house and then he locked the door and put the keys — '

'Would you recognize the knife?' the police prosecutor interrupted.

I turned towards him, unsure. 'Yes, I think so. It was long, it had a long blade, and a old, beaten handle.'

'Is this the knife?' The prosecutor put his hand into a bag and held up a knife.

I stiffened. I hadn't known the police had the knife. 'Yes.' I looked at the knife. It was so much smaller than I remembered.

'I told him I didn't have any more money,' I continued, 'I told him to take the car. Then the rapist said, 'I want vagina' . . . ' I waited for the translator to repeat what I had said but she looked mortified. She opened her mouth but nothing came out. She fiddled with a bracelet round her wrist. She opened her mouth again, her eyes avoiding the rapist, mumbling.

'That is not what she said,' the magistrate rebuked her in English. The translator tried again but she just could not bring herself to say the word for vagina in Setswana. She was being forced to say something that traditionally people just couldn't say and she was getting increasingly upset. In the end she repeated what I had said, but in English not Setswana.

I looked at her in sympathy, angry that she was being made to suffer too. But I had to keep on talking; I had to get to the actual rape. With one part of my brain I spoke and with the other I prepared myself to say what I had been advised to. I would have to say the rapist put his penis into my vagina and moved up and down.

'Then he undid his belt,' I said, 'and took out his penis and — '

The magistrate interrupted. 'He raped you?'

'Yes,' I said.

'Well, then, that's all you have to say,' said the magistrate.

I was taken aback and I threw an angry glance at the lawyer.

The police prosecutor stepped forward and coughed politely. Then he turned to me. 'What colour was your underwear?' he asked.

'Red,' I mumbled. I felt uncomfortable and in a sudden flash of memory I thought about the day, years before, when I had bought underwear in Francistown and how the salesman had been shocked that I wanted to buy anything other than white. What would the magistrate think now, about my red underwear?

'Would you recognize it?' asked the police prosecutor.

I wanted to say of course I would, but I felt sick. The prosecutor had a small plastic bag in his hands and I could see he was about to take my slashed underwear out and hold it up in court. I remembered hearing about rape trials in Maun where the woman's underwear was brandished in court, and everyone present burst out laughing.

'Yes,' I said, at last. 'I would recognize it. It was Marks and Spencer. Size fourteen.'

The prosecutor bent to take the underwear out of the bag but the magistrate waved his hand impatiently. The prosecutor didn't appear to understand that he was being stopped. He bent again to take the underwear.

'We don't need to see it,' the magistrate snapped.

I returned to my testimony, describing how I had locked Ruby and myself in the bathroom after the rape.

'Your baby was with you?' the magistrate asked.

'Yes.'

'All that time?' The magistrate raised his

eyebrows, he looked incredulous.

'Yes. From the moment I picked her up from her cot she was on my hip.'

The magistrate wrote something down, perhaps he didn't believe me.

'I heard the back door close,' I continued, 'and then I looked out of the window and I saw the rapist coming round the side of the house . . . '

'In what direction is the gate to your plot?' the magistrate asked.

'It's sort of at an angle to the house,' I said, hesitating.

'How far?'

I looked across the courtroom and out of the window opposite, desperately trying to think in terms of distance, in terms of metres. 'It's like from here to that first tree outside, but sort of on the right, at an angle to the house, if you see what I mean.'

'No,' snapped the magistrate, 'I do not.'

I tried again, until finally the magistrate looked like he'd heard enough.

Half an hour later I finished my evidence. I swallowed hard; I relaxed my grip on the wooden box. I hadn't broken down, I hadn't cried. I had left nothing out.

'Does the accused have any questions?' the magistrate asked.

Now I gripped the box again. This was the part I dreaded. I had no idea how the rapist would cross-examine me, what he would say, what he could possibly ask. The lawyer had said he might ask me detailed questions about his penis — was it big, how big? Was it hard, how hard? Had I enjoyed it?

The rapist stood up; he pulled at his trousers, hitching them up. He stuck his chest forward like a cockerel. He began to speak and his voice gave me the chills.

'If it were to be established that you didn't live in Matlapaneng,' he rasped in Setswana, his hands laid out on the dock, his body straining forward, 'then would you agree this alleged attack hadn't happened?'

I knew what he had just asked, but I kept my face blank. I looked at the translator, waiting for her to speak. This was how I would do it, I decided. I would listen to his question, then I would wait for the translator to ask it in English and that way I would have more time to think.

The translator finished the rapist's first question. I nodded that I had heard and then I frowned. This wasn't a straightforward question. I thought I knew what he was getting at. My address in court had been given as Matlapaneng, yet really we lived in a place that had no official name at all. It could be considered Matlapaneng, but it also could be considered as part of Sedie Ward.

'Officially I live in Matlapaneng,' I said. 'That is where you raped me. My bills, my water bill, they give the address as Matlapaneng.'

The rapist drew himself up and he pointed at me. He was very close; if he got down from the dock he would be on me within a couple of steps. 'I asked if it were to be established that you didn't live in Matlapaneng then would you agree this alleged attack hadn't happened?'

'I don't understand the question,' I said, looking to the magistrate for help.

'Just answer yes or no!' the rapist roared.

I opened my mouth. I just couldn't think what answer to give. The question didn't really make sense, so how could I be forced to answer it? 'No,' I said at last.

The rapist nodded as if he had proved a point. He rustled his papers. He flexed his arms.

'Do you know me?'

'Do you mean did I know you before?'

He shook his head impatiently, as if I were deliberately annoying him.

'Before you came to my house I didn't know you. I know you now because you tried to kill me, and you raped me.'

'What shoes was I wearing?' he asked, leaning forward, a smile on his face.

I resisted the impulse to stand back in the box, to move away from him. I wondered if he would be allowed to ask and do anything he wanted, whether the magistrate would stop him, or whether this would just go on and on.

'I can't remember,' I mumbled. 'Boots, I think. But I can't be sure.'

The rapist laughed and looked around the courtroom.

'Describe the shoes I was wearing.'

'I can't. They were boots, I think. I can't describe them because I can't remember them exactly. They were probably brown.'

'Describe the shoes!' The rapist was furious now. He was as furious as he had been when he'd first broken into my home, when he had said he would stab me.

I looked at the magistrate but he appeared to be doodling on his paper.

'They were brown boots,' I sighed, 'I think.'

'How much money did I take?'

'I'm not sure. I had just been to the bank so I had about two hundred pula in my purse. I saw when you emptied the purse.'

'*How much money?*' Now the rapist was shouting, his voice booming across the courtroom as if it were he who was in charge. I stood rigidly, convinced that at any second he would step out of his box. I looked at the courtroom door, my heart thumping, wondering if I would be able to make it out in time. 'I'm not sure. Perhaps around fifty pula? I saw some of the money fall on the ground. I saw some of it later on the floor. I showed the police.'

'*Tell me how much money!*' the rapist yelled. 'She is not answering the question!'

'She is trying to be honest,' the magistrate said suddenly, his head snapping up. 'She has said she doesn't know.'

The rapist sucked his teeth and bent to consult his handwritten notes. Then he looked up. I could feel he was trying to make me look at him but I was looking determinedly at the magistrate.

'Can I sit down?' I asked.

The magistrate ignored me.

'Can I sit down, please?' My voice was weak, it sounded as if I were begging. My legs were feeling wobbly; I had been standing in the same spot for nearly three hours. The magistrate nodded. I sat down and realized immediately what a terrible mistake I had made. Now that I was sitting down I felt even more vulnerable. The rapist was towering over me and when he spoke I had to look up, like a small child looking up at a huge, angry adult.

'What do you think when you look at me?'

'What?' I asked, confused.

'Do you think I am a Christian or a sinner?'

I bit the insides of my cheek. He wasn't going to do this to me; he wasn't going to make me as afraid of him here, in this courtroom, as I had been at home. 'You want to know what I think when I look at you?' I asked slowly, choosing my words. 'I feel pity for you,' I spat. 'I pity you because you are a person who can rape someone, and you can rape someone while they are holding a baby in their arms.'

The rapist scowled. I could see spit forming around the corner of his mouth. 'You must say whether I am a Christian or a devil!'

I felt a chill run down my spine. I remembered how I'd asked the rapist if he believed in God, how he had said he didn't. This was what he was referring to now. It was as if he were playing with me, reminding me that he had raped me, that he and I knew we had had this conversation.

'It's not for me to say,' I stammered. 'I can't say if you're a Christian. God can decide what you are.'

'No!' the rapist roared. 'You must say whether you think I am Satan.'

'You are Satan,' muttered the magistrate and I turned to look at him, to see whether he really had said this or not.

The rapist drew himself up on the box, looking pleased. Then he laid his hands out, the fingers splayed, and leaned towards me again.

'You say you took the knife off me?'

'No . . . ' I responded immediately.

'You say you took the knife off me,' the rapist repeated, his arm out, his hand pointing down at me.

'No. I said you put it down and I picked it up.'

'Why didn't you kill me then?'

'You want her to do a Bosch?' the magistrate burst out and he roared with laughter. I felt my face redden. The magistrate and the police, the lawyer and the rapist, were all laughing. This was the second time I had been compared to Mariette Bosch, the white woman on death row.

The rapist finished laughing and he leaned forward again with a smirk. 'Why did you go to a private clinic?'

'I don't understand the question,' I answered, knowing this would anger him.

'Why did you go to a private clinic and not the government hospital?' The rapist looked around the court. 'Does this not show that you were undermining government doctors?'

I sensed an air of tension in the courtroom. The implication was that, as a white person, I didn't trust the doctors that everyone else had to go to, that I was rich and I considered myself above everyone else. 'Time was of the essence,' I explained to the magistrate. 'I knew I'd have to wait ages at the hospital. I didn't know if they had anti-retrovirals or not. I knew the clinic did,

505

I had to get them quickly, because of AIDS.'

'You have not answered the question!' roared the rapist. 'Were you undermining government doctors?'

'No,' I said, 'I wasn't.' I was about to say that I had given birth in the local hospital when the magistrate interrupted.

'You have five more minutes,' he said a little wearily.

After almost four hours of giving evidence and being cross-examined, I was told to leave the dock. The case was adjourned for lunch. I walked unsteadily outside and joined Ron who stood with Gabs and Anne Sandenbergh and the two men from Med Rescue who were due to give evidence later in the day. I was quivering as I walked, elated that the worse was over, but not sure how to act, how to speak or how to stand now that I was out of court. I turned as I felt someone behind me. The rapist brushed against me, a leer on his face. Then he took a few steps forward and stopped, standing to face me in the courtyard, legs apart, his whole posture aggressive. Unconcerned, the police stood in a group on their own, chatting and laughing, sharing a cigarette. Keep him away from me, I wanted to cry. He's standing there deliberately intimidating me, someone do something. But I was trembling too much to speak. The energy needed to face the cross-examination had suddenly evaporated.

That evening I sat on the porch. It was a cool spring evening but while I could see the beauty of the place around me, it didn't touch me, the trees, the river, the sinking sun, all seemed far away as if I were living in a bubble without feelings or smells or sounds.

The next day one of the Med Rescue officers took the stand.

'Are you friends with this *Caitlin Davies?*' the rapist asked and, sitting at the back of the courtroom I felt my body go cold. How dare he use my name? The fact that he knew my name, that he could pronounce it properly, that he could speak it so casually made me feel all my defences had been taken away from me. 'Are you friends with this Caitlin Davies?' he asked again.

The Med Rescue man seemed to hesitate. As with the day before, I could feel the tension in the room, the Med Rescue man was white, the raped woman was white, people thought we knew each other.

'I had never met her before in my life,' said the Med Rescue man easily.

The rapist looked furious.

'I had only arrived in Maun the day before the incident,' continued the Med Rescue man. 'I'd never been to Maun before either. This was my first call out.'

I sat back on the bench and smiled in satisfaction. But then Ron was called to the stand and I felt my heart leap in anxiety. I watched as Ron walked to the box, his shoulders squared, his eyes on the rapist. And I felt terrible for him. Ron was not involved in the rape, he hadn't been there, it was not his fault. And yet now he was having to stand up in court and face a cross-examination by the man who had raped his wife. And the rapist was looking excited; I saw him lick his lips as Ron took the oath. He was looking forward to this.

I prayed that Ron wouldn't get annoyed, that he wouldn't let the rapist bait him, that he wouldn't become angry. I inched my way forward. There was no back to the bench; I couldn't sit properly. I looked around and saw, at the back of the courtroom, at the end of the aisle between the benches, a proper chair with a back. I got up cautiously and moved over to the chair, looking around in case anyone was going to stop me. I was sitting directly between them now, down at the front on my right was Ron and opposite him, on my left, was the rapist. Both had their arms folded, I could see the muscles twitching in each of their faces.

Ron began his evidence in English, but then he grew impatient with the translator, she wasn't being exact enough so he went into Setswana himself. I sat there nervously, they were speaking too quickly, I was losing track of what was being said. Ron was speaking too formally, his language ornate. I followed as best as I could but again I felt as if I were floating. The hours went by. I could hear people outside the courtroom walking by and laughing. The rapist was yelling and waving his arms. He demanded yes or no answers. He demanded to know the exact colour of the shirt he had been wearing. He demanded to know how much money had been stolen. Finally, after almost two hours of questioning, the rapist announced he was finished and sat down. Ron returned stiffly to the bench, and I watched him go, his face unreadable.

★ ★ ★

At home I became difficult to live with. I got angry over small things, I felt impatient, unable to tolerate anyone or anything except Ruby. All I talked about was the attack and the trial. And Ron no longer responded when I talked, he just sat and hung his head or walked out and stood on the porch. He was becoming a stranger to me now. We slept apart; neither of us could bare to touch the other.

★ ★ ★

We returned to court a few days later to listen to an army officer give evidence. But the officer grew confused and contradicted himself, and the magistrate became annoyed. And I realized that I no longer wanted to be in court. Each time the case continued I became more and more drained. I began to have cramps. Once, while other cases were being heard for mention, I excused myself from the courtroom to go to the toilet. But when I came out of the toilet the rapist was there, waiting for me. He had seen me leave; he had told the police he needed the toilet too. And then he had stood outside, leaning casually up against the wall, waiting for me.

★ ★ ★

A few weeks later I was standing in a clothing shop in the Old Mall, flicking through children's clothes, listening to the lunchtime news on Radio Botswana.

My cell-phone rang and I saw it was Ron.

'What happened?' I asked, my heart pounding.

'Guilty.'

'Guilty?'

'*Ee.*'

I held the phone tightly in my hand wanting to feel something, to feel satisfaction, to feel happy. But I felt nothing at all. I felt no pleasure in the man being found guilty. He was guilty, I knew that anyway.

'Has he got AIDS?'

'They're sending him for a test.'

I put the phone back in my pocket and continued looking through the children's clothes.

A few days later the rapist was back at court. Again I was in a shop in the Old Mall when Ron rang.

'He's negative.'

'He hasn't got AIDS?'

'No.'

I looked around the shop, people were listening to me. I shifted from one foot to another. If the rapist wasn't HIV positive, then nor was I. But I had had three tests. And they hadn't been necessary. All the months of uncertainty, the blood tests, the waiting for the results, had been unnecessary. He didn't have HIV at all. And to my horror I realized I wished that he did. I wanted him to have AIDS.

'How many years?'

'*Mma?*'

'Ron, how many years did he get?' The rapist

had already been found guilty, both of armed robbery and rape. The minimum sentence in each case was ten years, I knew the rapist was facing at least a twenty-year jail sentence.

'Twelve for armed robbery . . . ' Ron paused. 'Ten for the other . . . '

I gave a bitter laugh. 'More for armed robbery than for rape?'

'*Ee*. And he's done it before.'

'What, rape?' I clutched the phone.

'*Ee*. Everything. He has a string of records.'

'So that's twenty-two years?' I asked.

'No, I don't think so. The magistrate said twelve years.'

'But it *can't* be, they can't run the sentences concurrently because it's two minimum sentences. Did they say concurrently, or consecutively?'

'I don't know.' Ron sounded miserable.

'But they've got it wrong!' I wailed. 'It can't be that. They can't run the sentences together.'

That afternoon I told Alice the news. 'Alice,' I said, putting my head round the corner of her bedroom door.

Alice looked up, she was lying on her bed surrounded by exam papers, none of which she was reading.

'Alice. He got sentenced today, the man who attacked me. He got twelve years.'

Alice looked up.

'I just thought I'd tell you. It's over.' I smiled reassuringly. 'It's good, isn't it?'

'*Twelve years?*' Alice sat up. She didn't look pleased.

'Yes.'

'But that's too long!'

'What?' I stiffened in the doorway. I thought I had misheard.

'That's too long,' Alice repeated.

'Too long? For someone that stabbed and raped your mother? No sentence would be too long!'

Alice shook her head. 'It's too long,' she said, 'just for that.'

# 31

Winter seemed to come early that year and by August the nights were bitterly cold. In the mornings I wrapped Ruby in her warmest clothes, struggling to get her reluctant body into socks and shoes, jumpers and coats. But Ruby was bigger now, and stronger. She was one and a half years old and she was determined not to wear clothes. She could take off shoes and socks as quickly as I could put them on. 'Naughty Mama,' she scolded me as I pulled trousers on to her legs. 'No! Naughty Mama!'

I desperately wanted Ruby to be okay, not to show any sign that the rape had affected her, and as far as I could see she feared nothing and no one. And yet so much of my mind was still taken up with the rape, I was on constant alert, as if I were a sniper on a twenty-four-hour shift that never ended. I wanted Ruby to feel safe, when I didn't feel safe at all.

At night I woke in the early hours and couldn't get back to sleep. I knew the rapist had been transferred several hundred kilometres away to Francistown prison, but still I expected him to come back. I lay and thought about what I would do if he did. In the mornings Ruby went to Woodland nursery where she cuddled everyone and asked if they were her friends. She went there every day now, while I went to work. Before the rape trial had finished I had got a new teaching job at a small school called the Chicken House. My students were bright and articulate. They wanted to learn and I wanted to teach them, but I felt I was leading a double life. The rape trial had never really finished; there were too many loose ends. The police were unhelpful when I protested that the magistrate had given the wrong sentence, that he hadn't applied the law. I was told the sentencing was nothing to do with them, their job was over. It was up to the magistrate to admit the mistake himself, and forward the files to the court of appeal for review. But I couldn't seem to be able to establish if this had been done or not. And then I was told the case files had gone missing. No one knew where they were; no one in authority seemed to care. Several people suggested it was witchcraft; the rapist had used witchcraft to make the files disappear. The morning I heard about the files I arrived a little late for work and when I walked into the classroom the students were talking excitedly. Irritated about the missing court files, I told them to get down to work, we were revising the causes of World War One. 'What did you think about the planes?' one of the students asked.

'What planes?'

'Yesterday, in New York.'

'What happened yesterday in New York?'

'The terrorist attack . . . '

'You're kidding?' I asked. I had stopped paying attention to what went on around me, let alone what was happening in other countries. I didn't seem connected to other people any more.

The evening of 12 September, Bashi and Pearl came round. Pearl was upset, she couldn't believe what had happened in New York, she had been praying constantly. We sat outside by the fire Alice had built, roasting meat and talking just like old times. But it wasn't like old times, for I could see that Bashi was sick. His skin was patchy, with little white marks like watery clouds. He coughed frequently. But he made no mention of being ill, of what could be wrong. Instead he laughed a lot, a forced laugh that dared anyone to talk of anything serious. As the evening wore on, Bashi and Ron went to the far end of the plot to try to track down a snake. I had seen the tracks of a puff adder in the afternoon and Ron had his gun in his hands.

'Are you okay?' I asked Pearl who, as the men wandered off, put down her plate and gave a heavy sigh. Alice had gone back into the house and I could see the light was on in her room. Outside Pearl and I were alone with the dogs.

'*Ee.*'

'The kids okay?'

'*Ee.*'

'Bashi?'

'He is ill,' Pearl said, and she looked over her shoulder as if someone was listening.

'Has he been to the doctor?' I asked.

'It is nothing,' Pearl said suddenly, drawing a cardigan round her shoulder. 'It is something that started last year, in the stomach. That's all.'

I nodded. I thought Bashi had AIDS. I had not noticed him growing ill, but now it seemed obvious. I moved my chair nearer to the fire.

Pearl and I had known each other nearly ten years. We had done everything together, laughing and dancing at Maun picnics, going on trips to the bush. We had seen each other through pregnancy and childbirth, through affairs and through deceit. I couldn't bear the idea that still there were things we couldn't talk about.

'Why didn't you come to my trial, Pearl?' I asked. As soon as the words came out I regretted them. I had wanted to ask about Bashi. I had wanted to say that if he got tested and it was HIV then he could take anti-retrovirals. The Botswana government was about to issue the drugs for free, making it the first country in Africa to do so. But instead of asking about Bashi I was once again thinking of myself.

Pearl shifted closer to the fire too, so that we sat side by side, our chairs nestled together. She looked at me and then she looked away. 'Which trial?'

'The rape trial.' I leant forward and poked a fallen stick back into the fire. 'I told you the dates; I thought you would have come. I wanted you there.' My heart began fluttering as I spoke. The fact that Pearl hadn't come had bothered me for a long time, as had the fact that not a single relative on either side of the family had come to show support. Not my mother- or father-in-law, not any of my sisters- or brothers-in-law, none of the assorted uncles or cousins or aunts. But I felt that while I couldn't ask them, I could ask Pearl.

Beside me Pearl gave another heavy sigh. 'I couldn't.'

'You couldn't?'

'*Ee*. I wanted to, but I couldn't . . . '

'Because?'

'Because,' Pearl echoed. She said it flatly, as if the word were the end of a sentence not a beginning. 'Because it happened to me.'

'What?' I asked, but I had seen her face and I knew.

'With my first-born. The father of my first-born.'

'He raped you?'

'*Ee*.'

I shivered. I remembered when I saw the rapist in court for the first time how I had wanted to spit, how I had thought at once of Pearl and her ex-boyfriend. Now I knew it wasn't a boyfriend at all, it was a rapist. And she had kept the child, Pearl had been raped and she had kept the child.

'I'm sorry,' I said, 'I didn't know. I'm sorry.'

★  ★  ★

I continued to teach at the Chicken House, but I felt I was still struggling to function. One night I was sitting on the porch, arguing with Ron. He had left mud on the floor, then he had walked across the mud, not bothering to stop and clean it. He was standing at the back door, he had just finished cutting some wires and he had a knife in his hand. As we argued, he gestured impatiently with the hand that held the knife and I began to scream. 'Get out, get out!'

Ron stopped speaking.

'The knife,' I yelled. 'Get rid of the fucking knife. Get out!'

'Get out where?' Ron asked, perplexed.

'Just get out.'

'It's me,' Ron said, coming towards me.

'Get away!' I screamed again. 'You're standing just like *him*, with the knife.'

'I don't look anything like him,' Ron objected.

'The knife, the way you're standing, it's just like him.'

Ron turned and went back inside the house. Why don't you understand? I thought. Why can't you do everything the way I want you to?

It had been almost six months since the rape and still I felt unsafe. I stuck rigidly to my routine, leaving at the same time each day, picking Editor up, dropping Ruby at nursery, getting to work. And if anything threatened to alter the routine I panicked.

One day Editor was not where she usually was, standing outside her house, ready for the lift to nursery. And the next day she wasn't there either. I knew things were getting worse in Zimbabwe, I knew she had her own daughter there, and her mother. I knew that food was scarce, that Mugabe's thugs were accosting people, beating and raping them. I thought perhaps Editor had gone home, but I couldn't understand why she hadn't told me. And then a week later she returned. She said she'd had to go to the border to get her permits renewed. And now the gardener Mactracy left, and I hired another gardener, a woman called MaStar. But sometimes she didn't come to work either and in the mornings I paced the living-room, watching for her familiar figure at the gate, only feeling able to leave the house once I could see she had arrived. And now I realized I had turned into an expatriate. I had come to Botswana with little, I had had a job but I had lived in a two-room house without a bath or hot water, without a fridge or a TV or a computer. Now I had my own house, my own car, along with all the trappings, all the household equipment most people aspired to. And I had staff. I had a woman who looked after my child, and I had a gardener who watered my plants. I had become a Madam.

And while I was in charge of things at home, Ron had fallen back into his old routine. He no longer came home before it was dark; he was once again juggling office with family and farm. As night fell I would grow increasingly fretful, not allowing Alice or Ruby out of the house, insisting we were inside, with the doors locked. I felt safe to go outside only once Ron came home. But there were always delays, and always dramas to explain the delays. There were more and more funerals to attend, goats were killed by lions, computer networks crashed, there was always a reason.

'Where have you been?' I asked one night as soon as Ron came in the door.

'Where's Phuthumphi?'

'She's sleeping. It's dark! She went to bed hours ago. You *know* that. Why couldn't you have called?'

'No coverage.' Ron held up his cell-phone.

'So why didn't you use the home phone?'

'The line's dead, Cait.'

'It is?' I went to check the phone. Every week the phone line went dead, sometimes for a few minutes, sometimes for hours, sometimes for days. And when it went dead then I felt uneasy; it meant that there was no line from the house to the rest of the world. 'But why can't you just come home before it's dark?' I asked the back of Ron's head.

'Look' — he turned — 'I worry too. I *hate* thinking of you all here on your own. I drive like *crazy* to get back here, I worry about it all the time.'

'So just come back here from work, then.'

'Cait, I have things to do,' Ron said and slammed a computer manual down on the table. 'I'm not your babysitter.'

I stopped where I was in the living-room. 'I don't want you to be my babysitter,' I protested. But I did.

As the nightmares intensified, as the feeling of being constantly afraid didn't appear to lessen, I went back to see Beata, the psychologist. I had thought that after the trial I didn't need any more help. I had been determined that the rape would not ruin my life; I had wanted it behind me as soon as possible. Beata told me I wasn't accepting what had happened and I snapped at her, 'You want me to *accept* rape?' But Beata was trying to help me, she was the only person I could talk to about the violence in vivid detail, the only person not afraid to ask me questions.

I left Beata's in a rush, hurrying to pick Ruby

up from nursery and then Alice from Ron's mother's in Moeti. If we got home quickly then Ruby would nap and I would have time to mark exams. I drove into Moeti, flinging the car into the yard. I looked around for Alice, expecting her to be waiting for me on the step to the main house. But I couldn't see anyone at all. I beeped the horn, then cursed myself in case it woke Ruby. At last I saw Alice walking slowly from round the back of the house. Her sleeves were rolled up; it looked like she were washing clothes.

'Let's go,' I called out of the car window.

Alice stopped where she was, she didn't move forward, she didn't move back.

'Alice! Come on, I said I'd be back in two hours, I need to get home.'

Alice scuffed at the sand with her shoes.

'Are you washing?'

'*Ee.*'

'Clothes?'

'*Ee.*'

'Alice!' I said in exasperation. 'Okay, okay, finish what you've done and hang them up. Please, get a move on. I want to get back while Ruby's still asleep and I've got so much exam-marking to do.'

'I have finished.'

'Okay, good, then get in the car.'

Still Alice didn't move, she just turned her head to one side. I followed her gaze and saw Ron's mother emerging from a neighbour's compound.

At last Alice clambered into the back of the

car, but before she had even settled herself down, Eliah marched into the yard.

'Ao!' she said, seeing Alice in the car. 'What are you doing?'

'We've got to go,' I told Eliah. 'Alice knew I was coming back to pick her up.'

'But she hasn't eaten,' Eliah said, putting her hands on her hips.

'She can eat at home.'

'Ao! She hasn't eaten!'

'She can eat at home,' I repeated, putting the car into gear. But in the rear-view mirror I saw Eliah move round to the back of the car. 'Get out,' she told Alice.

Alice hesitated, about to stand up.

'We are going,' I objected. The car was moving now; this was dangerous.

'Get out!' Eliah ordered.

I turned and looked at Alice. She was glancing from me to Eliah, unsure which one to obey. Quickly she decided to obey Eliah and leapt out of the car.

Then Eliah came round to the passenger seat, walking slowly, deliberately. She bent down slightly and looked in through the open window. I turned and saw the smile on her face was triumphant. She had won; her expression said she had won. She had made my own child disobey me. She had never forgiven me for arguing with her when she had tried to confine me after Ruby was born. Now, nearly two years later, I could see she had been holding this close to her, waiting. The fact of the rape hadn't altered her view of me, if anything it appeared to have made things worse. In my mind, it was as if she blamed me for what had happened.

I sucked my teeth and drove off, shaking with fury. I didn't know what was happening any more, I didn't know if I had the right to be angry or if I were over-reacting to everything because of the rape. These days I seemed to get incensed so easily; only the day before a driver had overtaken me in Maun and I had wanted to kill him, to literally kill him, to take out a gun and to shoot him, to see his blood splattered on the tar road.

As I drove home I wondered what Ron would make of the exchange with Eliah, for his mother would get to him first, she would explain her side long before I had the chance to explain mine.

'How was the day?' I asked brightly when Ron returned with Alice.

'Fine,' he said over his shoulder, heading for the bathroom and shutting the door.

A few moments later he came back and went outside on to the porch.

'Alice,' I called, 'can you watch Ruby for a second?' I waited while Alice came slouching into the living-room and then, a little anxiously, I followed Ron out.

'I've got to go to Charles Hill,' he said.

'What? That's on the other side of the country. You mean, you'll have to stay there too?'

'*Ee.* It's a two-day job, at least.' Ron was worried about work. Already the impact of September 11 was being felt in Maun. American tourists were cancelling their bookings, and safari companies were thinking more in terms of laying off staff than buying new computers. Now Ron had decided that he had to take on jobs that were further afield.

'But what will I do?' I asked, pulling up a chair. 'I can't stay here, on my own.'

'You've got the dogs,' Ron said. 'And the alarm. And Alice.'

I snorted in disbelief. 'You think that makes me safe?'

'Editor can move in.'

'I don't want Editor moving in,' I said. 'When exactly are you going?'

'Soon,' Ron said.

I got up from the chair and began pacing around the porch. 'So what does your mum say?'

'About Charles Hill?'

'No, about today. We had a fight.'

Ron leant against one of the porch pillars, looking out across the river. It was October now and the evening air was hot with the arrival of summer. 'My mother thinks Alice should move out.'

'Move out?'

'*Ee*. And my grandmother. They say Alice is not happy here.'

Ron wasn't looking at me, I couldn't see his face. I couldn't tell whether he was agreeing with Eliah and Madintwa, or simply passing on the message.

'What do you mean, not happy?'

Ron shifted from one foot to another. 'She says you're always ordering her to do things.'

'What?' I laughed. 'Since when have I ordered Alice to do anything? Come on, Ron, you know what Alice is like, she hates doing anything anyway.'

Ron nodded that this was true. Then he sighed and turned round. 'You know what my mum is like. Alice tells them these things, and they believe her.'

'Like what?'

'Like she doesn't get enough food . . . '

'What? Ron, you know that's not true!'

'Like you just want her to clean your house . . . '

'Oh come on! You know what Alice is like, you know I don't order her around, do I?'

'No.'

'Except today,' I added. 'Today I told her to get in the car. Your mum told her to get back out . . . '

'Really?' Ron raised his eyebrows.

'Yeah. I was late, I had to get home. It's a long story, but your mum told Alice to get out of the car.'

Ron shrugged; he didn't want to pursue this.

'It was a battle, Ron,' I told him. 'Didn't she tell you about it? Your mum was challenging me. And Alice had to choose between me and your mum. If you were a child, who would you obey, me or your mum? Who looks scarier to you?'

'My mum.' Ron laughed. 'My mum's definitely scarier.'

We both laughed and then started in surprise, as Alice stepped on to the porch. I had thought she was in the house, but she must have been standing outside, listening to our conversation. She ignored us both, dragging her feet, walking slowly to the back door.

'I thought I asked you to watch Ruby for a second?' I asked, realizing that Alice must have left the house through the front door. Alice didn't reply, she just shut the door and went inside. At once I heard Ruby cry and I rushed in, finding her sitting alone on the tiled floor of the kitchen.

'What's wrong, babe?' I asked, bending down and scooping her up. Ruby howled. 'What is it?' I asked, checking her over. I saw her right arm was red and a little swollen. For the past few days she had had a septic boil near the wrist, it had started as a small bite and then become infected. I had taken her to see a doctor, who had prescribed antibiotics and recommended I cover the boil with a plaster at night. But the boil didn't seem to be getting better and now I thought I would take her back the next day.

That night Ruby slept fretfully, waking and crying, holding up her sore arm, tears streaming down her face. By morning we were both exhausted. I sat in the living-room; it was early and the sun was just rising outside, Ron had not yet left for work. I tried to soothe Ruby, offering her a bottle of milk, giving her a cuddle. When she had finally settled, I carefully pealed back the plaster to see how the boil looked.

'Fuck!' I recoiled in horror.

Where the boil had been there was now a fat white maggot, half the length of my finger. Its body was jutting out of Ruby's arm and it was quivering to and fro as if in protest at being uncovered.

'There's a maggot coming out of her arm!' I yelled. 'Ron!'

'Calm down, calm down,' Ron said, rushing in. 'Stop yelling, you're going to frighten her.'

I bit my lip, he was right. Ruby was looking fearfully at her arm now, her eyes hooked on the waving maggot. Quickly Ron took the maggot between his fingers and pulled it out. 'Oh my God,' I whispered. 'It's *huge*.'

Ron ground the maggot on the floor with his shoe and I looked again at Ruby's arm. Where the maggot had been there was now a deep, black hole with perfect smooth edges, it was like looking down the inside of an empty metal cylinder.

'What was that?' I asked.

'Putsi fly.'

'What the hell is putsi fly?' And then, with a flash of recognition, I remembered. I remembered my Botswana orientation over eleven years ago at Farnham Castle in Surrey. I remembered the talk on health, about the certain type of fly that lays eggs on people and clothes. The fly had laid an egg on Ruby, it had hatched and for the last few days a maggot had been literally eating her, munching away on the flesh of her arm.

★ ★ ★

A few weeks later Ruby and I left for the UK. I wanted to spend Christmas and New Year in England; I wanted to be with my family and friends again. Part of me just wanted to show everyone that I was all right. It had been ten months since the rape and during that time I had stopped anyone from England coming to visit, though my mother had insisted she was getting on the next plane.

As I arrived at Heathrow airport I felt I had a new identity. I was a rape survivor; this was what had happened to me since the last time I had been to England. This was what was new in my life. In Botswana people didn't want to talk about my rape, about any rape. My in-laws never mentioned it, never referred to it in any way. Many friends were the same, even Pearl. Rape was something that happened and you kept quiet about it and you got on with your life. But I hadn't kept quiet about it; I was always talking about it. And now I would have to start talking about it all over again.

And I knew what people in England would wonder and perhaps even say; they would ask me why I didn't come home. And some people would think privately that this was what happened to white women that went to Africa. It was the Dark Continent, where dreadful things happened, like attacks by wild animals, like AIDS and like rape. But then that was the Africa of the British media, it wasn't the real Africa at all.

I returned to Botswana three weeks later feeling ready for a new year. But as the days went by I grew more and more anxious until finally I realized what I was dreading, the first anniversary of the attack. During the weeks in England the rape had seemed unbelievable, it had happened somewhere so far away that I couldn't be sure it was real. Now that I was back in

Maun, reminders were everywhere. The weather was the same as it had been during the rape, hot and muggy, long summer days without rain. The grass on the pathway was the same as it had been a year ago, long and green, providing easy cover for anyone who wanted to hide. The sounds were the same; the squeak of the gate being opened, the hoot of the lehututu birds along the riverbank, the sting of the cicadas at night. Again I felt unsettled and unsafe.

I had come back to Botswana to find that Alice had failed her school leaving exams and was now at the farm. When I asked Madintwa when Alice was returning home she explained that Alice was weeding. At last I realized that Alice was never coming home, her home now was the farm. The fact that I needed her was neither here nor there.

★　★　★

On 23 February, the day the rape had happened a year before, I spent the day at work. But that night I woke in the dark and I could feel the rapist in the bedroom as surely as if he were there. I could smell him, I could hear him, I could see him. It didn't matter that Ron was next to me, or Ruby asleep in her cot, I was rigid with terror. I was being haunted.

But once the night had passed I felt as if a weight had been lifted and I no longer felt quite so afraid. I decided to clean Alice's room, opening the wardrobe to find a mess. I could see her late mother's handbag, a stiff dusty black bag with a rusty metal clasp. I touched it, wiping it of dust, saddened that this was the only object Alice had as a memory of her mother. A year after her death, her mother's possessions had been divided up among family, as was the custom, and this was what Alice had been given: a broken handbag. I put the bag on the bed as gently as possible. When I went back to the wardrobe a pile of photographs fluttered out. I picked them up, smiling, seeing immediately that these were old photos from Sowa that I thought had been lost. But then I saw what Alice had done to them: in each group photo she had cut out my head. And behind the photos, further in the wardrobe, I could see a pile of clothes that I now saw were mine: a orange patterned top that Ron had once given me for my birthday, a scarf I had worn during winter in England, a scrunched-up bra. She hates me, I thought, stuffing the photos and the clothes back into place. My own daughter hates me.

Two days later I heard that an Englishwoman I knew called Sarah had been attacked. She had been on her own at home, a few kilometres up the road from our house, when three men broke in. They beat her unconscious. She called the security company Coin Botswana while the men were breaking in, but by the time they got round to coming it was far too late. The attack had happened the exact day, a year ago, that I had been attacked. For the past year I had been trying to separate my fears from reality. Nothing bad had happened to me or anyone else I knew during the last twelve months. I was beginning to think that the rape had been one terrible, isolated incident. Botswana was still a peaceful country, Maun was still in some ways a village, it was far less dangerous than London. Now that Sarah had been attacked I was afraid again. I felt I had been right not to want to be alone at home; I had been right to feel unsafe.

Two weeks later another Englishwoman I knew, Kate, was gang-raped by three men while walking home along the main Maun road on a Sunday evening. The day I heard this I went out of my office, the hot air shimmering around me. In the garden MaStar and Editor were preparing to go home. I picked Ruby up, waved them goodbye, and then I rushed into the house. We had two Rottweilers now and I called them inside and locked all the doors. Ruby wanted to go outside and keep playing in the sand but I wouldn't let her. I was not thinking, I was not thinking things through rationally. Someone I knew had been raped and I was acting on fear. I had to make sure the doors were locked so that no one could get in. But the house still didn't seem safe, so I locked us both in the spare room. At each sound outside, I sat up, peering through the red blinds, checking and re-checking the bush.

In two weeks it was WAR's annual dinner and I had asked if they wanted a speaker. I knew how hard it was to get a woman to speak in public about being raped, so I had volunteered myself. Now here I was, crouched on the floor, locked in a room inside my house, convinced someone was coming to get me. I knew about post-traumatic stress, I knew that it existed; I knew that the effects of rape lasted a long time, but somehow I had thought that wouldn't happen to me. When people were raped in books, or on TV, when their rapes were reported in newspapers or magazines, there was never any after-effect. The drama was the rape; you rarely saw what happened next. Because what happened next was not dramatic, it was a day-to-day struggle. That's why people killed themselves, because that struggle just became too much. I tried to remember the joy I had felt when I had seen the rapist leave my house, the euphoria that I had not been killed, that I was alive. And I couldn't.

★  ★  ★

The evening of the WAR dinner the air was hot and oppressive. It was March, it should have been cool, but as Ron drove us to the venue all I could think of was how much I needed water. I was nervous as we walked in, almost as nervous as I had been just before the rape trial started. I thought perhaps it had been a bad idea, and wondered why I had suggested it at all. I walked through the dining area, in between the tables prettily set out with flowers and sparkling wine glasses. At the back was a small stage, dark but for a solitary microphone. Ron and I sat at a table to the right of the stage, Ruby sitting down between us. She knew that somehow this evening was special and she was subdued. I thought perhaps I shouldn't have brought her along. I had been selfish, wanting her near me this evening. I fiddled with a bread roll, watching the people on the table to the left of the stage. I could see Chibuya who had been in charge of MISA during my trial and was now the new WAR co-ordinator and a close friend. Next to Chibuya I could see the new Minister of Health, Joy Phumaphi.

I made my way to the stage and, as I stood in front of the microphone, I realized just how dark the stage actually was. I had written down what I wanted to say; now I thought I wouldn't be able to read it. But at once a spotlight was turned on and now I was blinded. I took the paper out of my pocket and then stopped. A man was setting up equipment in front of me, arranging a large camera, the sort I had only seen on television. And then I realized that Botswana's new national TV station was going to cover the speeches. I swallowed hard, my mouth dry. I peered towards the audience, searching for Ron. He was sitting just in front of me, Ruby snoozing on his lap. He smiled and I opened my mouth and began.

# 32

Ruby and I stood on the second floor of Maun airport. She was two and a half years old and just tall enough to be able to see out of the window. Outside we could see the usual row of small planes waiting to take tourists into the Okavango Delta. Most tourists still didn't spend any time in Maun; they flew in via South Africa and then were whisked by a safari company straight north and into the lushness of the swamps.

'Hey, Yarubi!' one of the airport cleaners, a relative, called out as she passed by with a big mop. Ruby went by several names now; I always called her Ruby but many relatives called her by her Seyei name Yarubi. Ron called her Phuthumphi; others called her MaMarama, a reference to her podgy cheeks. And people called me by different names now, whether MaRuby or MaYarubi and, to my surprise, I liked it, I liked being identified as the mother of Ruby.

Ruby had her tummy leaning against the coolness of the airport glass, her skin taut after eating a huge watermelon half an hour earlier. *Magapu* was one of the first words she'd said in Setswana and every time she saw people on the roadsides selling the giant redfleshed fruit she would clap her hands and yell, '*Mpha magapu!*' — Give me watermelon! I wondered what it would be like when Ruby became fluent in

534

Setswana and if there would come a time when I wouldn't understand what my own daughter was saying.

The airport was one of Ruby's favourite places. When I wanted to make her especially happy I either took her swimming to the pool I had swum in every day when I was pregnant, or to watch the planes at the airport. Today we were waiting for a big plane, as my brother Jake was arriving from England. This was the first time he'd been to Botswana since I'd arrived twelve years ago. He was coming with his partner, Rosa, and their daughter, Amelia, who was six months older than Ruby.

Ruby had met them twice at family Christmases in England. She was so excited now I thought she would pee herself.

'Where's Aunty Jake?' she asked. 'Where's Aunty Jake?'

'There!' I pointed, yelling over the sound of the Johannesburg plane landing on the tarmac outside. 'Look, see that plane? Jake's on that one. And it's uncle, okay? *Uncle* Jake.'

When we got downstairs Ron was there, holding open one of the doors into the Customs area. In the distance I could see my brother lining up to show his passport.

'Aunty Jake!' Ruby yelled and he turned, a little confused, and waved.

Then an airport official told us to close the door, that we weren't allowed in there. Since the new airport terminal had been built the staff weren't as friendly as they used to be. In the past, when visitors like the Duke of Edinburgh had jetted in, we had been able to stand on the airport apron to greet them. Now suddenly the staff were getting security conscious. Maun, it was rumoured, was a stop-off point for diamond smuggling and a place where planes involved in the illegal trade refuelled.

A few minutes later Jake popped his head around the Arrivals door. Every time I saw him these days I was surprised that he was my brother. He looked too much like an adult. He wore a green T-shirt and knee-length green trousers as if he was about to go on safari.

'What's the address?' he asked worriedly. 'They want the address where we're staying. I gave them yours and they said that's not an address.'

I laughed. There were still no addresses in Maun. There might be street names within the centre of the town, but there were none outside and post was still delivered to and collected from the central post office. It was impossible to give an address for a house in Maun. The customs people knew this; they must have decided to give my brother a hard time.

At last Jake, Rosa and Amelia emerged into the Arrivals area and we all hugged. Jake was wearing fancy-looking shades and he produced a pair for Ron as well. Together they picked up the luggage and headed to Ron's Land Rover. They looked like secret service agents.

I took Rosa, Amelia and Ruby in my new Toyota and we set off for home.

'Isn't it beautiful, all this sand?' asked Rosa, looking out of the window. 'What trees are those?

They're gorgeous. Look, Amelia, look at all the donkeys.'

I smiled as I drove. It had been a very long time since I had seen Maun through new eyes; everything was so familiar I no longer noticed it any more.

'What's that?' Rosa asked.

'An ant hill,' I said, looking at the sculpture of sand on the roadside, remembering how strange the hills had once seemed to me.

'Mum,' Amelia asked in a voice thick with anticipation, 'are we in Africa yet?'

★ ★ ★

For the first few days I took my brother and his family on the usual tourist treats. We swam at the safari lodges dotted along the Thamalakane River, made a visit to the local crocodile farm, and indulged in a helicopter trip over the Okavango Delta. Maun had now acquired official town status, with Internet cafés, a cinema, three shopping malls, plenty of bars and a handful of restaurants selling European food. And Botswana itself was now reasonably well known in England, with a Miss World and an Olympic running star. But it was also now known for having the highest HIV rate in the world. The Botswana government had recently announced that the country faced extinction if the epidemic could not be controlled. When I had arrived life expectancy for a woman was in the sixties, now it was just forty-seven.

A few days into Jake's holiday, I took him to

537

pay his respects to my in-laws. We had briefly been to Moeti where he had met Madintwa. She had given a lengthy welcome speech, ecstatic to finally meet my brother. The fact that he was Ruby's uncle gave him a special status, a unique role in traditional family life. In Setswana culture a woman's brother is expected to speak for her, and takes a leading role in any marriage preparations. If his sister has a problem, for example with her in-laws, then her brother is sent to discuss the matter. As my brother, and therefore Ruby's maternal uncle, Jake's relationship and authority over Ruby was also crucial.

We set off early in the morning in Ron's Land Rover. I hadn't been to the farm for almost a year and my new Toyota couldn't make it through the bush. The farm didn't hold good memories for me; when I pictured it I pictured the afternoon Ron had told the family I had been raped.

In the front of the car, Ron was smiling. He wanted to show Jake around. As I watched Ron steering the Land Rover confidently through the bush I realized that these days he rarely smiled. The demands of work and family, and the trauma of the rape and the court case, had toughened him. We drove past Maun airport and then took a right along the perimeter fence on to a route lined with dense mophane trees. Ron smiled at me in the rear-view mirror and I smiled back. The day after I had given the speech at the WAR dinner marked the first time I had spent a day alone at home since the rape a year before. Now I felt, finally, that I was recovering, that I was getting my old life back. I saw my brother's visit as a chance for a holiday, a chance to relax.

As we drove round the edge of the farm, and then parked in the shade of a tree, I was amazed at all the changes that had been made. We had entered the farm on a different route from the one I was used to and for a second I felt disorientated. I could see a new, neat, reed house on the left and further back a reed structure for the chickens and a blue water-container on stilts. In the distance there was a new goat kraal and as I looked around about twenty goats came tumbling out, rushing off into the bush. The cleared area on my right was much larger than it had been before. I could see washing hanging out on tree branches to dry, a large fireplace on the sand, a wheelbarrow piled high with farming tools.

But the farm didn't seem as busy as it usually did and there was a subdued air about the place. I could see Alice and her three sisters Gabs, Ene and Gosegomang, whom Ruby now called Gogo. They were sitting in a row against the wall of the house, their backs against the reeds. Alice was having her hair done; half was braided and the other half stood in an upright clump on her head. She looked thin and in need of a wash. Her face appeared older somehow, and as I looked at her I could hardly believe that she had ever been my child. I pictured her as the knobbly-kneed little girl I had first met at Last Chance bar, how shy and vulnerable she had seemed. And I remembered her as a schoolgirl in

Sowa, how she couldn't bring herself to reply to anything anyone said. And then how she had matured, how she had become fatter, healthier, more settled. I thought about how she had liked to wear her favourite wool hat when she did the washing-up at home in Matlapaneng, and how when she was happy she would laugh like a horse neighing. Now she was a scowling sixteen-year-old who didn't want to live with Ron and me any more, who was watching me walk past her as if we had never known each other at all. I wondered if she still thought I had stolen her from her mother, if she had always thought this and if her mother's death had somehow just confirmed it. I had not forgotten the hidden clothes I had found in her room, nor the way she had cut my face from the Sowa photographs. I could not believe how badly I had failed as her mother.

The girls looked up as Jake got out of the Land Rover, followed by Rosa and Amelia. But, as befitted Batswana children, they remained sitting in silence against the reeds.

Ron had parked just where his mother, Madintwa, and his great-aunt MaB sat. They were arranged in a row on an old blanket on the sand. In front of them was an empty wooden chair, the sort men took with them to the Kgotla. It was a low chair with a seat made from slatted rope and it was easy to fold up and carry from one place to another. Women were not supposed to sit on such chairs, and in twelve years I had never seen a woman do so.

'Which one's Ron's mum?' Rosa asked as we

540

walked forward. She had changed out of her shorts for this visit and was wearing a pretty yellow summer dress.

'In the middle,' I told her. Rosa's eagerness to behave appropriately reminded me of how I had been when I had first arrived in Botswana. I had wanted to know how to dress in order not to offend anyone, how to hold my hand out when meeting someone, how to give and respond to greetings.

Rosa took Amelia's hand and I turned to take Ruby's, but Ruby had already run off to play. A moment later I could see her heading for the goat kraal. One of the baby goats was hers and she loved to carry it in her arms and feed it.

'*Dumelang Bomma*,' I said as we got to the three women sitting on the blanket.

'*Ee*,' Madintwa replied.

Eliah sat staring ahead impassively. I wondered what was wrong, or whether everyone was just looking serious because this was an important visit, because they were meeting Ruby's uncle from England for the first time.

Jake shook Madintwa's hand while I introduced him to Eliah and MaB. Then Rosa and I sat down next to the women, with Amelia sitting on Rosa's lap, her sun hat pulled down over her face. Ron sat a little to his mother's left, on a white plastic chair. Ruby was off in the distance carrying her goat while Gogo watched her. Alice and her other sisters still sat motionless by the reed house. I wondered what they were waiting for. It was mid-morning; normally they would be busy by now.

Jake finished his greetings and sat down on the sand.

Immediately Eliah objected.

'*Nnyaa*,' she said, pointing to the Kgotla chair.

'It's fine, I'll sit here,' said Jake amiably.

'*Nnyaa*,' said Madintwa, instructing Ron to tell Jake to sit on the Kgotla chair.

'They want you to sit on that,' I said. 'It's the one reserved for men.'

Jake looked embarrassed, but as everyone was looking at him he sat down.

Madintwa clasped her hands together and cleared her throat. Then she leaned forward a little on the blanket, looking at Jake, her chin trembling slightly as she tried to keep her head upright.

'*Malomaagwe Yarubi*,' she said, beginning with my brother's proper title as Ruby's uncle.

Jake smiled. 'It's lovely here,' he said politely. 'What do you grow in that field?' he asked pointing to the distance.

Madintwa pressed herself forward a little more.

'She's making a speech,' I explained to Jake. 'It could go on for a while.'

So Jake sat back and listened while Madintwa spoke and then Ron translated.

'*Re ne la mathata*,' said Madintwa carefully.

What did she mean? I thought, with a stab of shock. What problem? She was saying we had a problem, but what was it?

'We have a problem,' Madintwa said again in Setswana, 'with your sister Caitlin.'

'Hold on,' I said, getting to my feet. 'What's

542

going on?' I asked Ron. He shook his head.

'She is not respectful any more,' continued Madintwa, her eyes on Jake.

'Stop it,' I said to Ron who had his mouth open, about to translate.

'Ao!' objected Eliah to my outburst, adding in Setswana that if I wanted to speak there would be a time when I could. I looked at her and saw this was her doing. It was Madintwa who was speaking but I sensed that it was Eliah's idea, that she had arranged this reception, that she had planned it for a long time.

'It's okay, Cait,' my brother said, unaware of why I was complaining. 'Let them speak.'

'No!' I said, because I could see that my in-laws were about to air a decade's worth of grievances. Jake didn't realize what was about to come but I did. They were reporting me to my brother. They had not prepared me for this; Madintwa had given no hint that a meeting had been called or what it would be about. I felt as if I had been ambushed. 'If they've got a problem with me then they should discuss it with me! I brought you here to say hello to them,' I said desperately to Jake. 'This isn't a Kgotla meeting you know.' I turned to Ron. 'Did you know about this?'

'No,' Ron said, hanging his head.

'Don't translate,' I pleaded.

Ron looked pained. His grandmother was asking him to put her words into English, I was telling him not to. I continued to stand on the sand, facing the women now, my head burning under the sun. I was being humiliated. I had brought my brother here as a matter of courtesy and walked straight into a trap. Although I had had problems with my in-laws, I had not always told my own family how bad these had become. They knew very little about my fights with Eliah, or of any conflict with Madintwa, or the fact that the family had refused to allow Alice to remain living with me. Now I wasn't going to be the one to tell them, it was all going to come out right here and right now, the way they wanted it to.

'I'm not doing this,' I said and I walked off into the bush. I walked past the reed house where Alice and her sisters still sat. How dare they, I thought, how dare the women do this in front of children? If there was one thing Setswana culture did not allow it was to scold an adult in front of children, especially their own children. I was so furious I walked around and around. But every few moments I was drawn back to the meeting, wanting and not wanting to hear what was going on. I wanted to order Jake and Rosa and Ron to stand up and leave but I was the only one pacing, everyone else was sitting down, waiting.

My brother was sitting very upright on the Kgotla chair. I could suddenly picture him in court, for Jake was a barrister and verbal sparring was something he was used to. I could see he was appalled at the idea that my in-laws were reporting me to him but that he wanted to see what would happen next.

'I think what the problem is . . . ' he began.

Eliah cut him off.

Jake looked at Ron. 'She says in Setswana

tradition a person is allowed to speak until they have finished,' Ron explained.

'Fine,' said my brother grimly.

As I walked around the perimeter of the meeting I could hear snippets of the conversation. Madintwa had finished and now I could hear Eliah's voice.

'Caitlin has forbidden Ruby to stay the night with us,' Ron's mother complained. 'She allows Ruby to stay with her sister Flora, but not with us.'

I stopped in my tracks. How did Eliah know that on my last visit to England Ruby had stayed the night with Flora? I must have mentioned it to Ron in passing, but I had no idea it was an issue with Eliah. And she had never asked that Ruby stay with her, so it was impossible that I had forbidden it. What? I wanted to shout. When did you ever ask Ruby to stay the night?

I marched on, getting sweaty, my ankles grazing against the thornbushes.

'Ruby says we are dirty,' continued Eliah. 'Her mother is teaching her to say these things about us.'

I stopped again, outraged. I had never spoken a bad word about any of my in-laws in front of Ruby. It was up to Ruby what she thought; I wasn't going to instil hatred in a child. And one of Ruby's favourite words was 'dirty'; she could easily have called someone dirty, she was two and a half years old. If someone had a spot of soot on their face she would point to them and say 'dirty'. How could Eliah take this as an insult from a child?

'If Caitlin wants to leave and return to England,' said Eliah, 'then she should go right ahead.'

Was that it? I wondered as I stood and listened. Was this what the meeting was all about, Eliah wanted to try to make me leave? I walked away and came back again. Now Jake was talking. 'It seems to me,' he said, 'that you are the ones who don't show respect. You are not respecting my sister. You're not even talking to her, you're talking to me!'

Madintwa looked utterly confused by this objection.

'The fact that she's stayed here shows respect, doesn't it? I think . . . '

But Eliah was interrupting now.

'Excuse me,' said Jake very nicely, 'but I thought that according to *your* culture, a person is allowed to speak until they have finished?'

Eliah pursed her lips and looked daggers at me.

'As I was saying,' Jake continued, 'the fact that my sister stayed here, after what has happened to her, shows respect, doesn't it?'

I walked closer to the group now. I just wanted the whole thing to stop. 'Let's go,' I said, but everyone was far too focused on what was being said. I went off to find Ruby and give her a hug. 'She's tired, and she's hungry, let's go,' I said, walking back with her.

But it was MaB's turn to talk now and she was trying to be placating. 'Because we cannot understand each others' languages,' she said, 'things might be being said and misunderstood. It is difficult. We should . . . '

But Eliah cut in. 'Caitlin is disrespectful . . . '

Now I couldn't hold back any more. She was asking for this, she was pushing me too far. I was being reported to my brother and I was expected to hang my head and accept the telling-off but I wouldn't. I walked towards her and then stopped. Eliah looked up and her face was stiff, she was looking at me and her eyes were cold. Without thinking I thrust my hand out, my fingers pointing down on her.

'You,' I said rudely, 'do you know everything I've done for you? Do you know how many compromises I've made for you and your family? We built you a *house*! Ron wanted to buy a car but *I* said no, we should build your mother a house first. So we did. I always put you first. When you were ill with malaria, it was me who told Ron to go and visit you in hospital. He didn't want to, I said he *had* to! And when he complained about you, it was me who said he shouldn't be disrespectful, I was the one who always told him to go and apologize. And I took you . . . ' I turned to Madintwa, 'to the doctor's every time you asked. I bought you every item of clothing you ever asked for. I even said you could move in with us, it was *Ron* who said no! I adopted your grandson's child for Christ's sake, not just Alice but Gabs as well.'

I drew in my breath. I had to speak rapidly or I would lose the momentum and be interrupted. I was aware that I was completely disrupting the proceedings but I had no desire to follow the conventions any more. I wasn't going to be put on trial by my family.

'When I was raped,' I spat, 'not a single one of you showed me any love, any support, any kindness. You did not visit. You did nothing for me. So don't talk to me about respect! You don't know the meaning of the word.'

I paused for a second and I could see Eliah shifting on the blanket, she was getting ready to respond. But I didn't want to hear her response. 'I'm going,' I said, 'I'm getting in the car with Ruby and I'm going.'

Jake got up as well and Ron followed.

'My cheeks are bleeding,' Ron said as he walked behind me to the car.

'What?'

'I've been chewing them the whole time. They're bleeding inside.'

I didn't reply.

'Did you know about this?' I asked again as I got into the car.

Ron caught my eye in the rear-view mirror. 'No.'

'Well, we fucking need to talk about this. And I can tell you Ruby will not be seeing them again. I've had it; I've totally had it. There is no way *in hell* she will ever, *ever* stay with them!'

'Let's not talk about it now,' Ron pleaded.

'Why?'

'Because things will be said in haste. Let's not say things we'll regret.'

I didn't reply.

'Where to?' Ron asked. 'Where do you want to go?' he asked again, both hands on the steering wheel.

'England,' I said, 'I want to go to England.'

# 33

I had discovered yoga. I stood in the middle of the living-room with my friend and teacher Jane, listening with pleasure at the sharp click in my leg as I stretched my hand down to my toes. It was mid-morning and Ruby was napping. There was no one around except for Dora, a new gardener I had hired. The day was silent and hot, even the donkeys appeared to be sleeping. I tried to focus on the next yoga position but, from the corner of my eye, I could see Dora leaning heavily on a rake, watching with an expression of bafflement the antics of the two white women inside the house.

As the session ended we lay down on the cool tiled floor. Jane told me to empty my mind, but it was full of thoughts of my in-laws, of what had happened at the farm, of what I was going to do now. Since Jake and his family had left I had not seen Eliah or Madintwa at all. But I had bumped into Ron's great-aunt MaB. I was shopping at Maun Fresh Produce and, while fighting my way through the crowds that came to shop at the month's end, I saw MaB sitting on the shop floor near one of the checkouts. I thought she hadn't seen me and I was about to walk down an aisle and ignore her when suddenly she began to wave.

'*Dumela Mma*,' I said, speaking the greeting quickly, ready to move on.

MaB beamed. Unlike Madintwa and Eliah, Ron's great-aunt had been placating during the meeting at the farm; she had seemed the only one to express some sadness at the confrontation. Now she took my hand, pulling me down towards her the way Madintwa always used to do. '*Jake o kae?*' she asked.

I told her my brother had left weeks ago.

She nodded, saying she had been happy to see him. Still she was smiling at me, hanging on to my hand.

'*O ya ko Moeti?*' she asked.

I told her, no, I wasn't going to Moeti. I shifted the shopping basket from one hand to another. Had she not noticed that I didn't go there any more?

'*Ga go na nama,*' MaB said pleasantly, letting go of my hand.

I stared at her. There was no meat. Did that mean she wanted me to buy her meat? I mumbled that I had no money, but I was lying.

MaB didn't seem to notice how upset I was, how coldly I was behaving towards her. And I wondered, as I did every day, just what Madintwa and Eliah had thought they had been doing at the farm. What had they wanted to achieve? Had they wanted me to be humiliated, to see me punished for what they perceived as a lack of respect towards them? Did they really think reporting me to my brother had been the right way to air their grievances? I could not get Ron to admit it had been wrong; as far as he was concerned the matter was over. It had been regrettable, but it was over. So I knew that whatever happened to me in the future, I could not expect any support from my in-laws. And at last I faced the dreadful realization that whatever Ron's doubts about his mother and the rest of the family, ultimately they would always, for him, come first.

I finished my yoga session and stood up. My head was spinning and there were flecks in front of my eyes. Outside I could see Dora begin to pull half-heartedly at a weed. As I walked Jane to the gate, Veronica pulled up in a car. She drove in quickly, parking haphazardly on the sand. In the back seat I could see her youngest son, Robin, fast asleep.

'Yes *mosadi*!' Veronica said cheerfully as she got out of the car. 'What are you wearing?' she asked, pulling on the cycling shorts I had been wearing for yoga. 'These look like old woman's pantaloons!'

'I suppose you're coming in to bother me?' I asked.

Veronica laughed and slapped me on the arm. 'Hey, I am hungry, what have you got to eat?'

I followed her into the house where she laid Robin on the sofa. He was a toddler now but of such a slight build that he looked younger. His eyes, so large when open, were shut tight and his face was smooth with sleep. The whiteness of a string of beads around his neck glowed against the darkness of his skin. His T-shirt with its logo of two laughing frogs had ridden up across his tummy, and on his feet the laces of his little trainers had both come undone. I bent and kissed him gently, not wanting to wake him.

Veronica busied herself in the kitchen making a sandwich, then she plonked a plate on the table and sighed.

'What is it?'

'Hey, this Ridge family . . . '

'They're giving you a hard time?' I smiled in sympathy. Two months earlier Veronica had been subjected to a family meeting after a vicious argument with Roy's sister Rita. The meeting had lasted from midday until it was dark and I couldn't see that much had been resolved. When I had left, just before dusk, everyone was as angry as they always were. 'Well, listen to this,' I said, 'you remember when my brother was here last month?'

'*Ee*,' Veronica laughed. 'Hey, I *like* your brother . . . '

'Well, I took him to the farm to say hello to Ron's mum and grandmother, and when we got there they hijacked me with this meeting. They told Jake I wasn't *respectful* . . . '

Veronica raised her eyebrows, the sandwich halfway to her mouth.

'They said all sorts of rubbish about Ruby. And they said that if I wanted to go back to England then I should just go ahead!'

'*Ao!*'

'So maybe I will,' I said. Then I sat back on the sofa, realizing that this was exactly what I intended to do. 'Maybe I will just go back,' I repeated, less sure of myself now. 'There's not much for me here any more. I don't see Ron. I don't even talk with Ron . . . I'm afraid all the time — '

'I've told him,' Veronica interrupted, 'I've told him so many times that he must spend more time at home. Every time I come here, he's not here!'

I leant forward on the sofa. 'They shouldn't have done that, should they, Veronica? I mean, call a meeting like that, not tell me anything and then just insult me. Tell me that's not the Setswana way. Because they seem to think they haven't done anything wrong at all. But they shouldn't have done that, should they? And they did it in front of the children. That's not right, is it?'

'No,' Veronica agreed. 'It is not right.'

We sat in silence for a while. I watched a man outside walking near the fence. Veronica finished her food. Then Robin woke and he sat up, rubbing his eyes. Veronica went to soothe him and he reached for her breast. 'Get me the Tabasco!' she cried.

'What?'

'Tabasco,' and she patted her breast.

'You're going to put Tabasco on your nipple?'

'*Ee*. He needs to stop breast-feeding, this one!' But Veronica said it with affection and when Robin began searching around her breast she happily began to feed him, cradling him in her arm as he curled his toes in pleasure.

'Mama!' I heard Ruby cry out from the bedroom and now it was my turn to get up.

Veronica and I sat outside on the porch, watching while Robin and Ruby sat on the sand, each absorbed in what they were doing, playing parallel games but every now and again turning to grab something from the other. As Ruby lunged for a plastic yellow spade, Robin turned towards me, his long face serious, his expression reproachful.

'Ruby,' I said, 'Robin was playing with that . . .'

Ruby's grasp on the spade tightened, then suddenly she changed her mind and handed it over to Robin. As he took it, Ruby followed up the gesture with a hug and, giggling, they began to grapple together. I watched them and thought how I wanted Ruby to grow up with this cousin, to spend her childhood with as many family members as possible. I didn't want her to grow up in a place of concrete rather than sand; I didn't want her to lose her family, her country, her father. But if I left for England then that was exactly what was going to happen.

*  *  *

I just couldn't decide what to do. I had been to England several times in the past few years, once for several months. Now I thought perhaps those trips had been a way of preparing myself for leaving altogether.

'I will pray for you,' Pearl said, arranging herself on a chair outside near the fallen tree trunk.

It was a Sunday morning and she was late for church. I had just told her I was going, that this time I wasn't coming back.

'No thanks,' I said.

But Pearl just smiled. '*Ee*, I will pray for you.'

I looked around the garden, it was a mess. Dora had been spotted at a shebeen drinking home brew; apparently this was what she did when I wasn't at home.

'Remember when we used to come here?' I asked, 'Before the house was built?'

'*Ee*,' Pearl said, beaming. 'We used to drive here and sit right there.' She pointed at the two palm trees to our right. 'And we used to drink Hunter's Gold and talk nonsense! Hey!' Pearl laughed and slapped one arm along the other, an old gesture I hadn't seen her do for a long time.

'You know what?' I said. 'A snake fell out of that palm tree the other day.'

'*Ijo!*'

'Yeah, Editor was sitting under it reading a newspaper while Ruby was asleep. Then this snake just plopped out of the tree and landed right by her foot and sped off.'

Pearl made the sign of the cross.

I stared across at the palm tree, thinking of Editor. Two weeks ago she had disappeared and someone had told me she'd been seen being bundled into an immigration vehicle. Then she had been put in prison in Francistown along with scores of other Zimbabweans. It was a crackdown on illegal immigrants, the papers said. And there had been reports of abuse, of the Botswana police beating people up. And then, although Editor had been jailed and deported across the eastern border, she had come straight back. That was how bad it was in Zimbabwe. She asked for some money and I gave it to her and, apart from the day the snake fell from the tree, I had not seen her again.

Pearl began slicing open a large soft pawpaw. She kicked at one of the Rottweilers as he came snuffling too close and the dog ambled away looking hurt.

'How's Bashi?' I asked.

Pearl shook her head. 'He is in bed.'

'He's in bed, the whole time?'

'*Ee*. He just sleeps. He has no energy. And he can't eat anything, he says it has no taste.'

'Has he been for a test?' I asked, speaking quickly, slipping the question in.

'*Ee*. He has been for a test. And he has HIV.'

I held my breath, not knowing what to say. 'And you?'

Pearl looked at me, her eyes clouded. 'If you can see him, how he is, the way he lies in bed. I don't need to test. Look at him, now tell me I don't have that too!'

'But now he's tested, he can get anti-retrovirals.' I tried to sound positive. 'The hospital has them; they're just about to start a pilot programme, giving them out for free. What you have to do is . . . '

But Pearl wasn't listening; she was gazing off across the river. I stopped speaking, I was telling her what to do when I hated other people telling me what to do. But I was leaving now; I didn't want to leave with anything unsaid between us. I shifted my chair back on the sand, the sun was moving, I had to follow the shade. I could remember the day I had met Bashi as clearly as anything, when we had met on the sand pathway as Ron and I went to visit Eliah for the first time.

That sand pathway was a tar road now; the traditional houses on either side had all gone and so had the trees. Last week I had heard that someone in that area was selling cocaine.

★ ★ ★

'I'm leaving,' I told Ron that evening. I was standing in the kitchen, stirring a pan of pasta on the stove. Ron was standing at the front door, cleaning an engine part with his old Clark T-shirt that was now a rag. 'I'm leaving. Me and Ruby are leaving. Ron, did you hear me?'

'What do you want me to say?' Ron stood with the rag in one hand.

'It's not what I want you to say. I'm just saying we're leaving. I can't think of any other way. Do you have any ideas?'

Ron looked out through the door, his eyes on the sunset outside.

'I mean, you and me we don't get on. You're never here; I don't see that's ever going to change. And when you are here, we either don't talk or we argue. Your family has betrayed me and you won't see that . . . '

Ron stiffened. 'Do we have to go over that?'

'No, we don't any more, because I'm going. I'm being driven to do this, do you see? Ron?'

But he didn't reply, he just sat down on the step outside.

'So I'm going to get a divorce.' I waited, my heart pounding a little. 'That makes it definite, doesn't it? And I want custody of Ruby.' Now my heart was really thumping. Ron could fight me on this, if his family heard I wanted custody then they would tell him to fight me. I knew that to leave Botswana legally with Ruby I needed a letter from her father giving his permission. If Ron didn't write the letter, then I could be stopped at the airport. And Ruby was a Motswana, she had been born here, and she had been born when I was a Motswana. If I was going back to England then I needed to reclaim my British citizenship, but whether Ruby would then get British citizenship as well wasn't certain. Eliah and Madintwa loved Ruby, I didn't know if they would let her go. They wanted me to go, but they wanted to keep her, I was sure.

'Ron?' I asked. I didn't want to beg, I just wanted him to agree. 'What do you say?'

'I think that yoga's really good for you.'

'What?'

Ron nodded. 'It makes you much calmer.'

I laughed in disbelief. 'So you agree?'

'Whatever you want.' Ron stood up, stretching out his legs. 'I've got to go to Charles Hill.'

'What, now?'

'Soon.'

'But, Ron, I've just told you we're leaving. Then you can go to Charles Hill or anywhere else as much as you want. Can't it wait a month or so, until I've gone?'

'No.'

'But what will I do?' I asked, fearful now, overcome with panic at the idea of being alone in the house. 'Please, can't it just wait?'

'It's work, Cait,' Ron said, shrugging. 'I have

to do it. I've been trying to go there for ages. I have to go.'

'Fine,' I said, ramming some mayonnaise into the bowl of pasta. I went to the pantry to get some tomatoes and I stopped in my tracks. If I was leaving, then what about the house? We had planned it and saved for it and built it. Ron had drawn up the diagrams; we had spent many evenings discussing the rooms, the porch, the roof. And Ron had built the foundation of the house himself, mixing the cement, watering the surface carefully every day to prevent it from cracking. And the day we had finally moved in there had been the thunderstorm. That was supposed to have been a good sign. And Ruby had been conceived in this house, she had spent her first night here after she was born, when we had been a family. And what of the garden, the hours I had spent watering and weeding. I had planted a jacaranda tree in the corner of the plot near the gate when Ruby had been born. Now I would never see it become a real tree, I wouldn't see its first shower of blossom falling like a vivid purple snowstorm on the sand.

★　★　★

A week later we sat in a lawyer's office on the second floor of one of Maun's four shopping malls. Ron's face was stony, his body language aggressive. It had been so easy getting married, now the lawyer was telling us how hard it would be to get divorced. We had to apply to the High Court, we had to appear in person, we had to

559

hire a lawyer, we had to give specific reasons for the divorce, we had to decide on maintenance.

'But I'm leaving in two weeks,' I said. 'Will the paperwork be done by then?'

The lawyer smiled and held his hands out; he couldn't give any assurances.

★　★　★

I woke to my last morning in Maun expecting sun. Ron was taking Ruby to the farm for the day and then we would meet at Moeti before my flight. I had not told my in-laws that I was leaving, nor about the divorce or the custody agreement. Ron said he would do it, but I knew he had not told them either.

I had the whole day to myself, to say goodbye to a place that had been my home for twelve years. But it wasn't sunny at all, it was dull and overcast. I had wanted to swim at the pool I had swum at when I was pregnant with Ruby, but now it felt too cold. It was December, the height of summer, I had never known a day in December to be like this. I hoped it would brighten up later as I walked around Maun, getting my divorce summons, trying to close my bank account, paying for three boxes of possessions to be sent to England. I would not take or send much on, I couldn't afford it. Instead I packed up everything belonging to Ruby and me and put it in my office. I laid piles of letters in cardboard boxes, took one photo from each of the photo albums, one pair of shoes Ruby had when she was a baby. The rest I would leave, it wasn't as if Ron were leaving too, he would keep an eye on them and one day I could get them sent on or return to fetch them myself.

★  ★  ★

I got to Sedie Hotel just as the rain started. It was a grey, drizzling sort of rain, the type that people called female rain. Male rain meant thunder and lightning, it made a lot of noise, but female rain actually fed the crops. The poolside was empty, a handful of tourists were sheltering under the shade-cloth by the bar. I slipped quickly into the pool and the water felt warm but I knew I would be shivering once I got out. As I lay in the rain with a damp towel around me Veronica arrived with Robin.

'I thought we said goodbye?' I asked.

'*Ee*. But I'm coming with you. I'm the first one to get in your suitcase.'

I laughed.

'You have to get me a job, in England,' Veronica said, sounding insistent. 'There are plenty of jobs there, aren't there?'

'I don't think so. I don't know. I haven't lived there for a very long time.'

'Get me a job,' said Veronica. 'Or I'll send this little one over to stay with you.'

I looked down at Robin; he was twirling his body round and round the bottom of an umbrella-stand laughing.

I went home, acutely aware that I was doing everything for the last time. Driving home along the pathway through the bush for the last time, opening the gate for the last time, walking into my home for the last time. I sat on the bed in the bedroom and went through my bags. I had my ticket, some money, my passport. But where was Ruby's passport? I went through my bag again. Her passport wasn't there. I emptied the bag on to the bed, searching through my belongings, my heart juddering. They had done it; Eliah had taken Ruby's passport. Now I wouldn't be able to leave. In tears I got up from the bed and tripped over the woven carpet on the floor. Ruby's passport was there; it had fallen when I emptied the bag.

I drove quickly to Moeti, wanting to get things over with, to get to the airport as fast as possible, to get on the plane. I didn't want to speak to Madintwa or to anyone else. But Madintwa and MaB and her boyfriend RaNjara were waiting for me. The women were sitting on the sand, the man on a lone Kgotla chair. Madintwa gave a nod to the elderly RaNjara and he stood up and cleared his throat. He called on the ancestors to assist my journey, he bid Ruby and I a safe trip. Then Madintwa took a mouthful of tepid water and she sprayed our faces. I didn't blink; in my mind I had already left Botswana, I was already on my way to England.

# PART SEVEN

# 34

When I arrived at Heathrow airport in December 2002 I came as a British citizen, my brand-new passport in my over-anxious hand. But Ruby arrived as a foreigner, as a Motswana, and the stamp in her passport said she had three months to stay in the UK. As we came through the Arrivals hall I could see my parents and sister waiting, but they hadn't recognized me. I hadn't told them I had shaved my head, that my hair was less than a centimetre long. Now I wondered why I had; it was winter, I was in a cold country.

As we drove through the dark empty streets of London, it was hard to tell what time it was. There was no sun, so I thought it must be pre-dawn, but I could see on the car clock that it was already eight o'clock. I had to get adjusted as soon as possible, I wasn't on holiday this time, I was back for good.

★   ★   ★

I spent the first few months at my parents' house, sleeping in the bedroom that hadn't been mine since I'd left home at the age of eighteen. Now I was a thirty-eight-year-old single parent. In Botswana there was no such term as single parent, although half of all households in the north were run solely by women. But in England I read all about single parents. I read that we were the latest trend in parenting and that we were responsible for many of society's ills. Our children were doomed to be maladjusted, with virtually every persistent juvenile offender coming from a 'broken' home. Family breakdown, I read in one broadsheet newspaper, was akin to child abuse.

I felt constantly irritable and I battled to do things everyone else seemed to find straightforward. In the mornings I pushed Ruby to the park in her buggy and I looked carefully at everything around me. I couldn't believe that people didn't have burglar bars on their windows, that their houses were so easy to break into. There were no signs for security companies, very few alarms, no barbed wire outside business premises. Did this mean people didn't fear being burgled, that they felt safe? But this was a city, how could people be safe? Then I read about how the body parts of two women had been found in bin bags nearby in Camden Town. No one seemed that outraged by the murder. They were shocked by reports of ritual murders in Africa, but closer to home they didn't seem to care. The women had been working as prostitutes; the media didn't seem to think their fate was so horrific as to almost be unmentionable. And not only did people not seem afraid that their houses would be broken into, but they didn't fear attacks like September 11. Yet when we'd left Botswana it had seemed obvious that England was going to be attacked — a suicide bomb perhaps, a missile strike. In my last week in Maun I'd heard of a new dance called the Bin Laden. People spoke of Bin Laden as they had done of Saddam Hussein. It didn't matter what either man had done, the popular image was that they were standing up to America, to the UK.

Out on the streets of London I was constantly jumpy: Several times I leapt away from a roadside bush at the sound of a rustling that I took to be a snake. For twelve years I had walked looking down, scanning the sand, learning to read the signs. Now I walked looking up, scanning the sky, wondering if I would ever see the sun again. I stood on kerbs and didn't know which way to go, which direction the traffic was coming until I realized there were signs written on the tarmac telling me to LOOK RIGHT.

Then I began to realize there was more security than I had first thought, for CCTV cameras were everywhere, though there were no notices explaining why. And I saw how the streets had changed in other ways as well. Most of the old corner pubs had been transformed into gastro pubs, the flowered carpets replaced with wooden floors, the old menus of plaice and chips replaced with French cuisine. And wherever I looked people were talking on mobile phones, in the pubs and on the streets and outside new fancy cafés that looked like they should be in Paris. It was December and yet people sat shivering on pavements outside these new cafés, drinking cappuccinos, huddled by outside heaters, as if desperate to pretend they weren't in England at all. And people kept on talking about the gym, a place that everyone seemed to go and everyone seemed to hate. I had no idea what people did there.

In the shops the food seemed very large and very expensive. One morning I spent an hour in a supermarket checking prices, translating them into pula and then back into pounds. I read labels about organic and 'non GM' and didn't know what either meant. I began to be repulsed by meat again, by the packaging of meat, by the way freezers held slab upon slab of flesh which bore no resemblance to anything that had ever lived, that had played and run.

I hesitated before shelves upon shelves of baby and toddler products, endless varieties of nappies; new-born nappies, big-baby nappies, swimming nappies, pull-up nappies, night-time nappies, pink bags to put smelly nappies in. There were creams and potions, drinks and foods. There were things I had never heard of and never needed, and now suddenly I wondered if I did need them.

'Is that Parmesan?' a fellow shopper standing at the check-out asked me. I held the package up, looked at it, not sure what sort of cheese I had actually picked. 'Yes,' I said, 'it's Parmesan.'

The woman inspected the label. 'That's a good price.'

'Is it?' I asked, relieved. 'Umm, how do I get the coin back out of this trolley?' I asked the check-out woman.

My shopping neighbour turned to me with a smile. 'Does someone usually do your shopping for you, love?'

No, I wanted to yell, I'm from here, I always do my own shopping, it's just that I've been in

Africa for the past twelve years. But then if I said this, the woman might think they didn't have supermarkets in Africa.

Night fell so quickly that by four o'clock it was dark and I felt fearful of leaving the house, although I knew there were no hippos here. Even during the daylight Ruby was afraid outside. She screwed her eyes up tight and held her hands over her ears. Motorbikes terrified her, she had never seen a bus before, or an ambulance, or a fire engine. She had never seen traffic that wasn't confined to a shopping area, but which went straight past people's doors. She thought the squirrels in the park were monkeys and that they were laughing at her. I began to think I had permanently damaged her by bringing her to England.

Ruby became more difficult and more upset. She insisted that the door to my parents' living-room be kept shut tightly at all times, slamming it when someone entered, shutting it with such force that it quickly became permanently stuck. And everywhere she went she carried bags, plastic bags, shopping bags, children's bags, packed with all her things: her dolls and bears and toys and books and pens. Each week the bags got bigger and bigger so that she began pulling them on a wooden trolley around the house. And she lashed out at people, scratching her cousin Amelia on the face, drawing blood.

'When are we going back to Africa?' she asked every hour, every day.

'We're living here now,' I said. She had her

British passport; legally there was nothing to stop us.

Ron rang from Botswana once a week. Each time I picked up the phone and heard the delay in his voice, the echo that sometimes came down the line, I gripped myself, fearing bad news. It was hard to talk trivialities on a long-distance phone call. It was hard to know what to say. I braced myself against the sound of loss in Ron's voice; I pushed images of Maun to the back of my mind.

But then slowly things became easier and I began to appreciate the conveniences of life in London. People complained a lot about things that seemed wondrous to me. Post was delivered each day, sometimes twice a day, right through a hole in the front door. I thought I would never have to go to a post office to get my letters again. And a letter posted one day arrived at the other end of the country the following morning. What were people moaning about? And as quickly as letters were delivered, rubbish was taken away. Trucks came to the house and took away the garbage; there were even separate collections to take away bottles and papers for recycling. There were people whose job it was to sweep the street, and many, I could see, were Southern Africans. Public transport was everywhere; there was no need for cars at all. Buses ran day and night, all over London, yet people complained that they'd been standing waiting for one for over five minutes.

The moment Christmas had passed, I got a job teaching at a local comprehensive school. I walked into the school on my first day feeling confident, I had experience, I was older, I was a parent now. But there was an atmosphere about the place that reminded me of when I had taught at Stanley Deason so many years before. The building looked like a zoo, a dark-grey concrete structure. There were no playing fields, no vegetable plots, few trees. In the foyer, the walls were full of colourful displays, including one about how students had raised money to fund a community project in southern Africa, but it was hard to lift the gloom. In the staff room the teachers all seemed younger than me and I thought they appeared happy and relaxed until I overheard an English teacher describe a nightmare involving her most difficult class.

'Why did you ever leave Africa?' the woman asked me. 'Why on earth did you want to come back here?'

I mumbled something; I didn't want to go into details. I had a new identity now; my court cases and the rape seemed light years away. The woman turned her attention to a tub of cottage cheese, mumbling out loud about how hungry she was.

As I fought my way through the corridors to the first lesson I tensed my shoulders, determined to enter the class in control, to begin as I intended to go on. But the door to the classroom was locked and at once I was surrounded by forty eleven-year-olds. They weren't called first-years any more, but I couldn't remember what I was supposed to call them. And the language they used confused me; I didn't know what a PlayStation was, or a DVD.

In my next class I found a half-empty room. Eleven adolescent boys were slouched at low white tables. Most of their faces were covered, by hats or by hoods. They wore their coats, as if they were only popping in for a moment and would soon be gone.

'We're the rejects, aren't we?' one boy asked.

'Shut up, you fucking Somali,' said his neighbour to the boy who was not Somali at all.

The first boy lunged, ripping mobile phone plugs out of the other's ears. As I opened my mouth to stop them, I saw another boy had got up and was walking around the room, picking up stray pairs of scissors and brandishing them in his hands. I thought of the classes I had taught in Africa, of how the students had behaved so well that I had almost been bored. And I thought about the pride of the students in Botswana, their belief that their country was the best in the world, their ingrained feeling of national identity. They knew who they were and they were proud of it, the students in London did not. And I realized that I had become, in little ways, a Motswana myself. Part of me expected the students to respect their elders simply because they were their elders. Outside school it was the same, I felt uncomfortable hearing a child calling an adult by their first name, I stopped one night in disbelief as three teenage girls called an elderly woman a 'cunt' on the street.

Now that I had a job, Ruby went to nursery. For weeks I had trudged around in the cold knocking at the doors of state schools. And these were security conscious, with buzzers and intercoms and heavy locked gates. But I was told there would be no state place available for a two-year-old for at least a year. So now I dropped Ruby off in the morning at a private nursery, leaving the house when it was still dark. By the time I picked her up after my school day it was dark again. I was working all day to pay for not seeing her all day and I didn't know how long I could keep it up.

'I've got a job,' I told Ron on the phone.

'That's good.'

'No, it's not. It's terrible. I don't want to be doing this.'

'You could always come back.' Ron's voice was low, as if he didn't want to be overheard. 'I should never have let you both go.'

I swallowed hard. 'I can't. I can't make a decision like the one I made and then change my mind. I've brought Ruby here now, we're staying here. I have to. Ron?' But there was interference on the line now, a thunderstorm was heading for Maun, the power was about to go, the phone line would soon be dead.

'Is everyone okay?' I asked hurriedly. 'At the farm and everything?' I felt I had to ask how Madintwa and Alice were, but part of me didn't want to know.

'Everyone is fine.'

'How's the garden?'

'I'll see at the weekend.'

'How do you mean, aren't you staying at home?'

'No, I'm staying at the farm.'

'Oh.' I thought about this. I thought about how that meant our house was empty now, how the sand had probably swept in through the windows and coated the floor with dust.

'How about Bashi, is he okay?'

'*Ee*. He's building some new houses.'

'He is? So he's really well again then?'

'*Ee*. He's taking these anti-retroviral things . . .'

'I always think, when you ring, that something has gone wrong.'

'You worry too much, Cait.'

The next day Ron rang again.

'What is it?' I asked. 'What's happened?'

'It's Robin.'

'Yes?' I smiled, thinking of Veronica's youngest son, picturing him at the swimming pool on my last day in Maun, twirling around the umbrella-stand.

'He's dead.'

I gasped and held my hand to my mouth. At the other end of the room my mother looked up, worried. 'He can't be.'

Ron didn't reply.

'He can't be. How can he be? What about Veronica, what about Roy? How did it happen?'

'He hanged himself.'

'He hanged himself. But he's only two . . .'

'I have to go,' Ron said. 'The funeral is on Saturday, I have to — '

'But how did it happen?'

Ron sighed. 'He was playing. Something happened. With the clothes' line.'

I put the phone down. Ruby was sitting on my

mother's knee, pointing at a book, asking questions. For twelve years I had been away from my family. While I had been in Botswana my grandfather had died. My aunt had died. Now I had been away from Botswana for a couple of months and my nephew Robin was dead. I could not take it in. I was too far away to make sense of it, to believe that it was true.

★　★　★

Eventually Ruby and I moved into a flat and one Saturday morning my boxes finally arrived from Botswana. I had sent three boxes, which had shared a space in a shipping container hired by a returning British teacher. I sat in my empty living-room and unpacked, wondering with each item that I took out and unwrapped why I had ever thought it necessary to send such junk across the world. I thought of the day I had arrived in Maun, of sitting in my tiny teacher's house unpacking my suitcases, realizing I had bought luxuries like books instead of necessities like sheets and cooking pots. I ripped open the boxes from Botswana, convinced there was something useful inside one of them, but it was a pile of trinkets: woven baskets, a candlestick, three pink plastic plates, a metal chameleon, a soap dish with a marble inside. I began to sort out the books I had packed, and at once a sprinkle of sand from the Okavango Delta rained down on to my blue carpet. I rubbed at it uselessly and then stopped as a long-legged spider stepped out from under a book and began to explore its new environment. But Ruby was happy, she began to sing a Setswana counting song, laughing as she popped the bubbles in the bubble wrapping.

Then she stopped. 'I don't like this house,' she said, trying to climb down into one of the boxes.

'Nonsense, of course you do,' I said. But I was worried; perhaps she could sense something wrong about the place.

I set to work unpacking my computer, frowning and swearing as I tried to work out which wire went where. I gritted my teeth, thinking of the afternoon, months before, in my office in Maun as Ron had colour-coded everything so that once in England I would be able to fix it up again. We had worked quietly, concentrating, the office cool compared to the searing heat outside. It was as if we had been working on something together, not packing up our lives ready for separation.

*　*　*

One day a surveyor from the council came to inspect a patch of damp in my new bedroom. It was my day off from work, Ruby was at school, so I was alone at home. At the door I asked for the man's ID, feeling foolish. He knew my name and address and the problem he had come to inspect, so surely he was from the council and not an impostor.

He followed me upstairs and I led him into the bedroom. He took a brief look at the wall and made notes. And then suddenly I began to tremble. The man, a middle-aged white man wearing a tweed jacket, was standing in front of the window explaining what the causes of the damp could be. I was facing him, my back to the open door. He had shown no sign of aggression, made no suggestive comment or movement, and yet I could feel the panic rising. As he spoke I looked around the room. When he tried to rape me, what would I be able to use as a weapon? The man took a step forward and I stiffened, rooted to the spot. I looked down at the cell-phone in my hand, wanting to call someone, anyone, so that it would feel as if there was another person in the room with me. But my fingers wouldn't do as they were told; they slipped around the keypad, trembling so violently I couldn't control them. The man was still speaking and I nodded and nodded, willing him to leave.

Afterwards I sat on the stairs as if I had had a near escape. I had been right back there, right back in the time and space in which the rape had happened. I thought I had left the rape in Botswana, but it had followed me here.

The following day I had to be back at school and I busied myself with my morning routine. I hoped having a routine would help both Ruby and me to settle. I woke and dressed her and then she wandered into the living-room with a just-warmed bottle of milk, while I made up her lunchbox in the kitchen.

'Do you want cheese or cucumber, in your sandwich?' I called out.

Ruby didn't reply.

I looked at the clock, it was 6.30 already. I didn't want to waste time making a sandwich she wasn't going to eat.

'Ruby?' I called out again.

Still she didn't answer, so I came out of the kitchen, irritated, feeling harassed. She had recently begun a new habit of blanking me, of not responding to a question until it was asked at least five times. 'You're getting just like your father,' I muttered under my breath.

As I strode into the living-room I saw that instead of sitting upright on the sofa, sucking from her milk bottle as I had left her, Ruby had keeled over to one side, her entire face hidden against a pillow. For a second I thought she was playing hide and seek. I bent forward, touching her on the shoulder, about to say 'peepo!' when I realized her body was completely rigid.

'Ruby!' I yelled in alarm. Her arms were bent at the elbow and held awkwardly up against her face. They were as stiff as board. Terrified I knelt down by the sofa. She was dead. 'Oh, my God, oh, my God,' I began to chant. I picked her up, almost roughly, wanting to see her body respond in some way. She was stiff but warm and her closed eyelids were flickering. I shook her a little, wanting to somehow shake her out of it, out of whatever sort of trance she had gone into. Perhaps she had eaten something, I thought, looking around, not seeing any sign of anything she had been doing but drinking her milk.

'What shall I do, what shall I do?' I said out loud, beginning to pace. I rushed into the kitchen, for some reason deciding Ruby had to have water. I began trying to wash water from the tap into her mouth, but her mouth was rigid, her jaw clenched. 'Oh, my God, oh, my God,' I ran back into the living-room. Then suddenly Ruby let out a gigantic sigh, a huge release of breath, and her body relaxed. I sat down abruptly on the sofa, and she flopped like a soft toy on to my lap. I pulled at the phone with my foot, dragging it along the carpet. I remembered that I was in England, that I could call 999.

Ruby didn't open her eyes until the ambulance arrived a few minutes later and when she did she appeared confused and panicky.

'It's okay, it's okay,' I soothed, lifting her into the ambulance, holding her tight while the driver backed out along my road. That day we spent eleven hours at Whittington Hospital. Ruby had recovered now, she was bright and cheerful and she did everything the staff asked of her: touching her nose, providing a urine sample, standing on one leg, giving a blood sample, following a finger moving in front of her face. No one said what they thought might be wrong with her and I didn't know what questions to ask. But I felt safe in the hospital, the children's ward was big and clean, the nurses were well dressed and efficient. They were busy but none of them scowled. The doctors bent down when they talked to Ruby, and they introduced themselves to her using their first names as if they were going to be playmates.

We were given a bed in a half-empty ward which had a television in the corner and a stack of children's videos. Down the corridor there was a play area, both indoors and outside, and at lunch hot food was served from a trolley. Ruby took a huge plate of chips and beamed, she couldn't believe her luck.

I was told that whatever had happened it was not a febrile convulsion, a fit that can follow a high temperature, for there had been no fever. There was the possibility that it was epilepsy, but as she'd only had one fit it wasn't clear and we were sent home.

The next morning Ruby woke up and turned towards me in the bed. It was a chilly morning; I pulled at the duvet to keep us warm. In a minute I would have to get up, I would have to get ready for work.

'Hello, Mama,' Ruby said and beamed, snuggling close. 'Can I watch cartoons?' And then suddenly she froze. Her eyes closed, her eyebrows quivered. Her body was as rigid as it had been the morning before. I sat up, watching her, willing her to become conscious again. This time I wouldn't shake her or try to force anything into her mouth. Two minutes later she came to, gave a shuddery sigh, and then fell into a deep sleep.

Again I called an ambulance, and again it arrived in minutes. Ruby and I sat inside while the ambulance man took her vital signs.

'Have they bombed Iraq?' I asked, remembering what day it was, how the night before the news had said a bombing was imminent.

The ambulance man nodded sadly. 'Let's hope it's over quickly.'

That afternoon, Ruby had her third fit, only

now I knew that I should be calling them seizures. This time her eyes were frighteningly open, staring blankly at me, not registering a thing. It was as if she wasn't my child, wasn't the person I knew at all, as if something had invaded her body, as if she had been bewitched. Now she was diagnosed with epilepsy and she began her anti-epileptic drugs.

Carefully I measured the thick red liquid into a syringe, knowing that this was a twice-daily procedure I was going to have to get used to, and so would she for at least the next two years.

That evening Ruby was in tears for half an hour, grief-stricken adult tears not angry toddler tears. 'I feel sad today,' she said, plaintively. 'I'm not well today.' That night she had seven seizures one after another and I knew I had to call Ron. Whatever Ruby had was serious, I had to tell him what was going on. 'She's having these fits, we've been in and out of hospital,' I said, speaking quickly, dreading that the line would go dead. 'They say it's epilepsy, Ron. Is there anyone in your family with epilepsy? There's no one in mine . . . the doctors keep on asking about it.'

'*Ee*,' Ron said, his voice sounding uncertain at first. '*Ee*. There is this one girl, my grand-mother's cousin's child.'

'Who?'

But Ron hadn't heard me, he was still speaking. 'She had fits. That was epilepsy, I think.'

'And what happened to her?'

'She's fine, I think. It happened at school.'

581

'So no one else?'

'No.'

'I'll ring you later, okay? To tell you what the hospital says.'

'Try not to worry, Cait. The doctors are good over there.'

★   ★   ★

The next day Ruby had an EEG, and she sat stiffly while twenty electrodes were fixed to her head, the attached wires hanging down like multicoloured hair extensions. I promised her more chips if she stayed still. Once the wires were in place the brainwave patterns showed on the screen. The woman in charge gave a sharp intake of breath and frowned.

'You look shocked,' I said, nervously.

'I am,' she replied. 'This pattern, it's *incredibly* abnormal . . . '

'Oh?'

The woman nodded, her face was drained of colour. 'It's not just epilepsy, there's something very serious causing it.'

Now it was my turn to go rigid, my heart convulsed as Ruby sat, oblivious on my knee, drawing on some paper. I had a seemingly healthy child on my lap, and no control at all over what was going on in her brain. I was totally powerless.

I left the EEG room trembling and made my way back to the ward upstairs, Ruby on my hip. An image of two years earlier flashed into my mind, of walking through Dr Patrick's clinic in

Maun after the rape, numb with fear, Ruby attached like a heavy limpet to my hip.

By now I was getting used to the fact that the nurses and doctors didn't want to commit themselves. They couldn't or wouldn't say what was wrong, only that Ruby would be having an MRI scan.

'Do you think she's got a tumour?' I asked. 'Is that why you're doing this, to see if she's got a brain tumour?'

The consultant murmured something and walked on to the child in the next bed.

That night Ruby slept restlessly. At midnight she gave an awful, high-pitched cry like a wild animal that has stumbled across a murdered mate in the bush.

'Have you had a bad dream?' a nurse asked soothingly.

'Yes,' said Ruby. 'Everything was going WHOOSH!'

The next day I left Ruby on the threshold of the scan-room, too fearful to go in with her, not able to watch her little body sliding into place. I walked up and down outside, while my mother sat patiently waiting beside me. At one point a woman rushed out of the screening-room and into the scan-room. I looked at my mother in terror; she tried to give a reassuring smile. Had they found the tumour then? Was this what was wrong? I was furious suddenly. Ruby was only three years old; she had lost her father and her sisters and her country. She had watched her mother be stabbed and raped. She had come to another country and now she had this, a lifelong condition. She would struggle in the future to get a driving licence or travel insurance; she would never be a pilot.

But the scan showed no major structural abnormality, no big masses lurking around in her head. It was epilepsy with no known cause.

I went home and rang Ron at once. 'She's fine. Well, she's not fine, but they can't see anything wrong with her brain.' I waited for Ron to react.

'My grandmother knows what it is.'

'What? Your *grandmother* knows about epilepsy?'

'It's not epilepsy. It's something else, it's . . . ' I could feel Ron struggling to find the right words.

'What do you mean, your grandmother *knows* what it is?'

'It's this thing, when your heart aches too much.'

'When your heart *aches* too much?'

'*Ee*. When you're heartbroken and you think about things . . . '

'Oh, so it's my fault? My fault for taking Ruby away from you lot?'

'No, no. I didn't say that. It's my fault.' Ron gave a heavy sigh.

'How, how is it your fault?'

'I've been thinking about her too much . . . '

'And that made her have fits? Come on Ron, they did an EEG, they looked at the brain patterns, they were totally abnormal.'

'My mother's going to send something, something for Ruby to wear.'

'Oh, so that's okay then?' I shifted in irritation. I had asked the hospital doctors, and the consultant, if there could be a psychological cause for Ruby's seizures and they had waved this away. The doctors didn't know why her fits had happened; they didn't know what was wrong. Perhaps Ron's theory was as good as any, perhaps someone's heart was aching too much.

# 35

Six months after Ruby and I returned to the UK, Ron said he wanted to visit. He rang one early summer's morning to say he was going to sell his car and buy a ticket.

'Don't tell Ruby,' I urged him. 'Don't tell her until you're actually on your way.'

And for several months, the visit wasn't mentioned again. Ron was tied up with the business, with the farm, and with the family. In England Ruby was adapting to yet another nursery, this time a free place at a state school. I left her there each day a little fearfully; what if she had another seizure, what if I couldn't get to the school quickly enough? The epilepsy seemed to be controlled now, but I watched her constantly, keeping up a running dialogue as I moved around the flat, rushing from one room to another if Ruby didn't reply.

'I'm an African,' she told her classmates and teachers at her new nursery. 'I speak African and I'm from Africa and I'm going back to Africa soon.' She had developed a little song too, and she danced for them, singing, 'I'm black, I'm black, I'm an African.'

'No, you're not,' said her friend Aysha.

'I am!'

'You're not black, Ruby,' Aysha said patiently. 'You're mixed race, like me.'

Ruby hesitated, torn between repeating her

argument and wanting to be like Aysha.

'Are you really going back to Botswana next week?' one of the teachers asked, taking me to one side.

'No!' I sighed and looked across the room to where Ruby was playing in the home corner, a tiny version of a living-room with cushions, miniature cookers and dolls. She never let up. Each night when I put her to bed the process was the same. First she wanted to read her favourite book, a tale of a hippo that has a party. I read the book a little reluctantly, hippos weren't like this in real life, they weren't cuddly creatures, they didn't wear hats and eat cake and dance. They were dangerous. And then, once the light was out, Ruby began the same conversation. 'I miss my dada. I miss him so much. And small grandma. And big mama. When are we going back to Africa?'

'We will go back,' I said carefully, each night giving the same response. 'But to visit. Okay? We will go back for a holiday. When you're older you can even go on your own.' Satisfied, she would then fall asleep.

On the weekends we picnicked in parks or went to the seaside. The days were more relaxed because it was summer, the people in our street began to talk to us, I began to recognize people in shops and in the post office. I had thought Londoners weren't friendly, that everyone lived their separate lives, but now with the sun out all this seemed to change. We went swimming with Bernie, the teacher I had travelled up to Maun with thirteen years earlier. She was back in

London too now, with Hassan and their two-year-old boy, Kai. We went to Wales to visit Stef who was no longer working for Women Against Rape in Maun but looking after her baby twins while her husband Bryn studied at Bangor. And we saw Sarah, the woman who had been beaten to a near coma in Maun a year to the day after I had been attacked. She was teaching in England but already she wanted to return to Botswana. She said what she missed most was the light. I spoke to Kerrin when she came over for a visit to England too. She and Andrew were living in Gaborone now, where Andrew was working for the *Voice*. Kerrin had been the recent victim of two assaults, once held up at knife-point in a Gaborone shopping mall and once when a group of men with guns burst into a friend's house during a hen night.

But while we sometimes saw people from Botswana, when Pearl or Veronica or Beauty rang it always threw me. Veronica was still deep in mourning for Robin and her voice sounded heavy and flat. Sometimes Ruby would answer the phone and I could see her frowning. It bothered her, the fact that she couldn't understand Setswana any more, that she no longer knew how to respond to greetings. But at school she was learning new languages and now she could sing a song in Bengali and greet people in Somali.

★  ★  ★

Ron arrived in England on a bitterly cold December day. The flight landed at six in the morning and Ruby and I took a cab to the airport to meet him. In my bag I had a letter formally inviting Ron to stay with his ex-wife and daughter in London for two weeks. The British Embassy in Botswana said he needed this or he wouldn't be allowed in the country. In the cab Ruby sat alert, endlessly pointing out the bright lights of the fake Christmas trees shining from window after window, in street after street. She was excited to be up so early, to be going on a trip.

'We'll get the tube back,' I told her. 'I don't know if your dad's ever been on a tube.'

Ruby sat stiffly beside me now, not answering.

I bent nearer, she was sitting a little too awkwardly, and in the gloom of the back of the cab I couldn't see any expression on her face at all. For a second I thought she had had another fit. But she was concentrating on her fingers, enjoying the shadows they made on the back of the seat.

The airport was deserted when we arrived, the Arrivals area empty. Ruby slid up and down the shiny floor asking where her father was. Two women arrived and smiled at Ruby indulgently. And then, without any announcement or warning, Ron came through the double glass doors. His head was freshly shaved and it looked vulnerable somehow, too exposed for Christmas in England. He wore a light green jacket, the sort a person might wear on an English summer's day. Over his shoulder he carried a black holdall.

His face looked around, his lips quivered a little. He was middle-aged, I realized, which meant that I was too.

'There he is!' I told Ruby. 'See!'

Ron stopped where he was, put down his bag, and Ruby ran to meet him. He scooped her up and held her, smelling her hair, smiling, his eyes wet with tears. She clung to her father, holding on tight, her eyes closed. Then suddenly she drew back, appraising him, wriggling to show she wanted to get back down on her own two feet.

'Has she changed a lot?' I asked.

But Ron was too emotional to respond.

'We'll get the tube,' I said. 'This way . . . '

Ron followed as I led the way to the Underground, standing back while I bought the tickets. Expertly I pressed the buttons, deposited the money, took two tickets and handed one to Ron. I did it without thinking, as easily as if I had been using such machines all my life.

'This way,' I said again, and Ron followed as I tried to find the right line going home. He seemed uncertain, the way he stood there waiting when for so many years it was he who had been in control. He hadn't been out of Africa for thirteen years; he had forgotten how to function in a country like England. He would have to rely on me. I turned my head, about to get on an escalator to the Northern Line when I saw Ron in the distance half-swallowed up in a sea of black-suited commuters.

'You have got a coat haven't you?' I asked. 'A proper coat?'

Ron smiled sheepishly. 'Just this one.'

'But that's as thick as a crisp packet! You're going to freeze.'

'I know.' Ron shivered though it was warmer now that we were underground. 'I just forgot about what cold feels like. I forgot it was even possible to feel as cold as this.' He leant forward to smile at Ruby but she was scowling now. She insisted she sat next to me, and that I sat next to Ron. She didn't want to sit between us; she didn't want to sit next to her father, just to watch him.

When we left the tube we emerged into a crisp day, so cold that we slipped on the ice that coated the pavements. It was almost nine o'clock but it was still dark, most of the shops were still closed.

Later that day we went to Hampstead Heath and Ron pushed Ruby on the swings. No other children were playing there; it was too overcast, too cold. But Ruby didn't mind the cold, she just wanted to ride on Ron's shoulders, and Ron didn't mind either for he had borrowed a warm jacket off my brother. We went to a pizza place for lunch and Ruby sat between us, quiet, not interrupting, just eating and sometimes laughing. I thought how differently she was behaving now she had two parents, she was less demanding, less confrontational. She seemed like more of a child, I had been getting too used to talking to her as if she were an adult.

'So how's business?' I asked.

Ron shrugged. 'It looks like I'm going to be an MP.'

'You are?' I put down my fork.

'*Ee*. I got elected for one of the Maun wards, Maun is split into all sorts of wards these days.'

'So, what, you're standing for government now?'

'*Ee*, in the general elections, next year.'

'You'll be good at that, I always thought you should have been a politician . . . Rra Nama would be pleased,' and then I realized that if he were so certain of becoming an MP it was because he was standing for the ruling party. 'You mean, you're in the BDP now?'

'*Ee*.'

'But when did that happen?' Ron had a different life now; I no longer knew what he was doing or what he hoped to do. For a second I couldn't believe that we had ever been intimate, that we had once been married. I wondered, if it hadn't been for his family, if it hadn't been for the rape, whether we would have still been together today.

'A while ago,' said Ron, 'I joined the BDP a while ago.'

'That's the party that put me on trial . . .' I tried to sound casual but I was annoyed; it felt like Ron had joined the enemy. 'Twice.'

'It wasn't the party, it was an individual.'

'It was?'

'*Ee*.'

'But why the BDP? You remember what some people said, don't you? That the rape was a set-up? That someone was out to get me. That it was the same as the court cases, the rape was a set-up, a way to shut me up, and that's why the case files went missing . . .'

Ron sat back and pushed away his plate. 'I never knew that.'

'You didn't?'

'No.'

I shrugged. 'It probably wasn't true . . . but, anyway, why the BDP?'

'You have to get into power, Cait, if you want to change things.'

'And get corrupted on the way, you mean?'

Ron scowled. 'Let's not . . . '

'Yes, you're right. Sorry.' Being with Ron meant slipping back into old ways; every conversation had the potential to lead to an argument. 'So, how's Alice and everyone?'

'Fine,' Ron spoke carefully, his eyes on the table.

'Your mum?'

'Fine.'

I sighed and lifted my fork again. I had never finished with Eliah, I still wanted Ron to take sides, to apologize for his mother and for his grandmother on the day of the confrontation at the farm.

'Madintwa? How is she?'

'She's had an eye operation.'

'She has? But I tried for years to get her to have her eyes done! Has it worked, can she really see again?'

'It doesn't look too good so far.'

We left the pizza place and set off for home again. 'Which way?' Ron asked, standing on the pavement, Ruby on his shoulders.

'Dada!' she called, patting his head.

'Yes?' Ron tried to crane his face up.

593

But Ruby hadn't anything to say; she was just enjoying the word 'dada'.

'Which way, Cait?'

'The way we've just come,' I said. 'We're going up that hill, the hill we just came down.'

Ron began trudging up the hill, Ruby hanging her arms around his neck, his body stiff against the wind and the cold. I walked beside him, unable to believe that he had lost his sense of direction. In Botswana he knew Maun inside out, he knew all the pathways between the different wards, he knew the farm and the bush, he could distinguish every tree, every track on the sand. But he was in London now and he'd lost his familiar landmarks.

Ron slept early that night, so used to going to bed when it was dark. He slept on the floor next to Ruby's bed, so that he would see her at once when she woke. But the next day Ruby was unsure how to respond to him, behaving as if she had to choose to favour either me or her father but not both together. At times she cuddled and patted him, other times she pushed him away. The anti-epilepsy drugs seemed to have given an edge to her temper. At school she often lashed out at other children, swore violently and smashed things. I had been introduced to an educational psychologist; a health visitor suggested Ruby undergo art therapy; a social worker came round and paid a home visit, checking up on odd behaviour at school. It had been almost ten months since she'd been on the drugs. Now I couldn't distinguish what was drug-related behaviour and what was just an expression of her distress.

And Ron was distressed too, everything in England was strange to him. But to me everything now seemed normal: the way people spoke, the traffic on the streets, the goods in the shops. I had become careless about things, leaving a tap running while I brushed my teeth or cleaned out a pot, almost forgetting how precious water was.

Each night Ron went to bed earlier and earlier. Once Ruby was asleep we had little to talk about. He didn't want any arguments, he refused to discuss old resentments, and had become almost as silent as he had been when I'd first met him in the United States.

'You know I'm writing a book,' I said one night as we sat watching *Top Gear*.

'So you told me.'

'It's about my life in Botswana, that means it's going to have you in it, and your mum and everyone.'

Ron nodded.

'Is that okay with you?'

'You're an adult. You can write what you like.'

★   ★   ★

As the days passed I discovered how I had become used to being a single parent, and how much I now liked it, not having to consult or negotiate with another adult. I wasn't used to asking someone else what they wanted to do, or having to think about how they were, if they wanted food or a cup of coffee. And Ron was used to being served; now that he was living full-time on the farm everything was handed to him on a tray — his tea, his lunch, a bowl of water to wash his hands. He had forgotten how to work in a kitchen or how to clean up after himself.

And still Ruby alternated between wanting him and not wanting him. We went to her nursery's Christmas play where Ruby refused to let Ron sit anywhere near her, or even to show him around the home corner where she had taped up a photo of her father for the other children to see. That night Ron drank a shot of whisky, his first alcoholic drink for several years.

The day Ron left to return to Botswana we went to Camden Town and shopped in the snow for shoes and presents for Alice and Gabs. On the way home I complained because we had been waiting for a bus for seven minutes and I realized how much I complained these days, about London transport, about the frequent electricity cuts, about letters that were never delivered.

It was nearly dark by the time Ron's cab arrived. We hugged in the hallway, both saying 'sorry' at the same time but neither of us saying what we were sorry for. Ruby and I stood by the window watching as Ron crossed the road to the cab. He had his head turned, waving back at us. He stooped to get into the car and still his head was turned, searching the window for our figures.

'Bye bye Dada!' Ruby called and she pounded on the glass.

I picked her up and hugged her. I didn't belong in Botswana and Ron didn't belong in England but I hoped that Ruby could belong in both.

★　★　★

In January 2004 Ruby turned four. Her brainwave patterns had normalized and I wanted her withdrawn from the drugs. It looked like she didn't have epilepsy at all. I started work again and I went to an NHS psychotherapist who treated people suffering from post-traumatic stress. As I left after the first session I stood in the street outside, checking my pockets. I felt as if I had been wearing a rucksack and had left it behind in the psychotherapist's office. When I realized I hadn't had a rucksack to begin with, I began checking my pockets with the feeling I had lost something, misplaced it somewhere. But it was simply the sense of being unburdened.

Now I saw how I still avoided any reminders of the rape. I could not have a knife, however blunt, visible in the house. In the kitchen I shoved all my knives to the back of a drawer, and was careful to put away screwdrivers too. Scissors, on the other hand, didn't bother me at all. Sometimes, in the park or on the street, I would feel a physical reaction to a man I didn't know. The figure could be far away, his face indistinguishable, but if he resembled the rapist in height, or gait, or complexion then adrenaline began pumping through my body, my heart beating with juddery, irregular beats.

A few months after Ron had visited us in London, our old house in Maun was broken into. There had been several break-ins since I had left Botswana because the house was largely empty. This time Ron rang to say my office had been ransacked too. All the things I had left behind me, the twelve years' worth of photo albums and letters and writings, Ruby's first clothes and her first toys, my pregnancy clothes, my books and my paintings, had gone.

I imagined the house on the peninsula returning to nature, the sand blowing in through the windows, the grass creeping back up to the porch, the lehututu birds strutting in single file right next to the fence now there were no dogs to scare them. I could picture the hippo making its nightly stroll past the gate and perhaps over the gate and into the plot. I could see the snakes coming back and breeding in their old holes.

It was only when I heard that the office had been broken into that I began to feel any sense of loss. It was as if I had been trying to block out memories of the house where I had been happy and loved, where I had given birth and been confined, where I had been raped. I had blocked the years out because the good things were too painful to think about now that I had lost them, and the bad things were just too painful.

People in England often asked me what I missed about Botswana and normally I said nothing. But some days I thought perhaps it was everything. It was the consistency of the sun outside in the morning, the way it came up and went down at the same time every day. There was a surety in this, a guarantee as to how the day would go. I missed the leisurely way people greeted each other, the way they hung on each other's words with as much intensity as they hung on to each other's hands when strolling down a pathway in the sand. And I missed the sound of frogs bouncing in the air at night, fire smoke in a darkened compound, the pleasing exactness of a wall made from reeds.

'Mum?' Ruby asked one morning. 'When we go back to Africa, can I take all my toys with me?'

'Yes, you can take some.'

'Are we going next week?'

'No, we are not going next week.'

Ruby slammed her hand on the table. 'But I *miss* Africa, I miss it so much.'

I put a bowl of cereal before her. I wanted to tell her not to expect too much, not to think that Africa was any better or any worse than anywhere else.

'And, *actually*, do you know what, Mum?'

'What, Ruby?'

'I'm black, I'm black, I'm an African,' she began to sing as she danced around the room.

The events portrayed in this book are true, but some names have been changed and, in some cases, fictional characters used in order to protect certain individuals.

We do hope that you have enjoyed reading this large print book.

Did you know that all of our titles are available for purchase?

We publish a wide range of high quality large print books including:
**Romances, Mysteries, Classics
General Fiction
Non Fiction and Westerns**

Special interest titles available in large print are:
**The Little Oxford Dictionary
Music Book
Song Book
Hymn Book
Service Book**

Also available from us courtesy of Oxford University Press:
**Young Readers' Dictionary
(large print edition)
Young Readers' Thesaurus
(large print edition)**

For further information or a free brochure, please contact us at:
**Ulverscroft Large Print Books Ltd.,
The Green, Bradgate Road, Anstey,
Leicester, LE7 7FU, England.
Tel:** (00 44) 0116 236 4325
**Fax:** (00 44) 0116 234 0205

## RELATIVE STRANGERS

### Hunter Davies

On 18 May 1932, Kate Hodder gave birth to a baby girl at Birchfield House Infirmary near Sevenoaks in Kent. Three and a half hours later, a baby boy was born. And then, forty minutes on, a second girl was delivered. But the joy at the birth of triplets — a very rare event in the 1930s — was to prove short-lived. Kate died the following day. Her husband Wills was soon struggling to cope with their six previous children, so the decision was made to offer the triplets up for adoption. Remarkably, aged sixty-nine, the three triplets were reunited. Here, their astonishing story charts their three different upbringings, and the struggles and detective work that brought them back together.

# CHILDREN OF WAR

## Susan Goodman

The novelist Susan Goodman, herself a child of the Second World War, appealed for stories to commemorate the experiences of a special generation. This remarkable book is the result. A rich tapestry of the dramatic, poignant and everyday, its compelling first-hand stories reflect not only British life during the Second World War, but also the experience of refugees from the *Kindertransports*. Nostalgic, funny, tragic, positive, bleak, and evocative — these voices form a narrative that is hard to put down, and bring back to life an era that shaped a generation.

# TICK BITE FEVER

## David Bennun

Africa has a rich history of heroes and trailblazers. David Bennun is neither. He belongs to the dark continent's less celebrated tradition of accidental adventures. Throughout his 1970s African childhood, and despite the best efforts of his long-suffering family, David manages to get himself in more trouble than one person has any right to survive. Here is the story of how a bemused and clumsy small boy discovered Africa. A day rarely passes when he doesn't run the risk of getting eaten, crushed, poisoned, drowned, trampled, shot or impaled. Even his dog, Achilles, seems to have a death wish. David Bennun's writing is evocative, touching and so funny that you will find it hard not to laugh out loud.